US public diplomacy in socialist Yugoslavia, 1950–70

Manchester University Press

Key Studies in Diplomacy

Series Editors: J. Simon Rofe and Giles Scott-Smith

Emeritus Editor: Lorna Lloyd

The volumes in this series seek to advance the study and understanding of diplomacy in its many forms. Diplomacy remains a vital component of global affairs, and it influences and is influenced by its environment and the context in which it is conducted. It is an activity of great relevance for International Studies, International History, and of course Diplomatic Studies. The series covers historical, conceptual, and practical studies of diplomacy.

Previously published by Bloomsbury:

21st Century Diplomacy: A Practitioner's Guide by Kishan S. Rana
A Cornerstone of Modern Diplomacy: Britain and the Negotiation of the 1961 Vienna Convention on Diplomatic Relations by Kai Bruns
David Bruce and Diplomatic Practice: An American Ambassador in London, 1961–9 by John W. Young
Embassies in Armed Conflict by G.R. Berridge

Published by Manchester University Press:

Reasserting America in the 1970s edited by Hallvard Notaker, Giles Scott-Smith and David J. Snyder
Human rights and humanitarian diplomacy: Negotiating for human rights protection and humanitarian access by Kelly-Kate Pease
The diplomacy of decolonisation: America, Britain and the United Nations during the Congo crisis 1960–64 by Alanna O'Malley
Sport and diplomacy: Games within games edited by J. Simon Rofe
The TransAtlantic reconsidered edited by Charlotte A. Lerg, Susanne Lachenicht and Michael Kimmage
Academic ambassadors, Pacific allies: Australia, America and the Fulbright Program by Alice Garner and Diane Kirkby
A precarious equilibrium: Human rights and détente in Jimmy Carter's Soviet policy by Umberto Tulli

US public diplomacy in socialist Yugoslavia, 1950–70
Soft culture, cold partners

Carla Konta

Manchester University Press

Published by Manchester University Press
Oxford Road, Manchester M13 9PL
www.manchesteruniversitypress.co.uk

British Library Cataloguing-in-Publication Data
A catalogue record for this book is available from the British Library

ISBN 978 1 5261 4075 3 hardback
ISBN 978 1 5261 8243 2 paperback

First published 2020
Paperback published 2024

The publisher has no responsibility for the persistence or accuracy of URLs for any external or third-party internet websites referred to in this book, and does not guarantee that any content on such websites is, or will remain, accurate or appropriate.

Typeset in 9.5/12 pt Minion Pro by
Servis Filmsetting Ltd, Stockport, Cheshire

For my mom. She knows I would never have done it without her, and I have no way of rewarding her.

Contents

Acknowledgements

Gratitude teaches us to be humble and learn from others. Investigating, questioning, and picking the best ideas drove my motivation in writing this book. The faults are mine, whereas I remain in debt to so many.

First, thanks to the Department of Human Studies at the University of Trieste. Elisabetta Vezzosi and Marco Dogo have been tremendous mentors and an inexhaustible inspiration. Having believed in me, Elisabetta taught me to approach history with enthusiastic and open-minded commitment. Working next to her made me grow personally, professionally, and intellectually in so many ways.

Two dear friends and colleagues from the University of Trieste, Annalisa Mogorovich and Luca Manenti, played a special role in my personal and intellectual maturity by listening, advising, and encouraging. We share beautiful memories and experiences. Other department members helped with comments and suggestions to keep my research on track, especially Tullia Catalan and Elisabetta Bini, while my colleagues provided a challenging, stimulating, and supportive community. With Elisabetta I share many recent research projects, and she keeps supporting and teaching me to always give my best. I am grateful to Matteo Pretelli for introducing me to the debate about public diplomacy free of easy interpretations and stereotypes; and to Gaetano Dato for supplying me with well-grounded preparations on the US National Archives. The research was funded thanks to generous support from the Italian Ministry of Foreign Affairs and International Cooperation-Unione Italiana-Università Popolare di Trieste, while my home department covered archival stays and conferences abroad.

One of the greatest pleasures of investigating a multinational topic is the opportunity to spend time abroad. I got invaluable support from staff at the US National Archives at College Park (MD) – David Langbart, Richard Peuser, David Fort, and Amy Schmidt. My stay in Washington, DC benefited from the good company of Sara C. Leonard, Marija Mladenović, Nikola Mladenović, Liz Fisher, Klaudio Jadrić, and Taikei Okadia. I had a profitable and great time researching Belgrade's archives thanks to Branko Pusica, Slobodan Mandić, and Dragan Teodošić – especially Dragan, who helped me with the Archives of Yugoslavia materials in unimaginable ways. My stay at the Croatian State Archives was productive thanks to the help of the archival staff, especially Ivona Fabris, and the directorship that provided me with access to unregulated folders. Special thanks are due to scholars Mark A. Lewis, for interesting conversations at Croatian State Archives, Zagreb, and for reading parts of my writings, and to Simone Selva, who supplied me with additional sources from the National Archives when I had already returned to Europe. Thanks to the staff of the University Library of Rijeka, the National and University Library of Zagreb, Antonia Parić, Svetozar Marković at Belgrade's University Library, and Strossmayer Art Gallery. The American Embassy in Belgrade, Zagreb, and Ljubljana answered all my questions: my appreciation extends to Saša Brlek, Public Affairs Officer (PAO), and Marica Bahlen, Information Resource Center Director at the American Embassy, Zagreb, Charlotte Taft, Alumni Coordinator at the American Embassy, Ljubljana, and Information Resource Center staff from the American Embassy, Belgrade.

The Roosevelt Institute for American Studies (RIAS) in Middelburg, the Netherlands, supplied me with a research grant at its Microfilm Collection. My experience at the RIAS was inspiring in every way; I am indebted to Giles Scott-Smith, Dario Fazzi, Hans Krabbendam, Leontien Josse, and particularly Marleen Roozen, who made my stay there feel like home. Meeting Dario Fazzi at the RIAS was a lucky occurrence. Many times, and at many conferences, I have appreciated his friendship, humour, but also his scientific scrutiny and advice in reading pieces of my work.

This book would not have seen light were it not for Giles Scott-Smith believing in it while the research was only in its infancy. From our first discussions about the US Foreign Leader Program at the RIAS back in 2015, Giles read chapters of this book as they emerged. Always finding time to discuss its weak and strong points, he offered true guidance and mentoring. His intellectual humility, combined with deep knowledge and devotion to young scholars, makes me truly admire him.

I was lucky to meet many advanced career scholars during these years. Their comments, suggestions, and criticisms laid the groundwork for this book. Some of them are already mentioned elsewhere, but I cannot forget David J. Snyder, Randall Woods, Nancy Snow, Justin Hart, Raffaella Baritono, Umberto Gentiloni Silveri, Sarah E. Graham, Vladimir Kulić, Ljubica Spaskovska, Vladimir Unkovski-Korica, Ljubodrag Dimić, Milan Ristić, and Igor Duda. Tvrtko Jakovina patiently (and with no delay) answered my enquiries many times over these years, and Vanni D'Alessio, my PhD external reviewer, provided advice and suggestions. Among others, Radina Vučetić gave me valuable insights, support, and recommendations. Radina's research on Yugoslav 'Coca-Cola socialism' inspired me to look for its diplomatic and bilateral contexts; her generous assistance and insightful understanding of the 'Yugoslav experiment' meant so much to me. The Diane D. Blair Center of Southern Politics and Society (University of Arkansas, Fayetteville) sponsored my participation at the conference 'J. William Fulbright in International Perspective,' in September 2015, and made possible my research at the University of Arkansas Library. Here I met such devoted and easy-going staff and scholars: Geoffrey Stark, Vera Ekechukwu, Jeanne Short, and Misti Harper. I am mostly grateful to Alessandro Brogi from the University of Arkansas for timely and compelling insights about my research, and to his son Sam: I truly enjoyed their good company and care during my stay in Fayetteville.

My interviewees, Nada Apsen, Danica Purg, Zdenka Nikolić, Petar Nikolić, Rade Petrović, Sonja Bašić, and Fulbright alumni Taib Šarić and Ranko Bugarski, deserve special mention for sharing their personal memories with depth and emotion. I know it is never easy to talk to a stranger. David Corrales Morales and Deborah Bessenghini accompanied me at the 2016 Transatlantic Studies Association annual conference:

I greatly profited from our insightful discussions and friendship. The 2017 SHAFR (Society for Historians of American Foreign Relations) Summer Institute had more of an impact on my intellectual and professional growth than I could imagine; among others, special thanks go to Andrew Preston, Mario Del Pero, Jayita Sarkar, Craig Malcom, James Bradford, Gaetano Di Tommaso, Aileen Teague, and particularly Michael Graziano for taking time to read parts of the manuscript and giving me confidence to finally get the book proposal out.

In 2017, I started a research fellowship at the University of Trieste. Working on the Yugoslav nuclear civil programme and its transnational networks, I met and learned from many great scholars and scientists who broadened my perspective regarding our academic commitment: Carlo Rizzuto and Jana Kolar from Sincrotrone Elettra, and Valerio Cappellini from the International Centre for Theoretical Physics, but also younger friends and colleagues such as Ilaria Zamburlini, Stefan Guth, and Fabian Luescher. Working as a postdoctorate lecturer at the Department of Italian Studies, University of Rijeka, had an impact I cannot adequately express. While I was lacking confidence about my writing pace, Luka Skansi provided insightful suggestions and motivation. Writing a manual on academic writing with Luca Malatesti proved a real relief, both for solving many writing problems and for having Luca giving me the right advice when my morale was low. Thanks to Anna Rinaldin for being a patient and supportive listener, and to Maja Djurdulov and Iva Peršić for days full of humour and discerning discussions on our academic life. To Gianna Mazzieri Sanković and Corinna Gerbaz Giuliano, my special thanks for taking care of me in every single way. They were, and will always remain, my teachers and my inspiration.

My proofreader, Joseph Molitorisz, did more than he should by encouraging me to search for the right word, pointing out problems in the narrative flow, but also by discussing my work from his lifelong experience. James Hayton helped me to better understand and obviate the problems we, as scholars, deal with daily regarding the academic writing process.

Thanks to Simon Rofe from the SOAS University of London for believing in this book and my project from its very beginning, and to the whole Manchester University Press team – former Senior Commissioning Editor, Tony Mason, today's Senior Commissioning Editor, Jonathan de Peyer, as well as to Robert Byron, Jen Mellor, and Deborah Smith. I was backed by a supportive, attentive, and timely team. I would also like to thank my copy-editor, Anthony Mercer, for his patience, professionalism, and expertise.

In the days of hard and apparently unending work, my friends encouraged me in every way: Ana and Luka, Monika and Goran, Sonja and Marko, Larisa and Jakov, Minka and Mario, Mario and Ivana, Dajana and Bozo, Dario and Kristina, Patricia, Andrijana, Kristina, Ewa, and my dear friends from Associazione IPSA Trieste. Last, but not least, I thank my family for always being there for me. My truly special parents, my dad and, foremost, my mom, for their unmeasurable support and love. I would never have made it without them. My sister Ana made me laugh when times were tough, and accompanied me babysitting Gabriel in Belgrade. My parents-in-law helped me with devotion and care by babysitting, encouraging, and assisting.

This book would not have seen the light of day if it wasn't for my husband Dario who, passionate about management, leadership, and engineering, taught me to approach investigations in a timely, constructive, and precise manner. No words can describe his patience and support. As far as our life together is concerned, I would not be who I am without him. Last, but not least, our children, Emanuela, Clara, Gabriel, and Larissa have my deep heartfelt gratitude: patient and supportive, with smiles, humour, and overwhelming love, they made everything around this book so meaningful.

Notes on translation, pronunciation, and archival references

The translations from Serbo-Croatian, Slovenian, French, and Italian are mine. The title of documents originally in Cyrillic is always provided in the Latin alphabet. In the text, I use the diacritic signs of the Serbian (Latin) and Croatian alphabet. Serbo-Croatian is completely regular in pronunciation, and there are no silent letters. Eight Serbo-Croatian consonants do not feature in English, and four consonants appear identical but are pronounced differently. They are: Č is *ch* in 'church'; *ć* is *t* in 'mixture'; *dž* is *j* in 'jam'; *dj* is *d* in 'duke'; *š* is *sh* in 'shoe'; *ž* is *s* in 'treasure'; *lj* is *ll* in 'million'; *nj* is *n* in 'new'; *c* is *ts* in 'Tsar'; *j* is y in 'yet'; and *h* and *r* are always pronounced. Of the remaining consonants, *g* is always hard (as in 'gag'), and so is *s* (as in 'sack'). The vowels in Serbo-Croatian sound as follows: *a* in 'father'; *e* in 'pet'; *i* in 'machine'; *o* in 'hot'; *u* in 'rule.'

I opted for the US National Archives criteria, which follows the exact opposite sequence of the Archives of Yugoslavia, the Historical Archives of Belgrade, and the Croatian State Archives criteria.[1] This means I give the references in this order: the type and title of the item, originating office, addressee, date, file number, box and/or files by name and number, series or entry title/name of the collection, record group, and name of the repository. This rule has been respected in all cases, except for the records of the League of Communists of Yugoslavia's (LCY) Central Committee, which have a special identification number (a sequence of Roman and Arabic numbers) that has been inserted between the box number and the entry title. At the time that I accessed the Republican Commission for Cultural Relations with Foreign Countries at the Croatian State Archives, the record group was still unregulated. Therefore, I refer to it by the Archives' temporary references.

Note

1 L. Benson, *Yugoslavia: A Concise History*, 2nd edition (Houndmills, Basingstoke; New York: Palgrave Macmillan, 2003), x–xi.

List of abbreviations

Archival abbreviations

AY	Archives of Yugoslavia / Arhiv Jugoslavije
AYBT	Archives of Josip Broz Tito / Arhiv Josipa Broza Tita
CDF	Central Decimal Files
CFPF	Central Foreign Policy Files
CK SKJ	Centralni komitet Saveza Komunista Jugoslavije / Central Committee of the League of Communists of Yugoslavia
CSA	Croatian State Archives / Hrvatski državni arhiv
HAB	Historical Archives of Belgrade / Istorijski arhiv grada Beograda
KMOV	Komisija za međunarodne odnose i veze / Commission for International Relations
KPR	Kabinet Predsednika Republike / Cabinet of the President of the Republic
KPVI	Kulturno-prosvetne veze sa inostranstvom / Cultural-educational relations with foreign countries
MC	Manuscript Collection
MIC	Microfilm Collection
NACP	National Archives and Records Administration at College Park
RG	Record Group
RIAS	Roosevelt Institute for American Studies
RKKV	Republička komisija za kulturne veze s inostranstvom / Republican Commission for the Cultural Relations with Foreign Countries
RSK SRH	Republički sekretarijat za kulturu SRH / Republican Secretary for Culture, Socialist Republic of Croatia
RSPKFK	Republički sekretarijat za prosvjetu, kulturu i fizičku kulturu / Republican Secretary for Education, Culture and Physical Culture
SNF	Subject Numeric Files
SNK FNRJ	Savet za nauku i kulturu Vlade Federativne Narodne Republike Jugoslavije / Council for Science and Culture of the Government of the Federal People's Republic of Yugoslavia
SSOK	Savezni sekretarijat za obrazovanje i kulturu / Federal Secretary for Education and Culture
UAL	University of Arkansas Library
USIA OR	USIA Office of Research

USIA ORA   USIA Office of Research and Analysis
USIA ORMR   USIA Office of Research and Media Reaction

Acronyms

AEC   Atomic Energy Commission
ANTA   American National Theatre and Academy
BFS   Board of Foreign Scholarships
CAO   Cultural Affairs Officer
CC   Central Committee
CPP   Cultural Presentation Program
CU   Bureau of Educational and Cultural Affairs
EC   Executive Council
FCCR   Federal Commission for Cultural Relations with Foreign Countries /
               Savezna komisija za kulturne veze s inostranstvom
FEC   Federal Executive Council / Savezno izvršno veće / vijeće
FLP   Foreign Leader Program
FNEC   Federal Nuclear Energy Commission
FO   Foreign Office / Državni sekretarijat za inostrane poslove
GLCA   Great Lakes College Association
IBS   International Broadcasting Division
ICA   International Cooperation Administration
ICS   Information Center Service
IIA   International Information Administration
IMG   Informational Media Guarantee Program
IOA   Office of Administration
IPS   International Press Service / Press and Publication Service
LCC   League of Communists of Croatia / Savez komunista Hrvatske
LCY   League of Communists of Yugoslavia / Savez komunista Jugoslavije
MAP   Military Assistance Pact
MDAP   Mutual Defense Aid Program
MFN   most-favoured-nation
MSA   Mutual Security Agency
NSC   National Security Council
OWI   Office of War Information
PAO   Public Affairs Officer
RFE   Radio Free Europe
RL   Radio Liberty
SAWPY   Socialist Alliance of Working People of Yugoslavia / Socijalistički
               savez radnog naroda Jugoslavije
SEC   Secretariat for Education and Culture
SFRY   Socialist Federal Republic of Yugoslavia / Socijalistička Federativna
               Republika Jugoslavija

TCA	Technical Cooperation Administration
UDBA	Uprava državne bezbednosti / State Security Administration
USIA	United States Information Agency
USIE	United States Information and Education (Program)
USIS	United States Information Service
VOA	Voice of America
YCP	Yugoslav Communist Party

Introduction

'No event could be more momentous for the attainment of our [US] foreign policy objectives than the permanent alienation from the Soviet Union of this key regime.'[1] These words, spoken by American counsellor R. Borden Reams in Belgrade only a few days after the Tito–Stalin split of June 1948, seemed to capture perfectly the profound significance of that moment. The news about the expulsion of the Yugoslav Communist Party (YCP) from the Cominform erupted on the front pages of worldwide newspapers. *Borba*, *Vjesnik*, and *Politika* – as the main Yugoslav Party's 'spokespersons' – expressed consternation and disbelief.[2]

The Information Bureau of the Communist and Workers' Parties, more commonly known as Cominform (Communist Information Bureau), founded in September 1947 as a political response to the Marshall Plan to unify the European communist parties under Soviet auspices, expelled the YCP from its ranks with the accusation of disloyalty to Marxist and Leninist ideals. In fact, it was Tito's expansionist ambitions over Greece, Bulgaria, and Albania that irritated the Soviet dictator and caused the Soviet–Yugoslav impasse.[3]

Soon it became clear that there was no return from the break-up and no way around its long-term consequences. The Soviet–Yugoslav rupture would lay the ground for the Yugoslav 'way to socialism,' its socialist self-management economy, and its non-aligned foreign policy. In the years following 1948, the Yugoslav leadership started searching for new geostrategic partnerships, alliances, and military backing. By 1950, Yugoslavia would turn towards the United States, and the United States towards Yugoslavia, a process that transformed Tito's regime into the 'American Communist ally,' in the words of historian Tvrtko Jakovina.[4]

Walter Smith, the US ambassador to Moscow during those stormy days of 1948, rightly observed that the 'Cominform resolution, which the Yugoslav Communist Party has now rejected, indicates [the] first really serious crisis in the new "family" of Soviet states erected since the war's end, and will be a *God-send to our propagandists*.'[5]

This story starts from Smith's 'God-sent' propaganda issue. In this new situation, it was not obvious what Yugoslavia would do. The Yugoslav choice was a surprise for the international community and for the Yugoslav leadership as well. The Soviets expected that they would return to the fold with their head bowed, while Truman did not envision Tito's turn towards the United States for help. Indeed, Yugoslavia became the first communist-ruled state that defied Soviet domination and deviated from the Soviet model. As Yugoslav expert Dennison Rusinow explained, Tito's regime experimented with market mechanisms and gradually replaced a command economy with decentralized decision-making, broader personal freedom, new forms of political participation, an open frontiers policy, and wide-ranging integration into the Cold War international arena.[6] By the early 1950s, Yugoslavia embraced what its ideologist and leader Edvard Kardelj called the doctrine of 'active peaceful cooperation' with foreign countries, including the Western ones, foremost the United States.[7] In foreign policy, Yugoslav State Secretary Koča Popović followed a path of neutrality that, only after the 1956 Soviet occupation of Budapest, moved boldly towards non-alignment. Together with Indian president Jawaharlal Nehru and Egyptian leader Gamal Abdel Nasser, Tito signed the Declaration of Brioni in July 1956, giving birth to the Non-Aligned Movement organization (NAM).[8]

Yugoslavia became a top priority for Washington's public diplomacy creators after 1950. First the Truman and then the Eisenhower administrations adopted a policy of 'keeping Tito afloat.' The State Department policymakers coined the term 'wedge strategy' to indicate the foreign relations approach to Yugoslavia. The strategy consisted in supporting Yugoslav nationalism to instigate divisions between the Soviet Union and other communist countries and demonstrate that socialism was possible outside the Soviet sphere. Nevertheless, using Yugoslav nationalism as an example for other Soviet-dominated, communist states, the American government, argues Lorraine Lees, jeopardized its strategy by futile attempts to change Tito's regime. While Lees meant short-term political overturns, overtures, and a greater influence on the Eastern bloc, Tito's regime partially, but truly, reformed in the following decades.[9]

After Stalin's death, Yugoslavia took a liberalization shift, embodied in a more liberal and less Soviet-like 1953 constitution. From the mid-1950s onwards, and more intensely in the 1960s, the country began importing Western-style cultural and social models, American jazz and British rock, Hollywood movies, and Italian San Remo pop melodies. By the early 1960s, a marked increase in family incomes helped spread an American-style advertising industry and a Yugoslav way of consumerism. Such a modernization novelty was apparent in new household appliances, culinary arts, urban architecture, and, of course, in Yugoslav supermarkets.[10]

'America' arrived in Yugoslavia through many informal channels and entered Yugoslav daily life as part of a modernization process. Culturally, Yugoslavia opened up to the West, and Western fashion, music, and art styles penetrated its public sphere, thus adapting to local tastes and traditions. Such a modernization flow from the United States – defined by Serbian historian Radina Vučetić as 'Coca-Cola socialism' and simplified as pure and simple Americanization – was largely caused by cultural influences that came through private channels, mostly led by business and economic interests.[11]

Still, something planned by the United States government came to Yugoslavia from the 1950s onwards. Backed by US military, technological, and economic aid to Yugoslavia, the State Department, from the early 1950s onwards, and the United States Information Agency (USIA) from 1953, envisioned a long-term policy aimed at exerting a cultural but, most of all, political influence on Yugoslavia. Soft power played a key role in this undiscovered, and, up until the present day, untold story. This book examines a neglected aspect of the American–Yugoslav special relationship that helped foster the mutual partnership: namely public diplomacy.

Based on US and Yugoslav archival sources and periodicals, as well as written and oral testimonies, *US Public Diplomacy in Socialist Yugoslavia* reveals a wide network of lobbies and operations conceived by the USIA from its headquarters in Washington, DC and implemented by the United States Information Services (USIS) in Belgrade and Zagreb and, from there, in the Yugoslav territory. This network penetrated the Yugoslav Party leadership, intelligentsia, students, and public opinion, and influenced policy outcomes.

For the State Department, public diplomacy entailed 'government-sponsored programs intended to inform or influence public opinion in other countries' such as 'publications, motion pictures, cultural exchanges, radio and television.'[12] Even today, public diplomacy influences 'public attitudes on the formation and execution of foreign policies' and 'encompasses dimensions of international relations beyond traditional diplomacy.' This study follows Nicholas Cull's definition of public diplomacy, and looks specifically at 'the cultivation by governments of public opinion in other countries,' 'the interaction of private groups and interests in one country with another,' 'the reporting of foreign affairs and its impact on policy,' 'the communication between […] diplomats and foreign correspondents,' and 'the process of intercultural communications.'[13]

In 1945, the US government opened its USIS post in Belgrade, in 1948 in Novi Sad, and in 1951 in Zagreb. USIS Ljubljana opened its doors in 1970, Skopje in 1972, and Sarajevo in 1973. These American information centres housed a public library and reading room that provided American journals and specialized periodicals, lectures, exhibits, concerts, and English lessons. They arranged the Cultural Presentation Program (CPP) that provided the arrival in Yugoslavia of American artists, usually choirs, jazz, blues, and classical music performers, vanguard theatre groups, then painters, athletes, and academic lecturers. By broadcasting Voice of America (VOA), the US government reached thousands of Yugoslav citizens. Likewise, the American pavilions at the Zagreb and Belgrade international trade fairs further enhanced the idea of American wealth, knowledge, and technological expertise. What is more, the Cultural Exchange Program, by including an extraordinary variety of more than fifty exchange platforms, such as the Foreign Leader, Fulbright, and Ford programs, provided by public, private, or state–private funds, generated intense interest and impact on the part of Yugoslav politicians, academics, and university students, by introducing an alternative and, for them, insidious *forma mentis*.

The period of almost three decades investigated in this book tracks intense transformations of Tito's regime from the late 1940s to the early 1970s – a period in which US influence played a crucial role. The book closes with the early 1970s. Leonid Brezhnev's firm grip on Eastern Europe in the early 1970s increasingly caused

Yugoslav concern. President Nixon's bold support for Yugoslavia, and tangible Soviet threat, induced the Yugoslav leaders to invest, more than ever before, in cultural and economic cooperation with the United States. Nevertheless, by the early 1970s it became evident that the US success in terms of public diplomacy entailed an uncalculated risk: namely, influencing Yugoslav political and intellectual leaders with Western values emboldened internal dissent that sometimes could not change the regime from within, but was rather suppressed for challenging the Party's monopoly. The early 1970s represent, therefore, especially with the 1974 constitution, a closing chapter of a two-decade-long Yugoslav transformation from a Stalinist state to a socialist regime open to foreign influence.

In shaping the American 'battle for the hearts and minds' of Yugoslav citizens, soft power played a crucial role. In the famous Joseph Nye definition, soft power is a country's 'ability to obtain the outcomes it wants in world politics' and 'to shape the preferences of others' through the attractiveness of its values, prosperity and openness.[14] If the United States designed a vast 'visible' and 'invisible' network among Yugoslav citizens and leaders, what do we know about its influence on Yugoslav–US foreign relations? Put in reverse, how did US public diplomacy interests respond to bilateral Cold War downturns and crises? To what strategic goals did the US concerns in Yugoslavia respond? How did US field officers challenge the rather piqued Yugoslav government officials, at micro and macro level, and hit the targeted population? How were operational goals met? What were Yugoslav attitude patterns towards American propaganda in Yugoslavia? How did the communist hierarchy and USIS field officers embody Yugoslav–US cooperation and dissimilarities?

Needless to say, soft-power resources are never monolithic, unidirectional, and uncritically received. American public diplomats in Yugoslavia knew that, and in the process of intercultural communication they used both official, state-directed channels of communication, attraction, and influence, and private actors speaking for governmental goals. In the collective Yugoslav imaginaries, the US cultural mission represented an iconic United States and its *way of life*. Geographically immobile and stationary, USIS centres relied on VOA, the exchange programs, the cultural exhibitions and lectures, the mobile libraries, and the mobile movie theatres for rural propagation. In this book, relations between 'centres' and 'peripheries' are essential to understanding the Yugoslav case: those between USIS centres and the Yugoslav territory (the Socialist Republics); those of Yugoslav executive officials with local administrators; those between the USIA and the Department of State.

The research covers historiographical gaps primarily as a case study of the political role of culture in diplomacy, neglected today in US–Yugoslav foreign and bilateral relations;[15] secondly, as a statement on fluid relations between information and propaganda and unintended effects (consequences) that propaganda can produce beyond the control of both producers and receivers.[16] This study rejects the presumption that US propaganda in Yugoslavia was an avowal of cultural imperialism, as Tomlinson and others have argued,[17] somehow underestimating the capacity of negotiation and refusal as well as of reciprocal cultural 'creolization.'[18] Neither is the question of 'Americanization' as a concept addressed, which prevents us from grasping the multi-polarity of cultural and political relations between the United States and Yugoslavia.[19] In the spring of 1980, Ivan Pongračić entered the American Library in Zagreb and found on its desk Russell Kirk's *The Conservative Mind*. Fascinated by the author, he returned looking for more books. Soon after, he applied to an international conference organized by Kirk in Pennsylvania, which he found out about in another American Library magazine. In the United States, Pongračić became first Kirk's friend, then his assistant, and, ultimately, ended his career as professor emeritus of Indiana University.[20] This example, among many others, suggests that the impact of public diplomacy often transcends the main reason for which it was established. For this motive, this book looks at resource attractiveness and the behavioural outcome in public diplomacy, through the perspective of the sender (the US government and its private partners), the receivers (Yugoslav citizens – first and foremost the cultural exchange grantees), and the observers and receivers (Yugoslav officials and Party leaders). The State Department, its Bureau of Educational and Cultural Affairs (CU) from 1961, and the USIA, searched for soft-power solutions that would include a proper strategy and the desired outcome. Their position presumed knowing the final recipient of power and communicating in his terms, while not trespassing the established framework of the political diplomacy strategy.

Yugoslav diplomats interpreted Yugoslav openness as the 'starting grid' of Yugoslav exceptionalism.[21] Similarly, Slavenka Drakulić, a world-known Yugoslav feminist, upheld that 'the system of "self-management", that Yugoslavia was so proud of, was a ruse, invented to make you believe that [...] it was the most perfect system among the one-party states, set up [...] to make you feel that you had more freedom than anyone in Eastern Europe.'[22] Indeed, conscious of the Yugoslav crucial position between the two superpowers, the regime's policymakers used the country's cultural avant-garde as a soft-power instrument to affirm the Yugoslav image, prestige, and value – its distinctive 'way to socialism' or 'socialism with a human face' – at the international exhibitions, festivals, and contests in the Western European cultural capitals.[23] In many notable studies pertaining to Yugoslav history, scholars have used the Yugoslav 'exceptionalist model' to comprehend its boundary position between East and West, capitalism and communism, namely the 'Coca-Cola' socialism, and the 'socialism on the American grain.' By unifying two opposite qualities of the Yugoslav regime, symbolically appertaining to both the capitalist and communist ideology, they enhanced the idea of a Yugoslav oxymoron. So, for instance, Patrick Patterson and Igor Duda examined the socialist consumer and well-being of society;[24] Hannes Grandits and Karin Taylor studied the ideological role of mass, Western-like, tourism in shaping the Yugoslav worker;[25] Tvrtko Jakovina emphasized the Yugoslav nation-building process on the 'American grain';[26] while Radina Vučetić wrote about the 'American dream in the Yugoslav way.'[27]

Seen as 'exceptional' by its authors and as an 'exception' by its scholars, the Yugoslav exceptionalist model does not work for this book. In its engagement with US public diplomats, the Yugoslav side acted pragmatically, which corresponded, in fact, to the US attitude as well. While usually guided by realpolitik stances, the Yugoslavs reacted in accordance with the type of *identity* they were trying to construct in the face of the foreign world – usually flaunting openness that was limited when it was perceived as challenging to the regime's power. Dejan Jović's assessment is very helpful in this scenario. He argues that there were two 'Others' against which Yugoslav socialism tried to construct itself – liberal representative democracy and Soviet-style socialism – both antipodes and 'mirror images.' These potential threats had their domestic representatives in, on the one hand, the 'liberals' and 'techno-managerial forces,' and, on the other, 'dogmatists,' 'unitarists,' 'bureaucrats,' and 'Stalinists.' Several circumstances led the Yugoslavs to declare the Soviet-type statist socialism as their main threat and danger. Consequently, the Yugoslav political elite opposed, with much less vigilance, the liberal democrats and the pro-Western groups and, when the Soviet Union collapsed, they were left without the existence of the Soviet 'Other' on which they constructed their own identity. Ultimately, liberalism, together with nationalism, 'entered the Yugoslav identity-making arena and emerged victorious.'[28] Here, I want to analyse how the liberal democratic 'Other' evolved in Yugoslavia through US public diplomacy agents and agencies, by appealing to target groups, exploring, negotiating, and contributing to the Yugoslav experiment in the early Cold War period.

Soft power through foreign relations: the cultural Cold War and public diplomacy

> One of the reasons reciprocation can be used so effectively as a device for gaining another's compliance is its power. The rule possesses awesome strength, often producing a 'yes' response to a request that, except for an existing feeling of indebtedness, would have surely been refused.
>
> Robert Cialdini[29]

From the early 1990s, historians Akira Iriye and Frank Ninkovich pioneered the rise of a cultural analysis within the fields of diplomatic history. Iriye defined culture in the study of international relations as 'the sharing and transmitting of consciousness within and across national boundaries, and the cultural approach as a perspective that pays particular attention to this phenomenon.'[30] Ninkovich went further: not only were cultural relations a minor form of diplomacy, it was the whole foreign policy process that seemed imbued with larger cultural dynamics. Or expressed otherwise, 'penetrating the source of cultural processes, […] might shed some indirect light on the nature of cultural influences, external and internal, upon foreign policy.' Studying the American cultural programs abroad is beneficial in many ways: through the authors of such programs we sense not only their need to change society, but also their inner anthropological values. The State Department cultural policies were 'an organic development, not simply an intellectual response,' of institutional and societal environment. They mirrored the domestic factors on foreign policy, underpinning connections between foreign policy and society.[31]

Looking at cultural relations in the American–Yugoslav partnership is even more necessary because public diplomacy reveals that Cold War partnerships were a matter of domestic debate, policymaking and, therefore, foreign confrontations. What looks like inner contradiction of the US–Yugoslav alliance, under the public diplomacy perspective becomes a symptom of mutual engagement through various channels of cooperation: economy, science, military, and finally culture.

As Cull remarks, public diplomacy is 'an international actor's attempt to conduct its foreign policy by engaging with a foreign public in five main ways: listening, advocacy, cultural diplomacy, exchange diplomacy, and international broadcasting.'[32] Each of these elements have a different source of credibility, attractiveness, and infrastructure. Therefore, they have been treated in different chapters. Whether it is a government, an international organization, a non-governmental organization, or even an individual, the core idea is to advance foreign policy by engaging with foreign audiences. Specifically, such engagement differentiates public diplomacy from propaganda: public diplomacy listens (or should listen) to what people have to say, while propagandists listen to target groups only to deliver their message more effectively. Propaganda has a short-term range and looks for immediate impact, while public diplomacy is open for cultural exchange with foreign audiences and perpetuates long-term objectives. In a way, 'public diplomacy provides the mechanism by which international actors communicate their culture and values to an international audience.'[33]

Public diplomacy scholars have extensively used Nye's theorizing on soft power to enhance their interpretations. For Nye, a country's soft power rests on three resources: 'its culture (in places where it is attractive to others), its political values (when it lives up to them at home and abroad), and its foreign policies (when others see them as legitimate and having moral authority).'[34] Such theorizing has been largely criticized by many authors. While Niall Ferguson declined soft power as not being really a 'power' as it was 'too soft,' Janice Bially Mattern asserted that attraction, as a sociolinguistically constructed 'representational force,' makes soft power a continuation of hard power, only by different means.[35] To counter these critics, in *The Future of Power* Nye introduced the *smart power* concept, a combination of both hard and soft power. Along this line, culture is soft power 'only when it rests on a foundation of hard power. Increases in hard economic and military power produce enhanced self-confidence, arrogance, and belief in the superiority of one's own culture or soft power compared to those of other peoples and greatly increase its attractiveness to other peoples,' argues Samuel Huntington.[36]

I argue that the Yugoslav leadership opened towards the United States for reasons of pragmatism – economic and technological – and accepted the presence of the USIA on Yugoslav territory as a side effect of such a decision. On the other hand, the USIA won over the Yugoslav and worldwide public mainly by publicizing a people's way of life (customs, values, ideals); elite artistic expressions (literature, fine arts, performing arts); and popular culture (the products of the commercial entertainment industry). Paraphrasing Su Changhe, soft power, as cultural power, was a crucial component of American foreign policy in Yugoslavia. It has been used in all areas and levels of bilateral diplomacy. It has been used reciprocally, as this book proves. In a way, soft power between these two actors meant translating Gramsci's hegemony thesis into a value-neutral concept for policymakers of that time, Americans and Yugoslavs.[37]

US public diplomacy in the Cold War

> Our task is to present the truth to the millions of people who are uninformed,
> or misinformed, or unconvinced. Our task is to reach them in their daily lives,
> as they work and learn. [...] Our task is to show them that freedom is the way to
> economic and social advancement, the way to political independence, the way
> to strength, happiness, and peace. The task is not separate and distinct from other
> elements of our foreign policy.
>
> President Truman, 20 April 1950[38]

The experience of World War I changed the attitudes towards propaganda within
the United States when Wilson's Committee on Public Information (the Creel
Committee) got involved in information activities abroad. While the post-war isola-
tionist policy dismantled the governmental backing of 'propaganda,' which continued
to rely on private initiatives such as the Rockefeller and Ford foundations,[39] it was only
with Franklin Roosevelt's presidency that the administration moved again towards
domestic and foreign propaganda. The presidential radio 'fireside chats,' logos and
posters, rallies and parades, publicized his New Deal programs, to the extent that in
1934 FDR created the United States Information Service (USIS) within the National
Executive Council. After war broke out in Europe, President Roosevelt engaged in
an overall effort to pawn the effects of Axis propaganda. Especially in Latin America,
he entrusted Nelson Rockefeller to counteract German and Italian propaganda with
the newly established Office of the Coordinator of Inter-American Affairs.[40] Soon
after the Japanese attack on Pearl Harbor and Germany's declaration of war against
the United States, the State Department inaugurated VOA broadcasts in February
1942. In June, the Office of War Information (OWI) came to life.[41] On the flow of an
expanding foreign propaganda, the years between 1943 and 1945 saw a tremendous
increase of American Libraries abroad: from Sydney to Johannesburg; from Cairo
to Istanbul; from London to New Delhi.[42] For the first time in US history, ideas and
images of the United States not only 'mattered to foreign policy,' they *were* the US
foreign policy, Justin Hart suggests.[43]

The increased Cold War tensions, and the conviction over Soviet superiority in
the war of ideas, convinced Congress that VOA was necessary and legitimate, even
in peacetime. Nevertheless, many doubted that a democratic country should maintain its robust propaganda effort after World War II. The liberals feared that the US
government might begin to direct propaganda towards American citizens; others
believed that the post-war status of the United States alone would induce the world to
reject communism, with no need to spend taxpayers' money. Influential policymakers
believed that everyone would want to emulate the US freedom, social mobility, and
superior quality of life, without the interference of state initiatives.[44] The controversial
US Information and Education Exchange Act of January 1948 (Public Law 402),
popularly referred to as the Smith-Mundt Act, legalized peacetime propaganda, but
restricted the State Department (and later the USIA) officials involved with public

diplomacy from engaging in operations within the United States. Proposed by Senator Alexander Smith and Congressman Karl Mundt, the law intended 'to promote the better understanding of the United States among the people of the world and to strengthen cooperative international relations.'[45]

Containment doctrine and public diplomacy

Truman's decision to continue American warfare propaganda in peacetime was closely linked to the embracing of containment. Known also as the Truman Doctrine, and conceived by American master diplomat George Kennan, the containment strategy meant to counter Soviet geopolitical expansion in Germany, Italy, Turkey, the Eastern Mediterranean, and Asia. Faced with the Soviet threat, 'U.S. officials came to believe that they have to offer economic assistance […], establish linkages with foreign elites […] incur strategic commitments and assume political-military responsibilities in places they had not contemplated.' In other words, the containment tactic established a 'configuration of power that safeguarded U.S. security and […] institutionalized Washington's preponderant influence in the international system.'[46]

Truman retained the wartime information apparatus as a resource for post-war American foreign policy and decided to use American power to forge an international environment conducive to the American way of life. He believed in the United States' exceptional mission as 'God's country, the city on a hill, the exemplar of a superior civilization based on personal freedom, private property, entrepreneurial opportunity, and limited government.'[47] By executive order 9608 of 31 August 1945, the President wrapped up the Office of War Information (OWI), which was transformed into different organizations before becoming the USIA.

In late August 1945, the Secretary of State, James Byrnes, persuaded his friend William Benton, an expert from the world of advertising, to accept the post of Assistant Secretary of State for Public and Cultural Relations. Preparing the country for a prolonged confrontation with the Soviet Union, in early 1947, the administration introduced a National Security Bill to establish a Central Intelligence Agency, a National Security Resources Board, a Joint Chiefs of Staff, and a single Defense Department. Above all, the newly created National Security Council (NSC) would become the key senior figure in foreign and defence policy to coordinate the US foreign relations approach.[48]

Then, from 1950 to 1951, Truman led the way to a major overseas propaganda, deliberately named 'the Campaign of Truth.' Launched in April 1950 in a speech at the American Society of Newspaper Editors, he announced that the Cold War was 'a struggle, above all else, for the minds of men,' in which 'forces of imperialistic communism' could be overcome by the 'plain, simple, unvarnished truth.'[49] For its author, Edward Barret, the new Assistant Secretary for Public Affairs after Benton, the Campaign would open up a 'worldwide war of ideas' fought as a 'dirty street-corner battle,' countering the 'Big Lie with the truth.'[50] Barrett directed what, at the time, was called the United States Information and Educational Exchange Program (USIE).

In its final administration year, Truman's policymakers struggled with mounting pressure to remove the information agency from the Department of State. Therefore, before leaving office, Truman reorganized the information and exchange program under the semi-autonomous US International Information Administration (IIA), the last step before the USIA's creation.[51]

'The primary purpose of the United States Information Agency,' established a National Security Council directive, 'shall be to persuade foreign peoples that it lies in their own interest to take actions which are also consistent with the national objectives of the United States,' and consequently, 'to harmonize wherever possible the personal and national self-interest of foreigners with the national objectives of the United States.' Such goals required that 'the United States find out what other peoples want, relate their wants to those of this country, and explain these common goals in ways that will cause others to join with the United States in their achievement.'[52] The Reorganizational Plan no. 8 launched the United States Information Agency on 1 August 1953, 'a new, independent information and propaganda agency at the sub-cabinet level.' Under the USIA umbrella, President Eisenhower merged the International Information Administration (IIA), the Mutual Security Agency (MSA), and the Technical Cooperation Administration (TCA), but left the exchange programs within the State Department.[53] President Eisenhower's Committee on International Information Activities – the so-called Jackson Committee – provided important recommendations for the new agency, namely to adapt broadcasting and information activities to the target needs of each country; to avoid US self-praise; and to use non-attribution tactics.[54] The USIA mission was to convince uncommitted and communist-dominated people that their aspirations could be best achieved in a free society. In Yugoslavia, this meant emphasizing the ideological aspect of the East–West struggle, the defence against Soviet aggression, and the maintenance of independence from the Soviets, so that 'every effort be made to present a sober and true picture of the United States, to the end that the Yugoslavs shall respect and understand us, rather than [...] selling freedom to them [which] [...] connotes the subversion of their system, with the likely risks to U.S. security interests.'[55]

In its tormented history, during which it struggled for a deserved place at executive level, the USIA would became the spokesperson and interpreter of American foreign policy and the promoter of anti-communist stances and positive themes about the United States. This first global information agency sold the American dream abroad through cultural propaganda, celebrated democratic values and practices, criticized communist ideology that permitted forced-labour camps and restricted both individual freedoms and consumer goods, and advocated American capitalism. In doing so, VOA became one of its prime weapons of influence.[56] Partially covert, the USIA planted news in newspapers, programmes on local television channels, and used personal contacts to influence foreign journalists and influential opinion leaders.[57]

Yugoslavia ... my target, my friend

The Yugoslavs need the technical knowledge which the West has. Moreover, they could not entirely prohibit our activities in this country without forfeiting their claim to independence of both East and West. Consequently, there has been certain relenting in their resistance to the spread of information about the United States in Yugoslavia. Their own need for us, however grudgingly admitted, opens a narrow but indispensable door in the wall of ideological hostility – and through this door ideas can pass.

Letter from Inspector Lawrence Morris to USIA Director George
Allen, Belgrade, 20 November 1959[58]

The American Libraries abroad were the direct product of Washington's public diplomacy. 'Like the fresh new U.S. embassies,' argued lifelong USIA officer Richard Arndt, 'libraries themselves showcased an aspect of U.S. democracy. Their content, access, user-friendly classification systems, furnishings, ample lighting, knowledgeable and cheerful staff, open shelves, alternative or critical viewpoints, and free lending, showed how a free citizenry gets its information.' Indeed, the USIS libraries made a strong political statement about America. Nobel Laureate Wole Soyinka, haunting USIS libraries in Nigeria as a youth, learned that books are 'objects of terror to those who seek to suppress the truth.' Umberto Eco, Italian leftist intellectual and philosopher, like other young intellectuals around the world, devoured every book in his USIS library in Milan, tasting free access to a wealth of books, including those critical of the US government.[59] In the 'war of ideas against [communist] totalitarianism,' claimed an USIA early report, USIS overseas libraries were essentially 'instruments of persuasion,' appealing to leadership and opinion-moulding groups. The American Library abroad represented, almost simultaneously, a *place* and an *idea* that attracted those in a position to influence others. There were demonstration models and training centres. In Yugoslavia, as in other countries, they targeted editors, translators, public officials, teachers, intellectuals, and students.[60]

Not surprisingly, USIS centres were power in the sense Nye intended it: the power to get others 'to want the outcomes you want' and to 'shape the preference of others.'[61] In other words, the USIS centres were intended to explain and interpret to foreign people 'the objectives and policies of the United States government' by depicting the correlation between US policies and those of other countries; '[by] unmasking [...] hostile attempts to distort [...] the objectives and policies of the United States'; and by portraying the 'life and culture of the people of the United States.'[62] This book attempts to reconstruct how the US cultural power operated in a semi-opened socialist country where it became an adhesive rather than a dividing wall, proving how the soft approach was the only successful and most persuasive in the Cold War cultural struggle. It, therefore, opens many unanswered questions. Why did the United States invest so much in Tito's Yugoslavia? Was the US government successful in attracting Yugoslavia to the United States? How did Tito and his leadership cope with being an 'American' partner?

Why did Yugoslavia open to US cultural penetration? How did US public diplomacy adapt to a socialist environment? This book explores the cultural background of the Yugo–American Cold War alliance. I argue that, while being ideologically problematic for Washington policymakers to 'sell America' in a socialist society without criticizing the dictatorship, the US cultural programs succeeded in attracting the Yugoslav academic, intellectual, artistic, and political leadership, and created cooperation networks that strengthened pro-American and Western sentiments.

Yugoslav political attitudes towards USIA-USIS public diplomacy policies drastically changed from one program to another. American participation at Yugoslav trade fairs, as Chapter 3 explains, was highly endorsed and appreciated. Considered by the organizers a matter of prestige, it improved US–Yugoslav economic and trade relations and helped Yugoslav entrepreneurs gain precious technological know-how. The US Cultural Presentation Program (Chapter 4) was equally welcomed. The American artists, musicians, actors, ballet dancers, etc. were not perceived as a political danger, but rather as politically neutral. The Yugoslav standpoint over the Cultural Exchange Program with US universities and institutions seemed more controversial. The exchange program (Chapter 5), counting around fifty different models between state and private initiatives – the most popular and effective being the Ford, Fulbright, and Foreign Leader programs – was on one hand appreciated as a means of modernization and a way for Yugoslav affirmation in the United States. It was less prized for trying to politically influence groups of cultural (academics and scientists) and political (of middle-high and middle rank positions) leaders. But the Yugoslav authorities were mostly reluctant in relation to USIS field activities (Chapter 1 and 2) and the broadcasts of Voice of America (Chapter 4). Why was this the case? The reasons are stratified. The stance towards field operations, which included VOA broadcastings as well, was more conservative. In the 1950s, but also in the 1960s and beyond, the American cultural centres in Belgrade and Zagreb represented a 'nail in the head' and 'thorn in the side' of Yugoslav organizations such as the Socialist Alliance of Working People of Yugoslavia (SAWPY), since they personally contacted large masses rather than carefully picked categories, as was the case with the exchange programs. And VOA, by reaching a large slice of the population, was considered even more harmful. The USIS regarded its work as successful both because of its popularity among the audience and because of the liberal cultural trends that, following the approbation of the 1953 constitution, left them more freedom in working with Yugoslav cultural leaders. Finally, by providing new insights into porous borders between freedom and coercion in Tito's communist regime, I argue how public diplomacy programs acted as an external input for Yugoslav liberalization and dissident movements.

Notes

1 Reams, Chargé in Yugoslavia, to Secretary of State, 30 June 1948, *Foreign Relations of the United States* (hereafter FRUS), 1948, Vol. IV, Eastern Europe; Soviet Union, doc. 700.

2　See *Borba*, 30 June 1948, 4–5; *Vjesnik*, 30 June 1948, 1–3; and *Politika*, 30 June 1948, 1–2.
3　Jeronim Perović, 'The Tito-Stalin Split: A Reassessment in Light of New Evidence,' *Journal of Cold War Studies* 9, no. 2 (2007): 32–63, https://doi.org/10.1162/ jcws.2007.9.2.32.
4　Tvrtko Jakovina, *Američki komunistički saveznik: Hrvati, Titova Jugoslavija i Sjedinjene Američke Države 1945–1955* (Zagreb: Profil, 2003).
5　Smith, Ambassador in the Soviet Union, to Secretary of State, Moscow, 1 July 1948, FRUS, 1948, IV, 1082. The emphasis is mine.
6　Dennison I. Rusinow, *The Yugoslav Experiment 1948–1974* (Berkeley: University of California Press, 1978). From the same author, but giving in-depth analysis, see *Yugoslavia: Oblique Insights and Observations* (Pittsburgh: University of Pittsburgh Press, 2008).
7　Edvard Kardelj, 'Nova Jugoslavija u savremenom svijetu,' *Komunist*, 1 (January 1951): 1–32.
8　Rinna Kullaa, *Non-Alignment and its Origins in Cold War Europe: Yugoslavia, Finland and the Soviet Challenge* (London; New York: I. B. Tauris, 2012). Unlike Rinna Kullaa, Svetozar Rajak claims that the 'conceptualization of non-alignment was underway by the early 1950s' ('No Bargaining Chips, No Spheres of Interest: The Yugoslav Origins of Cold War Non-Alignment,' *Journal of Cold War Studies* 16, no. 1 (2014): 146–79, https://doi.org/10.1162/JCWS_a_00434) and that, together with Nehru and Nasser, 'Tito was instrumental in transforming the idea of passive neutralism into a universal movement of Third World countries with an ambition to play an active role on the global stage' ('From Regional Role to Global Undertakings: Yugoslavia in the Early Cold War,' in *The Balkans in the Cold War*, ed. Svetozar Rajak et al. (London: Palgrave Macmillan, 2017), 73–4).
9　Lorraine M. Lees, *Keeping Tito Afloat: The United States, Yugoslavia, and the Cold War* (University Park, PA: Pennsylvania State University Press, 2005).
10　See for instance Hannes Grandits and Karin Taylor, eds, *Yugoslavia's Sunny Side: A History of Tourism in Socialism (1950s–1980s)* (Budapest; New York: Central European University Press, 2010); Patrick H. Patterson, *Bought and Sold: Living and Losing the Good Life in Socialist Yugoslavia* (Ithaca, NY: Cornell University Press, 2011); Breda Luthar and Marusa Pusnik, eds, *Remembering Utopia: The Culture of Everyday Life in Socialist Yugoslavia* (Washington, DC: New Academia Publishing, LLC, 2010); Francesca Rolandi, *Con ventiquattromila baci: L'influenza della cultura di massa italiana in Jugoslavia (1955–1965)* (Bologna: Bononia University Press, 2015).
11　Radina Vučetić, *Coca-Cola Socialism: Americanization of Yugoslav Culture in the Sixties* (Budapest; New York: Central European University Press, 2017). Even if *Coca-Cola Socialism* represents an extraordinary contribution to the history of American influences in Yugoslavia, the book oversimplifies the 'Americanization' of Yugoslav society in the 1960s by including in this term various modernization inputs from the United States, Italy, Great Britain, and France.
12　'Public Diplomacy,' *Dictionary of International Relations Terms* (Department of State Library, 1987).
13　Nicholas J. Cull, 'Public Diplomacy before Gullion. The Evolution of a Phrase,' in *Routledge Handbook of Public Diplomacy*, ed. Nancy Snow and Philip M Taylor (New York; London: Routledge Taylor&Francis, 2009), 19.

14 Joseph S. Nye Jr, *Soft Power: The Means To Success In World Politics*, 2nd ed. (New York: Public Affairs, 2009), 21–2.

15 Besides Jakovina's works, other authors have inquired into Yugoslav–US relations under the frame either of economic relations (John R. Lampe, Russell O. Prickett, and Ljubiša S. Adamović, *Yugoslav–American Economic Relations Since World War II* [Durham: Duke University Press, 1990]); or Cold War strategy (Lees, *Keeping Tito Afloat*); or traditional diplomatic relations (Nick Ceh, *US Diplomatic Records on Relations with Yugoslavia during the Early Cold War* [New York: Columbia University Press, 2001]; Dragan Bogetić, *Jugoslavija i Zapad 1952–1955: Jugoslovensko približavanje NATO-u* [Belgrade: Institut za savremenu istoriju, 2005]; Dragan Bogetić, *Nova strategija spoljne politike Jugoslavije 1956–1961* [Belgrade: Institut za savremenu istoriju, 2006]; Dragan Bogetić, *Jugoslavensko-američki odnosi 1961–1971* [Belgrade: Institut za savremenu istoriju, 2012]; Dragan Bogetić and Aleksandar Životić, *Jugoslavija i Arapsko-Izraelski Rat 1967* [Belgrade: Institut za savremenu istoriju, 2010]; Dragan Bogetić, *Jugoslovensko-američki odnosi u vreme bipolarnog detanta 1972–1975* [Belgrade: Institut za savremenu istoriju, 2015]; and Darko Bekić, *Jugoslavija u Hladnom ratu: Odnosi s velikim silama 1949–1955* [Zagreb: Globus, 1988]).

16 Jonathan Auerbach and Castronovo Russ, eds., *The Oxford Handbook of Propaganda Studies* (New York: Oxford University Press, 2013), 5–11.

17 John Tomlinson, *Cultural Imperialism: A Critical Introduction* (London: A&C Black, 2001); for another perspective, see Christian G. Appy, *Cold War Constructions: The Political Culture of United States Imperialism, 1945–1966* (Amherst: University of Massachusetts Press, 2000).

18 Mel van Elteren, 'Rethinking Americanization Abroad: Toward a Critical Alternative to Prevailing Paradigms,' *The Journal of American Culture* 29, no. 3 (2006): 345–67.

19 Volker Berghahn, 'The Debate on "Americanization" among Economic and Cultural Historians,' *Cold War History* 10, no. 1 (2010): 107–30, https://doi.org/10.1080/14682740903388566.

20 Ivan Pongračić and Russell Kirk, 'Prolog,' in *Politika razboritosti* (Zagreb: Večernji list, 2015), 11–16. In the 'Prologue' of Russell Kirk's Croatian translation, *The Politics of Prudence*, Pongračić reveals that he had been a member of the American Library since his law studies in 1961, and usually borrowed music magazines and disks.

21 Leo Mates, *Međunarodni odnosi socijalističke Jugoslavije* (Belgrade: Nolit, 1976).

22 Slavenka Drakulić, *How We Survived Communism and Even Laughed* (New York; London: W. W. Norton & Company, 1991), 6.

23 Miroslav Perišić, *Diplomatija i kultura: Jugoslavija: prelomna 1950* (Belgrade: Institut za noviju istoriju Srbije, 2013).

24 Patterson, *Bought and Sold*; Igor Duda, *U potrazi za blagostanjem: o povijesti dokolice i potrošačkog društva u Hrvatskoj 1950 – ih i 1960 – ih*, 2nd ed. (Zagreb: Srednja Europa, 2014) and *Pronađeno blagostanje: svakodnevni život i potrošačka kultura u Hrvatskoj 1970 – ih i 1980 – ih*, 2nd ed. (Zagreb: Srednja Europa, 2014).

25 Grandits and Taylor, *Yugoslavia's Sunny Side*.

26 Tvrtko Jakovina, *Socijalizam na američkoj pšenici* (Zagreb: Matica Hrvatska, 2002); Jakovina, *Američki komunistički saveznik*.

27 Vučetić, *Coca-Cola Socialism*.

28 Jović claims that the Yugoslav elites' 'commitment to Marxism prompted them to underestimate the chance for liberal democracy or nationalism to compete with socialism as a vision of the future society. By declaring alternative models of socialism, especially the Soviet model, as the only real threat (since socialism was "the only game in town"), they ended up exactly where they did not want to be, more dependent than ever on the existence of the Soviet Other.' Dejan Jović, 'Communist Yugoslavia and its "Others",' in *Ideologies and National Identities: The Case of Twentieth-Century Southeastern Europe*, ed. John Lampe and Mark Mazower, Hors Collection (Budapest: Central European University Press, 2013), 277–302, http://books.openedition.org/ceup/2438.

29 Robert B. Cialdini, *Influence: The Psychology of Persuasion* (New York: HarperCollins, 2009), 34–5.

30 Akira Iriye, 'Culture and International History,' in *Explaining the History of American Foreign Relations*, ed. F. Costigliola and M. Hogan (Cambridge: Cambridge University Press, 1991), 215. Some illuminating debates on these issues are Akira Iriye, 'Culture,' *Journal of American History* 77, no. 1 (1990): 99–107; Jessica C. E. Gienow-Hecht, 'Shame on US? Academics, Cultural Transfer, and the Cold War: A Critical Review,' *Diplomatic History* 24, no. 3 (2000): 465–94, https://doi.org/10.1111/0145–2096.00227; Volker Depkat, 'Cultural Approaches to International Relations: A Challenge?,' in *Culture and International History*, ed. Jessica C. E. Gienow-Hecht and Frank Schumacher (New York; Oxford: Berghahn Books, 2004), 175–97.

31 Frank A. Ninkovich, *The Diplomacy of Ideas: US Foreign Policy and Cultural Relations, 1938–1950* (Cambridge; New York: Cambridge University Press, 1981), 2–3.

32 Nicholas J. Cull, *The Cold War and the United States Information Agency: American Propaganda and Public Diplomacy, 1945–1989* (Cambridge; New York: Cambridge University Press, 2009), xv.

33 Francisco J. R. Jimenez, Lorenzo D. Gomez-Escalonilla, and Nicholas J. Cull, *US Public Diplomacy and Democratization in Spain: Selling Democracy?* (New York: Palgrave Macmillan, 2015), 2–4. In scholarly debate on public diplomacy, several books made a difference: Nancy Snow and Philip M. Taylor, eds, *Routledge Handbook on Public Diplomacy* (New York; London: Routledge Taylor&Francis, 2009); Jan Melissen and Jian Wang, *Debating Public Diplomacy: Now and Next* (Leiden; Boston, MA: Brill, 2019); and Ellen Huijgh, *Public Diplomacy at Home: Domestic Dimensions* (Leiden; Boston, MA: Brill, 2019).

34 Joseph S. Nye Jr, *The Future of Power*, Reprint (New York: PublicAffairs, 2011), 123.

35 Niall Ferguson, 'Think Again Power,' *Foreign Policy*, February 2003; Janice Bially Mattern, 'Why "Soft Power" Isn't So Soft: Representational Force and the Sociolinguistic Construction of Attraction in World Politics,' *Millennium: Journal of International Studies* 33, no. 3 (2005): 583–612, https://doi.org/10.1177/0305829805033003160 1.

36 Samuel P. Huntington, *The Clash of Civilizations and the Remaking of World Order*, 3rd ed. (New York: Simon & Schuster, 2011), 141.

37 Su Changhe, 'Soft Power,' in *The Oxford Handbook of Modern Diplomacy*, ed. Andrew F. Cooper, Jorge Heine, and Ramesh Thakur (Oxford: Oxford University Press, 2013), 544–58; Craig Hayden, *The Rhetoric of Soft Power: Public Diplomacy in Global Contexts* (Lanham, MD: Lexington Books, 2011), 27–76. For more discussions, look

into Philip Seib, *Toward a New Public Diplomacy: Redirecting US Foreign Policy* (New York: Palgrave Macmillan, 2009) and Jan Melissen, *The New Public Diplomacy: Soft Power in International Relations* (London: Palgrave Macmillan, 2005).

38 Howland H. Sargeant, The Overt International Information and Educational Exchange Program of the United States, 31 March 1952, Box 2245, Central Decimal Files (hereafter CDF) 1950–54, Record Group 59 (hereafter RG), National Archives at College Park, Maryland (hereafter NACP).

39 Sarah E. Graham, *Culture and Propaganda: The Progressive Origins of American Public Diplomacy, 1936–1953* (London; New York: Routledge, 2016), 17–48.

40 Justin Hart, *Empire of Ideas: The Origins of Public Diplomacy and the Transformation of US Foreign Policy* (Oxford; New York: Oxford University Press, 2013), 72. For pre-Cold War studies on public diplomacy see also Wilson P. Dizard Jr, *Inventing Public Diplomacy: The Story of the US Information Agency* (Boulder, CO: Lynne Rienner Publishers, 2004), 1–62; Allan M. Winkler, *The Politics of Propaganda: The Office of War Information, 1942–1945* (New Haven, CT: Yale University Press, 1978).

41 Study of USIS libraries, August 1967, E-4-67, Box 1, Estimates and Evaluations 1966–78, USIA Office of Research and Evaluation, RG 306, NACP, 3–6.

42 Study of USIS libraries, August 1967, 3–6.

43 Hart, *Empire of Ideas*.

44 David F. Krugler, *The Voice of America and the Domestic Propaganda Battles, 1945–1953* (Columbia: University of Missouri Press, 2000); Gregory M. Tomlin, *Murrow's Cold War: Public Diplomacy for the Kennedy Administration*, Kindle (Lincoln: University of Nebraska Press, 2016), Introduction.

45 Psychological Board Briefings, 6 November 1950, 511.00/11–650, Box 2238, CDF 1950–54, RG 59, NACP.

46 Melvyn P. Leffler, *A Preponderance of Power: National Security, the Truman Administration, and the Cold War* (Stanford, CA: Stanford University Press, 1993), 498. For more detailed analysis on the theory and implementation of containment, see Melvyn P. Leffler, 'The Emergence of an American Grand Strategy, 1945–1952,' in *The Cambridge History of the Cold War*, ed. Melvyn P. Leffler and Odd Arne Westad, Reprint ed., vol. 1 (Cambridge: Cambridge University Press, 2012), 67–89; and John L. Gaddis, *Strategies of Containment: A Critical Appraisal of American National Security Policy during the Cold War*, Kindle (New York: Oxford University Press, 2005).

47 Leffler, 'The Emergence of an American Grand Strategy, 1945–1952,' 68.

48 Cull, *The Cold War and the United States Information Agency*, 23–34. On the role of the NSC and the CIA covert propaganda operations during Truman's and Eisenhower's years much has been written. Notable overviews can be found in Lori Lyn Bogle, *The Pentagon's Battle for the American Mind: The Early Cold War* (College Station: Texas A&M University Press, 2004); Sarah-Jane Corke, *US Covert Operations and Cold War Strategy: Truman, Secret Warfare and the CIA, 1945–53* (New York: Routledge, 2007); and Kenneth Osgood, *Total Cold War: Eisenhower's Secret Propaganda Battle at Home and Abroad* (Lawrence: University Press of Kansas, 2006).

49 'Address on Foreign Policy at a Luncheon of the American Society of Newspaper Editors,' 20 April 1950, in *Public Papers of the Presidents of the United States: Harry S. Truman, 1950* (Washington, DC: Government Printing Office, 1965), 260–4.

50 Barrett to Flanders, 16 June 1951, 511.00/6-951, Box 2242, CDF 1950–54, RG 59, NACP. Officially, the campaign's main goal would be to protect and maintain 'peace, freedom, stability, promotion of spiritual and social well-being, and respect for the rights of individuals in a free society' (Department of State Publication 3927, August 1950, 511.00/9-2250, Box 2238, CDF 1950–54, RG 59, NACP).

51 Cull, *The Cold War and the United States Information Agency*, 22–3, 81–2.

52 Radius and Sargeant to Bowie, 15 July 1953, FRUS, 1952–54, II, 2, doc. 343.

53 Hickenlooper to Dulles, 9 May 1953, 511.00/5-953, Box 2248, CDF 1950–54, RG 59, NACP. These changes brought into the USIA the previous IIA divisions: International Broadcasting, Overseas Information Centers/Information Center Service, Private Enterprise Coordination Staff, Information Media Guaranty Program, and International Motion Pictures (9th Semi-annual Report of the US Advisory Commission on Information, 2 February 1954, 511.00/3-2554, Box 2249, CDF 1950–54, RG 59, NACP).

54 'Coordination of unattributed propaganda is vital, and as a general rule [...] a much greater percentage of the information program should be unattributed,' stated the NSC proposal directive on the USIA in 1953 (Radius and Sargeant to Bowie, 15 July 1953, FRUS, 1952–54, Vol. II, part 2, doc. 343).

55 Despatch 680 Embassy Belgrade to Dept. of State, 7 June 1955, 511.68/6-755, Box 2204, CDF 1954–59, NACP.

56 Laura A. Belmonte, *Selling the American Way: US Propaganda and the Cold War* (Philadelphia: University of Pennsylvania Press, 2010); Greg Barnhisel and Catherine Turner, eds, *Pressing the Fight: Print, Propaganda, and the Cold War* (Amherst and Boston, MA: University of Massachusetts Press, 2012).

57 Richard Nelson and Foad Izadi, 'Ethics and Social Issues in Public Diplomacy,' in *Routledge Handbook of Public Diplomacy*, ed. Nancy Snow and Philip M. Taylor (New York; London: Routledge, 2008), 336.

58 Morris to Allen, 20 November 1959, Box 10, Inspection Report and Related Records 1954–62, USIA Inspection Staff, RG 306, NACP.

59 Richard Arndt, *The First Resort of Kings: American Cultural Diplomacy in the Twentieth Century* (Washington, DC: Potomac Books, 2007), 150, 156.

60 Report on Operations of the Overseas Book and Library Program, 15 July 1953, Box 1, Interagency/Congressional Reports, USIA Office of Administration, RG 306, NACP.

61 Nye, *Soft Power*, 1–5.

62 Telegram 144 Dept. of State to all USIS Posts, 28 October 1953, 511.00/10-2853, Box 2249, CDF 1950–54, RG 59, NACP.

1

Strategies of persuasion

On 31 January 1946, the Federal People's Republic of Yugoslavia proclaimed a constitution embodying six constituent republics and five constituent peoples – Serbs, Croats, Slovenes, Montenegrins, and Macedonians.[1] The Five-Year Plan, adopted on 28 April 1947, set grandiose targets for growth. Wholesale nationalization of the economy occurred by the end of 1946, including the seizing of all foreign assets. Industrial production was scheduled for 5 per cent and agriculture for a 150 per cent increase, while 200 major investment projects were planned. The Cominform blockade of Soviet credits and aid reshuffled the deck of cards on the table. The Yugoslav famine crisis turned out to be very serious and, in September 1949, the Export–Import (EXIM) Bank granted Yugoslavia's request for a $20 million credit, while the International Monetary Fund approved a $3 million drawing for Tito's government.[2]

In the following years, US assistance to Yugoslavia would cover three fundamental aspects for Yugoslav independence from the Soviets and their linking with the United States: economic aid, military assistance, and cultural influence. On 10 November 1950, the State Department announced US food relief to Yugoslavia. Before asking Congress for an official grant-aid program, the State Department decided to employ the EXIM Bank, the Marshall Plan, and Mutual Defense Aid Program funds to send $30 million for food purchases. US policymakers accentuated the humanitarian aspects of the aid while masking the self-evident strategic importance of an independent Yugoslavia. On 23 May 1951, the State Department's policy advisory staff advised to publicly dismantle every aspect of US support for Tito's regime, or put pressure on Tito for military alliances.[3] No doubt, such aid played a crucial role in the economic recovery of the Yugoslav regime. Between 1950 and 1964, the 'American assistance, broadly defined, covered sixty per cent of Yugoslavia's payment deficits on the current accounts,' and 'added perhaps two percentage points to a rate of growth in national income during the 1950s which averaged 7.5 percent.'[4] In a letter to Secretary Dean Acheson, Ambassador George Allen wrote from Belgrade in 1950: 'Such economic assistance as we have given Yugoslavia [...] [supporting] its resistance to the Soviet Union and satellite pressure,' was a 'small price [to] pay for benefits already enjoyed and expected from Yugoslav independence of Kremlin dictation.' And he continued:

'This independence from the West, as well as East, is [...] essential to our immediate purpose of promoting disharmony in the ranks of world Communism and thus weakening Kremlin's aggressive power.'[5] US military assistance provided Yugoslavia with the essential prerequisite to protect its borders and stabilize its national security system from possible Soviet attack. In early 1951, the Yugoslav Army's Chief of Staff, Koča Popović, arrived in the United States to secretly discuss military aid to Yugoslavia. Envisioned to enhance what Eisenhower defined as the 'South NATO wing,' the Military Assistance Pact, signed on October 1951, included the Yugoslav Army in the Mutual Defense Aid Program providing T-33A aircraft, artillery, machine guns, radars, and electronic equipment. And thanks to US Army training, the Yugoslav Army transformed itself from a guerrilla-like one to a regular one.[6]

Even Project TROY, a special report on how American information could get through the Iron Curtain and reach Russian people, contemplated Yugoslav independence as a top priority policy. Commissioned by the State Department in late 1950, and named after the legendary wooden horse operation, Project TROY brought together twenty-one scholars from MIT and Harvard, who gathered for the first time in October 1950. Submitted on 1 February 1951, the final report 'urged for the unification of political warfare' at 'our national power, political, economic,' and military levels. The section on Tito's Yugoslavia made a strong point: among all the communist-dominated countries, Tito's regime was the most successful, economically, politically and socially. Its value was manifold. First, even if Yugoslavia could not become an 'American puppet,' by welcoming Tito into the Western camp without forcing him to change his ideology, the United States would ensure a partner of strategic relevance. Second, the MIT group recognized that there were 'some indications that the Tito regime may slowly be growing less doctrinaire.' The decentralization of industry, the abolition of privileges for Party members, and admission of foreigners, stressed the report, were 'all point[ing] to a general liberalization.' While partly inaccurate and partly overestimating the chance for the regime's prompt liberalization, Project TROY emphasized how the United States should give Yugoslavia 'every possible support in developing an economic and political life independent of Russia.'[7]

The third aspect of US involvement in Yugoslavia – its public diplomacy strategy and soft-power policies – worked to increase Yugoslav orientation, especially in 'official circles,' towards 'the foreign policy objectives of the United States.'[8] The first USIE Country Plan, issued for the years 1950 to 1953, reflected these major objectives. It envisioned supporting the emergence of Yugoslavia 'as a democratic, independent member of the world community, cooperating with and adhering to the United Nations.' The Plan was predicated on the view that 'Titoism should continue to exist as a corrosive and disintegrating force within the Soviet power sphere' to 'extract the maximum political and propaganda advantage from this quarrel.' But most importantly on the cultural edge, US public diplomacy would encourage in Yugoslav people their 'democratic and independence aspirations' and their desire for 'freedoms and the material advantages of Western forms of government and society.' Such a *wedge* public diplomacy strategy incurred several criticisms from the field officers in Belgrade who thought that supporting Titoism in the short-term would not achieve democracy in the end. The Embassy and USIS posts disagreed with the IIA on the abandonment of anti-Titoist rhetoric since it helped to 'keep alive democratic aspirations' and proved to 'the international Communist movement that Yugoslavia' had not become an US 'puppet.'[9] But the IIA policymakers remained firm in their judgements: the communist regime, except for small groups of dissidents such as peasants and former aristocracy, had no serious political alternative, and its young middle class was mostly consentient to the regime. So even if the government failed in observing basic human rights, the IIA decided on a neutralist policy and focused its propaganda in 'associating the United States [...] with [favourable] trends in Yugoslavia.' Like a rope pulled in two directions, the apparent dilemma continued to worry US administrations in the following decades. On the one hand, US policy included military and economic assistance, while on the other, IIA/USIA cultural policies could 'result in [...] political disaffection and contribute towards weakening the loyalty of party members.'[10] IIA and USIS uncertainty reflected the administration's hesitations towards the Yugoslav case. Because of Tito's willingness to resist Stalin and slacken his posture towards the West, the United States and its international aid agencies, like the Agency for International Development, assured the economic support needed to withstand Cominform pressure. Possible Soviet reprisal provided the United States and its allies with reasons for military assistance to Yugoslavia. But, as Lorraine Lees underscored, such an arrangement was full of tensions. In 1950, for instance, when Dean Acheson informed the Yugoslav government that recognition of the Ho Chi Minh government of North Vietnam would provocatively disrupt American public opinion and reduce extraordinary aid, Tito lost his temper. 'Yugoslavia had refused "to bow to the Soviets" or to the West and would not "beg" Washington for loans,' declared the Marshal in Titovo Užice, Serbia.[11] Indeed, Tito would never take an active role in a possible European war or Western defence system.[12] The wedge strategy would work better in the arena of political bilateral relations between the two countries, rather than for the application of NATO's military alliance network in southeastern Europe. But both Yugoslavia and the United States were capable of genuine pragmatic 'ability [...] to base a foreign policy on national security requirements rather than ideological imperatives.'[13]

By 1952, Yugoslavia officially agreed, though 'grudgingly and slowly,' to American cultural penetration. The joint USIS–MSA Country Plan recognized that Yugoslav 'openness' followed the US economic and military support, and the famine-relief aid. By playing the role of 'ambassador[s] of good will,' US military items such as textbooks, lectures, specialists, trainees, journals, or CARE boxes, proved American 'genuine interests' in assisting Yugoslavia.[14] The first USIS Country Program recognized the Party activists, the youth, the non-communist officials, the rural population, the religious groups, the Army officers, the industrial workers, and the educators as the first targets of US public diplomacy in Yugoslavia. At this point, the Program envisioned the most diverse channels of persuasion such as books, magazines, newspapers, exhibitions and movies, press materials, networks of private American organizations, Voice of America radio broadcastings, and the English language teaching program.[15] With seventeen American officers and forty-one local employees in Belgrade,

Zagreb, and Novi Sad, from the early 1950s on, USIS policies shaped the contours of Yugoslav–American foreign relations while being, reciprocally, forged by Yugoslav internal ideological adjustments.

Waging public diplomacy in the 1950s

George Allen replaced William Benton at the head of the information agency in 1948, and held the post until 1949. When he departed to his ambassadorship mission to Belgrade, he was well ready to set up the USIS mission in the new, post-1948 Yugoslavia. In Belgrade, where he remained in service until 1953, he did an extraordinary job. The new margins of liberty in which the USIS now operated astonished the field officers there. In this regard, Allen recalled: 'Ample evidence that our VOA radio programme is heard comes to us daily through letters from every nook and corner of the country. America is reaching directly into homes of Yugoslavs in villages and hamlets from Slovenia to Macedonia.' And he concluded, 'we must fight armed aggression with armed might, we can only fight bad ideas with better ones. [...] This is what USIE is trying to do and is doing with increasing success in Yugoslavia.'[16] The 'tremendous interest and response' in USIS activities increased exponentially. In only three months, from April to June 1952, around 50,000 Yugoslavs entered USIS Belgrade, in a city that, at the time, counted around 440,000 inhabitants.[17] Staff numbers increased accordingly: in August 1951, two Americans and eight Yugoslavs worked in Belgrade, and one was staffed at the Novi Sad library.[18] In 1953, in USIS Zagreb, total numbers increased to seventeen Americans and forty-one Yugoslavs.[19]

USIS Belgrade was in Čika Ljubina Street at n. 19 in the central pedestrian zone, at the crossroads of the historical Knez Mihaila and Čika Ljubina. It was a prominent business and university district, in the proximity of the Republican Square, the Faculty of Humanities and Social Sciences, and the Serbian Academy of Sciences and Arts. Indeed, part of the USIA strategy consisted in finding locations of easy access by public transportation and ground-floor exhibit rooms. Opened in March 1945, before World War II officially ended, the Belgrade post operated almost continuously until 1998.[20] The American Center in Zagreb was not lacking in elegance compared to the one in Belgrade. Opened in May 1953 in the aristocratic Zrinjevac green area, the old park of Zagreb's high-town, it intersected Hebrang and Braće Kavurića Street n. 13 (today Zrinjevac Street).[21] Situated within the General Consulate's building, USIS posts appeared vis-a-vis the Modern Gallery and opposite the Croatian Academy of Sciences and Arts. Owned by the US government, it consisted of 403 m² located on the ground floor, with ten rooms and a forty-seat reading room. By contrast, the American Belgrade Center was leased by USIS and consisted of nine rooms distributed on 290 m².[22] Both the centres were opened during the morning and evening, six days a week, which provided enough time for working and retired people, university students, white-collar workers, and academics, to visit.[23] As for the American Library in Novi Sad, it functioned as Belgrade's branch and not an information centre, which, nevertheless, occupied a privileged geostrategic position as the capital of the Vojvodina autonomous region, situated in the proximity of the Rumanian and Hungarian borders.[24]

In contrast to the British Council's separate status abroad, the State Department decided to house USIS offices in whole or in part within the same building as the diplomatic mission. What mattered was the liaison between the Public Affairs Officer (PAO), leader and front runner of every mission, and the ambassador with whom he cooperated closely. The PAO confirmed or modified the Country Plan, set up the cultural policy guidelines, managed the budget, administered the staff, combined analysis and communication with a country target group, and represented the USIS towards the Yugoslav government.[25]

From 'Business is booming …' to the Trieste question

Between 1950 and 1953, many factors – both in bilateral relations and Yugoslav internal developments – repaired shattered Yugo–American relations. Truman's support of Tito's independence from Moscow was essential in drawing Yugoslavia closer to the West, as scholars agree.[26] Better bilateral relations soon resulted in less anti-Americanism, both in Yugoslav newspapers and in the Party's public declarations. The positive atmosphere immediately influenced the position of USIS in Yugoslavia. Crowds previously just staring at exhibit windows – because 'comfortable anonymity' was more 'politically safe' – suddenly began visiting the Library and taking books away, reported Bruce Buttles, the USIS PAO in Belgrade. The numbers continued to surge enormously between 1950 and 1953. A 1950 report showed that, in January, around 3,000 Belgrade citizens visited the post in Čika Ljubina and borrowed 700 books.[27] In June, there were already 4,061.[28] Their number jumped to 9,700 in October 1951 and reached 16,500 in October 1952, with almost 3,000 books circulating.[29] The number of officially registered borrowers increased from 150 in 1950, to 700 in 1952.[30] Activities inside the USIS centre were accompanied by analogous work outside. Already, in the late 1940s, USIS Belgrade inaugurated a library extension service, which provided press and publication materials to Yugoslav cultural institutions like the Academy of Sciences and Arts and the Bibliographic Institute, and to the university and its faculties of science and technology, humanities and art. Quite surprisingly, the American Library supplied Yugoslav government institutes and ministries with law materials, and industrial plants with technical bulletins, as in the case of the chemical company Hempro, the glass factory Pančevo, and the aircraft factory in Zemun. Yugoslav periodicals and newspapers regularly received USIS press material – reviews like *Tehnika Narodu!* (Technology to the People) and *Prosveta* (Education), and the famous newspapers *Republika, Borba, Politika*, but also publishing houses such as Kultura.[31]

Nevertheless, in the early 1950s the USIS program in Yugoslavia remained 'flexible and modest,' identical to those in Western Europe, only without the exchange programs. Only VOA broadcasts were comparable to those of Eastern European countries for their wide audience reach. The flourishing of the American cultural program in Yugoslavia was due less to USIS management than to Yugoslav antipathy towards the Stalinist regime. This was acknowledged by field officers who 'carefully avoid[ed] anti-communist propaganda,' but extensively served 'much anti-Soviet material [...] to the Yugoslavs.' But this did not mean life was easy for US public diplomats in Belgrade and Zagreb. As PAO Buttles remarked, Yugoslavia presented a 'cyclical atmosphere for USIS operations' that varied from active official resistance to relaxations and even cooperation.[32] As long as Yugoslavia remained a communist state, 'the free circulation of Western ideas' continued to be considered 'inimical to the maintenance of [power].' Such a pattern would perpetuate itself through the 1950s, 1960s, and 1970s, and submit USIS operations in Yugoslavia to 'continuous frustrations, interruptions and delays stemming from the resistance of communists inside and outside the government.' While Yugoslav officials acted with reserve, ordinary people usually expressed welcome attitudes to the US cultural representatives. In November 1952, when Bruce Buttles attended the 105th foundation anniversary of the Žika Popović People's Library in Šabac (at that time, a leading commercial town in northwest central Serbia), the audience received him with such enthusiasm 'that the master of ceremonies had to [restrain] the applause to go on with the rest.' The audience, consisting of 'students and townspeople,' was obviously 'pro-American.'[33]

The USIS Zagreb experience of the early 1950s followed Belgrade's trends. After the opening of the Brace Kavurića Library, staff reported 'stimulating and invaluable experience' and 'greater understanding' that was deepening 'the friendship between Americans and Yugoslavs.' At the time, an average daily attendance of about 1,000 people had some 100 books circulating every day. In June 1953, when the post had some 3,100 registered borrowers, the library stopped the initial program of magazine and newspaper circulation because of unexpected crowds. 1953 saw an extension service established providing the possibility for out-of-town borrowers from Croatia, Slovenia, and Bosnia-Herzegovina to borrow the books by mail. Spurred on by rising activity levels, the library decided on a far-reaching program of sending letters of invitation to customary and potential borrowers, inviting them to ask for books without any postage fee, and proposing special subject lists to particularly interested borrowers. The response was immediate and wide-ranging. Since of the 250 extensive borrowers in June 1953, 150 were from Ljubljana, USIS Zagreb decided to donate more than 100 books to their university. In the early 1950s, USIS observed with satisfaction that Yugoslav users went crazy for periodicals such as *Life*, *Time*, and *Newsweek*, the *Saturday Evening Post*, *House Beautiful*, and fashion magazines.[34] In the same year, the library started serving outside its facility; this met with success when the Končar factory trade union asked USIS to provide English teaching lessons, films, recordings, periodicals, and newspapers.[35]

The year 1953 was revolutionary in Yugoslavia's relations with the world. In February, Belgrade, Ankara, and Athens agreed on the Treaty of Friendship and Assistance that would, in 1954, become the Balkan Pact. The treaty with Greece and Turkey saved Tito from the embarrassment of formal military ties with NATO, while linking with two important members of the Atlantic Pact.[36] In March 1953, Tito made his first visit to a democratic Western country, staying in London from 16 to 21 March. The visit came at an auspicious moment: Yugoslavia had just broken diplomatic ties with the Vatican (late 1952), and its relations with Italy's De Gasperi's government was 'in a bottle' because of Trieste.[37] Stalin's death in March, and the end of the Korean War, relaxed Cold War tensions. On the international front, Tito began to look for new allies, and from 1953 onwards he engaged in long trips to Chile, Brazil, Burma, and India, trying to reinforce the non-aligned, anti-block voices in the international arena.[38] Internally, at the Sixth Congress, in 1952, the Yugoslav Communist Party changed its name to the League of Communists of Yugoslavia (LCY), the National Front became the Socialist Alliance of the Working People of Yugoslavia, and more power was given to local, now LCY, Party organizations. The 1953 constitution endorsed the partial abandonment of centralism, reinforced the autonomy of republics, and introduced self-management for many organizations, institutions, hospitals, universities, and enterprises. It was an 'historical turnover' in which 'state-owned and bureaucracy monopoly' conceded the 'larger autonomy of economic and political subjects as well as local and regional communities.'[39]

Although USIS business boomed in the early 1950s, and US–Yugoslav foreign relations were on a stable, even increasing, drift, occasional attacks, both in words and actions, reminded USIS staff in Yugoslavia that this was an ideologically and politically hostile country. In September 1951, *Omladina*, the official organ of the League of Communist Youth of Yugoslavia, became alarmed about tremendous Western infiltration in the Yugoslav press and called for anti-Western pressures on editors. On 20 February 1952, a handmade bomb was thrown at USIS Belgrade, causing fire and material damage. Almost two months later, the Belgrade authorities started an anti-USIS campaign warning YCP members against using the American reading room because of improper, 'bad influence.' Soon after, the politburo member Blagoje Nešković, who the chargé d'affaires Jacob Beam defined as the 'most intolerant communist,' visited the USIS exhibit room and scrutinized every bulletin, map, picture, and display. In the meantime, the Belgrade post acknowledged that the Yugoslav authorities had arrested, and held for twenty-four hours, a Yugoslav woman carrying a copy of the USIS *Bilten* (Radio News Bulletin). The officers interpreted the attacks as a counteraction to a favourable VOA listeners' survey carried out months before. Then, on 22 April, the Foreign Office called Beam for a talk. Jakša Petrić, director of Western Hemisphere and British Commonwealth Affairs, complained about the distribution of *Atomic Energy for War or Peace* pamphlet and 'inappropriate' USIS movies sent to Yugoslav schools.[40]

In the following months, and also in 1953, similar incidents reoccurred. In summer 1952, the Yugoslav authorities prohibited Thereza Mravintz, Zagreb's Cultural Affairs Officer (CAO), from participating in the Novi Vinodolski summer school for English teachers.[41] On 10 March 1953, Milorad Peršić, President of the Yugoslav Federation of Students' Central Committee, criticized those 'reactionary students' who used 'Western propaganda literature' and maintained 'connections with their libraries.'[42] In June, *Duga* and *Omladina*, the first a children's and the second a youth periodical, eliminated Western-supplied materials.[43] *Timok*, Zaječar's newspaper, published an attack on William King, information officer of USIS Belgrade, calling American propaganda 'aggressive,' 'cruel,' 'damaging,' 'insolent,' and 'misusing our democracy.'[44] Similar tones appeared in *Politika*, which denoted, with heavy-handed and surly humour, USIS visitors as old, ignorant, and anti-regime.[45] Criticism came even from the highest communist ranks. In his speech in Montenegro, Djilas accused 'weaklings and men without character' of spreading 'foreign, bourgeois, anti-socialist, anti-Yugoslav ideas for foreign money.'[46]

Such occasional incidents gravely escalated with the Trieste question. On 8 October 1953, the ambassadors of the United States and United Kingdom announced the end of the military occupation of Zone A (Trieste and surroundings) that would pass to Italy. Yugoslavia reacted immediately by sending troops to its Western borders, bloody protests occurred in Trieste by both nationalities, while formal and spontaneous massive demonstrations gathered in many Yugoslav cities. A Cold War breeze returned between Belgrade and Rome, while sour and harsh anti-American narratives arose again in Yugoslav newspapers. The Trieste question became an international incident that provoked an immediate decline in USIS activities. Nada Apsen, former director of USIS Zagreb, at the time acting as a librarian, recalled: 'the demonstrators gathered around the [USIS] building yelling "Trst je naš!" (Trieste is ours!) and "Dole Papa, dole Rim i Pella skupa s njim!" (Down with the Pope, down with Rome and Pella together with them!); then they threw torches at the library, broke the exhibit windows and threw torches inside, destroying the books and shelves.'[47] Only after the London Memorandum was signed on 5 October 1954, and the new border ratified, did relations return to normality, also thanks to the softer approach of the new Italian Prime Minister Mario Scelba.[48] The Memorandum restored political acceptance of the American Libraries in Belgrade and Zagreb, which counted their damages and the toll taken. And indeed, because the program closed for a while, many funds allotted by the USIA for the fiscal year 1953 were simply returned to Washington.[49]

Resisting American 'propaganda'

> When they wanted to lay accusations against [me] because I am campaigning for Americans, because I said that Tito, now that he is with the Americans, will give a better life to the people and will come over to the West [...]. I was in UDBA (security police) for three months and then brought to court. They asked me did I say that, and I said, Yes I did. We are not in 1947 when Tito was with the Russians and they would chop off my head; but we are in 1950, and Tito is with the Americans, and we are no more afraid of you, I said. So, they let me go home.
>
> Letter of a Yugoslav villager to USIS Belgrade, March 1953[50]

From their establishment in the late 1940s, USIS activities in Yugoslavia encountered varying degrees of official political opposition, but the following analysis will show that the reasons for Yugoslav bias and counteractions depended on several key factors: an anti-American attitude based on its Marxist communist ideology, the Yugoslav positioning as a neutralist, independent country in the bloc's competition, and opposing internal policy views as to what was the 'Yugoslav way to socialism,' especially after the Sixth Congress in 1952.

After the Tito–Stalin split, Yugoslav policymakers needed time to familiarize themselves with the new circumstances where they were deprived of Soviet support, both ideological and economic. Independence remained a Yugoslav prerogative in foreign policy, but their relying on American assistance was hard to accept. As Yugoslav diplomat Cvijeto Job put it, 'Tito never "hived" on the United States, but as a realist statesman, he never threw the US card from his hands.'[51] Nonetheless, this only partially explains Yugoslav apprehension over foreign 'propaganda' during the 1950s and the 1960s. Such a preoccupation persisted despite mounting trends towards openness in Yugoslav society from the mid-1950s onwards that facilitated foreign cultural influence. Among the Yugoslav policymakers troubled by foreign 'propaganda missions,' the Yugoslav secret services or UDBA (Uprava državne bezbednosti, the State Security Administration) expressed the most severe concerns. In fact, a 1953 report emphasized: 'Such American propaganda [...] is becoming a huge political problem which we as UDBA, and only with our measures, aren't able to resolve.' It continued: 'The Americans today want to penetrate every pore of our political and social life, especially [...] among the youth, throughout schools, universities, organizations of the People's Front, etc. What is more, they are trying to enter the Army and our press.'[52] The State Secretariat of Foreign Affairs articulated similar views: 'The question of [foreign cultural missions in Yugoslavia] must be treated as a high policy. Every measure must be applied to its consequences. [...] We think it would be better to have fewer measures, but more decisiveness to carry them out.'[53] Radina Vučetić argues that, after the 1949–50 Yugoslav conciliation with the United States, the USIS in Belgrade and Zagreb operated undisturbed.[54] Yugoslav archival records, on the other hand, reveal a vivid debate, enduring fearfulness, and test control systems that fluctuated over time. At a time when the Yugoslav regime vaunted a high level of consolidation and consent, between 1952 and 1966, several Yugoslav executive agencies struggled for years to find the right counteraction policy to limit foreign propaganda efforts.

And indeed, most of the Yugoslav reports on propaganda from the early 1950s emphasized the lack of law regulations as the 'Achilles heel' in the control of foreign propaganda. The first official attempt in that direction came in 1953 when an inter-committee, composed of members from the Foreign and Internal Affairs Secretariat, produced a report on American, British, and French missions and their 'political propaganda against our country.' The report criticized Yugoslavia's apathy and its laissez-faire attitude, and emphasized the political influence of foreign 'reading rooms and cultural centres.' The inter-committee report depicted a serious problem regarding Yugoslav schools, cultural institutions, 'and even the Army,' which collaborated with the propaganda missions by playing their movies or dispatching their magazines. The Yugoslav policymakers complained about the protests of the diplomatic corps that 'often prevented us from undertaking ulterior restraint.' They objected to the lack of reciprocity since 'for several sacks of books that we import by diplomatic mail on behalf of the Embassy, they import several wagons; for our weekly newsletters of a few hundred copies, they issue daily bulletins in total circulation of 20,000 copies.'[55] On the other hand, mass organizations like the Socialist Alliance of Working People of Yugoslavia (SAWPY)[56] and its Commission for Foreign Relations criticized the English teaching courses as 'political propaganda against our country' because they allowed foreign professors to induce Zagreb, Belgrade, and Ljubljana university students by way of 'easy and cheap leisure and jazz music.'[57]

But, contrary to mere declarative intents, UDBA acted promptly in the field to limit the dissemination of American 'propaganda.' On 31 August 1953, after the American cultural missions increased their publications' copies, the secret service intervened covertly in Yugoslav institutions to decrease subscriptions. Of 1,550 active subscriptions, they managed to eliminate around two hundred. Of course, these actions were not always successful. While 1,300 people rejected USIS materials in August 1953, another 1,500 new customers demanded USIS magazines. And despite strong field efforts, the process of combatting American propaganda in rural areas had contradictory results. In Niš, the number of receivers decreased from 200 to twelve, in Svetozarevo from 100 to ten, while elsewhere, like in Kragujevac, Čačak, and Zrenjanin it rose by more than 100 per cent. The fact that the American publications reached even the smallest Yugoslav villages – like Krupanj, Negotin, Sremska Mitrovica, and Titovo Užice, where Yugoslav newspapers did not – made the secret services extremely frustrated. In some rural districts, emphasized the report, villagers talked more 'about life in the USA and England' and felt more 'enthusiastic about the degree of Western agricultural development' than about internal Yugoslav policies. The fact that some receivers of American publications were members of the Party was unacceptable. The report also complained about USIS Zagreb publishing *Bilten* to the tune of 8,000 and the *Agricultural Bulletin* to the tune of 7,000 copies. The Americans, emphasized the UDBA, 'exploited personal contacts with journalists to insert pro-American materials in the Yugoslav press.'[58] Such concerns appeared in almost all secret service investigations. That USIS attracted 'politically very sensitive groups,' like students, professors, and intellectuals, was even more provoking. The UDBA abhorred the book donation program as a means of increasing personal contacts, and it despised the American exhibits at USIS because, according to their view, it affirmed US political and economic superiority and underscored American assistance to Yugoslavia. By attracting more than 4,000 visitors per day, these exhibits implied 'that if Yugoslavia had a similar [capitalist] system, it would enjoy all the benefits of it.'[59]

Yugoslav employees at USIS posts were victims of UDBA pressures as well. Another 1953 report defined Belgrade's PAO Buttles as the 'the biggest enemy of Yugoslavia in the American Embassy' because his employees, like Slavko and Radmila Todorović, were monarchist and anti-Yugoslav reactionaries.[60] Over the years, USIS local employees often suffered harassment, some of them were briefly jailed, while during the 'Trieste riots' they were even socially marginalized for being 'associated with the Americans.' The early Yugoslav employees in Belgrade were fierce anti-communists, looking with sympathy to the United States and with great suspicion at their own government, recalls Petar Nikolić. They belonged to the pre-war middle and higher bourgeoisie and aristocracy; many of them had relatives shot and their property confiscated after the war. 'I remember those old ladies in elegant and somewhat aristocratic outfits coming to work with a poodle, some of them very troubled because the communists nationalized their family enterprises. A lady called Ruža Todorović was such a woman, always wearing a cocktail dress and with fresh coiffure.'[61] Working for the American Center in Belgrade or Zagreb was not an easy task in Yugoslav communist society. Employees often felt overwhelmed by work and the expanding services.[62] Some of them encountered difficulties in finding a job elsewhere. 'I wanted to leave the Library [...] because the working hours were tough, but after an unsuccessful search, I gave up. And our phone was tapped until 1990,' Zdenka Nikolić, librarian in Zagreb, recalls.[63] On the other hand, USIS provided higher salaries, and female employees were sometimes granted fashionable outfits from the United States.[64]

In the early 1950s, Yugoslav policymakers defended the restrictions on foreign cultural missions, even if in a veiled manner, by affirming Yugoslav independence in internal affairs and neutrality in foreign policy. Balancing between restrictions and relaxation was part of the Yugoslav approach, and it was due to gradual liberalization trends in Yugoslav political life between 1948 and 1953. Between the Fifth and the Sixth Congress of the YCP (1948–52), the Yugoslav leadership conceived the idea of a self-managed socialist society. Slovenian leaders Edvard Kardelj and Boris Kidrič envisaged an economic reform that would strengthen the autonomy of the working councils and leave the enterprises, while remaining state-owned, to partially dispose of their profits.[65] For Boris Kidrič, 'These changes would put the enterprises in freer market competition where, exempted from state planning, they would gain profit.'[66] In the meantime, other cracks appeared following the Yugoslav abandonment of the Stalinist line. In 1951, the Fourth Central Committee Plenum condemned the 'dogmatic politics of education,' while in 1952 the Congress of Writers expanded the framework for freer 'intellectual and spiritual production.' However, by accepting the self-management conceptions, so argues Croatian historian Dušan Bilandžić, the Yugoslav leaders created a discrepancy between existing social relations built on autocratic and centralistic assumptions and the new anti-statistic and anti-bureaucracy conceptions of the LCY. And, while according to the spirit of the Sixth Congress, the Party would become an 'educator' and not 'ruler of the masses, many leaders did not know how to act, while others interpreted these trends as power-losing.'[67]

But these liberal trends evolved together with dictatorial practices of power. Between October 1953 and January 1954, one of Yugoslavia's highest Party leaders, Milovan Djilas, published nineteen articles in *Borba* arguing that a new ruling oligarchy formed by Party bureaucrats had established its power in Yugoslavia. Later his thoughts were collected in the first world-renowned Yugoslav dissident bestseller, *The New Class*, that forced him into his first, six-year-long, imprisonment.[68] The Djilas case unveiled the duality of the Yugoslav reform system that, while withdrawing from Stalinism, established an experiment that never abandoned its totalitarian and autocratic tendencies.

Eisenhower's bolder strategy and US public diplomacy

As Kenneth Osgood demonstrates, President Eisenhower significantly expanded every aspect of America's information programs, integrating them into the foreign policy process. Propaganda, media manipulation, and public relations followed Eisenhower's bolder strategy against communism, which resulted in stronger psychological warfare worldwide and, consequently, in USIS posts in Yugoslavia.[69] The President's Secretary of State, John Foster Dulles, a fierce anti-communist, wanted to replace the 'static doctrine of containment' with 'roll-back' and 'liberation' for the 'captive nations' of Eastern Europe. Certainly, he was careful to caution against war because, as he declared in a 1952 *Life* article, 'We do not want a series of bloody uprisings and reprisals [in Eastern Europe].' For Dulles, Tito's peaceful separation from Moscow was an important sign. 'We can be confident that within two, five, or ten years,' he argued in the same article, 'substantial parts of the present [communist] world can peacefully regain national independence.' For this reason, Dulles continued the roadway forged by Truman's administration and worked to encourage Yugoslavia's independence from Moscow. The fact that Tito was a communist thoroughly opposed to democracy played no role.[70] During a break in the foreign ministers' meeting in Geneva, in November 1955, Dulles joined Tito at his villa on the Brioni Islands. He remained fascinated by the Marshal and the meetings only enhanced his commitment to supporting Yugoslavia.[71] In the meantime, the Eisenhower administration conceived the 'New Look,' a foreign policy strategy that consisted in a more forceful response to communist aggression and affirmation of US nuclear superiority.[72] More assertively, 'Tito *would* be enticed to join NATO,' he '*would* also be convinced to inspire, if not lead, a Titoist liberation movement in the satellites.'[73]

The 'New Look' influenced USIS strategy in Yugoslavia as well. When, in 1954, Joseph Kolarek became Belgrade's PAO, he was advised to pursue a more compelling policy. Reaching Yugoslav intellectuals, opinion makers, and Party prime leaders became a priority. Kolarek started the so-called Personal Contact File campaign in which each USIS officer, after approaching any influential communist official, would create an information card on his career, interests, attitudes, and friends. Among these, some would be chosen as *Pregled* or *Bilten* recipients, others invited to events at the post. Of course, among others, the highly ranked communists – those who knew where the political decisions were made, by whom, and why – remained the main targets of American public diplomats.[74] Thanks to the first USIA investigation at the Belgrade post of May 1954, produced by Robert Byrnes from the USIA, we know that the 'USIS program was gaining ground within Yugoslavia,' and enjoying good relations between USIS and Embassy staff. The chronic lack of housing facilities was the negative side of the permanence in Belgrade, but it regarded the capital's population as a whole and would persist for decades.[75] In January 1955, the USIA established the Inspection Staff as a successor to the former Foreign Service Inspection Corps of the State Department that would in future provide regular biennial overseas inspections.[76] However, it was only under George Allen, USIA director from 1957 to

1960, that the evaluation of USIS became a high priority. The USIS 1959 inspection, completed in both Belgrade and Zagreb by inspectors Lawrence Morris and Robert Beliveau, presented a complex and fluid situation. 'Yugoslavia must constantly resort to balancing off East against West, and which way the pendulum swings depends upon whether it is her hunger for technology or her fear of becoming a "battleground of the Cold War".' The report stressed that when American cultural material was 'satisfying Yugoslav hunger for new technologies' it was permissible, but then controls were tightened when the USIS reminded of Russian and Chinese totalitarian practices.[77] Yugoslav balancing between East and West became a centrepiece of its foreign policy, especially after Stalin died in March 1953 and the Soviets extended a hand of reconciliation. The latter led to the Soviet–Yugoslav rapprochement that culminated in the signing of the Belgrade (1955) and Moscow (1956) Declarations.[78] For Yugoslav foreign policy leaders, the mid-1950s meant a search for alternatives, so Tito shifted towards Third World nations with which he engaged in intense personal diplomacy activities. At the 1956 Brioni Conference with Nehru and Nasser, Tito explored options to bipolar bloc politics, and shaped, in the final document, the conceptual guidelines for non-alignment, namely peaceful cooperation, anti-colonialism, and disarmament.[79] Non-alignment, as Phil Tiemeyer suggests, 'allowed Yugoslavia to forge deep political ties and economic relations with similarly situated countries in the Global South,' but, more than anything, it offered Yugoslavia the opportunity to place itself at the 'world's crossroads between East, West, and South.'[80]

For USIS, this inevitably caused a sense of disorientation. As Walter Roberts, Belgrade's PAO in the early 1960s, remembers the Yugoslav Foreign Office telling him in 1960, 'They told us, "confidentially," that this was done to rein in the Soviets. I personally had no doubt they told the Soviets that they did it in order to rein in the Americans.'[81] Roberts's point correctly underscores what the 1959 investigation report mentioned as Soviet pressure. 'They have examined,' noted Morris, 'the books on the shelves of the USIS Library in Belgrade,' and protested to the Yugoslav authorities on 'dissemination in a friendly country of anti-Soviet propaganda.' USIS staff rightly felt that they had to balance between advancements and retreats, as 'we never know how far we can go.' In other words, the game was 'to determine the point at which the other will be provoked to drastic action.' The USIA's primary cultural focus was on bringing about the process of 'first true understanding, then sympathy and finally adaptation,' to weaken the Soviet position in Yugoslav society, and by US economic aid to keep the Yugoslav 'standard of living rising above that of the satellite countries' in order 'to show the Yugoslavs themselves the advantages of dealing with the West.'[82] The 1959 Country Plan, approved by the USIA in September of the same year, emphasized four major tasks: to explicitly encourage Yugoslav independence; to explain the democratic motivations of Washington's foreign policy; to demonstrate US political, economic, and cultural dynamism, and freedom; and to set out a peaceful and prosperous future assured by US scientific advancements. For the first time, the Plan foresaw the Monthly Themes, projects on which the entire USIS team had to work and shape its exhibits. The *Pregled* periodical that started in 1958 would reflect, in smiley and cheerful tones, themes related to the American way of life – from education to university;

from the benefits of the free enterprise system, the supermarkets and the advertising industry, to the mass media; from the social welfare services, to the advantages of the American bipartisan system. Even though USIA materials were poorly accepted on Yugoslav national radio and television, Inspector Morris evaluated the American program in Yugoslavia as being 'developed with vigour and imagination,' appraised the PAO attitude as assertive and the relationships with Yugoslav leaders as mostly positive. Above all, US public diplomacy was 'contributing to a gradual process of westernization in Yugoslavia' and the USIS penetrating among influential Yugoslavs and the Party's top bureaucracy.[83]

Such goals were achieved with a detailed persuasion program crafted at USIA headquarters and adapted to local audiences. The Agency pursued psychological objectives capable of influencing 'attitudes and behaviours,' in order to realize political purposes 'through the resources available at USIS.' For every country, policymakers identified Priority Target Audience Groups considered capable of influencing the country's political and social structure.[84] Basically, the USIA distinguished between three types of leaders: opinion creators, 'whose prestige causes them to influence the opinion of the group'; controllers of communication, in charge of 'a group's special channels'; and decision-makers – also defined as prime movers – those 'empowered to act for the group.' The public diplomacy actions themselves embraced three types of operations, such as direct operations focused through the mass media, indirect operations towards the communication leaders, and operations seeking to influence the leaders.[85] How did the USIS library manage to achieve this kind of influence? The 'USIS libraries,' argues Richard Arndt, 'had slow-acting influence.'[86] They were special-purpose libraries as they selected materials and designed services to reach certain reader groups. In contrast to public libraries in charge of expanding their book collection, USIS proposed true circulating libraries where new collections from Washington substituted the old ones, usually then donated to museums, universities, libraries, or cultural leaders. In such a way, ideas took individual, uncertain, everyday life paths through people capable of taking political or economic actions, or simply transmitting information. But USIS was also a community centre serving local needs that incarnated 'a visible U.S. presence and an institutional base for furthering U.S. objectives.'[87] In a way, the USIS was a multitasking centre. Besides routine library activities, the American Centers organized movie evenings and lectures, arranged thematic exhibits, produced radio broadcasts, and distributed books and leaflets. The officers in Belgrade and Zagreb organized translations of American authors, coordinated the arrival of American classical artists and jazz performers, welcomed US specialists, and searched for candidates for the exchange programs. Of course, this meant, or at least required, some personnel holding broad skill competencies, from public relations, press and publication, library, film and exhibition management, to radio programming and exchanges. Largely staffed by female librarians – in 1964, 70 per cent of USIS Zagreb employees were women – the American centres personified domesticity and 'accessibility to all.'[88]

This was especially important in Yugoslavia where the media remained under strict government control, leaving culture as a relatively free channel. USIS libraries owned large collections of periodicals, publications, leaflets, films, and photos, as well as radio receivers, production and recording equipment, film strips and projectors. Yugoslav cultural leaders, academics, film producers, painters, writers, and students loved coming and working at USIS. As Sonja Bašić, professor emeritus of Zagreb University, recalls: 'In a certain way, we went there like on a pilgrimage, the place was so important.'[89] It 'was a vanguard home for Belgrade's intellectual circles,' confirmed Petar Nikolić, a former employee of USIS Belgrade.[90] Many, nowadays famous, Croatian cultural leaders were assiduous visitors of USIS from the 1950s onwards. Among them, the linguist Stjepko Težak; the writer and literature professor Tomislav Sabljak; the writers Branislav Glumac and Luko Paljetak; the painters Josip Vaništa and Mirko Rački, and sculptor Milena Lah; the composer Bruno Bjelinski; the film director Obrad Gluščević (whose wife Maja worked in the library), and his colleague Krsto Papić; the cinematographer Goran Trbuljak; the music critics Dražen Vrdoljak and Mladen Raukar; the lawyer Vladimir Ibler; the art historian and academic professor Vera Horvat-Pintarić; the ballet artists and married couple Ana Roje and Oskar Harmoš; the jazz musicians Boško Petrović and Dubravko Majnarić; Đurđica Barlović, the first singer of the pop group *Novi Fosili*, later a soloist; the deaf-mute mime actor Zlatko Omerbegović; the writer Igor Mandić; the well-known academic and intellectual Predrag Matvejević; professors of the English Department like Željko Bujas, author of the major English–Croatian dictionary; prominent doctors, priests, and so on. Most of them belonged to the young generation, while communist-oriented scientists rarely, if ever came to the American Center. This fundamental detail was confirmed by all the former employees of USIS Yugoslavia I spoke to: 'Some of them came only once, and fearfully asked to be cancelled from the sign-up sheet,' recalls Zdenka Nikolić.[91] The former Library director, Nada Apsen, remembers personalities such as Franjo Durst, the famous gynaecologist and professor; scientists from the Meteorological Institute; the painter Ivo Vojvodić, from Dubrovnik; the directors of Strossmayer Gallery, Ljubo Babić and Vinko Zlamalik; the political scientist Štefica Deren-Antoljak; Anton Bauer, former director of Glyptoteque Museum (the HAZU sculpture museum); Radovan Ivančević, art historian and professor; Radovan Vukadinović, professor of international law and senior fellow, in 1970–71, at the Research Institute on Communist Affairs at Columbia University; the jazz conductor, composer, and drummer Silvestar Silvije Glojnarić – and many more.[92] Vida Ognjenović, Serbian theatre director, writer, diplomat, and, in 1989, among the founders of the Democratic Party, the first opposition party in Serbia, shared the USIS experience in Belgrade, together with film director Branko Bauer, Belgrade students, and Olja Ivanjicki, a Serbian contemporary artist who, thanks to a Ford Foundation cultural exchange, brought pop art to Yugoslavia and inspired a whole generation of young artists.[93]

Certainly, USIS's success in attracting the Yugoslav cultural vanguard, academia, and intellectual leaders relied on distinctive communication approaches. Informal, interpersonal contacts with individuals played a major role, but then meetings, conferences, and lectures delivered even stronger messages of American democracy, personal freedoms, wealth, or artistic creativity. The USIS extension service – materials distributed to the republics' executive governments, councils for science and culture, universities, high schools, cultural institutes, newspapers and publishing houses, theatres and film studios – conquered Yugoslav 'hearts and minds' outside the library perimeter. From Zagreb, USIS covered Croatia, Slovenia, and Bosnia-Herzegovina, while Belgrade concentrated its efforts on Serbia, Macedonia, and Montenegro. Above all, Voice of America attracted massive, delighted audiences. USIS owed its success to the way ideas were presented – in a simple but fascinating manner, centred on 'one important basic idea,' understandable to large audiences, even the less educated, and appealing to emotions and intellect. According to Washington's policymakers, USIS messages had to 'give hope for the future,' 'strengthen foreign countries' national pride,' and 'avoid giving the impression of [US] self-interest.'[94] Backed by USIA guidelines, in the field USIS spread carefully constructed cultural narratives of freedom, progress, and abundance that introduced new, politically challenging points of reference, but which ultimately, as Laura Belmonte emphasized, safeguarded US national security.[95]

Stopping American 'propaganda'

The Yugoslav authorities reacted quite convincingly to USIS's bolder strategy of the Eisenhower era. The secret services continued to survey 'hostile activities' and 'enemy propaganda,' condemning many students that were in touch with the 'foreign reading rooms.'[96] The SAWPY went even further. In 1956, the agency created an ad hoc commission to investigate the statutes of the information centres, coordinate their activities, and assess if they were pursuing Yugoslav interests. The SAWPY report acknowledged that foreign publications were not directly attacking Yugoslavia, but instead delivered 'large scale anti-communist propaganda.'[97] Soon after, the Foreign Office advisory board issued a new regulation on foreign press, publications, and books that could now be distributed in Belgrade, Zagreb, Ljubljana, and Rijeka, only by the state enterprise *Jugoslovenska knjiga*, and in numbers decided by the Secretariat of Information and the Foreign Office. Content supporting the criminal and harmful education of the young and adverse views towards Yugoslavia were forbidden.[98] A 1957 survey on *Politika*, *Borba*, and other newspapers, demonstrated that foreign press materials, including those of USIS, were spreading sensational, unaesthetic, and tasteless views, and developing feelings of 'inferiority and colonialism,' so they were strongly disapproved for use.[99]

Almost concurrently, discussions at the League of Communists of Yugoslavia's ideological commission, chaired by Veljko Micunović, a leading communist and government member, affirmed in more conciliatory tones that cultural contacts with foreign countries cannot be avoided. Yet, the commission requested that tougher restrictions should be applied and urged to create an institution that would perform as a foreign cultural centre.[100] The Belgrade Cultural Centre (Kulturni centar Beograd), founded as an information-propaganda institution to neutralize foreign propaganda activities in 1956, began to operate in 1957, and then expanded in 1958. While planned as a reading room supplying foreign periodicals, the Belgrade Center remained at an infant stage for years – even though provided with a photo, audio, film, and art section – mostly for financial reasons, and there was little public interest since its services were charged.[101]

In 1957, USIS Belgrade had already published around 20,000 copies of *Bilten*, while the movies section retained sixty projectors and 8,000 movies. For the Yugoslav authorities, such 'long-term, intensive, and organized' propaganda needed an ideological counteraction 'to affirm our views and our praxis, to paralyze the ideological influence' from the United States (but also other Western countries and the Soviet Union).[102] The Yugoslav authorities further enhanced restrictions over foreign propaganda in late 1958. First, in September, when the Foreign Office obliged USIS publications (and those of all the other countries) to be approved by the Republic's Internal Affairs. The new provision also compelled USIS to publicize film events only by way of personal, and not mail, invitation. Lastly, the posts were forbidden to donate printing paper to Yugoslav publishing houses for the publication of American books in translation. Then, in November, further restrictions were applied. All published or imported press material had to be sent to Internal Affairs. USIS Belgrade sent two pamphlets, *The USA on Disarmament* and *The Reward of Independence*, which were both rejected. The new regulation obliged USIS to report the names of the English teaching students to the authorities, to ask for movies to be approved by the Federal Commission for Film Review, and to rent them only through the Federal or Republican Center for Cultural-Education Film (or, in case of the capital, through the Belgrade Cultural Centre). Even if many Yugoslav institutions continued to borrow directly from the American posts, the restriction nevertheless reduced such activities by more than 30 per cent.[103]

The Second Plenum of the Party's Central Committee of November 1959 accused foreign 'enemy propaganda' of operating through foreigners' visits to industrial production plants, through Yugoslav citizens on exchanges abroad, and through the foreign cultural centres.[104] Then, in late 1960, the Secretariat of Information presented a draft of the Press Law and other Views of Information to the Federal Assembly.[105] The law proposal declared that importing foreign press was free, except for materials 'explicitly destined for the Yugoslav people' and, therefore, 'propaganda.'[106] Articles 67–79 sanctioned the restrictions introduced two years earlier, including a new prescription that forbade negative criticism of one country to another, targeted specifically at American critics of the Soviet Union. Articles 100–115 obliged the foreign cultural centres to register with the Yugoslav government and administrate expenses and activities. In addition, they were prohibited from being placed within a diplomatic mission, and the control of their movie program was delegated to the Secretariat of Information, now responsible for the permissions of the movie screenings at USIS. Finally, article 52 established the criteria for censorship by prescribing that political offenses 'against the people and state' of Yugoslavia, materials 'abusing moral' and those offending 'the citizens and insulting the public order and peace,' should be censored.[107] The law was approved and became operational on 9 November 1960, with the information centres given six months to adapt and negotiate the new rearrangements with the Foreign Office.[108]

But, as I explain in the following pages, the implementation was neither completely successful, nor easy.

The Yugoslav Press Law induced the USIA to radically rethink its cultural strategy in Yugoslavia. On the one hand, USIS officers were convinced that the motivation for 'harassment' of USIS posts was Yugoslav 'hyper-sensitivity vis-à-vis Russians and Chinese,' and their way of showing 'that all countries must obey the same laws.'[109] This was certainly one reason for Yugoslav anxiety towards foreign propaganda. Another was the mounting trend of cultural imports in Yugoslavia, not only from the United States. As Francesca Rolandi shows, Italian pop melodies started conquering the Yugoslav musical arena from the late 1950s on, when the Sanremo festival became a symbol of modernity. From 1957, the authorities permitted foreign tourists to enter Yugoslavia. Soon, they relaxed the border crossings with Italy, and by the end of the decade Yugoslavs started to shop in Trieste. Western consumer products and practices, from music discs to nylon socks, erupted in Yugoslav daily life.[110] Larger cultural freedoms were recognized in the Embassy's reports. Secretary Stephen Palmer describes his conversations with painter Milica Lozanić-Petrović and vanguard sculptors Ana Bešlić and Jovan Soldatović in 1956, that proved the privileged position of Yugoslav artists to 'express themselves in the way they wish.' On the other hand, writers and filmmakers, since they produced for large audiences, were frequently censored.[111] The Seventh Party Congress of 1958 promised to 'emancipate creative arts from dogmatism' and pledged 'to exempt art and science from being used as instruments of political interests.'[112] Even *Politika* and *Borba* defended modernist art against the attacks of the 'dogmatists' and requested democracy for Yugoslav art.[113] This gradual cultural liberalization endorsed USIS work in the field. In 1958, USIS Belgrade created *Pregled* [*Horizon*], a new colourful periodical whose contents improved the engaging narratives of American freedom, democracy, and economy, and in which it looked like American citizens lived full, happy lives in a classless society and shared the economic bounty. By the end of the decade, USIS strategy certainly became subtler and more target-centred. The 1959 Country Plan defined Yugoslav students as 'the only true hope for greater democratization,' the art leaders and personalities as 'those best prepared to listen,' and the Yugoslav managerial class as those who made vital decisions, but possessed little technical knowledge and education.[114] It was clear as daylight that it was a 'battle for hearts and minds,' and no surprise that the LCY ideologues, preoccupied with surmounting liberal trends in society, put pressure on foreign propaganda, trying to limit its influence.

Waging public diplomacy in the 1960s

From the early 1960s on, USIA strategy in Yugoslavia became, more than ever, entangled in US–Yugoslav bilateral affairs, the evolving 'Yugoslav experiment' with its bolder strategy of non-alignment, and the developments of Cold War confrontation. In January 1961, John F. Kennedy became president of the United States. In his inaugural address of 20 January, he promised to defend 'freedom in its hour of maximum danger' and 'struggle against the common enemies of man: tyranny, poverty, disease, and war itself.'[115] Kennedy replaced Eisenhower's deterrent strategy over the nuclear arms threat with his 'Flexible Response' doctrine to 'extend the means available to deter undesirable shifts in the balance of power.' Considering Eisenhower's foreign policy establishment slow, bloated, and unwieldy, he resolved to 'cut back the National Security Council staff' as the main national security decision-making body, and rely on direct contacts with individual departments and task forces.[116]

Like his predecessors, Kennedy believed that American-style institutions and values, and the free market, would enable other nations to become more prosperous, modern, stable, and friendly.[117] Immediately after becoming president, he nominated journalist Edward Murrow to lead the USIA. By the time George Allen left the directorship, the Agency was in good 'shape.' The USIA had 200 posts in eighty-five countries; it employed 3,771 Americans and a further 6,881 foreign nationals, while the VOA daily audience was around fifty million. The USIA director sat on the National Security Council (NSC), attended cabinet meetings, and by 1960 was meeting the President at the White House every three weeks. Allen's leadership gave a positive shift to the Agency by maintaining excellent relations with Congress, initiating jazz ambassadors to go abroad, and pushing for broader English teaching activities.[118] Both Kennedy and Murrow had very clear ideas on how to use information abroad, and were interested in renewing the American image with television. Indeed, Murrow was familiar with its power and the impact television had on public opinion and policies. In the wake of the McCarthy purges in early 1954, as the anchorman of CBS, he initiated the *See It Now* series (remembered for their 'Good night, and good luck' closing) by which he contributed to discrediting McCarthy's tactics in rooting out communist elements within the government.[119] In Murrow's years (1961–64), the USIA played a role in major foreign policy stories such as Berlin, Cuba, and Vietnam. The agency's research department boomed under Leo Crespi, its polls found wide circulation and, every day, President Kennedy read USIA's digest of world editorials. Nonetheless, Murrow's era demonstrated growing incompatibility between USIA and VOA, since Murrow expected the broadcasts to be able to manipulate its content as policy dictated. Murrow believed the Agency should not just inform but persuade, and personally oversaw propaganda operations during the tensest Cold War moments: Operation Mongoose (a covert sabotage program of Castro's regime in Cuba), the disastrous Bay of Pigs incident, and the Cuban Missile Crisis in 1962.[120] To Murrow's misfortune, executives left USIA 'out of the loop' in one of the most precarious covert actions, the landings at the Bay of Pigs. According to Nicholas Cull, 'Murrow spent much of the next three years recovering from the implications of that single decision.'[121]

Under Murrow's directorship, USIA produced the most ambitious Country Plan for Yugoslavia that predicted a radically different, leaders-oriented, cultural agenda. Approved in 1962, and released in 1963, the new USIA plan, crafted on the State Department's *Guidelines of U.S. Policy and Operations for Yugoslavia*, emphasized the USIS crucial role to link Yugoslavia to the West. USIS objectives were to 'influence the evolution of Yugoslavia's political, economic, and social institutions along more democratic and humanistic lines and with increasing association with the West'; and 'to maintain and expand the channels of communication with the Yugoslav people and to use these channels to help them understand the United States' policies.' According to the Plan, the wedge strategy continued to be operational. Even USIS's aim was, after all, 'to assist Yugoslavia to build a firm, secure base of national independence'; to bring the United States the 'maximum benefits' from 'the divisive effects of Yugoslavia's independent status' both upon the international communist movement and upon other Soviet-dominated Eastern European governments. The Plan took a sharp leader's shift. Yugoslav leaders were 'most likely to be influenced towards a true understanding of American systems and policies,' and they could, consequently, 'influence others.' More specifically, the Plan recommended that they be persuaded to promote objective information about the United States. It envisioned that USIS would enlarge its policy of cultural contacts with Yugoslav policymakers, editors, publishers, and spokespersons. The USIS goal, stated the Plan unambiguously, was to influence Yugoslav government and intellectual leaders to adapt Tito's regime to Western values and standards.[122]

The Country Plan enlisted 2,000 Yugoslav leaders to whom the USIS would send unrestricted, 'un-sanitized' bulletins. This group included parliamentarians and assembly members (from the Federal People's Assembly, the republican assemblies, and those of the autonomous regions, Vojvodina and Kosovo); the executive councils' leaders (from the Federal Executive Council and the republican executive councils); ministries, agencies, and commission leaders (officials at the Foreign Office and Secretaries of States offices, republican secretaries and undersecretaries, and presidents and secretaries of commissions and committees at all government levels); and press and information leaders (editorial boards of newspapers, radio, and television).[123] The new plan urged the enlargement of the US Foreign Leader Program that had commenced in 1958, and realization of the Fulbright agreement whose negotiation started the same year (concluding in 1964).[124] Indeed, while the Yugoslav Press Law reduced USIS margins of freedom, it inspired a new shift towards a leader-oriented policy with greater emphasis on Yugoslav politicians, academics, intellectuals, and opinion makers that would provoke unpredictable and controversial outcomes in the decades to come.

Applying and resisting the Yugoslav Press Law

At the time USIA approved the new Country Plan for Yugoslavia, Yugoslav–American bilateral relations were at a serious impasse. Tito delivered a harsh anti-colonial speech at the UN's fifteenth General Assembly in New York, in September 1960.[125] It was a statement of non-alignment that would, in years to come, become a sort of Yugoslav recognition flag – its 'nation-building' course, as William Zimmerman put it.[126] A year after New York, in early September 1961, Tito gathered in Belgrade India's first prime minister, Jawaharlal Nehru; Indonesia's first president, Sukarno; Egypt's second president, Gamal Abdel Nasser; Ghana's first president Kwame Nkrumah; and twenty other state delegations. Opened just two weeks after the Bay of Pigs invasion, and Soviet Yuri Gagarin's space success, the First Non-Aligned Conference in Belgrade only inflated Washington's anti-communist mood.[127] Tito's anti-Western and anti-American conference speech left Ambassador Kennan constrained. 'Tito's statements on Berlin and on the Soviet resumption of tests,' telegrammed Kennan to Washington, 'came as a deep disappointment [...]. The passage on Berlin contains no word that could not have been written by Khrushchev; and that on [Soviet resumption of nuclear testing], is weaker and more pro-Soviet than even those of Nasser and Nkrumah.'[128] Kennan suggested Washington should carefully reflect 'on its implications for our treatment of conference and, in more long-term, our attitude towards the role of Yugoslavs.'[129] But then, Secretary of State Dean Rusk, and Assistant Secretary of State for European Affairs, Foy Kohler, especially after his reassuring meeting with Ambassador Marko Nikezić on 19 October, calmed the troubled waters, so that the pragmatic line seemed to prevail.[130]

Nonetheless, voices contrary to US softness towards Yugoslavia urged the stopping of economic aid, and anti-communist hardliners in Congress and the Senate prevailed. During the Aid Act voting of 6 June 1962, the US Senate adopted the Frank Lausche (Democrat, Ohio) amendment which restricted American economic aid to all communist countries, including Poland and Yugoslavia. On 12 June, the House's Ways and Means Committee, while considering the Kennedy administration's request for broader authority to negotiate trade agreements, reported legislation (H.R. 1818) that included a provision withdrawing most-favoured-nation (MFN) status from Poland and Yugoslavia. The bill passed the House on 28 June by a vote of 298 to 125. For Yugoslavia, this meant doubling or tripling import tariffs on Yugoslav export commodities. Foreign Secretary Popović and Ambassador Nikezić rushed to meet Rusk, who assured them that such a retreat 'was contrary to the wishes of the Administration.'[131] But the damage was done, and between 1961 and 1963 a Cold War 'breeze' descended on relations between Belgrade and Washington. In a meeting with Rusk, Veljko Mićunović, appointed Yugoslav ambassador in October, expressed 'Yugoslavia's sense of bewilderment and consternation,' and lamented the political harm to 'Yugoslavia's international reputation and prestige,'[132] especially when Yugoslavia was rising as a prominent leader of non-aligned nations. The State Department interpreted Khrushchev's most cordial visit to Tito in October 1962, and Tito's visit to Moscow in December, a result of US–Yugoslav distancing.[133]

Such bilateral relations heavily impacted USIS's activities in Yugoslavia and reinforced already existing resentment. In 1961, Belgrade's City Committee recommended applying the Yugoslav Press Law in order to 'paralyze and limit these [foreign] influences,' and prevent the 'weaknesses of Yugoslav institutions' and 'the lack of communist consciousness.'[134] Several local parties' ideological commissions, acting at Belgrade's surrounding municipalities, excitedly discussed the impact of counterpropaganda measures and the outcome of the Press Law. Savski Venac, Zvezdara, Palilula, Zemun, Stari Grad, Vračar, Novi Beograd, and Voždovac took almost universal positions, and agreed to develop systematic activities to counteract these measures. They warned against 'members of the League of Communists that [...] are not able to take a proper attitude towards foreign propaganda and foreigners,'[135] and admonished those 'who continued to visit the reading rooms, receive foreign propaganda publications and participated in various competitions of foreign radio stations,' that 'strong Party measures would be taken.'[136] The local ideological commissions criticized the 'film and entertainment press for spreading a foreign way of life, mentality and traditions,'[137] and emphasized the lack of critical appraisal of young people towards foreign artists and cultural workers. They urged the representatives of *Avala-film, Kolo, Interfarm, Metropola, Jugoinvest, Automobil-Beograd,* and the other Belgrade enterprises to establish a more severe regulative stance to foreign visitors.[138] Finally, they insisted that all bulletins, publications, and press sent by foreign embassies or cultural posts be returned to senders, or destroyed.[139] Belgrade University's Committee expressed an equally critical attitude by instructing 'students to avoid the foreign reading rooms,'[140] and obliged foreign professors and students on exchanges, wishing to lecture at the university, to ask the Rectorate and State Secretariat for approval.[141]

But for USIS, it was not only a war of words and ideas. The ideological pressures broke out in violent acts over the posts and their users. On 19 May 1961, the Interior Affairs office of Novi Sad called a part-time USIS employee and warned that carrying *Bilten* from the train station to the reading room constituted 'a criminal act.' Ambassador Kennan, while waiting to settle the Press Law question, recommended that *Bilten* for Novi Sad be temporarily discontinued, and instructed the post to stop lending films or projectors. Meanwhile, Interior authorities in Belgrade questioned the Yugoslav CAO assistant in a two-hour interview. On 6 June, 'a local employee at the reading room in Belgrade observed individuals' from 'the Interior who have appeared from time to time in the past.' Two days later, Kennan decided to temporarily close the post, waiting for Yugoslav assurances that the 'American reading rooms' were 'not contravening Yugoslav law.'[142] This highly embarrassing situation was resolved when both parties signed an agreement on 14 June 1961.[143]

Nevertheless, tensions resurfaced again in 1962 when the Municipal Committee of Palilula strongly criticized a Belgrade professor and Party member who received US publications by mail, and whose wife was employed at the US Embassy.[144] In January 1962, the authorities stopped a telegraphist from the Belgrade train station 'because he participated in the prize contest of the American reading room.'[145] Two months later, this time in Zagreb, Danilo Pejović, a philosophy professor at Zagreb University who was a Party member, Djilas sympathizer, and former Ford grantee, was warned by UDBA to stop contacting USIS Zagreb officers, and prohibited from having luncheons with Ambassador Kennan if not via official visits. In his last conversation with Consul Joseph Godson, Pejović recalled how the Consulate telephones were 'tapped' and all 'mail inside [the] country' was opened. While Godson concluded: 'It was a sad meeting and an even sadder parting, a sharp reminder of unrelenting totalitarian police control of its citizens.'[146] In June, another incident occurred, this time when Tomislav Kuzmanović, an art student at Sarajevo University and frequent visitor of the Consulate's magazine facilities, was called to a four-hour session with the Party's faculty members. He was strictly warned against any further use of American magazines among other students because the exhibition of *House and Garden, Holiday, Look,* and *Arts* would 'make them prone to make comparisons between life in Yugoslavia and life in the United States. Yet, while shaken by the interview, Kuzmanović 'retained sufficient courage to borrow two more art magazines.'[147] Periodic harassment persisted until early 1963 when, in January, Branko Karadjole, assistant director for the Western Hemisphere at the Internal Affairs, warned the Embassy that some *Bilten* articles on Cuba, published days before, presented 'controversial, slanted, and one-sided cold war material for broad public dissemination.' The issue was not banned, because it was the first violation of the law, but Karadjole requested more circumspection for the future.[148]

How did USIS cope with the Yugoslav Press Law and coercion on the field? On the one hand, compared to other Eastern European countries, Yugoslavia permitted a relatively wide range of freedoms for USIS. But among all the foreign missions, USIS was the most determined in avoiding the new Yugoslav regulations. USIS officers insisted on contacting movie users directly, and were very tenacious in sending propaganda materials to Yugoslav industrial plants, even after several had been returned. With the authorities, they insisted on individual deregulation, temporary permits, and ad hoc negotiations.[149] To prevent financial supervision by the Yugoslav Information Secretariat, USIS transferred its financial sector to the Embassy. When, henceforth, USIS signed the agreement with the Yugoslav government in June, the number of registered field officers dropped from 108 to 22.[150]

To remedy the consequences of the Press Law, USIS started to negotiate with the Yugoslav government. Walter Roberts, a prominent US public diplomat who served at Voice of America from the late 1940s, and worked for the USIA from its inception, arrived in Belgrade in the spring of 1960 to operate as PAO, where he remained until 1966. 'If you read that press law from A to Z,' he recalls in an interview, 'it meant the end of USIS,' but not of the British Council, because the British Council was registered as a Yugoslav 'non-governmental organization.' 'USIS could never have done that,' underlined Roberts: 'I personally was convinced that my days were numbered, […] because the press law denied diplomatic status to any information or cultural program. […] And of course, we bitterly protested, but in vain.' Then, in Roberts' words, we 'started negotiations about how to make our program livable,' during which 'we used certain gimmicks, like putting an American resident in Belgrade in charge of our library. And as weeks and the months went by, the Yugoslavs became less interested in enforcing it. So, within a year or so, we were back to where we were before.'[151] Thanks to such field lobbying, USIS in Yugoslavia never separated from the Embassy and the Consulate and continued to act independently from Yugoslav government intrusion. Kennan pushed Tito to transform the Press Law into 'a non-law,'[152] and by the mid-1960s circumstances returned to normal.

Relaxed bilateral relations between Belgrade and Washington helped USIS to restore regular activities. In 1963, Secretary Dean Rusk visited Tito in May, and afterwards intervened with Kennedy on the question of sales of military spare parts to the Yugoslav Army.[153] Tito's first official visit to the United States on 17 October 1963, which was Kennedy's last meeting with a foreign statesman, sanctioned a good partnership and prepared ground for the Fulbright agreement with Yugoslavia, signed in November 1964. In the aftermath of the Kennedy–Tito meeting, Congress withdrew the MFN restrictions towards Yugoslavia.[154] In 1966, USIS was back to increasing trends. Compared to other foreign centres it supplied record numbers of printed materials (2.6 million of 3.7 million foreign printed materials distributed in 1965), frequently conducted public mail opinion surveys (angering the Yugoslav ideological commissions), and *Pregled* had the highest circulation of all foreign publications.[155] In the late 1960s, it would conquer many Yugoslav 'hearts and minds' and entice important societal changes.

The changing experiment

It was palpable to USIS from the late 1950s that profound changes were occurring in Titoist Yugoslavia. When, in May 1959, 3,000 Zagreb University students demonstrated because of bad food conditions at the university 'mensa' – the mess hall – the police blocked their way through the city and physical fights broke out. Two people died, while 150 students were injured, often suffering heavy blows from police truncheons, and many being arrested.[156] Following the demonstrations, some lost scholarships, and others were expelled from the university and Party. Shortly after, similar protests broke out in Belgrade, Skopje, and Rijeka. None of these were questioning communist power or inciting any political alternatives. But, for the US Consular officers, these first autonomous, non-governmental protests were deciphered as a signal of disagreement and dissidence, and, therefore, of liberalization. These demonstrations led to arrests and imprisonments, proving how the police authorities considered them politically dangerous.[157]

Liberalization occurred more evidently in literature but also in the newly approved 1963 constitution. In 1960, Miroslav Krleža, a prominent Croatian writer and Tito's friend, while welcoming Jean-Paul Sartre in Yugoslavia, proudly accentuated that the Seventh Congress 'liberated art from even the most insignificant administrative influence.'[158] Yugoslav artists, writers, and journalists were 'prohibited from making direct attacks upon, or from questioning, the domestic and foreign policy of the Tito government,' but they enjoyed a 'measure of freedom unparalleled in any other communist-ruled country, except Poland.'[159] The 1963 constitution institutionalized self-management practices in society, extended human and civil rights, and established constitutionally guaranteed court procedures.

The societal changes and the new regime's assets influenced the Yugoslav perception of the world outside. USIS results were already observable. Interviews of thirty Yugoslav refugees conducted in 1960 and 1961 showed that young male workers with medium income regarded 'freedom' in predominantly economic terms and the United States as an 'example of a democratic country.' Their image of America was shaped by American movies and VOA broadcasts. Indignant about the 'absence of political rights and freedom,' 'party control over life, and favouritism for party members' in Yugoslavia, they depicted American life where 'almost everyone has his home and television set,' 'You live like a human being,' and 'Freedom.'[160] In 1964, the Belgrade Institute of Social Science conducted a public opinion survey asking, 'Who is Yugoslavia's best-friend country?' While the United States came after the

Soviet Union, United Arab Republic, and India (a high score, given the presumable political caution of respondents), the results demonstrated that the 'younger the respondents, the more they favoured the United States and other capitalist countries.' Moreover, the majority replied that they were not politically active, nor wanted to become LCY members.[161]

Between March 1968 and January 1969, social scientists from Columbia University and Belgrade's Institute of Social Science worked together to research Yugoslav opinion leaders. They included federal legislators, administrators, mass organization leaders, enterprises directors, economic planners, and advisers, as well as editors from newspapers, television networks, radio stations, and publishing houses. The research involved leading journalists and commentators, intellectuals and university professors, leading literary writers, theatrical and film directors – a total of 517 individuals. The top twenty positions – the President and cabinet members – were excluded. The findings were remarkable. For instance, members of the federal government had 'conformist' attitudes to economic development, less propensity for freedom of criticism, and were less aware of public social criticism. On the other hand, participants at regional and local levels of power were more likely to endorse freedom of criticism and be more aware of the public mood. The most notable finding, however, was that in a society operating under a one-party government, influential leaders held a wide range of opinions and enjoyed a high level of mass media output and policy involvement.[162] This public opinion survey was comprised of the same group of leaders that USIS regarded as its primary target. They recognized the contribution of lower–higher hierarchy relations in Yugoslavia already in the early 1960s. 'We have evidence,' stated the 1963 USIS Country Plan, 'that leaders at the lower level exercised quite some influence on the higher echelon,' so that 'we had been able to convince at least lower echelons in the hierarchy of the necessity of continued close cultural relations with the West.' This was reflected in Yugoslav journalism as well. During the same period, USIS noted more objective news reporting, a distinction between news and editorials, and more openness towards foreign press agencies like Associated Press, United Press International, Reuters, Agence France Presse, and the USIS press service as well.[163] The Central Committee's ideological commission recognized this same trend as it affected Yugoslav journalism with 'market consumer mentality,' 'bourgeois aristocratism,' and the prevalent interest in Western over Eastern European countries.[164]

Despite occasional negative behaviour, USIS felt constructive when approaching lower ranked Yugoslav politicians and Party administrators. In 1966, USIS librarians undertook a large tour of Yugoslav cities and national libraries in Bosnia, Herzegovina, Dalmatia, Montenegro, and Serbia. Compared to the 1950s, the reception was warm, and it seemed 'that an old and enduring ice was broken.' At the National Library of Cetinje in Montenegro, Niko Martinović, the Library's director and president of the Yugoslav Association of Librarians, made a public toast to USIS, thanking them 'for your help to all Yugoslav libraries over these years.'[165] Compared to the severe and stern rhetoric of many Yugoslav ideological commissions, from the top to the bottom of the hierarchy, Martinović's standpoint seems opposed. It nonetheless illustrates the Yugoslav dichotomy between its projection outside – as a non-aligned leader – and its internal identity, which struggled between 'open' self-management socialism and the defence of a one-party dictatorship.

Yugoslav dichotomy and US public diplomacy

The Yugoslavs modified the Press Law in 1966 and 1968, but articles regarding foreign propaganda remained untouched. For instance, the 1968 amendments gave individual Yugoslav citizens the right to initialize a press publication, but expanded the reasons for prohibiting one that was deemed an 'attack on the social realities established by the Constitution, the social self-management, [...] and the violation of the honour and reputation of the nationalities of Yugoslavia.'[166] Such elusive definitions left the doors open for political manipulation and invisible boundaries of censorship.

Yugoslav balancing between openness towards the foreign world and the defence of its communist power emerged plainly in the approach towards American influence. 'We will never be able to solve propaganda. It is an octopus with thousands of tentacles [...]. But we can do a lot if we lead our propaganda in the direction that will, in a certain way, paralyze what we don't want to [...] exist,' stated Belgrade's City Committee in 1968.[167] The sharpest restrictions applied to Party members. 'Communists that participated in the contests of foreign radio stations, or who received gifts from foreigners or visited foreign reading rooms' were expelled.[168]

The Federation's bureaucracy and its institutions, associations, organs, agencies, leagues, trade unions, councils, and committees were not easily controlled. The ideological commissions felt that much had been done in the legislation, but the trends were intensifying, not diminishing. The Yugoslavs suspected that the sophisticated, long-term 'ideological influence' of American social norms, ideals, and moral concepts would change the outlook of young people and university students. They were irritated by the US's 'considerable cultural arrangements with organizations and individuals,' and by American infiltration of television, in the musical and entertainment press, film enterprises, and children's literature.[169] Against these penetrations, the Central Committee urged a stronger ideological battle. It was necessary to 'bring more order and intensify control.'[170] The ideological commission appointed a permanent working group at the SAWPY, the Commission for Political and Ideological-Educational Work, to monitor foreign propaganda. This added to other institutions and agencies which dealt with foreign propaganda – Internal Affairs, the Information Secretariat, the Commission for Cultural Relations with Foreign Countries, the Federal Secretariat for Education, the Office of Technical Assistance, and the Center for Scientific and Technical Movies. Representatives from these sectors were gathered in the Coordination Council for Information Activities (Koordinacioni savet za informativnu delatnost) established at Internal Affairs.[171] Juridicially, the foreign cultural centres were subject to the Information Secretariat, possessed no diplomatic immunity, and reported to the authorities their finances, new publications, press materials, and musical recordings. They could organize film screenings, but only with the authorities' permission. Internal Affairs officially controlled the film catalogues, while the Information Secretariat oversaw exhibitions. Nevertheless, 'the opening of our country towards the foreign world' emphasized Belgrade's City Committee, and the 'circulation of people' rendered these 'measures of limited impact.'[172]

The issue was on the table already from 1962 when the Central Committee's ideological commission stressed the dual view of the Party leaders on foreign propaganda. Some members considered foreign influences a weakening feature of the Yugoslav political scenario. Others regarded it as an internal problem, but not as its source. The commission concluded that Yugoslav political and social developments were both the cause and consequence of foreign propaganda operations. Because of its non-alignment, Yugoslavia was an open community, under attack by the 'psychological warfare' of 'block politics' and by 'moral pressure' that was exploiting Yugoslav weaknesses and popularizing foreign values and lifestyles.[173] This dichotomous vision of foreign propaganda tortured the Yugoslav leaders in subsequent years. In 1966, Leo Mates, a pro-Western Yugoslav diplomat, chaired the SAWPY's ideological commission. He stated: 'Our country has gradually liberalized its contacts with foreign countries and according to our Constitution Yugoslavia is a community open […] to foreign influence'; the latter, he pointed, could be only 'defeated by better living standards of Yugoslav workers.'[174] On the one hand, the highest ranked politicians tried to rationalize the propaganda problems as a side effect of Yugoslav non-aligned international policy. On the other, they identified a possible risk of Western 'infiltration' in Yugoslav society. While the SAWPY's commission defined the foreign propaganda as 'anti-socialist,'[175] the Federal Executive Council deemed it was impossible to restrict its dissemination without Yugoslavia losing international prestige as an 'open community.'[176] The story reported by PAO Roberts demonstrates the Yugoslavs' balancing between soft and hard approaches:

> We had a mailing list of our magazine called *Pregled*. One day, at some occasion, one of the Yugoslavs approached me and said: 'Have you discontinued *Pregled*?' And I said, no, not at all. 'Well, I didn't get my copy this month.' […] In the next two or three or four days, other people on the staff, both local employees, and Americans said they heard that *Pregled* was not distributed. So finally, I concluded that *Pregled* was not sent out to the post office. So, I took my jacket and went to the Foreign Office. […] One Sunday, a week later, […] Milan [Bulajić, who was the American desk officer] came over to my house and he said: 'I'm red-faced. I apologize. *Pregled* was thrown by the Ministry of the Interior into the Danube River.' […] But that was the only time.[177]

Certainly, among all the others, the middle echelons perceived and sought cooperation with the West from a mainly pragmatic, less ideological, point of view. We observe these phenomena in Yugoslav cultural exchanges with the United States. Because of this, they remained the major target of US public diplomacy in Yugoslavia. The American centres tried to change the Yugoslav regime from outside, and interpreted the liberalization processes of the 1960s as the result of American aid, and of its rapprochement with the West. What is more, they admitted that many other Yugoslav citizens shared this view.[178] This was, of course, only partially true, because internal, often opposing, Yugoslav movements also pushed for reforms.

As in other countries, USIS channels aspired to encourage democratic and Western cultural influence through books, magazines, newspapers, exhibitions, movies, cultural contacts, the English teaching program, and VOA broadcasts. However, unlike in Italy and France, where USIS mainly focused on the labour target group,[179] the USIA in Yugoslavia prioritized those mid-level leaders who could, in the future, be proponents of liberalization. And USIS did it using slow but continuous field work that, in a persuasive and creative manner, was trying to 'sell America' in a socialist society without criticizing the dictatorship.

Notes

1 Yugoslavia was a federation state comprising six socialist republics (Serbia, Croatia, Slovenia, Macedonia, Bosnia and Herzegovina, and Montenegro) and two autonomous provinces (Vojvodina and Kosovo), with Belgrade as its capital. Both the federal and republican governments had their own president, vice president, a parliament (the assembly), an executive council, the administrative agencies, and a judiciary.

2 Lees, *Keeping Tito Afloat*, 71, 83, 119.

3 Special Guidance 91 for the Mutual Security Program, 23 May 1951 in memorandum from Block to several Department of State offices, 24 October 1951, Box 2243, CDF 1950–54, RG 59, NACP, 7.

4 Lampe, Prickett, and Adamović, *Yugoslav–American Economic Relations Since World War II*, 72.

5 Allen to Secretary of State, 20 April 1950, FRUS, Vol. IV, 1950, doc. 799, 1404–5.

6 Jakovina, *Socijalizam na američkoj pšenici*, 32, 37–9.

7 Project TROY Report to the Secretary of State, vol. I, 1 February 1951, 511.00/2-151, CDF 1950–54, NARA, 1, 58, 61; Allan A. Needell, '"Truth is Our Weapon": Project TROY, Political Warfare, and Government–Academic Relations in the National Security State,' *Diplomatic History* 17, no. 3 (1 July 1993): 399–420, http://dx.doi.org/10.1111/j.1467-7709.1993.tb00588.x.

8 Foreign Service Circular 32, 10 April 1952, 511.00/4-1052, Box 2244, CDF 1950–54, RG 59, NACP.

9 USIE Country Paper Yugoslavia in circular 2 Belgrade to Dept. of State, 3 July 1950, 511.68/7-350, Box 2472, CDF 1950–54, RG 59, NACP.

10 IIA Plan for Yugoslavia 1951–1952, 15 January 1952 in Despatch 946 Belgrade to Dept. of State, 9 April 1952, 511.68/4-952, Box 2472, CDF 1950–54, RG 59, NACP.

11 M. S. Handler, 'Tito Warns Against Pressure,' *New York Times*, 19 February 1950; and Walter L. Hixon, *Parting the Curtain: Propaganda, Culture, and the Cold War, 1945–1961* (New York: Palgrave Macmillan, 1997), 16–17.

12 Ambassador Allen to Secretary of State, 20 April 1950, FRUS, Vol. IV, 1950, doc. 799.

13 Lees, *Keeping Tito Afloat*, 81–119.

14 USIS-MSA Information Plan for Yugoslavia 1952–1953, 1 August 1952 in despatch Belgrade to Dept. of State, 31 July 1952, 511.68/7–3152, Box 2472, CDF 1950–54, RG 59, NACP.

15 *Ibid.*; USIS Country Program for Yugoslavia 1952–1953, 3 December 1952, 511.68/ 12–352, Box 2472, CDF 1950–54, RG 59, NACP.

16 Telegram 1940 Belgrade to Dept. of State, 19 June 1951, 511.68/6–1951, Box 2472, CDF 1950–54, RG 59, NACP.

17 Telegram 291 Belgrade to Secretary of State, 4 September 1952, 511.68/9–452, Box 2472, CDF 1950–54, RG 59, NACP; Radmila Njegić, 'Razvoj Stanovništva Beograda u Posleratnom Periodu,' *Godišnjak Grada Beograda*, issue 11–12 (1964): 219.

18 Despatch 166 Belgrade to Dept. of State, 20 August 1951, 511.68/8–2051, Box 2472, CDF 1950–54, RG 59, NACP; Buttles to Barnett, 28 June 1951, 511.68/6–2851, Box 2472, CDF 1950–54, RG 59, NACP.

19 1954–1955 USIS Mission Prospectus, 3 December 1953, 511.00/3–1253, Box 2246, CDF 1950–54, RG 59, NACP.

20 Američki Informativni Centri u Jugoslaviji, 1973, Box 1, Records Relating to Culture Centers 1946–88, USIA Library Program Division, RG 306, NACP; Propaganda kapitalističkih zemalja u Jugoslaviji, 1953, 724/1953, Box 44, Materijali komisije za međunarodne veze 1950–59, SSRNJ, RG 142, Archives of Yugoslavia (hereafter AY); IRC US Embassy Belgrade, email message to author, 16 June 2015.

21 USIS Zagreb opened first in a small building on Kumičić Street in 1951. As for USIS Belgrade, it closed its doors in 1998. See Despatch 4 Consulate Zagreb to Department of State, 3 July 1953, 511.68/7–353, Box 2472, CDF 1950–54, RG 59, NACP; Marica Bahlen, IRC US Embassy Zagreb, email message to author, 18 June 2014.

22 Space occupied by US Information Center Overseas, 19 February 1969, Box 3, Records Relating to Culture Centers 1946–88, USIA Library Program Division, RG 306, NACP.

23 Summary Hours opened to Public, 17 February 1969, Box 3, Records Relating to Culture Centers 1946–88, USIA Library Program Division, RG 306, NACP.

24 Buttles to Barnett, 28 June 1951.

25 1954–1955 USIS Mission Prospectus; Airgram 398 Dept. of State to Certain Diplomatic and Consular Officers, 3 April 1953, 511.00/4–353, Box 2247, CDF 1950–54, RG 59, NACP; Hager to Arnold, 9 July 1953, 511.00/7–953, Box 2248, CDF 1950–54, RG 59, NACP; Message 1272 USIA CA to USIA circular, 22 November 22, 1957, Box 7, USIA Master Budget Files 1953–64, RG 306, NACP. From the PAO, the Country Plan passed to the Ambassador, and then to Washington. Here, at USIA headquarters, it waited for the final concurrence from the State Department. Only then, the Plan turned into an action document.

26 Bekić, *Jugoslavija u Hladnom ratu*; Lees, *Keeping Tito Afloat*; Jakovina, *Socijalizam na američkoj pšenici*; Ljubodrag Dimić, *Jugoslavija i Hladni rat* (Belgrade: Arhipelag, 2014).

27 Despatch 189 Belgrade to Dept. of State, 24 August 1951, 511.68/8–2451, Box 2472, CDF 1950–54, RG 59, NACP.

28 USIE Report 62 for June 1950, 27 July 1950, 511.68/7–2750, Box 2472, CDF 1950–54, RG 59, NACP.

29 Despatch 358 Belgrade to Dept. of State, 10 November 1952, 511.68/11–1052, Box 2472, CDF 1950–54, RG 59, NACP; Telegram 980 Belgrade to Secretary of State, 5 February 1952, 511.68/2–552, Box 2472, CDF 1950–54, RG 59, NACP.

30 USIE Report 178, December 1949–January 1950, 28 February 1950, 511.68/2–2850, Box 2472, CDF 1950–54, RG 59, NACP; Despatch 358 Belgrade to Dept. of State, 10 November 1952.

31 USIE Report 178, 28 February 1950.

32 Semi-annual Evaluation Report in despatch 44 Belgrade to Dept. of State, 13 July 1953, 511.68/7–1353, Box 2472, CDF 1950–54, RG 59, NACP.

33 Semi-annual Evaluation Report – Yugoslavia in despatch Belgrade to Dept. of State, 17 December 1952, 511.68/12–1752, Box 2247, CDF 1950–54, RG 59, NACP.

34 Report from USIS program in despatch 4 Consulate Zagreb to Dept. of State, 3 July 1953; USIE Report 610 for April and May 1950, 20 June 1950, 511.68/6–2050, Box 2472, CDF 1950–54, RG 59, NACP.

35 Despatch 267 from Zagreb to Dept. of State, 10 April 1953, 511.68/4–1053, Box 2472, CDF 1950–54, RG 59, NACP.

36 Bogetić, *Jugoslavija i Zapad 1952–1955*; David R. Stone, 'The Balkan Pact and American Policy,' *East European Quarterly* 28, no. 3 (1994): 393–405; Bojan Dimitrijević, 'Jugoslavija i NATO 1951–1958. Skica intenzivnih vojnih odnosa,' in *Spoljna politika Jugoslavije: 1950–1961*, ed. Slobodan Selinić (Belgrade: Institut za noviju istoriju Srbije, 2008), 255–74.

37 Katarina Spehnjak, 'Posjeta Josipa Broza Tita Velikoj Britaniji 1953. godine,' *Časopis za suvremenu povijest* 33, no. 3 (2001): 597–631.

38 Mates, *Međunarodni odnosi socijalističke Jugoslavije*; Dimić, *Jugoslavija i Hladni rat*, 16.

39 Dušan Bilandžić, *Hrvatska moderna povijest* (Zagreb: Golden Marketing, 1999), 333–4.

40 Despatch 798 Belgrade to Dept. of State, 21 February 1952, 511.68/2–2152, Box 2472, CDF 1950–54, NACP; Despatch 891 Belgrade to Dept. of State, 20 March 1952, 511.68/3–2052, Box 2472, CDF 1950–54, NACP; Telegram 187 Beam to Secretary of State, 1 April 1952, 511.68/4–152, Box 2472, CDF 1950–54, NACP; Telegram 1218 Beam to Secretary of State, 3 April 1952, 511.68/4–352, Box 2472, CDF 1950–54, NACP; Telegram 1232 Beam to Secretary of State, 5 April 1952, 511.68/4–552, Box 2472, CDF 1950–54, NACP; Despatch 992 Embassy Belgrade to Dept. of State, 22 April 1952, 511.68/4–2252, Box 2472, CDF 1950–54, NACP.

41 Despatch 46 Consulate Zagreb to Dept. of State, 1 August 1952, 511.68/8–152, Box 2472, CDF 1950–54, NACP.

42 Despatch 885 Belgrade to Dept. of State, 19 March 1952, 511.68/3–1952, Box 2472, CDF 1950–54, NACP.

43 Despatch 984 Belgrade to Dept. of State, 26 June 1953, 511.68/6–2653, Box 2472, CDF 1950–54, NACP.

44 Translation of 'Mr. King, We Had Enough of Your Propaganda,' *Timok*, 12 June 1953 in despatch 1033 Belgrade to Dept. of State, June 26, 1953, 511.68/6–2653, Box 2472, CDF 1950–54, NACP.

45 Despatch 43 Embassy Belgrade to Dept. of State, 12 July 1953, 511.68/7–1253, Box 2472, CDF 1950–54, NACP.

46 *Borba*, 14 July 1953; Despatch 52 Embassy Belgrade to Dept. of State, July 15, 1953, 511.68/7–1553, Box 2472, CDF 1950–54, NACP.
47 According to Apsen, some of the demonstrators were just library borrowers obliged by the authorities to participate in the demonstrations (Nada Apsen. Interview by author. Oral interview. Zagreb, Croatia, 31 May 2014).
48 Glenda Sluga, *The Problem of Trieste and the Italo-Yugoslav Border: Difference, Identity, and Sovereignty in Twentieth-Century Europe* (New York: SUNY Press, 2001); Bogdan C. Novak, *Trieste 1941–1954: La lotta politica, etnica e ideologica* (Milan: Mursia, 2013); John C. Campbell, *Successful Negotiation, Trieste 1954: An Appraisal by the Five Participants*, Reprint (Princeton: Princeton University Press, 2016).
49 Report on USIS Yugoslavia, April–June 1954, Box 10, Inspection Report and Related Records 1954–62, USIA Inspection Staff, RG 306, NACP.
50 Despatch 727 Embassy Belgrade to Dept. of State, 16 March 1953, 511.68/3–53, Box 2472, CDF 1950–54, NACP.
51 Tvrtko Jakovina, 'Razgovor s Cvijetom Jobom, dugogodišnjim diplomatom i veleposlanikom FNRJ/SFRJ,' *Časopis za suvremenu povijest* 35, no. 3 (2003): 1037.
52 UDBA Report, 20 May 1953, XI-109-VI-36, Komisija za međunarodne odnose i veze 1945–90, Centralni komitet SKJ (hereafter CK SKJ), RG 507, Archives of Yugoslavia (hereafter AY).
53 Pitanje propagandnih stranih misija u FNRJ, 3 June 1953, Pov. br. 92562, Box 44, Materijali komisije za međunarodne veze 1950–59, Socijalistički Savez Radnog Naroda Jugoslavije (hereafter SSRNJ), RG 142, AY, 18.
54 Radina Vučetić, 'Amerikanizacija u Jugoslovenskoj popularnoj kulturi '60-Ih' (PhD dissertation, Belgrade, 2011), 129–30.
55 Pitanje propagandnih stranih misija u FNRJ, 3 June 1953.
56 The Yugoslav acronym is SSRNJ and it stands for 'Socijalistički Savez Radnog Naroda Jugoslavije.'
57 Propaganda kapitalističkih zemalja u Jugoslaviji, 1953, 724/1953, Box 44, Materijali komisije za međunarodne veze 1950–59, SSRNJ, RG 142, AY.
58 Propaganda zapadnih kapitalističkih zemalja (UDB FNRJ III odeljenje), 31 August 1953, 723/53, Box 44, Materijali komisije za međunarodne veze 1950–59, SSRNJ, RG 142, AY.
59 Propaganda kapitalističkih zemalja u Jugoslaviji, 1953.
60 UDBA Report, 20 May 1953, XI-109-VI-36, Komisija za međunarodne odnose i veze 1945–90, CK SKJ, RG 507, AY.
61 Petar Nikolić. Interview by author. Oral interview. Belgrade, Serbia, 5 July 2014.
62 Byrnes to Kolarek, 1 June 1954, Box 38, USIA Master Budget Files 1953–64, RG 306, NACP.
63 Zdenka Nikolić. Interview by author. Email interview. Zagreb, 3–27 June 2014.
64 Nada Apsen. Interview by author.
65 Bilandžić, *Hrvatska moderna povijest*, 302–8.
66 *Ibid.*, 307.
67 *Ibid.*, 333–4, 337.
68 Until his fall from power, Milovan Djilas was Vice President of Yugoslavia, president of the Federal parliament, and member of the Politburo and Central Committee. He was imprisoned under the Monarchy (1933–36), and under Tito (1956–61 and

1962–66). Among his works, by 1990 only published abroad (the first in the United States), are *The New Class* (1957), *Conversations with Stalin* (1962), *The Unperfect Society* (1969), *Tito: The Story from the Inside* (1981), and *Rise and Fall* (1985). He lived as a freelance writer in Belgrade until 1995, uncensored, but occasionally harassed by the police.

69 Osgood, *Total Cold War*.

70 Tony Smith, *America's Mission: The United States and the Worldwide Struggle for Democracy*, Expanded ed. (Princeton: Princeton University Press, 2012), 189–90.

71 Lees, *Keeping Tito Afloat*, 173.

72 The nuclear deterrent was essential, Dulles argued in 1956, 'but that did not mean its invariable use against local aggression, or "nibblings".' (Gaddis, *Strategies of Containment*, chap. 6).

73 Lees, *Keeping Tito Afloat*, 122.

74 Inspection Report USIS Yugoslavia, 20 November 1959, Box 10, Inspection Report and Related Records 1954–62, USIA Inspection Staff, RG 306, NACP, 39.

75 Report on USIS Yugoslavia, April–June 1954.

76 Manual of Inspection Procedures, USIA, May 1955, Box 10, Inspection Report and Related Records 1954–62, USIA Inspection Staff, RG 306, NACP.

77 Inspection Report USIS Yugoslavia, 20 November 1959, 4–6.

78 Svetozar Rajak, *Yugoslavia and the Soviet Union in the Early Cold War: Reconciliation, Comradeship, Confrontation, 1953–1957* (London; New York: Routledge, 2011), https://doi.org/10.1080/14682745.2011.569155.

79 Dimić, *Jugoslavija i Hladni rat*, 123–87, 278–9; Tvrtko Jakovina, *Treća Strana Hladnog Rata* (Zagreb: Fraktura, 2011), 39–78; Vladimir Petrović, '"Pošteni posrednik". Jugoslavija između starih i novih spoljnopolitičkih partnerstava sredinom pedesetih godina,' in *Spoljna politika Jugoslavije: 1950–1961*, ed. Slobodan Selinić (Belgrade: Institut za noviju istoriju Srbije, 2008), 462–71.

80 Phil Tiemeyer, 'Launching a Nonaligned Airline: JAT Yugoslav Airways between East, West, and South, 1947–1962,' *Diplomatic History* 41, no. 1 (2017): 78–103, https://doi.org/10.1093/dh/dhv061.

81 Mark Taplin, 'Walter Roberts: US Public Diplomacy in Yugoslavia – "We Had Quite a Program There",' *Global Publicks* website, 22 February 2016, http://globalpublicks.blogspot.hr/2015/02/walter-roberts-us-public-diplomacy-in.html.

82 Inspection Report USIS Yugoslavia, 20 November 1959, 42–7. Beside political obstructions, the Belgrade post struggled with bad housing, lack of clothing, and the Embassy's incapacity for major administrative support (47).

83 Inspection Report USIS Yugoslavia, 20 November 1959, 48, 17–19.

84 Airgram 1188 Dept. of State to Certain Diplomatic and Consular Officers, 12 February 1953, 511.00/2-1253, Box 2246, CDF 1950–54, RG 59, NACP.

85 The target audience group included 'any number of individuals having in common certain interest which influence their politically significant behavior' and which, through its own channels of communication, advocated a 'common and distinctive ideology or systematic pattern of ideas.' (Airgram 882 Dept. of State to Certain Diplomatic and Consular Officers, 4 February 1953, 511.00/2-1053, Box 2246, CDF 1950–54, RG 59, NACP).

86 Arndt, *The First Resort of Kings*, 156.

87 Study of USIS Libraries, August 1967, E-4-67, Box 1, Estimates and Evaluations 1966–78, USIA Office of Research and Evaluation, RG 306, NACP, 1.
88 Zdenka Nikolić. Interview by author. As a field dominated by women, Suzanne Hildenbrand defined librarianship a 'gendered history.' (*Reclaiming the American Library Past: Writing the Women In* [Norwood, NJ: Ablex Publications, 1996]). The complete list of USIS Zagreb employees can be found in Spisak osoblja Američke Čitaonice u Zagrebu, 3 March 1964, 56/2–02, Box 29, Republički protokol, IVS SRH 1953–90, RG 280, Croatian State Archives (hereafter CSA).
89 Sonja Bašić. Interview by author. Telephone and email interview. Zagreb, Croatia, 26 November 2013.
90 Petar Nikolić. Interview by author.
91 Zdenka Nikolić. Interview by author.
92 Nada Apsen. Interview by author.
93 Radina Vučetić, *Koka-kola socijalizam: Amerikanizacija jugoslavenske popularne kulture šezdesetih godina XX veka* (Belgrade: Službeni glasnik, 2012), 53–8; Petar Nikolić. Interview by author.
94 Semi-annual Evaluation Report, 17 December 1952, 511.68/12–1752, Box 2247, CDF 1950–54, RG 59, NACP.
95 Belmonte, *Selling the American Way.*
96 Pregled neprijateljske aktivnosti u 1955 do sada – UDB FNRJ II Odeljenje, 20 February 1956, 1529/1, Box 44, Materijali komisije za međunarodne veze 1950–59, SSRNJ, RG 142, AY.
97 Zapisnik sa sednice Komisije za proučavanje pitanja primene propisa o inostranoj propagandi, 15 June 1956, 1651/1, Box 55, Materijali komisije za međunarodne veze 1950–59, SSRNJ, RG 142, AY.
98 Pravni položaj stranih kulturnih institucija, 1956, 1651/1, Box 55, Materijali komisije za međunarodne veze 1950–59, SSRNJ, RG 142, AY.
99 Uticaj inostrane propaganda u jugoslavenskoj štampi, 1957, 1839/1, Box 55, Materijali komisije za međunarodne veze 1950–59, SSRNJ, RG 142, AY.
100 Sastanak ideološke komisije CK SKJ, 28 June 1957, VIII/II/2-b-(85–98), Box 5, Ideološka Komisija, CK SKJ, RG 507, AY.
101 Informacija o Kulturnom centru Beograda, 1956, Box 537, Materijali o radu kulturno-prosvetnih institucija 1950–68, Gradski komitet SKS (hereafter GK SKS), Historical Archives of Belgrade (hereafter HAB).
102 Inostrana informativno-propagandna delatnost u Jugoslaviji, March 1959, 1935/1, Box 44, Materijali komisije za međunarodne veze 1950–59, SSRNJ, RG 142, AY; Rezime aktualnih zadataka na polju ideološke aktivnosti, 1959, 1966/1, Box 55, Materijali komisije za međunarodne veze 1950–59, SSRNJ, RG 142, AY.
103 Borba protiv inostrane propagande u FNRJ, 14 January 1959, 1989/1, Box 44, Materijali komisije za međunarodne veze 1950–59, SSRNJ, RG 142, AY.
104 O nekim vidovima neprijateljske propagande, 5 June 1961, Box 512, Materijali o delovanju inostrane propagande 1958–68 (hereafter MDIP 1958–68), GK SKS Beograd, HAB.
105 Predlog zakona o štampi i drugim vidovima informacija in Zeković to the President of Federal Assembly, 3 October 1960, Box 565, Javno informisanje 1955–60, SIV 1953–90, RG 130, AY.

106 Obrazloženje novog zakona o štampi in Zeković to the President of Federal Assembly, 3 October 1960.

107 Zeković to the President of Federal Assembly, 3 October 1960.

108 Micunović to SIV, 26 November 1960, 91628/10, Box 610, Međunarodni odnosi 1955–1970, SIV 1953–90, RG 130, AY.

109 Telegram 745 Belgrade to Secretary of State, 5 February 1959, 511.68/2-559, Box 2204, CDF 1954–59, NACP.

110 Rolandi, *Con ventiquattromila baci*, 67–90, 103–7; Breda Luthar, 'Shame, Desire and Longing for the West. A Case Study of Consumption,' in *Remembering Utopia: The Culture of Everyday Life in Socialist Yugoslavia*, ed. Breda Luthar and Maruša Pušnik (Washington, DC: New Academia Publishing, 2010), 341–77.

111 Palmer to Hooker in despatch 615 Embassy Belgrade to Dept. of State, 22 May 1956, 868.44/5-2256, Box 4846, CDF 1954–59, NACP.

112 Park to Cody, 27 March 1963, M-32-63, Box 1, Research Memoranda 1963–99, USIA Office of Research and Media Reaction, RG 306, NACP.

113 Despatch 82 Consulate Zagreb to Dept. of State, 28 May 1959, 868.44/5-2859, Box 4846, CDF 1954–59, NACP.

114 Inspection Report USIS Yugoslavia, 20 November 1959, 11.

115 'Inaugural Address of John F. Kennedy,' *The Avalon Project at Yale Law School*, 26 February 2018, https://web.archive.org/web/20070514235348/http://www.yale.edu/lawweb/avalon/presiden/inaug/kennedy.htm.

116 Gaddis, *Strategies of Containment*, secs 3827–9, 3909–11.

117 Frank Costigliola, 'US Foreign Policy from Kennedy to Johnson,' in *The Cambridge History of the Cold War*, ed. Melvyn P. Leffler and Odd Arne Westad, vol. 2 (Cambridge: Cambridge University Press, 2012), 114.

118 Cull, *The Cold War and the United States Information Agency*, 149–68, 186–8.

119 Thomas Rosteck, *See It Now Confronts McCarthyism: Television Documentary and the Politics of Representation*, 2nd ed. (Tuscaloosa; London: University of Alabama Press, 1994); Thomas Doherty, *Cold War, Cool Medium: Television, McCarthyism, and American Culture* (New York: Columbia University Press, 2005). For a remarkable film interpretation, see George Clooney, *Good Night, and Good Luck*, Drama (2005).

120 Dizard, *Inventing Public Diplomacy*, 123–8; Tomlin, *Murrow's Cold War*.

121 17th Review of Operations, USIA, 1 July to 31 December 1961, Box 1046, CDF 1960–63, RG 59, NACP; Cull, The Cold War and the United States Information Agency, 1945–1989, 189–91.

122 Country Plan for Yugoslavia 1963, 30 January 1963, Box 45, USIA Subject Files 1953–67, RG 306, NACP, 1, 5.

123 As in the 1950s, the target audiences remained the youth, the managerial and working classes, the press corps, the intellectual community, and professionals such as scientists, doctors, lawyers, judges, and translators (*ibid.*, 6).

124 *Ibid.*, 4–7.

125 Jakovina, *Treća Strana Hladnog Rata*, 46.

126 William Zimmerman, *Open Borders, Nonalignment, and the Political Evolution of Yugoslavia, Princeton Legacy Library*, 2nd ed. (Princeton, NJ: Princeton University Press, 2015).

127 Jakovina, *Treća Strana Hladnog Rata*, 51–61; Bogetić, *Jugoslavensko-američki odnosi 1961–1971*, 30–4.
128 Telegram Embassy Belgrade to Dept. of State, 3 September 1961, FRUS 1961–63, Vol. XVI, doc. 93, 202–4; 'Text of the Final Declaration of the Belgrade Conference of Non-Aligned Nations,' *New York Times*, 7 September 1961.
129 Telegram Embassy Belgrade to Dept. of State, 3 September 1961.
130 Kohler to Kennan, 19 October 1961, FRUS 1961–63, Vol. XVI, doc. 102, 212–16; Telegram Dept. of State to Embassy Belgrade, 20 October 1961, FRUS 1961–63, Vol. XVI, doc. 105, 220–2; David L. Larson, *United States Foreign Policy Toward Yugoslavia: 1943–1963* (Lanham, MD: University Press of America, 1979), 292–302.
131 Memorandum of Conversation, 12 June 1962, FRUS 1961–63, Vol. XVI, doc. 129, 273–4; Bogetić, *Jugoslavensko-američki odnosi 1961–1971*, 74–6.
132 Memorandum of Conversation, 23 October 1962, FRUS 1961–63, Vol. XVI, doc. 139, 290–2.
133 Bogetić, *Jugoslavensko-američki odnosi 1961–1971*, 85.
134 O nekim vidovima neprijateljske propagande, 5 June 1961.
135 Izvještaj o preduzetim merama, 24 January 1962, 2–6, Box 512, MDIP 1958–68, GK SKS Beograd, HAB.
136 Informacija o delatnosti strane propagande, 3 May 1962, Box 512, MDIP 1958–68, GK SKS Beograd, HAB.
137 Informacija o aktivnosti OK Savski Venac, 14 July 1961, Box 512, MDIP 1958–68, GK SKS Beograd, HAB.
138 Informacija o merama OK Palilula, 17 July 1961, Box 512, MDIP 1958–68, GK SKS Beograd, HAB.
139 Informacija Opštinskog komiteta SKS Voždovac, July 1961, Box 512, MDIP 1958–68, GK SKS Beograd, HAB.
140 O uticaju strane propagande, 17 July 1961, Box 512, MDIP 1958–68, GK SKS Beograd, HAB.
141 Informacija Univerzitetskog komiteta, 18 January 1962, 02–167, Box 512, MDIP 1958–68, GK SKS Beograd, HAB.
142 Telegram 1004 Belgrade to Secretary of State, 6 June 1961, 511.682/6–661, Box 1074, CDF 1960–63, RG 59, NACP; Telegram 1008 Belgrade to Secretary of State, 7 June 1961, 511.682/6–761, Box 1074, CDF 1960–63, RG 59, NACP.
143 Neka pitanja informativne-propagandne delatnosti SAD u FNRJ, 24 October 1962, Box 240, SAD, Kanada i Latinska Amerika 1953–67, Savezni sekretarijat za obrazovanje i kulturu (hereafter SSOK), RG 318, AY.
144 Informacija o merama preuzete na teritoriju Palilule, 1962, Box 512, MDIP 1958–68, GK SKS Beograd, HAB.
145 Informacija o aktivnosti OK SKS Savski Venac, 22 January 1962, 59, Box 512, MDIP 1958–68, GK SKS Beograd, HAB, 6–7.
146 Airgram 30 Consulate Zagreb to Dept. of State, 17 April 1962, 868.43/4–1762, Box 2708, CDF 1960–63, RG 59, NACP; Airgram 47 Consulate Zagreb to Dept. of State, 12 June 1962, 868.43/6–1262, Box 2708, CDF 1960–63, RG 59, NACP.
147 Despatch 122 Consulate Sarajevo to Dept. of State, 6 June 1962, 511.682/6–662, Box 1074, CDF 1960–63, RG 59, NACP.
148 Despatch 449 Embassy Belgrade to Dept. of State, 31 January 1962, 511.682/1–3162, Box 1074, CDF 1960–63, RG 59, NACP.

149 Informacija o delatnosti strane propagande, 2 February 1962, 232, Box 512, MDIP 1958–68, GK SKS Beograd, HAB, 19–20; Informacija o nekim pitanjima u vezi strane propagande, 20 January 1962, 02–19, Box 512, MDIP 1958–68, GK SKS Beograd, HAB.

150 Neka pitanja informativne-propagandne delatnosti SAD u FNRJ, 24 October 1962, Box 240, SAD, Kanada i Latinska Amerika 1953–67, SSOK, RG 318, AY.

151 Taplin, 'Walter Roberts: US Public Diplomacy in Yugoslavia.' Walter Roberts (1916–2014) was a long-serving USIS diplomat, deputy associate director of USIA (1969), and executive director at Radio Free Europe and Radio Liberty (1975–85). Both Presidents Bush and Clinton appointed Roberts to the US Advisory Commission on Public Diplomacy. In 2001, Roberts co-founded the Institute for Public Diplomacy and Global Communication and the Public Diplomacy Council. He is the author of *Tito, Mihailovic, and the Allies 1941–1945* (Durham, NC: Duke University Press Books, 1973), the first historical bestseller on the Tito-Mihailović talks of March 1943.

152 Mark Taplin, 'Walter Roberts: George Kennan and Public Diplomacy – "Basically, George Kennan was an Old-Line Diplomat",' *Global Publicks* website, 22 February 2016, http://globalpublicks.blogspot.hr/2015/02/walter-roberts-george-kennan-and-public.html.

153 Telegram Rusk to Dept. of State, 5 May 1963, FRUS 1961–63, Vol. XVI, doc. 160.

154 Bogetić, *Jugoslavensko-američki odnosi 1961–1971*, 139–62. See also Lampe, Prickett, and Adamović, *Yugoslav–American Economic Relations Since World War II*, 68–9.

155 Informacija o problemima vezanim za inostranu propagandu, 15 April 1966, 16/2–1966, Box 256, Komisija za politički i idejno-vaspitni rad 1966, SSRNJ, RG 142, AY.

156 Despatch 77 Consulate Zagreb to Dept. of State, 14 May 1959, 868.44/5–1459, Box 4846, CDF 1954–59, NACP.

157 Despatch 17 Embassy Belgrade to Dept. of State, 14 July 1959, 868.44/7–1459, Box 4846, CDF 1954–59, NACP; Predrag Marković, 'Najava bure: studentski nemiri u svetu i Jugoslaviji od Drugog svetskog rata do početka šezdesetih godina,' *Tokovi Istorije*, issue 3–4 (2000): 51–62.

158 Miroslav Krleža, 'Pozdrav Jean Paul Sartreu,' *Vjesnik*, 20 November 1960, 7.

159 Chronology of the Cultural Policy in Yugoslavia, 27 March 1963.

160 Yugoslav Refugee Attitudes, 2 April 1962, RN-10–62, Box 4, Research Notes 1958–62, USIA Office of Research and Analysis (hereafter ORA), RG 306, NACP.

161 Jugoslavensko javno mnijenje o tome koja nam je zemlja najveći prijatelj, 4 November 1964, Box 38, Series II-4-a (Političko stanje u zemlji), KPR, RG 837, AYBT.

162 Yugoslav Opinion Leader Study, 1968–69, YO6801, Box 41, Africa, Eastern Europe and Multi-Areas, USIA ORA, RG 306, NACP.

163 Country Plan for Yugoslavia 1963, 30 January 1963.

164 O nekim vidovima stranog uticaja u našoj zemlji, 20 June 1962, II/2-b-(162–169) K-10, Box 10, Ideološka komisija VIII, CK SKJ, RG 507, AY.

165 Message 44 USIS Belgrade to USIA Washington, 9 November 1966, CUL 9, Box 56, USIA Subject Files 1953–67, RG 306, NACP.

166 Informacija o dosadašnjem radu na pripremanju novog Zakona o štampi i drugim vidovima propagande, 24 January 1968, 01/172, Box 565, SIV 1953–90, RG 130, AY.
167 Magnetofonske beleške o propagandi, 28 October 1968, Box 257, O inostranoj propagandi i idejno-političkom radu 1968–70, GK SKS Beograd, HAB, 16, 19.
168 Informacija o delatnosti strane propagande, 3 May 1962, Box 512, MDIP 1958–68, GK SKS Beograd, HAB.
169 Zapisnik sa sednice Komisije za ideološka pitanja, 11 September 1965, Box 209, Zapisnici i materijali ideološke komisije 1965–67, GK SKS Beograd, HAB.
170 Uloga i zadaci sredstava informacija, 1968, n. 24, D-2950, Idejno-politička pitanja i ideološki rad, CK SKH, RG 1220, CSA, 7–13; O nekim vidovima delovanja neprijateljskih elemenata, 10 October 1967, D-2442, Idejno-politička pitanja i ideološki rad, Centralni komitet (hereafter CK) SKH, RG 1220, CSA.
171 O nekim vidovima stranog uticaja u našoj zemlji, 20 June 1962, II/2-b-(162–169) K-10, Box 10, Ideološka komisija VIII, CK SKJ, RG 507, AY; Informacija o problemima vezanim za inostranu propagandu u našoj zemlji, 15 April 1966.
172 Magnetofonske beleške o propagandi, 28 October 1968, Box 257, O inostranoj propagandi i idejno-političkom radu 1968–70, GK SKS Beograd, HAB; Objašnjenja za primenu propisa u oblasti inostrane propagande, September 1968, 36/1, Box 512, MDIP 1958–68, GK SKS Beograd, HAB.
173 Zapisnik sa sastanka Komisije za ideološki rad CK SKJ, 1 June 1962, II/2-b-(162–169) K-10, Box 10, Ideološka komisija VIII, CK SKJ, RG 507, AY.
174 Informacija sa savetovanja o političkom radu i stanju informiranosti, 21 May 1966, Box 256, Komisija za politički i idejno-vaspitni rad 1966, SSRNJ, RG 142, AY, 3, 9.
175 Stenografske beleške Komisije za ideološko-vaspitni rad SSRNJ, 5–6 May 1966, 16/6680, Box 256, Komisija za politički i idejno-vaspitni rad 1966, SSRNJ, RG 142, AY, 10/2.
176 Informacija: Donošenje posebnog zakona o inostranoj propagandi, 21 August 1969, 034–1564/1–69, Box 565, SIV 1953–90, RG 130, AY.
177 Mark Taplin, 'Walter Roberts: USIS Magazines and Exhibits in Yugoslavia – "I'm Red-Faced. I Apologize.",' *Global Publicks* website, 22 February 2016, http://globalpublicks.blogspot.hr/2015/02/walter-roberts-usis-magazines-and.html.
178 Neka pitanja informativne-propagandne delatnosti SAD u FNRJ, 24 October 1962, Box 240, SAD, Kanada i Latinska Amerika 1953–67, SSOK, RG 318, AY.
179 Simona Tobia, *Advertising America: The United States Information Service in Italy (1945–1956)* (Milan: LED Edizioni Universitarie, 2009); Alessandro Brogi, *Confronting America: The Cold War Between the United States and the Communists in France and Italy* (Chapel Hill: University of North Carolina Press, 2011).

2

The USIS in action

The American comedian Paula Poundstone once stated that while 'we think of libraries as quiet, demure places where we are shushed by dusty, bun-balancing, bespectacled women,' the truth is that they 'are raucous clubhouses for free speech, controversy and community.'[1] As sociologist Jeffrey Alexander explores, when the social nature of reading meets a communicative institution, the synergy of the two becomes capable, in a civil society, of providing information that regulates public discourse and influences political issues. This transforms libraries and reading rooms into places of political influence and activism, sometimes even dissent.[2]

When, in 1942, the Biblioteca Benjamin Franklin opened in Mexico City under the Good Neighbour program, it settled on 'a fine line between promoting dialogue and simply promoting the United States.' Like others that followed, these libraries, sponsored by the American Library Association and operating under the Office of the Coordinator of Inter-American Affairs, would embrace the methods of public diplomacy by beginning to care 'about the image the [US] nation projected to the world.'[3] From the early 1940s, the Council on Books in Wartime, a publishers' trade group, started working with the Office of War Information (OWI) to disseminate information 'about the war and the aims of the U.S. and its allies [...] holding book forums and fairs, and utilizing radio and films to promote its message'[4]. The newly established reference libraries, which passed to the State Department when the OWI went out of existence in 1946, prioritized books as 'purveyors of ideas' which, as 'window[s] on the West,' would resolutely strive for the 'reorientation of people.'[5] In April 1943, London got its American Library, the first under direct government control. Soon, the OWI libraries opened in all major world capitals, from Sydney to Cairo, Johannesburg to Madrid, in Stockholm, Paris, Oslo, Copenhagen, Brussels, and Rome – all the way to the Middle and Far East – Baghdad, Beirut, Istanbul, New Delhi, Bangkok – and back to Sofia, Moscow, and Belgrade.

Washington's public diplomats adopted a long-term book strategy. American books abroad, which disclosed 'the fullest (and most favourable) portrait of American culture,'[6] would persuade foreign audiences 'to adopt a predetermined set of American views.'[7] Unlike mass media content with a 'short cycle of life,' books would whet people's appetite to 'absorb [the] material [...] at a slower and more reflective pace.'[8] The American Libraries in socialist Yugoslavia typified such long-term goals. What was true for books proved valid for the entire library program. In Belgrade and Zagreb, students and professors came for foreign scientific and technical monographs, exam textbooks, and academic journals, while others came to read *The Times*, *Life*, *Better Homes and Gardens*, or the daily *New York Times*. Sometimes customers ordered a new book; other times they prepared a reference research, or simply sat down and studied. The reading room constituted a gathering community, mostly made up of intellectuals, scientists, doctors, students, retirees, and ordinary citizens, occasionally knowing each other, and predominantly unenthusiastic about the regime, as USIS director Nada Apsen recalls.[9] USIS's strength relied, as this chapter shows, on two key factors: first, the variety of program activities – from the reading room, the monthly exhibit, the English teaching, the occasional lectures, the translation program, to the movies and music section; and, secondly, on the program content. The latter certainly evolved over time; but, as Laura Belmonte has researched, its founding principles remained consistent. From Harry Truman to George Bush, US public diplomacy narratives promoted a substantial 'belief in the universality of American freedom, democracy, and free enterprise.'[10]

USIS books on Yugoslav shelves related to general subjects in the fine arts, literature, education, public opinion, history, architecture, and economy, and tackled ideas, facts, or promises of the American liberal tradition. Freedom was freedom to choose a job, a book, or friends, to vote according to one's own personal convictions, and to gripe about unjust wages.[11] The book program, crafted for foreign elites and intellectuals, had a 'pedagogical self-understanding' to 'teach about America' and, through the promotion of modernist authors, showcase American artistic achievement and prestige.[12] Of course, 'America's ideological offensive was not a ham-handed, one-size-fits-all model,' as Belmonte recalls, 'but a sophisticated endeavour utilizing the most advanced communications methodologies of the era.' The information program corresponded to 'a concerted effort to define the American national identity,' protect its national security, and justify its predominance in international affairs, through narratives of 'progress, freedom and happiness.'[13] What shaped the United States Cold War was 'American nationalist globalism,' defined by John Fousek as a tradition of 'thinking about American national mission and destiny,' deeply rooted in historic notions of 'chosenness, destiny, and mission,' that, in the post-war historic circumstances, conveyed powerful beliefs of national greatness, global responsibility, and anti-communism.[14] Nevertheless, the creation of an 'American character' and of its consensus emerged much earlier when, during the Great Depression and the ascent of Marxism and fascism, Americans of different political persuasions, economic backgrounds, religions, and ethnic and racial origins, launched into a single unifying *American Way* to rescue the American experiment. Under such circumstances, democracy, free enterprise, the Judeo-Christian tradition, and patriotism gained new meanings of ideals worth fighting for, as Wendy Wall explores.[15]

The cultural Cold War launched them globally, but USIA knew Yugoslavia was a different case from other Eastern European countries. Yugoslav communism was imposed by an internal, not an external, force, which gave Tito great political legitimation and provided his regime with a highly effective weapon in combating internal subversion and neutralizing overt opposition. The Marshal's legitimacy relied on a successful war against the German and Italian occupation; on his insubordination to Soviet domination, which made him a national hero, 'even in the eyes of anti-Communists'; and on the general perception of Yugoslav international prestige, much greater than the actual power and resources of the country. Nevertheless, 'it could hardly be said that the Yugoslav people are enthusiastic about their government,' and this was precisely what USIA intended to exploit with its library program. Yugoslav distrust of the government, inherited from the Turkish domination, the Serbo-Croat national controversy always 'in the air,' and the 'dire poverty and discontent,'[16] especially of young people and the educated, motivated US public diplomats to project an image of a rich, free, and opportunistic America that would change the Yugoslav regime from within. The American Libraries in Belgrade and Zagreb propelled these concepts onto the bookshelves, and faced the challenge of approaching (presumed) Marxists without criticizing Yugoslav communism.

Democracy, capitalism, and freedom on the Yugoslav bookshelves

In early 1953, USIS Belgrade went through a major reorganization as the library was equipped with a bright periodical room, two spacious reading rooms, and a work room.[17] With the exhibit windows on the ground floor, the library's open bookshelves on the second, the information office on the third, and the music and film section on the fourth, USIS Belgrade offered a complete cultural experience.[18] USIS had its library in Zagreb, with a reference and technical section and the reading room on the ground floor. Here, behind a large desk, crowds waited to pick up their copy of the daily *Bilten*, while glancing at the colourful exhibit windows.[19] Following the latest trends in library layouts, both posts organized the children's corner with low shelves, bright book displays, and two small benches.[20]

These libraries contained, apart from certain classics, no permanent bookshelf, as they were 'continuously responsive to new ideas and changing demands.' In USIA's vision, they projected 'the image of a democratic, dynamic, socially humane, and culturally significant United States,' portrayed the Americans 'as responsible and mature,' extolled 'the quality of American life, achievements, and ideals,' and fostered the understanding of US policy goals. In other words, USIS derived political benefits without being political in content because, in the centres, 'information' and 'culture' met, interacted, and became 'one program.'[21] USIS rhetoric and program content relied on different, transversal initiatives. Worldwide programs like Truman's 'Full and Fair Picture' (1946) and 'Campaign of Truth' (1950), Eisenhower's 'People's Capitalism' (1955), and Johnson's 'Great Society' (1965) were presidential projects, limited in time, and usually focused on special exhibit events.[22] Political crises that suggested the superiority of American democratic capitalism – such as the Soviet suppression of the 1956 Hungarian Revolution, the 1961 erection of the Berlin Wall, or the 1962 Cuban

Missile Crisis – inspired USIA's advocacy for American democratic traditions. The celebration of American historical anniversaries, remembrances of the founding fathers and past presidents, inspired storylines on American exceptionalism, while *Pregled* pages, USIS exhibit windows, and VOA radio waves delved into American life, domestic policies, and foreign relations. USIA recommended the posts abroad to explore the American 'economic system' and its 'resourcefulness,' and to depict the United States 'as a great hope [...] for all mankind,' 'based on freedom and dignity [for] every individual.'[23] As an early USIS pamphlet put it, America's unique 'combination of circumstances – free labour, free unions, social consciousness [...], sacred regard for individual human dignity, and economic capacity,' was the pathway to American workers' wealth and high living standards.[24] *Meet some Americans ... at work* (1951), a pamphlet released in Truman's 'Full and Fair' campaign and distributed in more than a million copies, depicted satisfied and fulfilled American workers of all kinds: African Americans integrated within US society, American farmers living the 'freest life on Earth,' and ordinary people free to pursue higher education in a system of scholarships and loans. Besides cheerful and smiling faces, the pamphlet made no mention of racial and gender discrimination, wage inequalities, or labour instability.[25] Soviet propagandists bombarded foreign audiences with 'reports on wide spread labour unrest, insoluble social problems, economic instabilities, and high unemployment in the United States.'[26] Since the early 1950s, countering such Marxist propaganda became USIS's top priority. The Yugoslav posts supplied pamphlets on the American labour unions (*The American Labor Movement*), on workers in free and totalitarian countries (*Free or Slave Labor*), and on miserable farmers in Czechoslovakia, Poland, and Red China (*The Farmer and His Land: Promises and Facts*).[27] By mid-1952, 28,000 copies of *The American System Works*, the Yugoslav version of *Consumer Capitalism*, reached readers in Belgrade and Zagreb.[28]

People's Capitalism, a campaign created by the long-serving president of the Advertising Council[29] and Eisenhower's close adviser, Theodore Repplier, was among the most notorious propaganda projects about the US free enterprise system. Repplier, who spent six months travelling to Burma, Cambodia, China, Hong Kong, Laos, Singapore, the Philippines, Pakistan, India, then Egypt, Greece, Italy, and England, under the Eisenhower Exchange Fellowship, became 'the first non-government American to study [...] information activities abroad.' Upon his return, he found 'capitalism synonymous with either colonial exploitation or restrictive practices,' and felt the United States needed an 'inspirational concept' to counteract this 'serious propaganda handicap.'[30] Repplier suggested that the USIA create an exhibit that would glorify the American middle class, its achievements, abundant opportunities, and ownership of capital.[31] On 14 and 15 February 1956, almost 25,000 people, including 100 invited foreign journalists, filled the main hall of Washington's Union Station to test the exhibit. Devised for trade fairs around the world, 'People's Capitalism' displayed two typical American homes: a 1776 common dwelling and a modern prefabricated house stocked with all kind of new furniture and labour-saving appliances. The exhibit defined capitalism as 'much more than an economic system' because it also embraced, beyond economic values, political, spiritual, and cultural elements.[32]

The exhibit departed for USIS posts abroad, along with press releases, magazine reprints, and glossy photographs of American bridges, highways, Hollywood divas, universities, and sport events. None of these were obviously concerned with domestic criticism of the American economy or aggravated forms of urban poverty. Certain that they could not answer such criticisms, 'the U.S. information officials tried to divert attention to the positive features of democratic capitalism.'[33] As a system in progress, the 'new American capitalism' was, unlike the Soviet Union, not an imposed *status quo*, nor the 'bloated selfish exploiter.' It generated, as in a free and creative process, owners, shareholders, small and medium enterprises, business people, and farm owners.[34] The capitalist theme was of strong impact on the Yugoslav working class, corroborated by a widespread economic dissatisfaction. Spiralling prices, housing scarcity, and excessive taxes seemed the main reasons for discontent, reported a USIA survey. Besides economic grievances, Yugoslavs accused the regime of restricting personal freedom and privileging Party members.[35]

The correlation between material wealth and freedom was soon recognized by Washington officials, particularly when 'Communist propagandists seized on international promotions of US consumer goods as evidence of materialism and immorality.'[36] This induced the USIA to link the American economy to its democratic traditions. Celebrated through major historical anniversaries, like President Abraham Lincoln's 150th birthday, USIS drew attention to many 'typical representative[s] of remarkable American qualities.'[37] In February 1959, USIS Belgrade received 10,000 copies of the *Lincoln* pamphlet.[38] The movie *Face of Lincoln* (26 minutes, black and white); Lincoln's biographies by Paul McClelland Angle, William Herdon, Jesse Weik, and Carl Sandburg; his speeches and writings, next to drama, literature pieces, and children's books, dedicated to 'the saviour of the Union,' appeared in the library. *Pregled* devoted its entire February 1959 issue to Lincoln's presidency. As the incarnation of US democracy, an inspiration for worldwide freedom struggles, an American of universal character but humble working-class beginnings, Lincoln was a symbol of patriotism and unity.[39] USIS in Yugoslavia regularly furnished material on *American Democratic Concepts*, a reference list covering the US political system, the constitution, the Presidency, Congress, the Courts, and the elections.[40] Next to capitalism and democracy, freedom constituted the third pillar of USIA propaganda in Yugoslavia. In articles such as 'The Spiritual Heritage of America,'[41] 'Freedom in America,'[42] 'Faith in Freedom and Democracy,'[43] 'Artistic Freedom for Everyone,'[44] 'The Role of Religion in a Free Society,'[45] and 'Protests in front of the White House,'[46] *Pregled* depicted the 'American way of freedom' where dissent was permitted, pluralism of opinions was allowed, and demonstrations and opposition attested to a healthy democracy.

Books – 'purveyors of ideas'

The book selection program was the most debated one among Washington's public diplomacy agents, especially during Senator Joseph McCarthy's anti-communist investigations at the IIA and, later, the USIA.[47] In fact, the first IIA directive, from the early 1950s, permitted controversial authors to be stocked at libraries abroad if they presented the United States in a positive light.[48] The IIA tried to appease McCarthy by setting a new directive in July 1953 which banned any material by 'controversial persons, communists, [and] fellow travellers,' unless for a specific program purpose.[49] This instruction created confusion for the Information Center Service (ICS) personnel and librarians abroad. On 4 April 1953, McCarthy's assistants, Roy Cohn and David Schine, flew to Paris for a ten-day tour of the European information centres. They inspected Bonn, Frankfurt, Munich, Vienna, Belgrade, Athens, Rome, and London. Between 19 February and 8 July, the State Department issued as many as ten separate confidential directives concerning materials in overseas libraries. By 23 June, 319 titles were removed from one or more of the US Information Centres. The charges of book burning inevitably resulted in a loss of prestige and credibility. Writers like Howard Fast, Dashiell Hammett and his partner, dramatist and screenwriter, Lillian Hellman, were called to testify before the House of Un-American Activities Committee for their ties with the Communist Party of America, and their books were pulled by anxious USIS librarians. The USIA banned African American sociologist, historian, and activist W. E. B. Du Bois for his socialist beliefs.[50] However, while the investigations slowed the pace of book arrivals abroad, they nevertheless drew major attention to the book program and re-established its centrality.

When, in the early 1950s, Washington's cultural policymakers bolstered a project aimed at a 'liberal understanding of American history,' they looked for narratives which depicted the centrality of freedom and individualism, specific cooperation between private enterprises and the government, and the role of cultural diversity for the greatness of the United States. Certainly, the USIA literacy agenda involved classic and contemporary works. Major figures of early American literature, such as Washington Irving, Herman Melville, Edgar Allan Poe, and Nathaniel Hawthorne, joined by the major writers of the later nineteenth century such as Walt Whitman, Emily Dickinson, Mark Twain, and Henry James, found their way onto Yugoslav bookshelves, together with more contemporary authors such as Willa Cather, William Howells, and F. Scott Fitzgerald. Ernest Hemingway appeared less acceptable (but not forbidden), while works by and about Ezra Pound, a controversial expatriated American poet, were forbidden in all programs after 1953. Histories of American literature, such as Wyck Brooks's *Flowering of New England* (1936) and Robert Spiller's *The Cycle of American Literature* (1955), provided narratives of an evolving literary tradition and the grand American nation.

The most innovative feature of the USIA book program was its 'modernism' agenda, claims Greg Barnhisel. Among the modernists, it was William Faulkner who played the major role and whose ascendance solidified the 'cultural dominance of literary elitism and liberal anti-Communism.'[51] No surprise then that the program lacked anything by Wallace Stevens, William Carlos Williams, Gertrude Stein, and Hart Crane, and predictably of John Dos Passos, Clifford Odets, and Langston Hughes, because of their earlier communist associations.[52] Another core theme concerned anti-communist literature, such as Czeslaw Milosz's *Captive Mind*, a formerly leftist poet who had worked for the Polish government, Arthur Koestler's *Darkness at Noon*, and George Orwell's *Animal Farm* and *Nineteen Eighty-Four*, while other anti-communist books focused on the most ominous aspects of Soviet communism such as the gulags, the Great Terror, and arbitrary imprisonments.

Frank Tannenbaum's *Philosophy of Labour* and Frederick Lewis Allen's *The Big Change: America Transforms Itself 1900–1950* attempted to dispel the harsh image of United States' capitalism abroad. Books such as Learned Hand's *Spirit of Liberty*; Carleton Coon's *Story of Man*; Robin Williams's *American Society: A Sociological Interpretation*; Carl Bridenbaugh's *Cities in Revolt: Urban Life in America 1743–1776*, and Arthur Breston's *The Restoration of Learning*, had intellectual and sociological pretensions.[53] And while the books, as 'powerful persuader[s],' were the library's 'focal point,'[54] it was in magazines that USIS saw the link between 'the realm of instant communications,' the daily news, and 'the world of books.'[55]

'Magazines play a vital role in the process of communication'

The USIA administration was particularly proud of the 'richness and diversity of American periodical literature.'[56] Considered as 'the vanguard of serious analysis,' and 'the springboard for introducing new ideas in the sciences, literature, and the arts,'[57] USIS Belgrade and Zagreb invested considerable effort in making this program efficient. They relied on surveys and statistical reports to detect audience preferences. Among almost 650 titles, Yugoslav readers mostly enjoyed magazines on politics, economics, and society such as *Reader's Digest, Time, Newsweek, Foreign Affairs, Atlantic Monthly, U.S. News & World Report*, and *Public Interest* (from 1965, the leading neoconservative journal). Their preference was for magazines dealing with history (*American Heritage* and *Current History*), with global business (*Fortune*), with masculine fashion (*Esquire*), with the building industry and architecture (*Architectural Forum*), with cultural issues (*Art in America, American Literature*, and *Opera News*), but also wellness and healthiness (*Today's Health*). The Yugoslavs especially loved American newspapers: the *New York Times*, the *Washington Post, Times Herald, New York Herald Tribune* (*International Herald Tribune* from 1967), the *Christian Science Monitor*, the *Washington Star*, the *Wall Street Journal*, as well as US domestic magazines such as *Saturday Review, National Safety News*, and *Business Week*.[58] Nevertheless, it was the colourful, illustrated, widely popular magazines that people loved most, but were not on the ICS core list: *Life, National Geographic, Sports Illustrated, Look, Scientific America, Holiday, Popular Mechanics, Popular Science Monthly, Better Homes and Gardens*, the *New Yorker*, and many more.[59]

The USIA press and publication service, the Agency's successful initiative to send out updated newsletters and magazines, including glossy pamphlets, pilot models, and kits, helped USIS to support its local publications, Yugoslav VOA broadcasts, and exhibits. Nothing was left to chance. When, in 1949, the Yugoslav government undertook an enormous plan of road building, and because Belgrade was 'using primitive [construction] methods,' USIS requested Washington to send 'airmail photos of [US] highway and roads construction methods,' 'equipment for cement, asphalt paving,' workers 'clothing, and particularly protective footwear.'[60] Visual representations of the United States, collected in projects such as *The Town Library of the U.S., 50 years*

*of U.S. Auto Industry, Typical U.S. High School Student, This is the United States –
Cities and towns, Rural Youth in the U.S. – Vermont Farm Boys, New Machinery
for U.S. Farmers*, impressed upon the Yugoslavs images of American infrastructural
development, general wealth, and captive richness.[61] The pamphlets of the highest
paper quality, underlined USIS Belgrade, had to prove American prosperity, prestige,
and 'standards of excellence,' and endure the hand-to-hand process.[62] Among a long
list of titles, the Yugoslavs preferred *Facts about the USA, Handbook on U.S. Economy*,
and *Elections USA*. A USIA 1960 survey revealed a prominent interest in various
aspects of the American way of life. Colourful and fascinating, USIA pamphlets
changed Yugoslav perceptions of the United States, countering what Washington
officials regarded as misrepresentations.[63]

USIS was particularly interested in reaching the Yugoslav press editors: they provided newspaper editors at *Politika, Republika, Borba*, and *Vjesnik* with reference
materials, while the feature *What is new in the United States?* [Šta ima novog u SAD]
was delivered to *Tanjug*, the Yugoslav press agency.[64] Background for editors was
personally sent to government officials. The *Review of the News*, printed in 13,000
copies, reached 8,600 homes by mail. In 1952, Zagreb's PAO, Bruce Buttles, proudly
announced that Ljubljana's *Slovenski Poročevalec* requested USIS photographs for
an exhibit seen by some 200,000 citizens.[65] The UDBA was particularly annoyed by
smaller USIS publications, so hard to track and stop.[66] No USIS publication, useful as
the *Agricultural, Economic*, and *Educational* bulletins were, could compete with the
radio news bulletin, *Bilten*, issued daily in Serbian, Croatian, and English. Long lines
and street crowds persisted for years in front of USIS during its distribution, which
always sold out. Starting in April 1953, with a humble 400 copies, the publication
reached 5,000 by June, and 11,000 in 1959.[67] Nevertheless, distribution met occasional
difficulties: postal officials and the police sometimes harassed the *Bilten* receivers,
while, at other times, local officials were more zealous than their superiors in Belgrade
and returned the delivered material.[68]

What was *Amerika* for the Russians became *Pregled* for the Yugoslavs. But *Pregled*
was not the first. In December 1951, USIS Belgrade started the *SAD* magazine (which
meant 'now' in Serbo-Croatian, but also abbreviated the USA) with 25,000 copies, and
consisting of sixteen articles over fifty-six pages, a map of the United States, and an
introductory note by Ambassador Allen.[69] As the first partially coloured magazine in
Yugoslavia, it became an immediate, huge success. The second issue reached 30,000
copies and alarmed the secret services. When, in 1953, USIS sent 5,000 questionnaires
to the readers and got a 42 per cent rate of return, the surprise could not have been
greater: the Yugoslav public was unaccustomed to any kind of survey, and the political
climate was not the most propitious. Ninety-nine per cent of respondents requested
more copies, and ordinary citizens and town libraries repeatedly voiced enthusiasm. 'The publication goes from hand to hand, and many are waiting impatiently
for their turn,' commented a reader, while others demanded copies for their friends
who 'have seen the publication and liked it very much.' Some of them addressed the
apprehension about political reprisals: 'Many of my friends would like to get your
publication, but they are afraid.'[70] The magazine appealed both to urban populations

which appreciated articles on the famous Broadway prize-winning play, *The Member of the Weeding*, and on 'Roots of Modern American Art,' or 'Vermont Symphony Orchestra,' while rural inhabitants preferred texts on 'Hybrid Corn' and industrialized food production.[71]

Although dropped in 1954 because of USIA's budget cuts during Theodore Streibert's directorship, the *SAD* project was not abandoned.[72] In 1957, American cultural officers in Belgrade resumed it under a new name, the monthly *Pregled*. Published in Serbo-Croatian, with the Serbian 'ekavica' variant, which prompted many complaints from Croatian readers, the magazine lasted until 1994. With an initial 12,000 copies, *Pregled* reached 25,000 only four years later, with eleven issues per year on more than sixty colourful pages, and was distributed to almost every Yugoslav who, in the past, had showed some interest in USIS activities.[73]

Between December 1965 and June 1966, USIA conducted a large survey of the *Pregled* readership: of some 4,500 replies, 99 per cent were 'favourable' or 'mostly favourable,' while separate letters of gratitude accompanied the survey returns.[74] *Pregled* enjoyed a broad appeal and an enthusiastic reception. It epitomized overall USIS propaganda in Yugoslavia. In addition to economic and political issues, it addressed social themes, such as the American woman, gender roles, and family images. Stories about 'average American families' living in private suburban homes with five rooms, a television, a radio, a fridge, and an automatic laundry machine, reinforced the gender and family narratives on affluence, prosperity, and free choice in the United States. Many American housewives lived their dream – a job outside their home – because the American way of life made their aspirations come true.[75] While changing narratives on American women are reflected in the changing female conditions in the United States, *Pregled* tended to idealize American society and American women as well: 'she is beautiful and youthful, vigorous and capable, independent, restless, confused and disappointed, but more than anything, happy.'[76] The comparison with Yugoslav society was implicitly present. In April 1964, *Pregled* produced a back cover portraying a beautiful young lady, in a relaxed and smiling pose, dressed in white with her nails coloured red.[77] Other times, the magazine emphasized women's new job opportunities, their access to university and academia,[78] or simply underlined current social developments: 'the family is democratizing' and 'women participate much more than ever in financial matters.'[79] To what extent did these stories impact the Yugoslav perception of the United States? Presumably, as Radina Vučetić suggests, the abundance of consumer goods in ordinary American life, the items at the supermarkets and their availability, as well as the household appliances that helped housewives' daily work, had the foremost effect of 'whetting appetites' in a socialist country where shortages of goods left the average consumer unsatisfied.[80] *Pregled*'s strategy to address American superiority in every endeavour was part of a silent and 'invisible' propaganda campaign. USIS knew that the Yugoslavs, 'fed up with propaganda in [their] state,' were fascinated by technical information about the United States and everyday American life. The officials in Belgrade and Zagreb were, therefore, advised to 'avoid any films, publications and exhibit material beset with straightforward propaganda,'[81] and *Pregled* did a good job with that. The Yugoslav Information Secretariat praised the magazine for its 'perfect illustrations,' its 'high-profile,' and the 'interesting and meaningful topics.' The magazine, admitted the Secretariat, intentionally chose trendy themes that were in vogue with Yugoslav public opinion – usually the pension, education, or welfare system – and presented them to give the impression 'that, thanks to American "free society" and its "way of life", these issues had long before been resolved in the United States.' Printed on glossy paper by the 'most modern American printing shop abroad,' *Pregled* remained the most read foreign magazine in Yugoslavia, according to a 1966 Yugoslav public survey.[82] The impact of the glossy paper and tempting illustrations cannot be underestimated. As Yugoslav feminist and activist Slavenka Drakulić evokes, 'For us, the pictures in a [US] magazine were much more important: we studied their every detail with the interest of those who had no other source of information about the outside world.' But 'inexperienced enough to read them literally,' she continues, 'we absorbed [them as] […] the other world was a paradise. Our reading was wrong and naïve, nevertheless, it stayed in the back of our minds as a powerful force, an inner motivation, a dormant desire for change, an opportunity to awaken.'[83]

Beyond the 'library'

An innovative feature of American public diplomacy consisted in meticulously planned 'outside' activities held in Yugoslav schools, education institutions, and even small rural villages. Among these activities, movies played a crucial propaganda role. In the 1950s and 1960s, cinemas were the most popular entertainment in Yugoslavia. Data from 1958 reveals that, for nineteen million Yugoslav inhabitants, mostly in rural and semi-urban areas, there were approximately 120 million paid admissions to the movies.[84] Tito himself was a 'movie addicted' personality: his private cine-operator recalls that there were years when the Yugoslav dictator watched one film per day, mostly Westerns, as his favourite pastime.[85] The Western gained such renown that Yugoslav filmmakers devised the 'partisan Western,' narrating the WWII national liberation struggle between partisans and fascist-Nazi forces as cruel dust-ups between 'cowboys and indians,' in John Wayne style.[86]

   Foreign movies could enter Yugoslavia through two channels: the *Jugoslavija film* enterprise and the foreign cultural missions. Every foreign movie had to first pass an examination by *Jugoslavija film* based on 'political and moral' norms; then they were evaluated by the Federal Commission for Film Review (a censorship board), and finally assessed by the republics' film commissions. By contrast, USIS movies were only authorized by the Federal Commission and then lent free of charge to any Yugoslav organization.[87] The *Jugoslavija Film* enterprise imported and paid for the Hollywood movies through the Informational Media Guarantee (IMG) Program. Administered until July 1952 by the Mutual Security Agency (MSA), and then by USIS, the IMG was a wide-ranging 'importing' program that granted Yugoslavia American books, periodicals, and films, and also projectors, school equipment, and printing papers, at affordable prices. To overcome Yugoslav dollar shortages, the IMG converted dinars owned by the US government at the Yugoslav National Bank, and acquired through the Surplus Sales Agreement, but paid in dollars for the American copyrights.[88] The exchange rate was very favourable: until 1962, when the rate jumped to 600 dinars for one dollar, and the real scale was 750 dinar for one, the IMG converted Yugoslav dinars at a rate of 300 to one dollar.[89] In 1958, for instance, the guarantee coverage was one million dollars, rising in 1963 to 300 million. Thanks to such support, American books, periodicals, and newspapers (imported throughout *Jugoslovenska knjiga*), American movies, documentaries, and TV releases (imported through *Jugoslavija film*, the National Radio-TV, the republican film centres or the Federal Centre for the Educational and Cultural Film [Savezni centar za prosvetni i kulturni film]), could reach any Yugoslav university, school, or other cultural institution upon request,[90] while copies of *Time, Life, Newsweek,* and the *New York Times* could be bought at Yugoslav newsagents. The IMG, which linked Yugoslav authorities with American publishing and film houses such as McGraw-Hill, Wiley & Sons, Pocket Books, Princeton University Press, Guaranteed Pictures Inc., the Motion Picture Export Association, the CBS/ITN News Film Service, NBC, and United Press TV, was intentionally not publicized by the Yugoslav government, so many Yugoslavs were unaware that 'they may order any American book, and pay for it in dinars.'[91]

While Hollywood movies immediately conquered the hearts and minds of Yugoslavs, USIS commercial movies proved a complete disaster, inducing the USIA motion picture service to focus on invitational showings and on film lending. These 'extremely short, of news-reel length' documentaries and educational movies on science, literature, art, and foreign relations, with its mobile motion-picture units, literally penetrated 'the back country to the end of the road,' and a bit beyond, 'bringing an American message to the silver screen to thousands of rural dwellers at a single showing, many of whom have never visited their own country's capital city.'[92]

The Yugoslav authorities and Party policymakers learned to live with the pervasive presence of American Hollywood in Yugoslav cinemas. 'We often tolerate artistic productions from the West,' explained Belgrade's ideological commissioner, 'because ours are not attractive enough.' And he underlined, 'it is the only way we justify the lower viewing numbers of our films.'[93] According to a USIA 1958 press survey, Yugoslav audiences preferred 'foreign films from the West to the local variety,' and disliked bloc films to the extent that they were 'even less popular that the domestic ones.'[94] Between 1952 and 1956, Yugoslavia imported more than 600 foreign movies, of which half were American, 15 per cent British and French, 10 per cent Italian, and only 5 per cent Russian. Eric Johnston, President of the Motion Picture Association of America, visited Yugoslavia in late 1948, and again in 1957, to meet Tito personally and lobby for an American–Yugoslav agreement on favourable movies import. Western cinematography, as Vučetić reveals, conquered Yugoslav audiences and became pivotal to public consent for the regime.[95]

While Hollywood movies attracted the masses, USIS picked its audiences carefully and deliberately, especially because two Yugoslav laws (the Law on Displaying Films for Public Display of 4 May 1953, and the Film Law of 18 April 1956), prohibited American posts from providing public movie showings.[96] Each spectator had to be personally invited. Initially, the USIS intentionally contravened by leaving invitations at the library desk, until the Yugoslav authorities protested that 'it was not in the spirit of the law.' USIS defined this 'game' played with the Yugoslav officials as 'a blatant commingling of etiquette and a lethal seriousness [...] [that] sometimes suggests a medieval joust.' So the posts decided to counterattack: first they obtained the names of clubs, associations, and individuals possibly interested in film showings; and later, through phone calls and personal visits, they started sending personal invitations to 'science enthusiasts, engineers, workers, painters, musicians, architects, doctors, photographic groups, [and] mountaineers.'[97] USIS Belgrade, which relied on more than 400 movies, two vehicles with integrated projectors, an automatic translation machine, and a machine for automatic photo slides, gave weekly projections all around Belgrade county, up to the north to Novi Sad, while USIS Zagreb, with two mobile units and twenty-seven projectors, covered Croatian suburban and rural areas. In 1959 alone, these mobile units performed 715 films in more than 4,700 showings attended by some 810,000 Yugoslavs.[98] To stop such propaganda, the Yugoslav government set up, from 1957 on, several film distribution centres in each republic, and, two years later, prohibited USIS from distributing movie catalogues directly to the users.

Newly established organizations like the Belgrade Cultural Centre (Kulturni centar Beograd), Zagreb's Centre for Cultural, Educational and Teaching Film (Centar za kulturno-prosvjetni film i nastavni film), or Sarajevo's Teaching Film (Prosvjeta film), were appointed, instead of the American Library, the British Council, the French Institute, and the Soviet Culture House, for movie lending, catalogues supply, communication with the foreign centres, and members' registration. Obliged to 'distribute only films of non-propagandist character,' the foreign centres perceived an instant decline in their lending activities, and, from 1962, new Yugoslav film regulations forced them to surrender their entire or partial film holdings to the Yugoslav distribution centres. USIS gave up some 250, the British Council almost 300, while the Soviet Culture House discharged its entire collection.[99] And while the foreign missions kept deliberately infringing Yugoslav laws (USIS persisted in keeping track of the film users and personal contacts), they once again adapted to the new circumstances, and the Yugoslav institutions became the channel for foreign centre movies. USIS performed particularly well under these circumstances. In 1964, the Croatian Secretariat for Culture registered almost 300 USIS movie lendings, and 1,000 film showings for some 95,000 spectators.[100] In that year, USIS Zagreb received more than 150 requests for educational documentaries from twenty-eight primary schools, twenty-seven institutes of adult education, eighteen faculties and research institutes, and more than thirty labour, sports, youth, and cultural associations, but also TV stations and industry councils. Interestingly, Catholic high schools and theology colleges made up almost 40 per cent of all high school and university requests. The medical institutes and medicine departments were likewise heavy users of this USIS program. The Institute of Histology and Embryology Medical Faculty in Ljubljana, for instance, demanded the *Nervous system* (1937), *Dividing cancer cells* (1933), *Disease of ear, nose and throat* (1946), *Midportion of oesophagus* (1947), and *Physiology of normal menstruation* (1948), for students' needs.[101] 'All the movies you loaned us,' stated the director of a gymnasium from Bosanska Kupa in Bosnia and Herzegovina, 'broadened the cultural horizon of our students,' adding, 'We would like to see more movies about the United States in the II WW, and more travelogues about America.'[102]

In *There is Music in the Town* (1954), USIA portrayed a New England high school musical ensemble practicing after-school activities, earning money to purchase instruments, cooperating for the final performance, to 'typify the genuine interest in many American secondary school students in developing their musical skills,' and to stress that music as 'an integral part of American education, brings to young people satisfaction of self-expression, broadened interest and deeper appreciation of the world around them.'[103] Indeed, USIS documentaries were modelled on the library's themes and its program. *People of the Western Shore* (1957, sixteen mm reel), for instance, described the 'geography, the people and the industries in the Pacific Coast,' while proving 'the interdependence of worker and farmer, of customer and producer, and of American and overseas counterparts engaged in foreign trade.' Suggested for government officials, schools and universities, labour and industrial groups, these documentaries were accompanied by pamphlets such as *United States Today*, *Pursuit of Happiness*, and *USA – Its Geography and Growth*.[104] *Man's Machines* (1957), tied to the People's Capitalism program, stressed the benefits of automatic machines on the American standard of living, and reassured that the advent of automation meant worker control 'over routine, repetitive operations,' thus liberating them 'from unpleasant toil.'[105] Besides themes of general curiosity such as popular science (*A is for Atom*, *Nuclear Ship Savannah*, *The Story of Fuel*, *Satellite Research*, *Atomic Power and the USA*), geography (*All about New York*, *San Francisco*), popular medicine (*The Story of Doctor Jucawi*), history (*The Face of President Lincoln*, *The Life of Indians*), art (*Museum of Art*, *The Art of Maya*, *Abstract Art*), music (*Pan-American Festival*, *The Boston Symphony Orchestra*), and agriculture (*Preservation of Fruit and Vegetables by Freezing*, *Farmer at his Job*, *Harvest Carried Out by One Man*), USIA documentaries also covered international and domestic US affairs. *Tito in the United States*, *Inauguration of President Kennedy*, *Kennedy's Journey to Europe*, and *The John Glenn Story*, became particularly popular in Yugoslavia.[106] USIA's *Tito in the United States* (1964) documentary worked on two parallel leitmotifs: on the one hand, it underlined excellent US–Yugoslav bilateral relations, reporting Kennedy's statement on 'different political philosophies' but a common understanding of 'basic policy and objectives,' and Tito's recognition of the 'principles of co-existence'; on the other, it emphasized Tito's astonishment with the United States and its glorious past. 'In Williamsburg, Virginia,' reported the documentary, 'Marshal Tito saw an America conscious of its revolutionary past,' a time when Americans 'dreamed of liberty' and 'fought for it.' The Yugoslav President could admire, continued the narrator, how the Revolution 'set in motion the creative forces,' like those of the press, which gave voice to people's 'protest and rebellion,' and, finally, shaped 'the dynamic society of twentieth century America.'[107] The message could not have been clearer: an audience accustomed to press censorship and hidden boundaries of coercion could only admire American liberties and dream of them.

As a powerful communication and entertainment medium, the movies became protagonists of the longest and most sophisticated cinematic conflict in history, namely that between the US and the Soviet film industries. As recent studies revealed, Hollywood entered the dispute for profit and propaganda reasons. Moreover, Hollywood–State relationships were far more consensual than those between film-makers and government in the communist regimes, simply because their owners and employees shared Washington's ideological world view. While, in some instances, the Washington propaganda agencies merely assisted in making or trimming movies, other times the FBI, CIA, and USIA financed, produced, and marketed films.[108] USIS documentaries, focused primarily on education, and secondly on political persuasion, struggled between political toleration and restraint, and institutional, often impercep-tible, forms of Yugoslav control, yet enjoyed wide appreciation and network growth.

USIS added English teaching, the Book Translation Program, and its music library as supplemental, but consistent, features of its agenda. The Fulbright Act (1946) and the Smith-Mundt Act (1948) inaugurated English teaching programs worldwide. As they were completely free of charge, the programs aimed 'to reach national teach-ers,' encourage them to 'include information on the United States' in their lectures, and provide the latest textbooks. When, in 1952, USIS launched Rapid Language Instruction and Georgetown University Language training, it generated a significant wave of subscribers. The USIA movie, *Teaching English Naturally* (1957), filmed at the American University campus, offered live dialogues and informational-drill techniques for teaching English conversation.[109] The 1959 USIS inspection report described teaching classes with more than seventy students, including teachers, doc-tors, lawyers, engineers, economists, journalists, and architects.[110]

Proud of its library's performance, USIS embarked on the Book Translation Program to subsidize the printing of American authors by Yugoslav publishing houses. The program, which operated under the IMG, granted publishers copyrights, translations, and even printed papers at ridiculously low prices. 'What seems at first like an unremarkable subsidiary-rights arrangement,' reminded Greg Barnhisel, 'was in reality generously underwritten by the middlemen, the U.S. government.'[111] By the end of the 1950s, the program involved more than thirty Yugoslav publishing houses, and ninety American translations. The program restrictions came from both sides. *Jugoslavenska knjiga* verified the books' suitability, and the 1951 Mutual Security Act excluded hobby, cook, and travel books not focused on the United States, plus materials 'patently lewd or salacious,' such as pornographic and sensational books, politically 'inimical to the best interests of the U.S.,' supporting 'unlawful purposes,' and, understandably, 'communist propaganda.'[112]

On the other hand, the USIS music library, as the first of its kind in socialist Yugoslavia, intended to stimulate 'worldwide interest in and knowledge of American music.'[113] Obviously, this was an understatement. As with the film industry, music became a Cold War weapon: the State Department sponsored worldwide tours to dispel Soviet propaganda over racial discrimination and promote a 'colour-blind democracy.'[114] Beyond political aims, American blues and jazz projected attractive images of the United States, especially to young people. 'Young Yugoslavs love American jazz, and every afternoon in the music library is like a little stateside jam session,' reported USIS in early 1950.[115] The musical collection contained both commercial long-playing phonographs and printed scores of American compositions. When, in the early 1950s, a few foreign records reached Yugoslav radio stations, USIS supplied them with spirituals, classics of Mozart and Bach, blues and jazz masters such as George Gershwin, and popular music composers like Jerome Kern and Aaron Copeland.[116]

USIS added one program after another, astounded by the eagerness of Yugoslav people to learn about America. The information centres, facing the main streets of Belgrade, Zagreb, and Novi Sad, with fancy libraries, photo and exhibit rooms, fanning persuasive newspapers and magazines, were literally small windows through which Yugoslavs could, and did, in ever increasing numbers, 'see America.' USIS reached every nook and cranny of the country, villages and hamlets from Slovenia to Macedonia, convincingly fighting bad ideas with better ones, confident that the more diverse the program, the more victorious it would become.

Notes

1 Jonathan M. Farlow, *I've Seen it All at the Library: The View from Behind the Desk* (Jefferson, N: McFarland & Company, Inc., 2015), 11.
2 Jeffrey Alexander, *The Civil Sphere* (New York: Oxford University Press, 2006), 53–92.
3 Hart, *Empire of Ideas*, 37–8.
4 Greg Barnhisel, *Cold War Modernists: Art, Literature, and American Cultural Diplomacy* (New York: Columbia University Press, 2015), 151.
5 Study of USIS Libraries, August 1967, E-4-67, Box 1, Estimates and Evaluations 1966–78, USIA Office of Research and Evaluation, RG 306, NACP, 3–6, 22.
6 Barnhisel, *Cold War Modernists*, 153.
7 Dan Lacy, 'The Role of American Books Abroad,' *Foreign Affairs* 34, no. 3 (4 April 1956), www.foreignaffairs.com/articles/united-states/1956-04-01/r-le-american-books-abroad.
8 Study of USIA Book Publishing Programs, January 1968, S-4-68, Box 24, Special Reports 1953-97, USIA Office of Research, RG 306, NACP, 6.
9 Nada Apsen. Interview by author. Oral interview. Zagreb, Croatia, 31 May 2014.
10 Belmonte, *Selling the American* Way, 23.
11 Airgram 3319 Dept. of State to Certain Diplomatic and Consular Officers, 24 April 1953, 511.00/4-2453, Box 2247, CDF 1950-54, RG 59, NACP.
12 Barnhisel, *Cold War Modernists*, 153–56.
13 Belmonte, *Selling the American Way*, 28–9. Many excellent scholarly works have successfully explored the USIA overall effort of telling America's story abroad. While Belmonte adopted a thematic approach on family, gender, race, capitalism, and democracy, Barnhisel focused on the USIA's promotion of modernism. Nicholas Cull (*The Cold War and the United States Information Agency*) favoured a chronological perspective, while Kenneth Osgood (*Total Cold War*) and Shawn J. Parry-Giles, (*The Rhetorical Presidency, Propaganda, and the Cold War, 1945-1955* [Westport, CT; London: Praeger, 2001]) concentrated on Truman's and Eisenhower's presidential propagandas. Scholars such as Simona Tobia

(*Advertising America*), Mikael Nilsson (*The Battle for Hearts and Minds in the High North: The USIA and American Cold War Propaganda in Sweden, 1952–1969* [Leiden: Brill, 2016]), and Francisco J. R. Jimenez, Lorenzo D. Gomez-Escalonilla, and Nicholas J. Cull (*US Public Diplomacy and Democratization in Spain*) privileged a national perspective in transnational context.

14 John Fousek, *To Lead the Free World: American Nationalism and the Cultural Roots of the Cold War* (Chapel Hill: The University of North Carolina Press, 2000), 187.

15 Wendy L. Wall, *Inventing the 'American Way': The Politics of Consensus from the New Deal to the Civil Rights Movement* (Oxford: Oxford University Press, 2008).

16 Refugee views on life in Yugoslavia, 30 April 1963, R-27–63, Box 13, Research Reports 1966–90, USIA Office of Research and Media Reaction, RG 306, NACP.

17 Despatch 44 Belgrade to Dept. of State, 13 July 1953, 511.68/7–1353, Box 2472, CDF 1955–59, NACP.

18 Manuscript for USIE Newsletter in despatch 189 Belgrade to Dept. of State, 24 August 1951, 511.68/8–2451, Box 2472, CDF 1950–54, RG 59, NACP.

19 In Zagreb, the US Consulate offices were on the second floor, while the film and music section, together with the Cultural Affairs Officer, occupied the third floor (Photograph No. 3, 'View of the new American Consulate Building and US Information Center in Zagreb, Yugoslavia,' 6 June 1953, Box 2472, CDF 1950–54, RG 59, NACP).

20 USIE Report 610 April–May 1950, 20 June 1950, 511.68/6–2050, Box 2472, CDF 1950–54, RG 59, NACP.

21 Study of USIS Libraries, August 1967, 22–3.

22 *Ibid.*, 1.

23 Recommendations for Scopes and Types of Programming in EUR Area Beginning FY 1957 or Earlier in Hickok to IOP and IOA, 15 August 1955, Box 16, USIA Subject Files 1953–67, RG 306, NACP.

24 *The Gift of Freedom*, January 1949, Box 10, Master Files Copies of Pamphlets and Leaflets 1953–83, USIA IPS/Publication Division, RG 306, NACP.

25 *Meet some Americans … at work*, 1951, Box 1, Publications 1950–2000, USIA Information Programs, RG 306, NACP.

26 Laura A. Belmonte, 'Selling Capitalism: Modernization and US Overseas Propaganda, 1945–1959,' in *Staging Growth: Modernization, Development, and the Global Cold War*, ed. D. C. Engerman et al. (Amherst; Boston: University of Massachusetts Press, 2003), 111.

27 Airgram 682 Dept. of State to Certain Diplomatic and Consular Officers, 7 October 1950, 511.00/10–750, Box 2238, CDF 1950–54, RG 59, NACP.

28 Semi-annual Evaluation Report Yugoslavia in despatch Belgrade to Dept. of State, 17 December 1952, 511.68/12–1752, Box 2247, CDF 1950–54, RG 59, NACP.

29 Commonly known as the Ad Council, this private, non-profit organization has, since 1942, created comprehensive and integrated communication campaigns, including consumer research, media outreach, public relations, and announcements, sponsored by non-profit organizations or federal government agencies (Ad Council, 'About us,' 15 November 2018, www.adcouncil.org/About-Us).

30 Dawn Spring, *Advertising in the Age of Persuasion: Building Brand America, 1941–1961* (New York: Palgrave Macmillan, 2011), 144–5.

31 Excerpt from speech by Sherman Adams, Assistant to the President, over the Mutual Broadcasting System, 1 December 1955, Box 13, USIA Subject Files 1953–67, RG 306, NACP; Hixon, *Parting the Curtain*, 133.

32 The People's Capitalism Exhibit: A Study of Reactions of Foreign Visitors to the Washington Preview, March 1956, IRI.G.7., Box 38, Research Memoranda 1963–99, USIA Office of Research and Media Reaction, RG 306, NACP; Belmonte, 'Selling Capitalism,' 119.

33 Belmonte, *Selling the American Way*, 224–5; for further analysis, see Hixon, *Parting the Curtain*, 133–41.

34 David M. Potter, *People's Capitalism*, Part I, 16–17 November 1956, Box 19, USIA Subject Files 1953–67, RG 306, NACP.

35 Refugee Views on Life in Yugoslavia, April 30, 1963, R-27–63, Box 13, Research Reports 1966–90, USIA Office of Research and Media Reaction, RG 306, NACP.

36 Laura A. Belmonte, 'Exporting America: The US Propaganda Offensive, 1945–1959,' in *The Arts of Democracy: Art, Public Culture, and the State*, ed. Casey N. Blake (Washington, DC; Philadelphia: Woodrow Wilson Center Press; University of Pennsylvania Press, 2007), 136.

37 David M. Potter, 'Lincoln i značaj Američke unije,' *Pregled*, February 1959, 2.

38 Message 1503 USIA CA to USIA, 28 November 1958, Box 7, USIA Master Budget Files 1953–64, RG 306, NACP.

39 *Pregled*, February 1959, 2–20.

40 Message 143 USIA CA to all principal USIS posts (and others), 17 July 1957, Box 7, USIA Master Budget Files 1953–64, RG 306, NACP; List of Reference Materials in Airgram 81 Dept. of State to All American Diplomatic and Consular Posts, 13 July 1962, 511.00/7–1362, Box 1046, CDF 1960–63, RG 59, NACP.

41 Dorothy Lafferty, 'Duhovno nasledje Amerike,' *Pregled*, January 1966, 2.

42 Walter F. Murphy, 'Sloboda u Americi,' *Pregled*, July 1966, 2.

43 'Vera u slobodu i demokratiju,' *Pregled*, January 1966, 8.

44 'Sloboda stvaranja za sve,' *Pregled*, July 1967, 14.

45 Charles P. Taft, 'Uloga religije u slobodnom društvu,' *Pregled*, March 1966, 13.

46 'Zaštita demokratije pred Belom Kućom,' *Pregled*, January 1966, 56.

47 The McCarthy investigations hardly hit the USIA inceptions. For a systematic overview, see Cull, *The Cold War and the United States Information Agency*, 82–94; Hart, *Empire of Ideas*, 178–97.

48 Airgram 218 Dept. of State to Certain Diplomatic and Consular Officers, 3 February 1953, 511.00/2–353, Box 2246, CDF 1950–54, RG 59, NARA.

49 Instructions for Selection and Detection of Material in Book and Library program, 15 July 1953 in Study of USIS Libraries, August 1967, 26.

50 Memorandum Prepared in the USIA 30 June 1953, FRUS, 1952–1954, II, 2, doc. 336; Louise S. Robbins, 'The Overseas Libraries Controversy and the Freedom to Read: US Librarians and Publishers Confront Joseph McCarthy,' *Libraries & Culture* 36, no. 1 (2001): 28–9, https://doi.org/10.1353/lac.2001.0021; Barnhisel, *Cold War Modernists*, 176–7.

51 Barnhisel, *Cold War Modernists*, 154–6, 185–6; Osgood, *Total Cold War*, 234, 302.

52 Barnhisel, *Cold War Modernists*, 187–94.

53 *Ibid.*, 180–6; Belmonte, *Selling the American Way*, 163–224.

54 Study of USIS Libraries, August 1967, 22.

55 Magazines at the American Center, Periodical list, 13 November 1973, Box 1,
    Records Relating to Culture Centers 1946–88, USIA Library Program Division,
    RG 306, NACP.
56 Study of USIS Libraries, August 1967, 24.
57 Magazines at the American Center, 13 November 1973.
58 Analysis of Periodicals, Table 3, 1 July–31 January 1959, Box 2, Reports and Studies
    1953–98, USIA Office of Administration, RG 306, NACP.
59 Study of USIS Libraries, August 1967, 24, 31–3.
60 Report of the IPS, 1947–49, Box 1, Special Collection Branch, Oversize Scrapbooks
    1947–58, USIA Library Program Division, RG 306, NACP.
61 Airgram 3319 Dept. of State to Certain Diplomatic and Consular Officers, 24 April
    1953, 511.00/4–2453, Box 2247, CDF 1950–54, RG 59, NACP.
62 Airgram 377 Belgrade to Dept. of State, 22 November 1950, 511.68/11–2250, Box
    2472, CDF 1950–54, RG 59, NACP.
63 Survey of Post Utilization and Assessment of IPS Materials and Services, February
    1961, PMS-45, Box 1, Program and Media Studies 1956–62, USIA Office of Research
    and Analysis, RG 306, NACP.
64 USIE Report 178, December 1949–January 1950, 28 February 1950, 511.68/2–2850,
    Box 2472, CDF 1950–54, RG 59, NACP.
65 Despatch 644 Belgrade to Dept. of State, 8 January 1952, 511.68/8–152, Box 2472,
    CDF 1950–54, RG 59, NACP.
66 UDBA Report, 20 May 1953, XI-109-VI-36, Box 6, Komisija za međunarodne
    odnose i veze 1945–90, CK SKJ, RG 507, AY.
67 Report from USIS program in despatch 4 Consulate Zagreb to Dept. of State, 3 July
    1953, 511.68/7–353, Box 2472, CDF 1950–54, RG 59, NACP.
68 Inspection Report USIS Yugoslavia, 20 November 1959, 21.
69 Propaganda kapitalističkih zemalja u Jugoslaviji, 1953, 724/1953, Box 44, Materijali
    komisije za međunarodne veze 1950–59, SSRNJ, RG 142, AY, 5.
70 Yugoslavian Reaction to SAD, a new USIS magazine, July 1953, IEV.YUG.1, Box 38,
    Research Memoranda 1963–99, USIA Office of Research and Media Reaction, RG
    306, NACP, 7, 14–15.
71 *Ibid.*, i–iii, 1, 8, 23.
72 Cull, *The Cold War and the United States Information Agency*, 100; Memorandum
    Belgrade to Dept. of State, 28 April 1954, 511.68/4–2853, Box 2472, CDF 1950–54,
    RG 59, NACP.
73 Country Plan for Yugoslavia 1963, 30 January 1963, Box 45, USIA Subject Files
    1953–67, RG 306, NACP, 6; Inspection Report USIS Yugoslavia, November 20, 23.
74 USIS Belgrade to USIA Washington, 27 January 1967, YO6601, Box 41, Africa,
    EE and Multi-Areas, USIA Office of Research and Analysis, RG 306, NACP.
75 'Profil prosečne američke porodice,' *Pregled*, January 1968, 9–11, 50–54.
76 'Američke žene,' *Pregled*, January 1965, 3.
77 'Back cover,' *Pregled*, April 1964.
78 'Žene radnice,' *Pregled*, January 1965, 12–24.
79 'Promene u američkoj porodici,' *Pregled*, January 1965, 25–26.
80 Vučetić, 'Amerikanizacija u Jugoslovenskoj Popularnoj Kulturi '60-Ih,' 138–48.
81 USIE Country Paper Yugoslavia in circular 2 Belgrade to Dept. of State, 3 July 1950,
    511.68/7–350, Box 2472, CDF 1950–54, RG 59, NACP.

82 Informacija o inostranoj pisanoj informativnoj-propagandnoj delatnosti prema Jugoslaviji, 17 June 1969, 01–624, Box 565, SIV 1953–90, RG 130, AJ; Memorandum of Conversation, 67049, Jan. 13, 1967, YO6601, Box 41, Africa, Eastern Europe and Multi-Areas, USIA Office of Research and Analysis, RG 306, NACP.

83 Drakulić, *How We Survived Communism and Even Laughed*, 27–8.

84 Inspection Report USIS Yugoslavia, November 20, 24.

85 Dragan Batančev, 'A Cinematic Battle: Three Yugoslav War Films from the 1960s' (MA thesis, Central European University, Budapest, 2012), 16.

86 Radina Vučetić, 'Kauboji u partizanskoj uniformi: američki vesterni i partizanski vesterni u Jugoslaviji šezdesetih godina 20. veka,' *Tokovi Istorije*, issue 2 (2010): 130–51.

87 Pitanje propagandnih stranih misija u FNRJ, 3 June 1953, Pov. br. 92562, Box 44, Materijali komisije za međunarodne veze 1950–59, SSRNJ, RG 142, AY, 15–17.

88 9th Semi-annual Report of the US Advisory Commission on Information, 2 February 1954, 511.00/3–2554, Box 2249, CDF 1950–54, RG 59, NACP, 17. The Agreement of the Surplus Agricultural Supplies was employed for any kind of US funding in Yugoslavia but was most effective in financing the cultural exchange programs. See Chapter 5 for more on this issue.

89 Popović to SIV, 18 January 1962, 9223, Box 640, Međunarodni odnosi 1953–70, SIV 1953–90, RG 130, AY.

90 ICS of the USIA, 4 December 1957, Box 9, USIA Master Budget Files 1953–64, RG 306, NACP; Roberts to Bulajić, 21 May 1964, Box 237, SAD, Kanada i Latinska Amerika, SSOK, RG 318, AY.

91 Inspection Report USIS Yugoslavia, 20 November 1959, 30, 46. For more on IMG cooperation in Box 99, Veze sa SAD i Kanadom, Savet za nauku i kulturu Vlade FNRJ (hereafter SNK FNRJ), RG 317, AY and Box 237, SAD, Kanada i Latinska Amerika, SSOK, RG 318, AY.

92 Robert E. R. Elder, *The Information Machine: The United States Information Agency and American Foreign Policy* (New York: Syracuse University Press, 1968), xi.

93 Zapisnik sa sednice Komisije za ideološka pitanja, 11 September 1965, Box 209, Zapisnici i materijali ideološke komisije GK SKS Beograd 1965–67, Gradski komitet SKS Beograd, HAB, 68.

94 Notes on film attendance in Yugoslavia, 2 June 1958, RN-26-58, Box 1, 1958–62 Research Notes, USIA Office of Research and Analysis, RG 306, NACP.

95 Vučetić, *Koka-kola socijalizam*, 89–101.

96 Pravni položaj stranih kulturnih institucija – Pravni savet DSIPa, 1956, 1651/1, Box 55, Materijali komisije za međunarodne veze 1950–59, SSRNJ, RG 142, AY, 22.

97 Inspection Report USIS Yugoslavia, 20 November 1959, 24.

98 Propaganda kapitalističkih zemalja u Jugoslaviji, 1953, 18–20; IMS Budget FY 1954, 7 July 1953, Box 8, USIA Master Budget Files 1953–64, RG 306, NACP; Prevođenje i štampanje knjiga američkih pisaca po BTP, 25 November 1962, Box 240, SAD, Kanada i Latinska Amerika 1953–67, SSOK, RG 318, AY.

99 Republički sekretarijat za informacije, 10 July 1964, 8/54–1964, Box 42, Kinematografija 1964–65, Republički sekretarijat za kulturu SRH 1963–65 (hereafter RSK SRH), RG 1414, CSA; Informacija o delatnosti strane propagande, 3 May 1962, Box 512, Materijali o delovanju inostrane propagande 1958–68, Gradski komitet SKS Beograd, HAB.

100 Dostavljanje godišnjeg izvještaja o korištenju filmskog fonda, 19 December 1964, 8/142–1964, Box 42, Kinematografija 1964–65, RSK SRH 1963–65, RG 1414, CSA.

101 Centar za kulturno-prosvjetni film i nastavni film, 3 April 1964, 8/38–1964, Box 42, RSK SRH 1963–65, RG 1414, CSA.

102 Despatch 156 USIS Zagreb to USIA Washington, 26 June 1956, Box 4, Europe and Canada, USIA Foreign Service Dispatches, RG 306, NACP.

103 Telegram 624 USIA CA to USIS posts, 31 March 1954, Box 8, USIA Master Budget Files 1953–64, RG 306, NACP.

104 Message 1260 USIA CA to USIA circular, 20 November 1957, Box 7, USIA Master Budget Files 1953–64, RG 306, NACP.

105 Message 830 USIA CA to USIA circular, 2 October 1957, Box 7, USIA Master Budget Files 1953–64, RG 306, NACP.

106 Box 42, RSK SRH 1963–65, RG 1414, CSA.

107 Transcript of 'President Tito in the US' (1964) in Conte to IMS/NY, 18 March 1964, Box 34, USIA Movie Scripts 1942–65, RG 306, NACP.

108 Tony Shaw, *Hollywood's Cold War* (Amherst: University of Massachusetts Press, 2007); Tony Shaw and Denise J. Youngblood, *Cinematic Cold War: The American and Soviet Struggle for Hearts and Minds* (Lawrence: University Press of Kansas, 2014). On this topic, see also: David W. Ellwood and Rob Kroes, *Hollywood in Europe: Experiences of a Cultural Hegemony* (Amsterdam: Vu University Press, 1994); Stanley Corkin, *Cowboys as Cold Warriors: The Western And US History* (Philadelphia: Temple University Press, 2004); Mark Glancy, *Hollywood and the Americanization of Britain: From the 1920s to the Present* (London; New York: I. B. Tauris, 2015); Rebecca Prime, *Hollywood Exiles in Europe: The Blacklist and Cold War Film Culture* (New Brunswick, NJ: Rutgers University Press, 2014).

109 Semi-annual Evaluation Report Yugoslavia in despatch Belgrade to Dept. of State, 17 December 1952, 511.68/12–1752, Box 2247, CDF 1950–54, RG 59, NACP; 1954–55 USIS Mission Prospectus, 3 December 1953, 511.00/3–1253, Box 2246, CDF 1950–54, RG 59, NACP; Message 3 USIA CA to all USIS posts, 1 July 1957, Box 7, USIA Master Budget Files 1953–64, RG 306, NACP.

110 Inspection Report USIS Yugoslavia, 20 November 1959, 34.

111 Barnhisel, *Cold War Modernists*, 169–71.

112 Propaganda kapitalističkih zemalja u Jugoslaviji, 1953; Barnhisel, *Cold War Modernists*, 164–6. Because of changed circumstances in the global publishing industry and US budget cuts, the program was ended by Congress in 1968.

113 Airgram 3319 Dept. of State to Certain Diplomatic and Consular Officers, 24 April 1953, 511.00/4–2453, Box 2247, CDF 1950–54, RG 59, NACP.

114 Penny Von Eschen, *Satchmo Blows Up the World: Jazz Ambassadors Play the Cold War* (Cambridge, MA; London: Harvard University Press, 2004).

115 USIE Report 62, 27 July 1950, 511.68/7–2750, Box 2472, CDF 1950–54, RG 59, NACP.

116 USIE Report 397, 11 April 1950, 511.68/4–1150, Box 2472, CDF 1950–54, RG 59, NACP.

3

'America' at Yugoslav fairs

In its 5 May 1947 issue, *Life* magazine displayed a photo-essay entitled 'Family Status Must Improve: It Should Buy More for Itself.' Ted and Jeanne Hemeke, parents of three children, lived, after World War II, in an unpleasant, rude cottage. Ted arrived home in workingman's clothes, and Jeanne struggled with a dirty coal furnace in the kitchen. By 1960, argued the Twentieth Century Fund economists, the US family would acquire 'a pleasant roof over its head, a vacuum cleaner, a washing machine, stove, electric iron, refrigerator, electric toaster and [...] matching dishes, silverware, cooking utensils, tools, cleaning materials, stationery and postage stamps.' Ted would come home wearing 'the middle-class badge of a suit,' the children would be 'fashionably dressed,' and Jeanne would approvingly survey 'a kitchen stocked with shiny new appliances.'[1] As Lizabeth Cohen highlighted, the majority of American post-war economic theorists and protagonists, from anti-New Deal big business and moderate liberal capitalists, to labour and its allies on the left, endorsed, albeit for different reasons, the importance of mass consumption as a highway to prosperity and middle-class wealth.[2]

Consumer goods, argues Rob Kroes, 'are living contradictions.' Although they 'are meant to be consumed, yet at the same time have reached consummation,' they attain 'a higher level of sense and meaning, of dreams and desire.' 'The automobile,' continues Kroes, 'as an object of consumption has a finite life [...]. Nevertheless, as a dream object, it keeps riding on.' The United States became the epitome of mass consumption society in the second post-war world; the American way of life developed as a euphemism for affluence, material wealth, and freedom of choice. Meaning more than just availability of products and services, the advent of the mass-consumption era bridged the separation between object and image, commerce and art, and transformed the advertising industry into an instrument for accommodating dreams and fantasies. 'The experience, or at least the promise, of freedom that U.S. citizens in their role of the consumer could share in, became the central ingredient of America's modernity. Shopping became a reassertion of one's identity,' claims Kroes.[3] In organizing American exhibitions at Yugoslav trade fairs, this ingredient remained an essential incentive of the US public diplomacy agenda.

Much of American mass culture consumption took place in private: people watched television in their living rooms, the youth paid to see Hollywood movies in quasi-private places of darkened movie theatres, the majority consumed American music via radio or records in homes or dance clubs. Outside private homes, the entertainment industry served effectively and successfully 'as a site of exposure to American mass culture' and proliferated worldwide under commercial auspices, 'creating the demand, if not the desire, for its consumption.'[4] At the international trade fairs and exhibitions, American mass culture met with the state intervention that used this very culture to gain audiences abroad.

The US national pavilions, assessed Robert Haddow, became favoured government vehicles for administrators and business supporters to counter communism through the promotion and transplantation of democratic capitalism overseas. At the 1950 Chicago International Trade Fair, the 1958 Brussels World's Fair, and the 1959 Sokolniki Park Fair in Moscow, US policymakers advanced the deployment of culture as a Cold War weapon, along with economic aid and military power. The trade displays and exhibitions placed on the same table government agencies, corporate associations, advertising firms, industrial designers, and the art world, but also opinion-makers, and obviously, designers and architects. As Haddow notes, these latter, who created exhibitions for the Department of Commerce, the USIA, or the Eisenhower White House Project, developed strong working relationships with business groups, including the Committee on Economic Development and the Advertising Council. Because of these interactions, a new generation of artists, architects, and designers, like R. Buckminster Fuller, Charles and Ray Eames, George Nelson, Peter Blake, Ivan Chermayeff, and Thomas Geismar, were trained to conceptualize and incorporate displays celebrating American capitalism and material abundance into public exhibitions and their art.[5] Washington used visual instruments to 'sell America's story abroad': commodity products charmed with their aesthetic appeal, technologically advanced appliances, and attractive technological aids. American exhibitions at Zagreb and Belgrade trade fairs advertised modern technology and consumerist abundance. But more than that, as Jakovina pointed out, every spring and autumn the Yugoslav international fairs became 'a promotional battlefield of two ideologically, economically, religiously and politically opposite blocs.'[6] Both the United States and Soviet Union, together with the communist-ruled countries of Eastern Europe, 'laid claim to the same cultural heritage, the same Enlightenment tradition, and the same concepts of human worth and social progress.'[7] The question of heritage became, therefore, enough of a political reason to engage in exhibitions worldwide. Yugoslavia, belonging to the socialist forces of the world, and endorsing the Non-Aligned Movement and Third World countries with its unique, often debated, American partnership, transformed the Zagreb and Belgrade trade fairs into an exemplary battlefield of cultural Cold War practices.

USIA's job was to provide foreign audiences with a picture of American life with 'familiarity and friendliness.'[8] The agency organized both USIS and trade fair exhibitions prepared specifically for Eastern Europe. In the Soviet bloc, but not Yugoslavia, these exhibitions operated under cultural exchange agreements and were concurrently managed by the Department of Commerce and Labor, and the

USIA from 1954 on. After 1965, the Smithsonian Institute took over the fine arts, while the USIA's ICS continued to manage other overseas showings. Only from 1966 onwards did the agency acquire the entire International Trade Fair program from the Department of Commerce. Finally, in 1968, a USIA directive limited participation in fairs principally to Eastern European countries.[9]

From the early 1950s, the IIA started contemplating using exhibitions and commercial enterprises at world fairs. 'We know of no more important instrument of psychological warfare than the actual display of America's industrial, economic and labour resources,' argued the policymakers in office.[10] In 1954, the US government launched the program built on close cooperation between government agencies and American individuals and businesses to 'patriotically [...] exhibit American industrial quality, progress, and power.'[11] The program championed American 'spiritual values [...] and reflect[ed] purposes beyond mere commercial expediency.'[12] As President Eisenhower said in his Congressional message on 10 January 1955, such exhibitions would 'impress upon the peoples of the world' that the United States had 'great productive capacity' and was 'dedicated to the preservation of peace and [...] the improvement of mankind's standard of living.' American owners, managers, and workers, 'living under a free political system and enjoying free enterprise,' Eisenhower underlined, would cooperate 'in the production of all kinds of goods and services not only for the benefit of our own people but for all with whom we trade.' By doing so, they would 'counteract and overshadow the efforts of the Soviet bloc countries in their intensive program to use international trade fairs as instruments to stimulate goodwill,' and, finally, 'supply tangible evidence that the United States is capable of, and willing to, expand mutually beneficial two-way trade pursuant to these objectives.'[13] Between 1954 and 1969 alone, USIA was involved in 343 separate showings abroad, visited by millions of people at expos and world fairs; its influence was deemed incalculable and its impact unmeasurable.[14]

Coming to Yugoslavia: the Atoms for Peace debut in 1955

In May 1950, the director of the Zagreb Fair sent the first invitation to the US Department of Commerce, pleading for American participation in September.[15] Poor coordination between the Yugoslav Embassy in Washington and the fair authorities caused a low involvement of American firms and the issue ended in stalemate. The fair ultimately displayed some mining equipment by Ingersoll-Rand, General Motors products, and CARE (Cooperative for American Remittances to Europe) packages, but none of the companies made any sales.[16] Between 1951 and 1954 the fair's director, Ivan Šnidaršić, repeatedly renewed its invitation to the United States: 'we all know how important it is that every possible effort is made to bring America and Yugoslavia closer together,' he claimed in 1951.[17] Between 1952 and 1954, the Zagreb Fair evolved from an exhibit of 'propaganda purpose' to a more 'regular international commercial show,' with increasing foreign participation. From 1953 onwards, Yugoslavia started liberalizing its trade policies so that other cities, such as Osijek, Novi Sad, Ljubljana, and Skopje got their fairs, the Soviets were allowed to take part after Stalin's death, while Yugoslav enterprises engaged in international expos in Milan, Brussels, Paris, and Casablanca.[18] But because USIS Zagreb was not allowed to participate near the American exhibitors until 1955, the US government declined any major participation in Zagreb, and the US companies exhibited only through European agents.

The Atoms for Peace program debuted at the Zagreb Fair in 1955 as the first US government-sponsored exhibition in Yugoslavia. The entrance inscription letters, ten centimetres high and topped by the title, were flanked by a two-metre-high portrait of President Eisenhower and an American shield of similar size. 'The United States pledges before you,' declared the inscription, 'its determination to help solve the fearful atomic dilemma, to devote its entire heart and mind to find the way by which the miraculous inventiveness of man should not be dedicated to his death but consecrated to his life.' Eisenhower's words were accompanied by Tito's statement delivered at the Federal Assembly in March that year: 'we are convinced that the only real way, which ensures the progress of humanity is the use of nuclear energy in peaceful industrial purposes toward the end of raising the standard of living and eliminating want and backwardness, which, to a great extent, are the cause of war.'[19] It was President Eisenhower who put the question of peaceful atomic energy to the UN on 8 December 1953. In a dramatic speech before the General Assembly, Eisenhower cited 'new deeds of peace' that could reverse 'the fearful trend of atomic military build-up' and develop it 'into a great boom, for the benefit of all mankind.'[20] By the time he announced his Atoms for Peace campaign, and proposed the creation of an international atomic energy agency, Stalin was dead and the Korean war was over. In August of that year, the Soviet Union proposed a Big Four conference in Western Europe. The moment seemed politically propitious. Following the 'New Look' doctrine, the Eisenhower administration achieved the heaviest weapons build-up in US history, from 841 nuclear weapons in 1952, to a stockpile of 18,638 in 1960. Atoms for Peace, as John Krige stressed, represented a genuine psychological warfare weapon and a 'polyvalent policy initiative.'[21] Beyond its propaganda dimension, Atoms for Peace pressured the US Atomic Energy Commission (AEC) to push forward legislative changes to promote a domestic civilian nuclear power industry, piloted by the American private sector. The relaxation of security arrangements facilitated the creation of the first International Conference on Peaceful Uses of Atomic Energy that opened at the UN palace in Geneva on 8 August 1955, gathering 1,400 delegates from seventy-three countries, and more than 900 journalists. The United States exhibited the working swimming pool fission reactor, designed and built at Oak Ridge National Laboratory, which had an enormous public diplomacy impact. The Soviets showed up with a power plant model, but it lacked the US exhibition's impact. On this occasion, many scientists, from East and West, met for the first time, and discussed in detail topics based on the common ground of scientific research.[22]

The Zagreb friendly atom show, intended 'to allay fears of the atomic bomb and to pressure the USSR indirectly into an agreement concerning the safe management of nuclear technology,' was a 'public diplomacy triumph.' The State Department's intent was to address Tito's 'widespread misunderstanding of the U.S.'s atomic position [versus] [non-aligned] countries,' to 'stress the identity of interests' of both sides, underline the peaceful character of nuclear power, and support Yugoslav development of peaceful atomic energy.[23] Toured by Yugoslavia's highest officers, like Aleksandar Ranković, major Yugoslav Party ideologist Edvard Kardelj, Central Committee member Svetozar Vukmanović Tempo, and Croatian Assembly President Vladimir Bakarić, the exhibit attracted 'more than a quarter of a million other Yugoslavs.' President Tito, together with Moša Pijade, Federal Assembly President, visited the US pavilion outside official working hours. A twenty-page USIS report recalled unprecedented success. Only two years before, in October 1953, demonstrators protesting the Trieste question smashed USIS windows and menaced security personnel. During its twelve-day output, Atoms for Peace attracted more than 150,000 visitors in Zagreb and some 108,000 at the Belgrade Kinoteka Film Museum, where it was moved afterwards. 'Long live America,' wrote a visitor in the guest book.[24] Never had a USIS publication seen such widespread distribution; 150,000 copies of *Atom – Nada Sveta* (Atom – Hope of the World), a handsome, colourful, illustrated pamphlet, was printed and widely distributed. Posters were put up in all major Serbian cities and USIS centres, insertions appeared in radio broadcasts and newspapers, and invitations arrived in schools and agricultural and technical organizations. The police and fair authorities fought back: films scheduled at the exhibit, such as *Introducing the Atom, Atoms in Medicine, Atoms in Agriculture* and *Industry and Power*, were prohibited. USIS Zagreb then installed a rear-view projector in one of its exhibit windows and scheduled continuous screenings for four hours from early evening. The first two days attracted around 800 spectators before the police stopped *Atomic Power for Peace* and *A is for Atom* showings because of 'crowds on the sidewalk and overflow on the street.' In Belgrade, the organizers were denied adequate indoor space, while the Zagreb Fair management insisted that Tito's speech inscription be placed next to Eisenhower's, less than a week before opening. The Zagreb Fair prohibited a refreshment reception for journalists and guests to USIS, blocked the telephone line for the pavilion, and intentionally shunned the US pavilion during the official opening procession.[25]

Beyond all expectations, Atoms for Peace received – as never before – abundant and decidedly favourable press coverage. Newspapers, magazines, children's weeklies, and economic periodicals praised it as 'the first and only one of this kind in Yugoslavia' and 'the greatest attraction at the International Fair,' while others celebrated 'the enormous power of atomic energy used for peaceful purposes,' which made 'people very thankful to the organizers.'[26] The aftermath was even better: thanks to contacts made at the exhibit, the Yugoslav Federal Nuclear Energy Commission (FNEC) sent twelve of the most prominent nuclear scientists to the United States in 1956; the Commission received the Atoms for Peace library collection at a high-level ceremony attended by Ranković, Vladimir Velebit, and other distinguished government members in 1957; while, immediately in the aftermath of the exhibit, the two governments initiated negotiations over the US nuclear aid program to Yugoslavia, concluding on 19 April 1961 with an agreement consisting of $350,000 aid for the Jožef Stefan reactor program and the Vinča Hot Laboratory.[27]

Supermarket USA and the Yugoslav 'kitchen debate'

With Atoms for Peace, USIA policymakers and USIS field officers inaugurated style-appealing displays rather than commercial revenues. The Zagreb Fair, along with Izmir, Damascus, and Plovdiv, was considered one of 'the best American exhibitions there to date' and a 'strategic show window,' successfully counteracting Soviet propaganda.[28] The fair had an old, prestigious pre-war tradition and a prominent place among southeastern European fairs. The American pavilion in Zagreb, at least by the late 1960s, was the largest permanent US pavilion in the world. As a split-level of excellent design, it was built in 1957, renewed again in 1967, and included 2,780 m² of covered space, 2,400 m² of outdoor area, plus some additional storage rooms. The rental space was covered by Embassy or PL 480 and ICA funds.[29] USIS filled the pavilion's thirty-metre-long exhibit window with photographic materials, prepared press releases, kits, diagrams, displays, and descriptions. Official Yugoslavia looked upon trade fairs, commercial exhibits, and cultural presentations as necessary concomitants to economic progress and cultural enlightenment. Viewing fairs as models for economic advancement, the Yugoslav authorities were less 'pleased with large displays of consumer goods,' especially if produced by more developed economies, because they whetted 'popular appetites that could not be satisfied.' On the other hand, ordinary Yugoslavs came 'to see a show and be amused. They want[ed] to see customer goods, cars, and recreational items.' US policymakers realized 'the value of whetted appetites in a country with a communist regime, which quite properly err on the side of pleasing the general public,' and coherently pursued such an agenda.[30]

This was certainly true for the US pavilion at the 1959 Moscow Sokolniki Park Fair which, as 'an epic propaganda battle,' 'mounted a massive exhibition of consumer capitalism,'[31] and 'bombarded Soviet visitors with multimedia images of American daily life and then deposited them in a multi-story warehouse overflowing with retail goods.'[32] Visited by 2.7 million visitors (and tens of thousands of gatecrashers), the US pavilion was dominated by a twenty-four-metre high, sixty-metre-long, gold-anodized geodesic dome that served as the information centre which displayed coloured pictures of American life, accompanied by a musical score and a voiceover commentary in Russian.[33] At the opening, Vice President Richard Nixon engaged in one of the most notable verbal Cold War sparring matches with Soviet Premier Nikita Khrushchev, known as the 'kitchen debate.' Standing in front of an American model kitchen and a sunshine yellow GE washer-dryer, Nixon and Khrushchev started a heated and lengthy dispute, not over missiles, bombs, and diplomatic diatribes, but over the relative merits of American washing machines, televisions, and electric ranges. Nixon argued that American superiority rested on the ideal suburban home complete with modern appliances and distinct gender roles of the male breadwinner and the full-time housewife. The labour-saving devices exposed the superiority of American freedom and free enterprise over communism.[34] The kitchen debate illuminated ideological diatribes, as Greg Castillo accentuated, 'over citizen enfranchisement, housework and gender equity, and the economics of mass consumption and planned obsolescence.'[35]

Yugoslavia got its 'kitchen debate' in September 1957 when the US Department of Commerce, along with the USIA and American business people, launched *Supermarket USA* at the Zagreb Fair. As Nada Apsen emphasized, 'Nobody knew what a supermarket was. And it was sensational.'[36] Indeed, most of the one million Yugoslav visitors had never seen a US supermarket, owned a mechanical refrigerator, or purchased pre-packaged convenience food before. The American planners expected that a radical transformation of Yugoslav consumer culture would follow.[37] John A. Logan from the National Association of Food Chains drew up the plans for a supermarket, stocking 4,000 items in a space of 1,000 m[2]. It was the first American supermarket in a communist country.[38] Fresh goods on display included yellow bananas, juicy grapes, and pre-packaged meats. The *New York Times* reported on the astonished and amazed women: 'Look at the meat, it's all packed and assorted, the price is marked on [it] and you just know it's clean.' A housewife emphasized, 'Why would it be so difficult for us to package meat this way? A little paper, that's all there is to it. […] Hygienic, it's wonderful.'[39] Just at the entrance, Eisenhower's huge poster recounted how 'all countries today stand on the threshold of more widely shared prosperity if they utilize wisely the knowledge of science and technology available to this age.' Next to the supermarket, the latest models of US air conditioners, fully power-equipped cars, automatic dispensers of candies, soft drinks, and pastries, and also home appliances such as a laundromat and a furnished American-style five-room apartment, captivated almost every person coming in.[40]

As the *New York Times* recalled, Party officials touring *Supermarket USA* with their Soviet comrades were reportedly 'visibly embarrassed.'[41] It was a revolution for the average Yugoslav consumer accustomed to rationing and shortages. Every hundredth visitor received a bag to be filled with free food. Female students, hired from the Zagreb University, acted as shoppers and cashiers. Young students, modelling the unknown self-service system, pushed carts around the store, often borrowing a baby from a mother in the crowd and surrounding the child with packages of processed foods. For a regime that struggled with cyclical famines and domestic shortages, *Supermarket USA* introduced a challenging industrial model of food production and distribution. It was, for Shane Hamilton, 'a demonstration of the systemic nature of American supermarketing and an exercise in techno-politics' that used 'technology as an instrument of power.'[42] The executives working on the exhibit anticipated an expansion of American economic hegemony in Eastern Europe generally, and Yugoslavia in particular. Steplock, the economic consultant, underlined how 'the changes in the Yugoslav economy over the last few years have been very substantial. The desire of the Yugoslavs to learn and improve their economy holds forth the promise of increased mutually advantageous trade.'[43] American food-processing corporations – including Armour, Campbell Soup, Kraft, Minute Maid, Pillsbury, Sunkist, and Wesson Oil – donated equipment and supplies, hoping to establish prosperous economic relations. The success was complete: the United States sold most of the supermarket retailing and food-processing machinery, from refrigerated cabinets and industrial freezers, to meat-wrapping machines, can and jar-making machinery, and other packaging machines.[44]

USIA's goal was soon achieved: the first American-style supermarket opened in Belgrade in April 1958, using a model bought at the fair by the *Vračar* enterprise; it was just the beginning, as similar supermarkets boomed unstoppably in the 1960s.[45] The American Embassy praised Belgrade's first self-service store; it offered the 'most varied foodstuffs and kitchen supplies, including frozen meat, fruit, and vegetables,' and was equipped with refrigerators, cash registers, display stands, and purchase trolleys, already used for the exhibition. The opening day attracted large lines of visitors deeply impressed 'by the huge quantities of packaged foodstuffs [...] in such cute and hygienic wrappings.' Ambassador Karl Rankin and Yugoslav ICA director Lloyd Larson attended the event. Larson applauded the new 'extraordinary progress' of Yugoslav food distribution, while the enterprise director, Milorad Jovanović, acknowledged his gratitude to the experts Rolin Moon and John Gallop who, funded by the US Department of Agriculture and the Colonial Stores Company, helped him get the store up and running.[46] Even though, in years to come, Yugoslav consumers adopted an American-style variant of supermarkets all over the country, and partially enjoyed the feeling of free (if limited) commodity choice, these Yugoslav supermarkets were American only in the sense that they sold branded goods at a central location. As Patrick Patterson suggests, the Yugoslav supermarkets remained small, sold only a limited range of groceries generally manufactured in Eastern Europe, and combined American self-service shopping with more personalized forms of retailing, such as open-air markets (*pijacas*).[47]

Selling the American market economy

'American industrial strength supports your freedom,' argued USIA policymakers in 1956.[48] Indeed, this agenda alleged that overall US exhibits displayed had a 'psychological impact on the audience.'[49] In 1960, USIS displayed *Marketing and Services in Industrial Economies*, attended by 1.2 million Yugoslavs (of 1.4 million total visitors), attracting 124 US companies and eighty-four exhibitors on an 8,483 m² pavilion. The fair, opened by Marshal Tito and other prominent government members such as Edvard Kardelj, Vladimir Bakarić, Ivan Gošnjak, Milentije Popović, and Zagreb's mayor Većeslav Holjevac, hosted foreign diplomats and George Allen, former ambassador to Yugoslavia and USIA director. After the entrance gate exposing (displaying) the President's message and poster, the exhibit consisted of photomurals of drugstores in America. The car section displayed the Corvair, the Falcon, the Lark, and the Valiant, while Shopping Centres USA displayed a community mall in America. The Space Exploration complex, where two satellite models, Pioneer V and Tyros I, portraying a 'man in space,' stood next to the 'Fashion' and 'Ampex Video Tape' sections. The 'Kitchen' sector shone as the star of the exhibit: three kitchens, one from the 1920s, one from the 1960s, and one from the future, featured design and technology that would simplify a housewife's chores. As for the US exhibit in Sokolniki Park, 'the kitchen of the future proved to be about the biggest attraction.'[50]

In 1961, the US pavilion presented *Productivity – The Key to Abundance*, a story of productivity and the worker, revolving around how technology could enhance the value of individuals, their work, safety, training, skills, education, and new job opportunities, to help them acquire and enjoy a higher standard of living.[51] Though it failed to attract the crowds of *Supermarket USA*, the Aeromobile 200–2, a ground-effect vehicle travelling on a cushion of air a few inches above the ground, developed by an Illinois country doctor, brought the pavilion the highest number of visitors. The machine, emphasized the exhibition, was an example 'of what individual initiative and genius, combined with the assistance of big business and government, can produce.' Some fifteen American companies donated parts for the machine, which was displayed as sufficiently well advanced to merit public presentation – in other words, a 'result of America's free enterprise spirit and technological opportunities.'[52] 'As the individual worker produces more,' reminded President Kennedy's inscription, 'his added contribution is reflected in greater material rewards and opportunities to cultivate a more meaningful life.'[53] US productivity growth meant, concisely, more jobs and higher living standards, increasing investments, and, finally, more welfare policies for the needy.

Months later, in spring 1962, the US pavilion hosted *Transportation USA*, a USIA exhibit arriving from the Soviet Union to the Belgrade Technical Fair, moving then to the Ljubljana International Electronics Fair in October 1962. Established in 1957, and highlighting US participation from 1960 on, the International Technical Fair in Belgrade on industrial equipment and engineering was Zagreb's strong rival, and the second Yugoslav fair in terms of status, with high commercial revenues. The event, held in high regard by USIS and the Embassy, drew mass audiences from the central and southern parts of the country. 'Workers and children, particularly those from rural areas,' otherwise difficult to reach by conventional media, but also 'key governmental officials, industrial bureaucrats, and the military,' flooded the fair, giving USIS a unique opportunity for new contacts.[54] Designed by George Nelson, *Transportation USA* was the second exhibition to travel to the Soviet Union. It featured a Cessna Skyhawk airplane, a Ford Thunderbird hardtop car, a four-metre model of a Boeing 707 passenger aircraft, and a scale model of a concept car on a circular track, with obvious focus 'on the range of choice available to the American traveller.'[55] USIS Belgrade ordered additional items, such as a Mack twenty-five-ton Dumpster, a caterpillar Traxcavator, a Desert Rat remote area vehicle, a Dodge pickup with a camper body, and an International Harvester Scout, displayed in 600 metres of outdoor space. The 1,200 m² of interior space displayed photographic panels, models, and mock-ups, a Ford station wagon, a Lincoln Continental, a Plymouth Coronado, an airstream trailer, a US rubber storage tank, a model of the Pan American terminal building in New York, and Tele-register, a model of automatic equipment for airline reservations. Mercury-Atlas 6, the first human spaceflight conducted by NASA in February 1962 by US astronaut John Glenn, and first to orbit the Earth, shined at the Belgrade show, and drew a major response. USIS projected three films on the flight and the rocket belt and distributed over 200,000 pamphlets.[56] PAO Roberts recalled about Tito coming to that fair: '[He] was very interested. I remember the capsule in which Glenn, later

Senator Glenn, circled the Earth; [...] I remember I showed it to Tito [who] said "Well, I'd have to lose a lot of weight to get into it."[57]

Concurrently with the Belgrade show, USIS organized *Constructive Use of Leisure Time* in Zagreb. That 1962 edition was an unparalleled hit, gathering thirty-seven countries from four continents, including nine African countries, and 1.6 million attendees. Ministers of commerce and industry from Italy, Norway, Poland, and Britain came, along with Soviet cosmonaut Gherman Stepanovich Titov. More than thirty important Yugoslav Party leaders attended the event. USIS chose the theme of 'mass appeal,' 'first class in every way,' improving 'the prestige of the United States,' not too narrow nor too specialized but 'representative of [...] the American way of life.' The 'Creative Home' portrayed Americans artistically enjoying their free time, in recreation rooms, with photo equipment, and paint spray cans; 'Outdoor Living and Recreation' exposed an A-frame ski lodge, a summer cottage, a plastic swimming pool, scuba diving equipment, archery equipment, and an American-made camp trailer; while 'Constructive Use of Leisure Time by Women' revealed sophisticated clothes and home beauty aids, mostly loved by American women. The Mercury capsule, although off topic, proved extremely popular, as did the space race generally. *Plastics USA*, the first US exhibition in the Soviet Union in 1961, found a place at the 1962 Zagreb Fair. Focused on the products in industry rather than the industry itself, the exhibition emphasized 'the variety and adaptability of plastics for use in automotive design, medicine, clothing, home furnishings, and houseware.'[58] Yet, USIS was misinterpreted; although intended to communicate that Americans work hard but still invest in their leisure time, visitors' feedback, reported the Consulate, was basically that 'Americans are very rich people with a great deal of spare time that they use for sports, arts, and crafts.' The Yugoslavs were getting accustomed to more sophisticated messages: 'they are no longer impressed by displays of consumer goods and luxury items'; and, USIS decided, 'our message should be more for the "eye" than for the "ear,"' with a major emphasis on sophisticated technologies.[59]

Intensive Farming: A Story of American Food from Field to Table, 1964, was a response to such a setback. Managed by Fritz Berliner and designed by Peter Muller from Munk Associates of New York, *Intensive Farming* recounted a technologically advanced history of the American agricultural triumph over nature. President Johnson's message stood sound and sophisticated: 'The toil of man to feed his kind is the struggle that unites all people. I know the sacrifices involved. I grew up on a farm. I return there whenever time permits, to the land, where human solidarity is a necessity and where progress through work of mind and body is hard to win.' The message was clear and effective: 'Eighty years ago, eighty percent of American labour farmed the fields to feed our forebears. Today in America less than eight percent suffice to feed all of us and more. If we, together, are to win our war on poverty, to win a world free of hunger, we must share our know-how.' County agents, irrigation, pesticides, egg production, automatic milking, hot feeding, grain, seeds, and feed equipment, rural electrification, milk processing, apple cutting, and chips production, were the highlights of the exhibition. Intensive farming meant 'a nearly constant amount of cropland to provide more than enough food for an expanding population […] by means of capital input.'[60] 'U.S. agriculture,' underlined the display, was 'productive because of free enterprise orientation and the government as a service, not a director.' USIS insisted on this point as 'private peasants in Yugoslavia [were] subject to harassment and discrimination in favour of the socialist sector of agriculture.' The exhibit clearly suggested that American technological superiority was an end product of its free institutions, while incentivizing 'the vitality and ingenuity of the individual.'[61] Indeed, Kardelj, who visited the exhibit on 11 September, remained 'very impressed with slides explaining the voluntary relationship between government and individuals.'[62]

USIS gets sophisticated (1967–70)

In 1967, USIA inaugurated four exhibits designed to show leadership groups and the Yugoslav public how a free-enterprise economy met consumer needs: *Modern Management and Marketing* (1967), *Packaging USA* (1968), *Research and Development USA* (1969), and *Industrial Design USA* (1970). *Packaging USA*, held in Zagreb in September 1968, moved afterwards to Budapest the following May, then to Poznan, Poland, in the June, was ultimately modified and updated for the Berlin Industries Fair in September 1969. Focused on packaging design, materials, and production, as well on distribution, marketing, and customer service, *Packaging USA* projected an image of American experts and leadership serving the end consumer. Visitors entered the exhibit over a plate-glass floor through a passageway surrounded by mirrors in which myriads of packages were projected into infinity. Next, forty-eight showcases displayed a variety of American packaging in terms of product protection and preservation, consumer convenience, innovation, and design. The pavilion facilities included a small lounge and library with USIS periodicals and reference materials. Bruce Wills, a former manager at the American Management Association in New York, conducted the exhibit seminars, well attended by Yugoslav managers and merchandisers, giving the opportunity for personal contacts with American packaging specialists and industry executives. *Packaging USA* was the second Zagreb Fair hosting a USIA director, this time Leonard Marks (serving 1965–68) who, accompanied by Ambassador Elbrick and President Tito, toured the exhibition on the opening day. On 12 September, when the fair hosted 'America Day,' the pavilion held a reception for 450 Yugoslav officials, dignitaries, and commercial leaders – an atmosphere light years apart from the incidents and frustrations surrounding the 1955 Atoms for Peace, when refreshments were denied.[63]

The exhibition Research and Development USA was presented for the first time at Zagreb in 1969; after the fair closed it moved to Budapest, then Poznan, and to Bucharest in 1970. The subject was dramatized by the display of an Apollo command space module, famous for having completed a manned flight to the moon, lent to USIA by the Smithsonian Institute, although it featured products, graphics, photos, and texts illustrating the vital role of research and development in response to consumer needs and preferences. President Tito and other Party leaders were among the more

than 800,000 visitors attracted by the Apollo 8 that made the pavilion an 'unprecedented success,' along with 125 leaders who attended the seminars and symposia.

The much-travelled *Industrial Design USA*, reshaped from the Brno International
Fair in Czechoslovakia and the Berlin Industrial Fair, was initially exhibited in the
Soviet Union, then moved to Zagreb, and proceeded on to Bucharest. By including
a wide-ranging array of products from American industry, the exhibition contrasted
older items with contemporary ones to expound on how US industry moved to min-
iaturization, new forms and materials, and mass production. Abbott Labs, American
Instrument Co., Bell Telephone Laboratories, Beckman Instruments, California
Computer, Corning Glass, Cyanamid International, Eaton Yale & Towne, General
Dynamics, General Electric, Parke-Davis Sunen, Uni-Royal, Vendo, and Xerox were
among the most appealing companies on display.[64] Eugene Smith, the American
designer of 'Why Ugliness? Why Not?' curated the exhibition by specific request of
USIA director Frank Shakespeare, personally besought at the Bucharest Industrial
Design exhibit. The seminars hosted leading designers such as Clare MacKichan from
the General Motors Design Studios, Yay Doblin from Unimark International, and
William Katavolos from the Parsons School of Design.[65] The Moon Rock Exhibit,
which arrived in Zagreb after the Belgrade Technical Fair in February 1970, gained
nationwide television coverage.[66] President Nixon nominated Robert Murphy, at the
time director of Corning Glass International and his personal adviser, to open the
gates on 10 September. Murphy was perfect for the assignment and was not new to
Yugoslavia: as a US diplomat, he played a critical role in negotiations between the Allies
and Tito's partisans at the end of World War II; while, in 1954, as Undersecretary of
State for Political Affairs, he helped defuse tensions between Yugoslavia and Italy.[67]

Soft-power commodities in Cold War battlefields?

While the USIA handled Yugoslavia separately from other Eastern European countries in policymaking and the executive agenda, the trade fairs were an exception, as
Yugoslavia recurrently hosted USIA's East European tours. The USIA was deemed
fundamental to shifting Yugoslavia's economic paradigm towards Western practices
like its Eastern neighbours. The American pavilions, very much consumer-care oriented, lectured on free enterprise benefits and explored new commercial routes for
American corporations. Commodity culture had a central place, not only in everyday
life, but in public and political discourse in Yugoslavia. 'Among the strongest individual memories of life under state socialism,' claims Slovenian scholar Breda Luthar,
was 'the lack of desired goods, the "culture of shortages" and the "dictatorship over
needs".'[68] On the political side, things were complicated. At the Seventh LCY Congress
of 1958, the Party decisively affirmed that, in the worldwide economic struggle of
socialism against capitalism, socialism 'had to win.' But the Congress concluded by
endorsing a rather 'capitalist' statement: the Yugoslav socialist goal, the 'individual
happiness of every man,' aspired to the 'maximum satisfaction of the individual and
collective needs of its citizens,' to 'private ownership [...] over different commodities,'

to an increased standard of living, personal consumption, and work productivity. Consumption, deemed the ideologists, would follow economic development along with increasing social control over trade, supermarkets, and commodity goods. The 1958 Congress, argues Croatian scholar Igor Duda, gave birth to the Yugoslav version of consumerism; only one year after *Supermarket USA* was delivered to the Zagreb Fair, the LCY engaged in the debate over consumer practices, criticized the bourgeois and snob mentalities, tendencies, and acts of the West, criticized Western bourgeois consumerism as an outcome of a snobbish mentality, but praised the rising incomes of Western workers and the increasing efforts put on work productivity.[69] Yugoslavs never stopped arguing about acceptable consumer practices and the immoral embourgeoisement of the working class. US historian, Patrick Patterson, concluded that the Yugoslav compromise around consumerism and Marxist mentality ended up in, what he defined as, the 'Yugoslav dream,' 'modern but modest, rewarding but reasonable.' The Yugoslav variant of consumerism promoted no social differentiation through consumption – at least not explicitly – as in the case of the freewheeling practices of the West. 'This was mass consumption, not massive consumption,' he asserts. The Yugoslav government used the rising standard of living and commodification of culture as a weapon of consent. While inside and outside official power circles a heated debate was going on over the contradictions between Marxist ideology and massive consumption, consumerism remained one of the critical factors that united the Yugoslav multiethnic society during the 'golden' 1960s and 1970s. For Patterson, it was the economic downturn in the 1980s that stripped Yugoslav of legitimacy and fuelled nationalist resentment which, ultimately, led to ethnic conflict and war.[70]

USIA championed and popularized American-style consumerism, both to spread American values while strengthening export trade relations for American business people and corporations. Even though Yugoslav restrictive commercial legislation prevented greater foreign trade relations, due to the lack of foreign currencies and intricate state permission systems (the latter ultimately disappointed American business people and executives), USIA was deemed the first objective and the highest priority.[71] The US pavilions as public spaces of mass culture consumption conditioned appetites and imaginary desires. They embodied the freedom of choice and freedom to choose that ultimately encouraged pro-American attitudes and frames of mind. For both sides, the exhibitions were intended to persuade. USIS cared greatly about the first impact: audiences tended to 'see everything in one day,' the exhibitions needed 'something truly dazzling or exciting' along with good demonstration techniques. Warren Peace, who presented the apple-peeling and coring machine at the 1964 *Intensive Farming*, was 'a showman with a captivating type of humour [who added a] chuckle [...] to an otherwise serious demonstration,' providing 'the illusive bridge that binds the human race together and thus creates [...] a more lasting impact.'[72] Nonetheless, familiar with propaganda, 'most Yugoslavs tend[ed] to be somewhat sceptical of obvious attempts to indoctrinate, and sceptical of slogans, charts, and statistics.' This drove USIS to keep the approach 'subtle and indirect.'[73]

USIS got periodical accusations of being overtly 'propagandistic,'[74] and the pavilion coped with occasional political complaints. In 1960, the fair director, Ivan Baćun, in a visit to *Marketing and Services* with Bogdan Crnobrnja, Deputy Secretary of State, accused three female students serving as demonstrators of treating him with disrespect. The incident escalated when Baćun requested that Consul Edward Montgomery dismiss the employees, while, concurrently, other employed students warned they would leave out of a sense of solidarity. Montgomery insisted on the reallocation of employees and warned about a possible US withdrawal from the fair. Baćun responded that he would contact the UDBA to get the students' names. In the end, the quarrel ended peacefully, and the students kept their jobs.[75] *Transportation USA* encountered another political incident at the Ljubljana International Electronics Fair in October 1962. USIS officer Dejan Kostić kept distributing questionnaires to visitors on relatives in the United States, travel habits and contacts in foreign countries, memberships in US associations, clubs and political parties, including the Communist Party. Yugoslav leaders were alerted, and Marko Nikezić, Undersecretary at the FO, demanded their urgent removal because such behaviour was 'transgressing all proper limits and [...] would not be permitted in the future.'[76]

But, beyond minor incidents, the Zagreb Consulate proudly emphasized how, year by year, the US pavilion was the most visited one. As long as USIA combined impressive architecture, commodity goods and, above all, human contact, in exhibits driven by consumer and commodity-oriented themes, along with sophisticated displays, its work was absolved. When, in late 2011, the Museum of Contemporary Art in Zagreb displayed *Socialism and Modernity: Art, Culture and Politics (1950–1974)*, a joint project on the Croatian socialist past, it underlined how Yugoslav society and culture, created in the context of a cultural struggle for hearts and minds, produced its own version of modernity. The distinctiveness of the West framed and conceptualized Yugoslav modernity in the spheres of architecture, urbanism, and home furniture.[77] The US Cold War pavilions publicized that kind of modernity and culture many decades before launching them in Yugoslav public places of both highbrow and mass-consumption culture.

Notes

1 'Family Status Must Improve: It Should Buy More for Itself,' *Life*, 5 May 1947, 32–3; Lizabeth Cohen, *A Consumers' Republic: The Politics of Mass Consumption in Postwar America* (New York: Vintage Books, 2003), 112–16.
2 *Ibid.*, 114–20.
3 Rob Kroes, *If You've Seen One, You've Seen the Mall: Europeans and American Mass Culture* (Urbana; Chicago: University of Illinois Press, 1996), 94–5.
4 The advertisements created economic demand while at the same time conveying imaginary Americas. In this way, they contributed 'to a European repertoire [...] a realm of reverie, filled with iconic heroes, setting standards of physical beauty, of taste, of proper behaviour' (Rob Kroes, 'Imaginary Americas in Europe's Public Place,' in *The Americanization of Europe: Culture, Diplomacy, and Anti-Americanism After 1945*, ed. A Stephan [New York; Oxford: Berghahn Books, 2007], 347). For an

interesting insight, see Beatriz Colomina, Ann Marie Brennan, and Jeannie Kim, eds, *Cold War Hothouses: Inventing Postwar Culture, from Cockpit to Playboy* (New York: Princeton Architectural Press, 2004).

5 Robert H. Haddow, *Pavilions of Plenty: Exhibiting American Culture Abroad in the 1950s* (Washington, DC: Smithsonian, 1997); for additional research, see Andrew J. Wulf, *US International Exhibitions during the Cold War: Winning Hearts and Minds through Cultural Diplomacy* (Lanham, MD: Rowman & Littlefield Publishers, 2015); Jack Masey and Conway L. Morgan, *Cold War Confrontations: US Exhibitions and Their Role in the Cultural Cold War* (Baden, Switzerland: Lars Müller Publishers, 2008); Greg Castillo, *Cold War on the Home Front: The Soft Power of Midcentury Design* (Minneapolis: University of Minnesota Press, 2010).

6 Tvrtko Jakovina, 'Narodni kapitalizam protiv narodnih demokracija. Američki super-market na Zagrebačkom velesajmu 1957. godine,' in *Zbornik Mire Kolar Dimitrijević*, ed. Damir Agičić (Zagreb: FF Press, 2003), 478.

7 Masey and Morgan, *Cold War Confrontations*, 15.

8 Study of USIA Operating Assumptions, December 1954, S-27-54, Box 6, Special Reports 1953–97, USIA Office of Research, RG 306, NACP.

9 Functions and Responsibilities and Recommended Organization for the ICS, 1 August 1973, Box 4, Records Relating to Culture Centers 1946–88, USIA Library Program Division, RG 306, NACP, 32–4; Special International Exhibition 7th Annual Report, 1 July 1968–30 June 1969, Box 13, USIA Director's Subject Files 1968–72, RG 306, NACP, 3–4.

10 Hummel to Arnot, 29 February 1952, 511.00/2–2952, Box 2244, CDF 1950–54, RG 59, NACP.

11 O'Connor to Thompson Jr, 2 March 1956, 511.00/8–1855, Box 2071, CDF 1955–59, RG 59, NACP, 3–4.

12 Titus to some IOP officers, 20 September 1954, 511.00/9–2054, Box 2250, CDF 1950–54, RG 59, NACP.

13 The Impact of the US Trade Fair Program, 25 April 1956, PMS-3, Box 13, USIA Subject Files 1953–67, RG 306, NACP.

14 Masey and Morgan, *Cold War Confrontations*, 11.

15 Despatch 566 Belgrade to Dept. of State, 29 May 1950, 868.191-ZA/5-2950, Box 5340, CDF 1950–54, RG 59, NACP.

16 Despatch 566 Belgrade to Dept. of State, 29 May 1950, 868.191-ZA/5-2950; despatch 172 Belgrade to Dept. of State, 9 September 1950, 868.191-ZA/9–950; and despatch 353 Belgrade to Dept. of State, 17 November 1950, 868.191-ZA/11–1750, Box 5340, CDF 1950–54, RG 59, NACP.

17 Despatch 145 Consulate Zagreb to Dept. of State, 12 April 1951, 868.191-ZA/4–1251, Box 5340, CDF 1950–54, RG 59, NACP.

18 Despatch 257 Belgrade to Dept. of State, 10 October 1952, 868.191-ZA/10–1052; despatch 746 Belgrade to Dept. of State, 18 March 1953, 868.191/3–1853; and despatch 49 Consulate Zagreb to Dept. of State, 14 August 1953, 868.191 ZA/8–1453, in Box 5340, CDF 1950–54, RG 59, NACP.

19 Report on the Atoms-for-Peace Exhibit, in despatch 006542 USIS Belgrade to USIA Washington, 15 December 1955, Box 21, Country Project Correspondence 1952–63, USIA Office of Research, RG 306, NACP.

20 Press Release, 'Atoms for Peace' Speech, 8 December 1953, DDE's Papers as

President, Speech Series, Box 5, United Nations Speech 8 December 1953 [pdf], 11 October 2019, www.dwightdeisenhower.com/DocumentCenter/View/2276/ Press-Release-Atoms-for-Peace-Speech-December-8-1953-PDF?bidId=.

21 John Krige, 'Atoms for Peace, Scientific Internationalism, and Scientific Intelligence,' *Osiris* 21, no. 1 Global Power Knowledge. Science and Technology in International Affairs (2006): 162; for major details, see Osgood, *Total Cold War*.

22 Krige, 'Atoms for Peace, Scientific Internationalism, and Scientific Intelligence,' 164–5, 174–8; for contemporary comments and scientists' feedback look at 'UN Conference on Atomic Energy, Geneva August 8–20, 1955,' *Bulletin of the Atomic Scientists* 11, no. 8 (1955): 274–313.

23 Message 122 USIA-State to Belgrade, 31 March 1955, 868.191/3–3155, Box 4841, CDF 1955–59, RG 59, NACP.

24 Report on the Atoms-for-Peace exhibit, 15 December 1955, 1, 5.

25 Report on the Atoms-for-Peace exhibit, 15 December 1955, 9, 15–16.

26 'Atomi za mir,' *Privredni Vjesnik*, 2 September 1955, 3; 'Atomi u službi čovječanstva,' *Glas Istre*, 14 October 1955, 3–4; *Naš Vjesnik*, 28 October 1955.

27 Despatch 453 Embassy Belgrade to Dept. of State, 6 March 1956, 868.1901/3–656; and despatch 654 Embassy Belgrade to Dept. of State, 4 June 1957, 868.1901/6–457, in Box 4841, CDF 1955–59, RG 59, NACP. For the US–Yugoslav negotiations look into Carla Konta, 'Yugoslav Nuclear Diplomacy Between the Soviet Union and the United States, 1950–1965,' *Cahier Du Monde Russe* 60, no. 3–4 (2020): forthcoming.

28 Hickok to Harris and Wilson, 1 October 1964, Box 21, Records Relating to International Trade Fairs 1951–66, USIA ICS/Exhibits Division, RG 306, NACP.

29 Telegram 49 Consul Zagreb to Secretary of State, 3 March 1967, CUL 4 US-YUGO, Box 335, CFPF 1967–69, RG 59, NACP.

30 Despatch 93 USIS Belgrade to USIA Washington, 1 July 1960, 868.191-ZA/7–160, Box 2705, CDF 1960–63, RG 59, NACP.

31 Hixon, *Parting the Curtain: Propaganda, Culture, and the Cold War, 1945–1961*, 185.

32 Castillo, *Cold War on the Home Front: The Soft Power of Midcentury Design*, xii.

33 Hixon, *Parting the Curtain*, 174.

34 Elaine T. May, *Homeward Bound: American Families in the Cold War Era*, revised ed. (New York: Basic Books, 2008), 10–14. For a challenging transatlantic perspective on the debate and its social and political implications, see Ruth Oldenziel and Karin Zachmann, *Cold War Kitchen: Americanization, Technology, and European Users* (Cambridge, MA: MIT Press, 2009), https://books.google.hr/ books?id=9dDgAAAAMAAJ.

35 Castillo, *Cold War on the Home Front*, xi.

36 Nada Apsen. Interview by author. Oral interview. Zagreb, Croatia, 31 May 2014.

37 *Supermarket USA* was not the first attempt to transform European food retailing. Beginning in 1953, a travelling Modern Food Commerce exhibit, funded by the Marshall Plan, introduced the basics of supermarkets to business people and consumers in France, Belgium, Holland, Denmark, and West Germany (Shane Hamilton, 'Supermarket USA Confronts State Socialism: Airlifting the Technopolitics of Industrial Food Distribution into Cold War Yugoslavia,' in *Cold War Kitchen: Americanization, Technology, and European Users*, ed. Ruth Oldenziel and Karin Zachmann [Cambridge, MA: MIT Press, 2011], 137–59).

38 'US Supermarket in Yugoslavia,' *New York Times*, 22 September 1957; see also *Vjesnik*, issues 6, 8, 19 September 1957.
39 'Typical American Supermarket Is the Hit of Fair in Yugoslavia,' *New York Times*, 8 September 1957.
40 'US Supermarket in Yugoslavia'; Jakovina, 'Narodni kapitalizam protiv narodnih demokracija,' 472–3.
41 'US Supermarket in Yugoslavia.'
42 Hamilton, 'Supermarket USA Confronts State Socialism,' 140, 143.
43 Telegram 761 Embassy Belgrade to Secretary of State, 3 September 1957, 868.191/ 9–357, Box 4841, CDF 1955–59, RG 59, NACP.
44 Hamilton, 'Supermarket USA Confronts State Socialism,' 152–3.
45 Vučetić, *Koka-kola socijalizam*, 367.
46 Despatch 656 USIS Belgrade to Dept. of State, 27 June 1958, 511.688/6–2758, Box 2204, CDF 1955–1959, RG 59, NACP.
47 Patrick H. Patterson, 'Making Markets Marxist? The East European Grocery Store from Rationing to Rationality to Rationalizations,' in *Food Chains: From Farmyard to Shopping Cart*, ed. Warren Belasco and Roger Horowitz (Philadelphia: University of Pennsylvania Press, 2010), 196–216.
48 Hickok to Dennis, 3 February 1956, Box 38, USIA Master Budget Files 1953–64, RG 306, NACP.
49 Hickok to Harris and Wilson, 1 October 1964.
50 Despatch 25 Zagreb to Dept. of State, 25 November 1960, 868.191-ZA/11–2560, Box 2705, CDF 1960–63, RG 59, NACP.
51 Draft Planning Paper, 21 March 1961, Box 5, Records Relating to International Trade Fairs 1951–66, USIA ICS/Exhibits Division, RG 306, NACP; despatch 411 Zagreb to Dept. of State, 27 December 1960, 868.191-ZA/12–2760, Box 2705, CDF 1960–63, RG 59, NACP.
52 Content and Theme of US Exhibition, 26 June 1961, Box 5, Records Relating to International Trade Fairs 1951–66, USIA ICS/Exhibits Division, RG 306, NACP; despatch 22 Zagreb to Dept. of State, 4 October 1961, 868.191-ZA/10–461, Box 2705, CDF 1960–63, RG 59, NACP.
53 Despatch 26 Consulate Zagreb to Dept. of State, 30 October 1961, 868.191-ZA/ ID-3061, Box 2705, CDF 1960–63, RG 59, NACP, 19.
54 Despatch 80 Consulate Zagreb to Dept. of State, 2 February 1960, 868.191/2–260, and despatch 26 Consulate Zagreb to Dept. of State, 15 February 1961, 868.191/2–1561, Box 2705, CDF 1960–63, RG 59, NACP.
55 Masey and Morgan, *Cold War Confrontations*, 304.
56 Airgram 270 Embassy Belgrade to Dept. of State, 19 September 1962, 868.191-BE/9–1962, Box 2705, CDF 1960–63, RG 59, NACP.
57 Taplin, 'Walter Roberts: USIS Magazines and Exhibits in Yugoslavia.'
58 Airgram 33 Consulate Zagreb to Dept. of State, 29 October 1962, 868.191-ZA/1–1663, Box 2706, and Airgram 251 Embassy Belgrade to Dept. of State, 29 December 1961, 868.191-ZA/12–2961, Box 2705, in CDF 1960–63, RG 59, NACP.
59 Airgram 717 Embassy Belgrade to Dept. of State, 16 January 1963, 868.191-ZA/ 1–1663, Box 2706, CDF 1960–63, RG 59, NACP.
60 Production Script for Intensive Farming Exhibit, 1964, Box 21, Records Relating to International Trade Fairs 1951–66, USIA ICS/Exhibits Division, RG 306, NACP.

61 Airgram 8549 Dept. of State to Belgrade, 25 February 1964, TP 8–1 YUGO (ZA), Box 21, Records Relating to International Trade Fairs 1951–66, USIA ICS/Exhibits Division, RG 306, NACP.

62 Clarke to USIA, State, Agriculture, Commerce, Labor and others, 25 March 1964; Telegram 55 Belgrade to Secretary of State, 20 March 1964; and Telegram 37 Consulate Zagreb to Secretary of State, 14 September 1964, in Box 21, Records Relating to International Trade Fairs 1951–66, USIA ICS/Exhibits Division, RG 306, NACP.

63 Special International Exhibition, 1 July 1968–30 June 1969, Box 13, USIA Director's Subject Files 1968–72, RG 306, NACP, 7, 35.

64 Special International Exhibition, 1 July 1968–30 June 1969, 15; 'How to build a corporate image and sell in an East European market,' *Business Abroad*, December 1969, in Dunlap to Shakespeare, 17 March 1970, Box 13, USIA Director's Subject Files 1968–72, RG 306, NACP, 18–20.

65 Dunlap to Shakespeare, 3 November 1970; Shakespeare to Dunlop, 23 July 1969; Shakespeare to Kichan, 14 October 1970, in Box 13, USIA Director's Subject Files 1968–72, RG 306, NACP.

66 Jenkins to Shakespeare, 26 January 1970, Box 13, USIA Director's Subject Files 1968–72, RG 306, NACP.

67 Informacije o dolasku Roberta Marfija na otvaranje Zagrebačkog Velesajma, 2 September 1970, 09 542, Box 44, Savjet IVS za odnose s inozemstvom 1967–73, RG 1409, CSA; 'Robert D. Murphy,' US Department of State Archives, http://2001-2009. state.gov/r/pa/ei/rls/stamps/67016.htm.

68 Luthar, 'Shame, Desire and Longing for the West. A Case Study of Consumption,' 341.

69 Igor Duda, 'Konzumerizmom do konzumizma? Potrošačka kultura u Hrvatskoj od 1950-tih do 1980-tih,' in *Potrošačka kultura i konzumerizam*, ed. Snježana Čolić (Zagreb: Institut društvenih znanosti Ivo Pilar, 2013), 85–6; Duda, *Pronađeno blagostanje*, 93–109.

70 Patterson, *Bought and Sold*, 148–96.

71 Despatch 411 Consulate Zagreb to Dept. of State, Dec. 27, 1960, 868.191-ZA/12–2760, Box 2705, CDF 1960–63, RG 59, NACP.

72 Hickok to Harris, 1 October 1964.

73 Airgram 251 Embassy Belgrade to Dept. of State, Dec. 29, 1961, 868.191-ZA/12–2961, Box 2705, CDF 1960–63, RG 59, NACP.

74 'Slabost najjačih,' *Ekonomska politika*, 17 September 1960, 867.

75 Despatch 9 Consulate Zagreb to Dept. of State, 19 September 1960, 868.191-ZA/ 9–1960, Box 2705, CDF 1960–63, RG 59, NACP.

76 Airgram 495 Embassy Belgrade to Dept. of State, 17 November 1962, 868.191-LJ/ 11–1762, Box 2705, CDF 1960–63, RG 59, NACP.

77 Ljiljana Kolešnik, ed., *Socijalizam i modernost: umjetnost, kultura, politika 1950-1974.* (Zagreb: Institut za povijest umjetnosti, 2012).

4

Art and sound diplomacy

All of Yugoslavia is singing today. [...] The Communist officials, the man in the street, the students, all are singing the songs of George Gershwin and the praises of the cast of the folk opera, 'Porgy and Bess,' which left this truly heartbroken country this morning.[1]

During the Yugoslav tour, the Nikolais group performed before enthusiastic capacity audiences [...]. The acclaim the group received in Skopje, Sarajevo, and Ljubljana was almost as great as in Belgrade. Certainly, not all people could appreciate what to many was rather new, revolutionary theatre, but this did not affect the enthusiasm they displayed in receiving it. Yugoslav audiences are grateful for the opportunity to see what is new, experimental or avant-garde and there is no question that they look primarily to the United States for this.

American Embassy Belgrade on the Alvin Nikolais
Dance Company tour in 1968[2]

On 27 July 1954, President Eisenhower asked Congress for five million dollars of additional funds 'to assist and encourage private musical, dramatic and other cultural groups' in tours abroad.[3] The President's Special International Program for Cultural Presentation – or, more simply, the President's Fund – was the forerunner of the Cultural Presentation Program (CPP), officially enacted in August 1956 and administered by the State Department through the Bureau of Educational and Cultural Affairs (CU). The purpose was to 'strengthen the ties which unite us with other nations by demonstrating the cultural interests, developments, and achievements of the people of the United States,' and to assist 'in the development of friendly, sympathetic and peaceful relations [with] other countries.'[4] In private correspondence, President Eisenhower reiterated that music was 'a psychological tool' able to 'counteract the stereotypical perception of Americans as "bombastic, jingoistic, and totally devoted to the theories of force and power",' while Elmer Staats, executive officer at the National Security Council (NSC), called it 'a secret weapon.'[5]

The program was amended in January 1961 by the Mutual Educational and Cultural Exchange Act, to a) 'provide tours in countries abroad by creative and performing artists and athletes from the United States, individually and in groups, representing any field of the arts, sports, or any other form of cultural attainment'; and b) represent the United States at 'international artistic, dramatic, musical, sports [...] and other cultural festivals, competitions, meetings, like exhibitions and assemblies.'[6] Supervised by the Secretary of State, the Cultural Presentation Program was jointly administered by USIA and State Department committees which handled and promoted performances abroad. Its main objective, to exploit US cultural prestige in the world and dismantle the prejudice of racial inequality in America, like Soviet propaganda suggested, coped with artists' personal motivations, usually looking for personal success, and race or gender equality. Scholars working on public or cultural diplomacy more broadly usually focused on specific musicians, genres, or groups. Penny Von Eschen studied Louis Armstrong, Dizzy Gillespie, and Duke Ellington's impact abroad;[7] Lisa Davenport and Ingrid Monson explored the value of jazz calling out the civil rights agenda in front of audiences worldwide;[8] while Clare Croft and Danielle Fossler-Lussier concentrated, respectively, on the consequences of using dancers and musicians to make political statements about American foreign and domestic policies.[9] This chapter investigates how the CPP linked American private artists sponsored by the CU, the Embassy, and USIS, with Yugoslav art directors, music commentators, journalists, and audiences, to encompass medium- and long-term psychological effects, particularly through enhancing artistic freedom and creativity.

The influence of American popular music – mainly jazz and rock 'n' roll – on Yugoslav pop culture has been addressed in many appreciated historical analyses over the last two decades. Most of them were determined to understand the hybridization process that occurred in Yugoslav popular music between American, British, and Italian traditions and the local folklore.[10] The Yugoslav leaders, Tito and Kardelj, personally engaged in lively debates about jazz and rock music. Tito was sensitive to 'rock's potential for rebelliousness,' and therefore hoped that by applying a policy of tolerance he would win the rock scene over 'to a supportive stance.' As Sabrina Ramet put it, 'His gamble paid off, and the 1960s, in particular, saw a rush of panegyric rock ballads praising him and his program of self-management.'[11]

The US State Department expanded the CPP to support American classical soloists, choirs and orchestras, drama, theatre and ballet groups, jazz and rock artists, as well as experimental performers on tour, to affirm the US leadership in classical music and vanguard artistic experimentation, and consequently to dismantle prejudices about the United States' supposed cultural backwardness. Its final goal was to inspire freedom of expression in a communist regime and disseminate heterodox ideas of art unconventionality by linking the Yugoslav cultural scene to the Western one. As a branch of USIA, Voice of America publicized the CPP and spread American music to every corner of Yugoslavia. US artistic performances abroad possessed 'mass appeal in their ability to transport an audience into a variety of emotional states,'[12] and created communication spaces between the performers and the gathered public. As Croft discovered, these events, crafted by the US government with its private partners, were 'to be simultaneously propaganda,' but also 'something more than propaganda.'[13]

From classic style to classy performances[14]

Eisenhower charged the American National Theatre and Academy (ANTA) with organizing the CPP. Congress established this New York-based institution in 1935 to serve as the United States' national theatre company. While the State Department arranged the finance and travel logistics, ANTA chose the music, dance, and theatre performers. According to Emily Ansari, the Music Advisory Panel 'was responsible for around 65 percent of the tours ANTA organized and a sizeable proportion of its $2.5 million budget.' Despite major historiographical interest in jazz musicians abroad, most of the US sponsored performers were neither jazz nor rock performers. Ansari's analysis demonstrates that, between 1954 and 1963, classical musicians accounted for 83 per cent of all performances abroad; jazz ensembles never made up more than a third of the groups approved.[15] The Music Advisory Panel, composed of more traditional musicologists and composers, discouraged jazz and folk music because there were 'no standards by which to judge "light music" except "charm," and charm is hard to judge, and it is not international in its acceptance.'[16] The choice of classical music certainly derived from its social prestige among the European cultural elites. Finally, what mattered most, argues Fosler-Lussier, was not only the music but its significance, since 'classical music and its avant-garde offshoot was part of a symbolic system in which the association with European elite culture was important to the value of music.'[17]

The Dubrovnik Festival, the Split Summer Festival (founded in 1954), and the Music Biennale Zagreb (founded in 1961) became major channels for US classical performers. USIS was there to organize, manage, finance, and give press support.[18] Between May and June 1955, Eleanor Steber, Metropolitan Opera soprano, performed in Zagreb, Belgrade, and Osijek, making an 'extraordinary effective work.'[19] It was one of the first high-class performances financed by the President's Fund.[20] The *New York Times* reported, 'she let her temperament show a bit' when she refused to sing *Madame Butterfly* at Belgrade's Theatre because 'they didn't have an obi [a Japanese sash]'; she then switched to *Tosca*, but nevertheless received 'critical acclaim,' 'made friends there,' and returned to Yugoslavia in August to sing Mozart's *Idomeneo* at the Dubrovnik Summer Festival.[21] Ruggiero Ricci, a prominent American violinist of Italian descent, prolonged his private European tour to perform in Ljubljana, Zagreb, Sarajevo, and Belgrade in February 1956 under the same fund.[22] Thanks to CCP sponsorship, the Zagreb Philharmonic featured renowned US classical artists in the 1960s; conductors such as Leopold Stokowski, Igor Stravinsky, Robert Kraft, and Zubin Mehta; pianists like Alexandar Brailowsky, Alexandar Uninsky, Shura Cherkasky, Byron Janis, and Jakob Lateiner, who, all except Janis, were East European immigrants; the African American André Watts, who had won over the world with his rhapsodic skills; violinists such as the legendary prodigy Roman Totenberg; and sopranos like African American opera star Martina Arroyo.[23]

In 1963, Josip Depolo, director of the Dubrovnik Summer Festival, spent three months in the United States under the FLP. After he returned, a boom of US cultural protagonists occurred in Dubrovnik.[24] Between 1966 and 1969, many US cultural elites attended the festival program: Curtis Davis, from the National Educational Television, Mark Schubart, from the Lincoln Center New York, and Samuel Rubin. During those years, Depolo enjoyed the visits and promotion of great US musical critics and editorialists: Paul Affelder, who served *Musical America*, *Opera News*, *Metropolitan Opera*, and the *National Observer*; Mort Gerberg and Mary Leatherbee from *Life*; Stabley Karnow from the *Washington Post*; Christopher Bird from *The Times*; Claire Sterling from *Harper's Magazine*; Jan Maguire from the *New York Herald Tribune*; and many more.[25] The CU co-financed the US artists performing on Dubrovnik stages, USIS Zagreb organized their arrival and stay, while the US Consul in Zagreb picked the names in accordance with festival authorities.[26] Cherkasky, Janis, Watts, and Mehta performed at the Dubrovnik Festival during the 1960s. Martina Arroyo featured in the Dubrovnik Summer Festival in 1961, 1962, 1964, and 1969. By 1971, the festival involved the elegant performances of John Browning, 'a great talent among young American pianists,'[27] and Van Cliburn, who achieved worldwide recognition in 1958, at the tender age of twenty-three, by winning the first quadrennial International Tchaikovsky Piano Competition in Moscow. The Russian-born pianist Alexandar Zakin, best known for being the accompanist of violinist Isaac Stern, performed at the festival as well. Dubrovnik hosted African American sopranos Mattiwilda Dobbs and Felicia Weathers, together with the Metropolitan Opera diva Blanche Thebom.[28]

American choirs, symphony orchestras, and glee clubs performed both on the Dubrovnik stage and the Music Biennale Zagreb, as well as in Belgrade and Ljubljana. In 1954, the Smith College Chamber Singers debuted in Dubrovnik and returned in 1958; in the same year, it was the turn of the Hora Smith College Chorus. The Minneapolis Symphony Orchestra played at the National Theatre in Zagreb in 1957, the same year that the Westminster Choir staged there.[29] The Robert Shaw Chorale performed in Zagreb, Belgrade, Sarajevo, and Skopje in October 1962, under the President's sponsorship, showing, according to PAO Roberts, 'a degree of precision and technical competence [...] unmatched by any other chorus; the artistry of Shaw himself as conductor was also given equally high praise.' The state–private network functioned for the CPP as it did for the cultural exchanges; acclaimed US musicians, touring Europe privately, were solicited by the State Department to prolong their stay and give performances in non-profitable countries. While on a private tour in Western Europe in 1963, the Yale Glee Club was invited to Yugoslavia (the Embassy's Press and Cultural Service covering expenses), and on 29 June they provided 'one of the most heart-warming performances we have ever witnessed in Belgrade.'[30] Between September and October 1964, USIS Belgrade arranged the American Festival of Music, and on 23 September Arthur Rubinstein captivated audiences at the Belgrade Trade Union Hall. PAO Roberts organized Rubinstein's flight from Bucharest by the US Air Force. His unexpected concert (it was arranged at the very last moment) was quickly sold out, and the involvement of Yugoslav TV, radio, and advertising turned out to be beyond all expectation. 'He performed magnificently and evoked great enthusiasm from the audience,' recalled Belgrade's *Politika*. The next day was the turn of Ruggiero Ricci who gave a private performance organized by Yugokoncert in an all-Chopin show. The New York Pro Musica choral, a vocal and instrumental ensemble specializing in medieval and Renaissance music, which performed at the 1963 Dubrovnik Festival, played in Belgrade and Zagreb between 27 and 30 September 1964; while the Pittsburgh Symphony Orchestra starred in Belgrade in early October. For PAO Roberts, it was the victory of USIS efficiency and capacity in the field.[31] In autumn 1967, CU sponsored the Los Angeles Symphony to visit Eastern Europe: they performed in Yugoslavia, Czechoslovakia, Romania, Turkey, Iran, Lebanon, and India, accompanied by André Watts and Zubin Mehta.[32] Outstanding US orchestras and choruses graced the Dubrovnik stages, especially in the mid and late 1960s. The festival starred the Cincinnati Symphony Orchestra, the Beaux Arts Trio, and the Sarah Lawrence Chorus in 1966 and 1968, the Harvard Glee Club – Radcliffe Choral Society in 1967, the Bach Aria Group in 1968, and the Amherst College Glee Club in 1969.[33] In 1970, the elite New York Chamber Soloists and world-renowned Juilliard Quartet, with the exclusive participation of Ruggiero Ricci and the Duke Ellington Orchestra, performed at the Dubrovnik Festival.[34] In 1971, the CU subsidized the University of California Chamber Singers, 'a very effective' student-singers group, to sing in Budapest, Belgrade, and Dubrovnik, in addition to their tour of other European countries.[35]

The LaSalle String Quartet, American Brass Quintet, and Juilliard Quartet were among the top US performers at the Yugoslav festivals. The LaSalle Quartet, best known for its *Second Viennese School* of Schoenberg, Berg, and Webern, played for the first time at the Dubrovnik Festival in August 1962 under the auspices of *Jugokoncert* and the Embassy. They returned to Belgrade, Zagreb, and Ljubljana in January 1963, this time under USIS sponsorship, where they gave five days of densely scheduled concerts, TV appearances, and workshops. As first violinist Walter Levin reported, 'the Yugoslav musicians [were] eager to learn the [modern] techniques.' For PAO Roberts, the LaSalle Quartet 'broadened the awareness of the excellence of American ensembles in the field of chamber music.' Finally, they performed at the 1965 Music Biennale Zagreb, thanks also to a contribution from the Yugoslav government.[36] The classical Juilliard String Quartet, founded in 1946 at the prestigious Juilliard School in New York, fascinated the Dubrovnik public in both 1964 and 1970. As for the American Brass Quintet, this innovative group – the first quintet to play music originally written for brass, but substituting a bass trombone for the conventional tuba part – starred at the Music Biennale Zagreb in 1966 and 1967.[37]

Concurrently to classical musicians, the State Department invested in an African American drama piece, *Porgy and Bess*, and a vanguard ballet group, to make political statements at cultural events. In December 1954, Gershwin's opera was performed at the Zagreb National Theatre, before moving to Belgrade.[38] This first ANTA tour literally 'welled up in joyous affection,' 'more than twenty curtain calls,' 'hundreds of letters [...] expressing gratitude in crude English and Serbian' and 'regret' for their departure, reported *Borba*.[39] In Belgrade, the members of the company 'surprised the citizens [...] by engaging in a match of "football" with a bunch of local young-sters in the street in front of their hotel.'[40] Written by Du Bose Heyward, George Gershwin, and Ira Gershwin, and debuted in 1935, *Porgy and Bess* told the story of a disabled beggar, his drug-addict girlfriend, her violent ex-boyfriend, and their long-suffering and hard-praying neighbours. With their white authors and African American characters, *Porgy and Bess* became a case study of the way white Americans 'craved stories about African Americans featuring earthy authenticity and unimpeded progress towards racial equality,' and the way African Americans 'had to manoeuvre within the cultural marketplace created by such white desires.' In other words, it was a history of collisions between white fantasy and black pragmatism before, during, and after the civil rights era.[41]

When *Porgy and Bess* came to Yugoslavia, it opened up 'with grace and charm,' 'new perspectives for a communist-led people sensitive to reports of American racial prejudice and exploitation.' To achieve such an impact, the artists entertained 'personal offstage contacts' on the streets, in the clubs, hotels, and private homes. They were invited to Serbian Orthodox saints' day ('slava') celebrations and sang Christmas carols and spirituals at the ambassador's reception.[42] In Zagreb, where the company received curtain calls and a half-hour standing ovation, a leading Yugoslav critic wrote: 'They have not only shown us a new kind of art, but a new world [...] which was unknown to us and more or less distorted through literature, I may say falsified [...]; they have come and have made it possible for us to feel friendship and closeness to a world so far away from us.'[43] While communist propaganda fostered 'the notion that United States culture consists of comic books and gangster motion pictures,' and that African Americans lived under conditions of *Uncle Tom's Cabin*, *Porgy and Bess* countered these stereotypes.[44] As Jack Raymond put it, that play was 'more than money and easier to take than political tracts.'[45]

ANTA supported dance and ballet groups because they spoke universal languages, reached and moved hearts, and undermined Soviet accusations of a lack of US cultural enlightenment. From the late 1950s on, the most eminent US ballet groups and dance performers displayed this kind of soft power on the Yugoslav stages. The Dubrovnik Summer Festival starred the American Ballet Theatre in 1958, the Jerome Robbins' Ballet in 1959, the New York City Ballet in 1965, the Alwin Ailey Dance Theatre in 1968, the American National Theatre of the Deaf in 1969, and the Glen Tetley Dance Company in 1969.[46] USIS reported exultant audiences after Jerome Robbin's play: 'It's you who are the revolutionaries!,' and 'the Russian Ballet is static – you are the country of the future!'[47] The renewed José Limon Company performed at the National Theatre in Zagreb in 1957, while the Martha Graham Company danced there in November 1962. These performances 'opened up new concepts of dance not before seen here,' and were truly admired 'for the tremendous accomplishment in training and disciplining the dancers to such high perfection.'[48]

In September 1968, one of the most groundbreaking US choreographers, Alwin Nikolais, visited Yugoslavia and performed in Belgrade, Skopje, Sarajevo, and Ljubljana (he returned to the Music Biennale Zagreb in 1969 and the Dubrovnik Festival in 1971).[49] Nikolais employed lights, slides, electronic music, and stage props to create environments through which dancers moved and blended. He made use of props, masks, and mobiles with aesthetic as well as functional purposes, and popularized modern multimedia theatre.[50] The Embassy attested to 'enthusiastic capacity audiences' and 'standing ovations.' The event, attended by Živan Berisavljević, Serbian Secretary for Education and Culture, and Belgrade's vice-mayor Milan Vukos, went beyond mere artistic interests: Nikolais was a 'person of such profound and various talents coupled with a modest, warm, genuine personality [that left] [...] a tremendous impression on all who meet him.'[51] During the group's stay in Belgrade, the Yugoslav theatre leaders, with Embassy support, organized several round tables: Nikolais met with Mira Trajlović, Belgrade International Theatre Festival, Atelje 212 director, and FLP grantee in 1962, the opera director Mladen Sabljić, and Belgrade's ballet dancers and actors.[52] Meetings such as this one engaged the US and Yugoslav sides in cross-cultural interactions that effectively used soft power for the purpose of gaining foreign audiences abroad. It was what public and cultural diplomacy were meant to do. In May 1969, the Glen Tetley Ballet Group, whose founder Glen Tetley majestically mixed ballet and modern dance, displayed 'fervid intensity, sinuous non-stop propulsion, and voluptuous physicality' when performing in Yugoslavia.[53]

On the back of State Department sponsorship, these ballet groups displayed innovative techniques in contemporary dance styles. Yet, what measurable effects and goals had the US accomplished by supporting otherwise expensive tours, and psychologically strengthening American prestige in highbrow culture? Were they increasing the appeal of the American dream? How could the State Department capitalize on these artistic performances, and to what extent did they gain obedience or political acquiescence to US foreign policies? Recent historiographical works have pointed to some major rifts in the US Cultural Presentation Program: the preference of classical music over jazz and other styles; the relevance of the selection process; the overcoming of musical diplomacy as a weapon of cultural imperialism and of musicians as its passive actors; the consideration of the spectators' responses; and the ways in which these musical actors were in fact 'performing the nation.'[54] Given the 'ready and enthusiastic audience in the Yugoslav community,' the CPP's final objective was to enable 'us [the Americans] to assure Yugoslavs of our continued interest in maintaining contact with its people through non-political activities.'[55]

Jessica Gienow-Hecht argues that the real importance of these orchestras and soloists performing abroad lies in the fact that they legitimized 'the nation's political influence and boosted its self-confidence to exert leadership abroad.' In her view, these performances were like 'a speech at the United Nations, a banquet at an embassy, or a handshake on the White House lawn.' She demonstrates the shift from pre-World War I symphony orchestras as culturally opened 'places of international encounter,' to post–World War II musical performances acting as 'stages of national self-representation.' The CIA's cultural officer, Thomas Braden, claimed that, in 1952, the Boston Symphony Orchestra 'won more acclaim for the United States in Paris than John Foster Dulles or Dwight Eisenhower could have bought with a hundred speeches.' Moreover, artists performing abroad rarely behaved as planned: by talking to audiences, pitching music and emotions against wars and weapons, they questioned the entire Cold War scenario and 'raised eyebrows across Washington.' Whether hailing from New York, Moscow, or Teheran, the political function of symphony orchestras, ballet, and drama groups abroad was not all in establishing a dialogue, but in displaying leadership and symbolizing the authority behind the orchestra in a foreign environment, while audiences remained quiet and attentive. A state-sponsored guest concert was, according to Gienow-Hecht, a way of saying *adsum* – 'I am present.'[56]

Jazz diplomacy or simply jazz?

'As long as I've been playing,' Miles Davis argued ironically, 'they never say I've done anything. They always say that some white guy did it.'[57] Unlike the classical musicians coming through CU sponsorship, jazz musicians had a stronger personal and political motivation to go abroad. Penny Von Eschen pioneered studies on the role jazz diplomacy played in the cultural Cold War. She explores how US officials, despite their misgivings about jazz, sent leading African American players abroad believing that they could save the tarnished American 'race problem.' By sending Dizzy Gillespie, Louis Armstrong, Duke Ellington, and Randy Weston overseas, Washington's bureaucracy suggested that talent and hard work, rather than skin colour, determined individual success in the United States. Jazz music encouraged individual creativity within established parameters and rendered the music an apt metaphor for liberal democracy. Yet, jazz musicians and US policymakers often spoke different languages. For the musicians the tours represented 'long-overdue recognition from a society that had previously failed to acknowledge' them. They toured, proud of representing the nation and helping the country, with shared patriot commitment for 'the edgy, competitive masculinity of Cold War America' not foreign to jazz culture, for the intrigue of adventure, and for 'the inherently secretive nature of covert action.'

The Gillespie tour began just as the five-month-old Montgomery bus boycott brought unprecedented national and international attention to American racism and the Southern civil rights struggle; therefore, the musicians championed jazz as a model of racial equity that they aspired to achieve, not as a faithful reflection of the freedom and equality offered by US society. While the government officials insisted on the music's universalism and its broadly American roots, African American artists promoted jazz as the creation of the black way of life. As the State Department tried to engender pro-American sympathies among ruling elites abroad, the musicians imposed their own agenda by frequently democratizing the tours, playing impromptu gigs for ordinary citizens, and jamming with local musicians. In 1956, Gillespie refused to play in Karachi, Pakistan, until the gates were opened to the ragamuffin children, while in Ankara he opened the gates declaring he had come to play for all the people.[58] The tour participants often articulated ideas more attuned to pan-African and Third World concerns than to those of US leaders. This inability to maintain a tight focus on national identities and priorities caused the program to be shut down in 1978.[59]

The CU jazz tours followed the Cold War hot spots. The 1956 Dizzy Gillespie tour began in Iran and culminated in Turkey, Yugoslavia, and Greece, with stops in Syria and the US military allies Pakistan and Lebanon. The Gillespie and the Dave Brubeck trip in 1958 moved through the Eisenhower conception of a 'perimeter defence' against the Soviet Union along the Northern Tier extending from Turkey to

Pakistan.[60] Yet, Davenport argues, 'while American jazz musicians who travelled on cultural tours sought to dismantle the structures of American racism,' the 'Russian youth, jazz lovers, and fans sought to surmount the political structures of Soviet Communism.'[61] To what extent does this apply to the Yugoslav case? 'For us to play jazz,' recalled Serbian jazz musician Duško Gojković, 'was a kind of freedom. The [Party] Commissioner could not tell me how to improvise on the trumpet. This was the only thing where I could choose what to play, and this was freedom for us.'[62] Equally, Goran Bregović, the frontman of *Bijelo Dugme* (White Buttons) Yugoslav rock group, once asserted something that worked for both jazz and rock 'n' roll: if we 'can't have any alternative parties or any alternative organized politics,' he claimed, 'there are not too many places where you can gather large groups of people and communicate ideas which are not official.' Jazz or rock 'n' roll, as in this case, was 'one of the most important vehicles for helping people in communist countries to think in a different way.'[63]

As Vučetić recalls, the post-war Yugoslav communist leadership identified jazz with Western decadence. In 1947, Djilas asserted, 'America is our sworn enemy, and jazz, as its product, as well.' However, the abandonment of Stalinism after 1950 gave Yugoslav jazz musicians more freedom to form jazz orchestras and arrange concerts. Despite Tito's softened, but still critical, opinion of jazz ('Jazz for me is not music, it is a racket,' he stated in 1962), in the 1960s the Radio-TV Belgrade Jazz Band played for his birthday celebration, on 25 May, the National Youth Day. During the 1960s, Yugoslav cultural authorities institutionalized jazz music; in 1960 they established the Bled Jazz Festival, while almost every larger town got its jazz orchestra. Such outcomes derived, concurrently, from the fact that, from the late 1950s on, the Yugoslav rulers stopped considering jazz politically dangerous, and from the popularization of jazz through concerts, sponsored privately or by the US government, and Voice of America influence.[64]

From the early 1950s on, jazz music conquered Yugoslav radio and TV, the record industry, and young audiences. Belgrade, Zagreb, and Ljubljana became special destinations for Hungarian, Romanian, Bulgarian, and Albanian jazz fans because they accommodated hundreds of American jazz concerts. The Dizzy Gillespie Orchestra played in Belgrade in 1956, while his quartet performed in late May 1961, and then in 1971, 1981, and 1990. The Glenn Miller Orchestra appeared at the Belgrade Kolarac Hall in April 1957, while the great Satchmo performed in 1959. Ella Fitzgerald sang in 1961 for the first time, and returned in 1971. Duke Ellington was scheduled to perform under CU sponsorship in 1963, but Kennedy's assassination cancelled the concerts. Ellington went to Belgrade's Trade Union Hall in 1970 under the joint sponsorship of the State Department, Belgrade's Bank of Commerce, and Radio-TV Belgrade.[65] Lionel Hampton came twice, in 1971 and 1979, while Casey Anderson was in Yugoslavia in November 1970. The Modern Jazz Quartet played in the Trade Union Hall both in 1960 and 1989. The Oscar Peterson Trio, with Ray Brown and Ed Thipgen, played in Belgrade in 1961 and 1973, and in Ljubljana in 1964. The great Miles Davis participated at the Newport Belgrade Jazz Festival in 1971 and 1973, and again in 1986. Yet most of these players came to Yugoslavia through private arrangements, mostly with the *Jugoslovenska koncertna agencija* (Yugoslav Concert Agency). As USIS specified in 1959, the post was not supposed to bring American musicians to Yugoslavia. Instead, they usually assisted *Jugokoncert* to do so, as in the case of the Louis Armstrong concert in 1959. In 1962, *Pregled* reported that the Jimmy Prat Trio, the Herb Geller Quartet, and John Lewis had participated in the Jazz Bled Festival, but without any US official sponsorship.[66]

From 1954 to 1971, the CU sponsored only four jazz performances in Yugoslavia, American participation at the 1966 Jazz Bled Festival, the folk-blues guitarist Casey Anderson concert in November 1970, and one rock concert from *Blood, Sweat & Tears* in 1971. The first two sponsored jazz bands were the Dizzy Gillespie Orchestra and Glenn Miller Orchestra in 1956 and 1957 respectively.[67] The third was the Woody Herman concert in Belgrade in 1966,[68] the same year that USIS provided a modest dollar honorarium trip to jazz trumpeter Art Farmer, as well as facilitative services to VOA's conductor Willis Conover for their participation at the Bled Festival. It was a good strategy, admitted acting PAO Hugh Sutherland, as Conover 'added his knowledge of jazz to the unofficial program,' 'spent night and day interviewing, being interviewed, listening and talking with Yugoslav and foreign jazz fans,' and discussing future performances of American jazz musicians in Yugoslavia.[69] The fourth CU sponsored tour occurred in late 1968 when the State Department sent the University of Illinois Jazz Band, a twenty-five-man band starring Don Smith and led by John Garvey, to an eight-week tour in Eastern and Western Europe. The band passed through Ljubljana, Zagreb, Belgrade, Novi Sad, Niš, and Skopje between 17 and 30 October. The tour proved successful: they showed 'the vitality, the imagination and talent of young American musicians,' opened to 'direct cooperation with the League of Belgrade University Students,' and advanced the 'objectives of the Embassy's cultural program.' According to Yugoslav newspapers, the Illinois band proved 'the best university band in the United States,' with a fabulous 19 year-old trumpeter that 'the entire Zagreb-Radio Television Orchestra should have gone to hear.'[70] *Blood, Sweat & Tears*, a nine-man band, was the only rock band sent abroad by the State Department for the purpose of bridging 'the generation gap' and identifying with young audiences. Aside from Yugoslavia, *Blood, Sweat & Tears* performed in Romania and Poland. An independent film crew accompanied the group and produced a TV documentary. According to the *New York Times*, the rock group brought 'more than 5000 Yugoslav music fans at a downtown stadium to their feet in roaring approval.'[71]

Although playing a supporting role to the American jazz masters coming to Yugoslavia, USIS had no major impact on the concerts, which were mostly staged through private arrangements. The extraordinary popularity of jazz rendered any official sponsorship redundant. Certainly, jazz was a cultural Cold War weapon in the broad sense, having the connotation of improvisation and freedom, but the State Department mainly sponsored classical tours due to two factors: the ANTA propensity for classical music and art; and the already high free circulation of jazz groups, LPs, radio stations, and orchestras, because of Yugoslav cultural liberalization drives from the late 1950s on. Jazz popularity surged with every concert. Ella Fitzgerald 'filled Belgrade's largest music hall [...] with a delirium of enthusiasm [and] [...] there were prolonged, angry shouts when the announcer said the concert was finished.'[72] For *Vjesnik*, Ellington's concert at the Dubrovnik festival 'was a sensation,' with 'excellent trumpeters, splendid soloists [...], who played with their whole body [...], showing at the same time great concentration and deep emotional involvement.'[73] The State Department only sustained tours that couldn't make private cost-return arrangements, and the financial assistance underwrote, as a rule, deficits like box-office receipts inadequate to meet costs, 'not to subsidize tours completely.' The Embassy established tickets prices 'at the going rate' since 'events requiring a token payment, however modest, gain prestige and major 'merit, artistically and otherwise, more so than completely free performances.'[74]

As for the Cultural Exchange Program, the Yugoslav authorities, while despising USIS person-to-person activities in the field, were more than constructive towards the CPP. Already in 1951, USIS received several requests from the Yugoslav Council for Science and Culture, soliciting them to bring to Yugoslavia 'American conductors and/or musicians,' even under Yugoslav guarantee for the artist's fee.[75] In 1952, the director of *Jugokoncert*, Veljko Bijedić, requested the assistance of the Embassy for obtaining top-rank American artists following 'enormous public demand.'[76] In 1952, the Federal Council for Science and Education contacted Albert Donnelly, the director of the Congress for Cultural Freedom, at the time sponsoring the Boston Symphony Orchestra in Western Europe, to organize a concert in Yugoslavia.[77] Moreover, in 1953, the Council eagerly accepted the proposed tour of the pianist Gary Graffman in Yugoslavia, for which USIS paid the travel expenses from Paris.[78] As ambassador in the United States (1962–67), Veljko Mićunović advised Janez Vipotnik, at the time President of the Federal Commission for Cultural Relations with Foreign Countries (FCCR), to invite more prestigious US cultural managers to Yugoslav festivals. In return, Micunović argued, it would be much easier to request more performances of Yugoslav artists in the United States.[79] The reciprocity never functioned on an equal basis, even though there were Yugoslav groups playing in the United States: in 1969, the Zagreb Philharmonic starred at the Music Festival in Philadelphia, while *Lado*, a Croatian national folk dance ensemble, toured the United States several times in the 1970s.[80] Although, as Vučetić suggested, the Yugoslav Party leaders used foreign jazz or rock concerts to create consent and show how liberal the regime was,[81] it also emerges from the latter evidence that at lower cultural echelons there were authentic interests in Yugoslav–US artistic cooperation motivated by reasons of cultural prestige, creativity, and public demand.

Voice of America speaks...

Voice of America played a special role in the public diplomacy endeavour, specifically promoting and widely disseminating what the CPP was doing on Yugoslav stages across the country. VOA focused on popularizing jazz, but did more than that, as we shall see. The first broadcast was put on the air in February 1942, followed by President F. D. Roosevelt's executive order in July that provided $5.4 million for the construction of transmitters. The desire to advance the Allied cause united all OWI propagandists, but ideological disputes soon emerged between New Deal liberals and their opponents. Critics continued to allege that Voice of America was a propaganda forum for the liberal domestic agenda and the President's personal ambitions. By the end of March 1943, VOA started broadcasting on Yugoslav territory and became a precious source of war information for Nazi-fascist occupied territories, along with the BBC.[82] In 1950, VOA already operated 'on a twenty-four-hour basis with a total of seventy daily programs in twenty-five languages' and had a 'potential listening audience of 295 million people.'[83] Twenty years later the US governmental radio broadcasted 780 hours per week in thirty-five languages; by contrast, the Soviet Union broadcasted more than 1,900 hours per week in eighty-four languages, and communist China and the United Arab Republic both transmitted more than 1,300 hours in thirty-eight languages.[84] In the mid-1960s, VOA's estimated weekly audience was around forty-two million, roughly distributed in communist Europe (seventeen million), Latin America (seven million), the Far East (six million), the Near East and South Asia (5.5 million), and Africa (2.2 million). The audience distribution tracked an anti-communist Cold War binary. The VOA feature consisted of mostly male listeners, aged 20 to 35 years, employed in middle to high-paid jobs, albeit 25 to 35 per cent were students.[85]

Together with Radio Free Europe (RFE) and Radio Liberty (RL) – the two fused in 1975 as Radio Free Europe/Radio Liberty – VOA spoke for the US government by broadcasting uncensored news and commentaries to people living in communist nations, using 'World War refugees from the USSR and Eastern Europe to communicate anti-Communist messages to their homelands.' RFE/RL was involved in the CIA's covert psychological warfare activities against the Soviet Union and its satellites. These Munich-based stations, founded in 1949 and 1951 respectively, received funds from the CIA until 1972, and were subjected to the CIA-State Department's policy directives.[86] The RFE/RL never broadcasted to Yugoslavia. Contrary to the praxis in the Soviet Union and its satellites, VOA jamming was forbidden here, which made the broadcasts extraordinarily popular, while concurrently making them the perfect USIA mass communication channel of US foreign policies. Generally, the Yugoslavs avoided committing themselves publicly and admitting to VOA listening; yet in private conversations, as an unnamed Party secretary confessed to PAO Kolarek in 1959, 'of course [he] listened to the Voice of America.'[87] VOA listening grew on the expanding radio production industry in Yugoslavia from the late 1940s and early 1950s on. Radio Industrija Nikola Tesla produced the first Yugoslav radio sets in 1947. By 1951, there were around 310,000 registered radios in Serbia, Croatia, and Slovenia; in 1957 they reached 711,000 for almost eighteen million inhabitants, and, according to *Komunist*, the Yugoslav government granted 1.3 million radio licenses, one to every third family, in 1959.[88] Still, radio sets remained luxury items for most of the 1950s; in 1955, one radio set cost the equivalent of 1,000 cinema tickets.[89] Yet, ten years later, a 1966 BBC–VOA joint survey revealed that 87 per cent of Yugoslavs had at least one radio or transistor, while in larger cities that number increased to 91 per cent. The differences among republics persisted; Serbia, Croatia, and Slovenia were above the national average.⁹⁰ Along with cinema, radio listening seemed the most preferred pastime in Yugoslavia in the early 1960s. Listeners mostly enjoyed light music – Italian and French romantic songs, South American folk, and obviously jazz – and radio listening appeared to be more popular among the rural population where there was less 'entertainment media available.'⁹¹

Criticized and investigated by McCarthy's Senate Permanent Subcommittee on Investigations in February 1953, in hearings which produced no evidence of communist infiltration, VOA shifted from hard-hitting anti-communist broadcasts to what the Jackson Committee recommended – to emphasise 'objective, factual news' and political 'commentary explanations,' but to reinforce its popularity with 'satire,' 'humour,' and 'music and entertainment.'⁹² Such a strategy ultimately led to Voice of America's recipe for success in Yugoslavia.

Listening in the 1950s

'To hear news from America makes me feel somehow warm,' admitted an anonymous VOA respondent in 1952.⁹³ USIS Belgrade conducted its first VOA survey in February of that year. The mail questionnaires were sent in five major Yugoslav languages. Of the 500 prepaid postage envelopes, 496 were returned to Belgrade. Although the questionnaires were individually sent, often the respondents collected answers from friends and fellow citizens. The final report by Columbia's Bureau of Applied Social Research revealed that more than half Yugoslav VOA listeners came from urban areas and were predominantly male and middle class – mainly bank managers, government officials, students, writers, teachers, engineers, and judges. Eighty per cent of them were between 20 and 30 years old. This convinced USIA policymakers that the program was hitting the young target and driving them towards pro-Western world views. The Yugoslavs enjoyed listening to Voice of America very frequently: 66 per cent of them reported daily listening, especially business and government officials and white-collar workers. Women, who were generally more at home in the afternoon, claimed to listen more than men.⁹⁴

Predictably, VOA respondents were openly anti-communist in their comments. The report listed many anti-Tito, anti-Soviet, and anti-communist remarks, and more than twenty favourable political references to the United States: 'I listen to VOA programs every day; I don't listen to enemies,' was one of them. A Yugoslav farmer wrote down, 'I do not work anywhere now. I am not a Communist, so they will not let me work as a grain merchant. Long live mother America who is delivering and freeing the whole world from communist Russia.' Some accounts recalled tragic personal stories after the communist takeover. A former teacher noted down, 'since May 1945 I was a professor of the First High School in Belgrade. I was dismissed for being an 'Anglophile' – at that time it was a big sin. For six years, I have lived in my village with my father and have a rather hard primitive life.' Some comments addressed the level of political coercion and protested against the authorities, although aware that there might be postal control over what they wrote. One respondent accused Tito and Moša Pijade of being 'liars, swindlers … a robber band.' Yet, young listeners loved

VOA, mainly for entertainment reasons: 'VOA is my great recreation for through its broadcasts I get to know the whole world and the life of different people.' Overall, Yugoslav listeners appreciated VOA, but pledged for more news on Yugoslavia and its culture, and to hear more American opinion on it, as in a sort of 'circuit of communication between themselves and the *Voice*.'[95] The VOA program, managed by USIA International Broadcasting Division (IBS), dedicated 32 per cent of the outputs to news, around 60 per cent to news analysis and documentaries, and only 10 per cent to the music programme, the favourite among Yugoslav audiences. The IBS provided USIS with of thousands of radio transcripts for Yugoslav national radio stations.[96] By the end of the decade, relations between USIS Belgrade and VOA became close; the post delivered weekly telegrams to the Yugoslav desk on the CPP, the US pavilions at Yugoslav fairs, and *Pregled* issues, making VOA more responsive.[97] Even the Yugoslav Central Committee admitted that there were, at least from the early 1950s on, no anti-Yugoslav biases in VOA's Serbo-Croatian broadcasts, except for minor issues, while being critical of the Soviet Union and its satellites.[98] The Yugoslav ideologists started their defamation campaign when, from the early 1960s on, the massive diffusion of radio sets provided VOA with a stronger cultural influence on Yugoslav youth.

Listening in the 1960s: political disapproval and American jazz

Voice of America 'had a mass appeal' and 'made an enormous difference' because it reached otherwise unreachable people.[99] Thanks to its program diversity, from news, sports, language lessons, science, life in the USA, to agricultural news, classical and popular music, and the youth program, VOA exerted a mass fascination over audiences. In the 1960s and early 1970s, the Serbo-Croatian desk broadcasted around thirteen shows from early morning to 10 pm.

VOA popularity surged from the early 1960s on: a survey collected between May 1960 and January 1961 revealed that 70 per cent of Yugoslav interviewers declared they enjoyed listening to foreign Western radio stations, and 69 per cent were regular VOA listeners; the corresponding figure for Czechoslovakia was 59 per cent and 62 per cent for Poland. At the same time, the BBC boasted 14 per cent of weekly listeners. The Yugoslavs, 33 per cent of them, deemed VOA's approach to communism as 'too soft.' The corresponding figure for Poland and Czechoslovakia was 27 and 16 per cent.[100] Such an anti-communist drift was common among VOA listeners. A 1962 survey of Yugoslav emigrants showed how listening to VOA meant, for them, defeating the regime's implicit boundaries of coercion; tuning to VOA and other Western broadcasts made them feel empowered to access unofficial news and dissent against political power. Predominately Croats and Slovenians, urban middle-high and highly educated, these emigrants looked to VOA (46 per cent), Radio Vatican (14 per cent), Radio Paris (13 per cent), the BBC, and the Italian RAI (11 per cent) to be informed about world issues.[101]

According to a 1953 comparison study, Yugoslavs preferred VOA to other foreign broadcasters because it was 'neither so carefully neutral as the BBC, nor so blatantly propagandistic as Radio Moscow.' For Radio Moscow, the world was 'black and white';

for the BBC it was 'grey'; while VOA strategy revolved 'around mutual security as the hope of the world.' It portrayed 'the United States as peaceful, defensively strong, and desirous of protecting human rights,' but without employing 'the detail and bright colours' that Radio Moscow used 'in describing the chief Cold War protagonists.' The stations differed in their basic approaches: VOA and BBC news tended 'to be direct and simple,' VOA scripts appearing 'on about the level of American commercial radio news'; meanwhile, Radio Moscow and the BBC were intended for 'highly-educated leader' audiences.[102] Compared to other foreign broadcasts, VOA was by far the most widely listened to foreign station; 'it attracted about three times as many listeners as its nearest competitor Radio Moscow, although Moscow beam[ed] twice the number of weekly hours – twenty-one compared to 10.5 [VOA] hours to Yugoslavia.' The BBC, which broadcasted eleven hours per week, captured only about one-seventh of the VOA audience in Yugoslavia. The fact that VOA transmitted by short and medium wave from Thessaloniki, while the other foreign broadcasters, BBC included, ran on short wave, assured VOA's dominant overall position among foreign broadcasters since most Yugoslavs tuned into medium wave.[103]

In September 1961, VOA announced the Transistor Contest: everyone could win a transistor by sending a letter containing their name, address, and information about age, sex, and occupation to the desk. The contest garnered more than 18,000 entries, an 'unexpectedly heavy response' that 'exceeded the total of any previous transistor contests.' USIS Belgrade reported 'some evidence that bags containing contest mails were burned [...] thus reducing the apparent number of entries.' The contest outcomes attested to a profound change in VOA audiences in only one decade: they were more female (46 per cent) due to women's major participation in society, and more working class, due to cheaper radio sets.[104] The Yugoslav local authorities were furious. On 15 November 1962, Radio Belgrade described contest participants as 'impulsive,' 'ignorant,' and 'traders in their pride,' with harsh words for 'those who [...] should strongly oppose such a practice.' The latter was a thinly disguised allusion to Party members and government officials who participated in the contest.[105] A previous 1961 declaration by the Municipal Committee of Belgrade warned against foreign radio stations as enemy propaganda which needed to be eradicated.[106] Members of the LCY who took part in the Transistor Contest were to be punished, by expulsion or verbal admonishment, deemed the local Party organization. When, in 1961, of 200 citizens from Krnjača municipality (today part of Belgrade city) who applied to a VOA contest, four Party members were found, the Party immediately expelled them. In most cases this also meant losing their job, social privileges, leisure-time benefits, and subsidized vacations. With foreign radio broadcasts, the Yugoslavs balanced between coercion and liberalization: VOA, the BBC, and RAI were not jammed in Yugoslavia, but local ideological commissions considered VOI 'highly problematic and dangerous propaganda,' and its listeners 'old pre-war politicians' and 'royal traders.'[107] No surprise then that the secret services regularly checked the mail listeners sent in response to contests.[108]

Despite negative perception of VOA listening, the adult weekly audience remained high: a 1966 survey estimated some 2.2 million Yugoslav listeners on 2.8 million radio sets. Twenty-two per cent of the Yugoslav urban population listened to VOA, half of them on a regular basis. The listeners tuned in to 'check on the news supplied by their own media, whose credibility they often suspected.' The Slovenian broadcasts, while costlier than the Serbo-Croatian ones, were overwhelmingly successful. Slovenians constituted 8.5 per cent of the entire Yugoslav population, but made up 5 per cent of the VOA audience; the Slovenian leadership, mostly attached to Western values, was essential to 'U.S. interests.'[109]

Not every VOA listening implied a political connotation. For young people, VOA meant *Music USA*, a legendary show, half dance half jazz, conducted by producer and broadcaster Willis Conover, which first broadcast in January 1955 and ran for forty years. With his recognizable deep voice, Conover was a jazz promoter and jazz star for audiences in Eastern Europe, the Soviet Union, and worldwide. When George Wein travelled the states of the Warsaw Pact as the producer of the Newport Jazz Festival, he was astonished by how 'Eastern Europe's entire concept of jazz [came] from Willis Conover.' Though little known in the United States, as VOA did not broadcast domestically, Americans travelling to Poland in the 1960s remained staggered that 'Conover's likeness was displayed as often and with as much affection as pictures of John Kennedy.'[110] VOA and its *Music USA*, followed mainly by Yugoslav students, raised an entire generation of Yugoslav jazz musicians whose production ended as one of the most vanguard and innovative in Europe. During a two-hour press interview with Duke Ellington, held in Dubrovnik in July 1970, Nikita Petrak from Radio-TV Zagreb, his American English emulating Conover's strong accent, reminded listeners how Conover was 'fondly considered to be the principal tutor and friend of a whole generation of Yugoslav jazz buffs,' the inspiration for 'thousands of Yugoslav youths,' and their 'teacher of English.'[111]

VOA was, argued a USIA 1972 report, 'a symbol of freedom that can give people hope, and we who enjoy freedom must not let them down.'[112] It tasted like freedom for many of its audiences. Vojo Šiljak, a Croatian talk-show host, remembered: 'my grandpa and father secretly listened to the Voice of America and the political news of the famous reporter Grga Zlatoper.' Milorad Bibić, journalist of *Slobodna Dalmacija*, recalled: 'Many times I could not hear the Italian songs till the end because my father asked for the Voice of America [...] for me [just] boring news. He would find the *Voice* and you'd hear: "Here is Washington, Voice of America, Grga Zlatoper speaks".'[113] As with other USIS field-centred activities in Yugoslavia, VOA remained in a limbo between approbation and restrictions, in a political space where boundaries of freedom and margins of coercion fluctuated. No firmly established criteria defined what was totally forbidden, tolerated, or implicitly not recommended. Such grey standards were negotiated in the political arena where decisions were made. The comparative analysis between CPP and VOA broadcasts highlight the discrepancy between the low perception of Tito's dictatorship and the mechanism of political violence and coercion put in place. The political anxieties that surrounded the listening to foreign broadcasts, and VOA in particular, frame the complexity of the Yugoslav leadership's polyarchy, its internal fractures, and differentiation of policy priorities that stemmed from such a wide bureaucratic state apparatus as the Federation. The spectacular popularity of

VOA subsisted as an effective public diplomacy story, probably less because of VOA's talents, and more because of a Yugoslav urban, young, and basically communist-disaffected, population.

Notes

1 'Yugoslavs Sing Praise of "Porgy"; US Troupe Earns Gratitude and Affection of Nation in One-Week Stand,' *New York Times*, 22 December 1954.
2 Backlund to Re, 19 December 1968, Folder 8, Box 21, CU, MC 468, Special Collection, UAL.
3 Joseph N. Acinapura, 'The Cultural Presentations Program of the United States,' in Galvin to Coe, 2 December 1970, Box 1, Records Relating to Selected USIA Programs 1953–99, USIA Bureau of Programs, RG 306, NACP, 16–17.
4 Special International Program, 10th Semi-annual Report, 1 January–30 June 1961, S-50–61, Box 17, Special Reports 1953–97, USIA Office of Research, RG 306, NACP, 29.
5 Emily Abrams Ansari, 'Shaping the Policies of Cold War Musical Diplomacy: An Epistemic Community of American Composers,' *Diplomatic History* 36, no. 1 (2012): 41, https://doi.org/10.1111/j.1467-7709.2011.01007.x.
6 Special International Program, 1 January–30 June 1961, 29; CPP – A Report to the Congress, 1 July 1963–30 June 1964, Folder 1, Box 49, CU, MC 468, Special Collection, UAL.
7 Von Eschen, *Satchmo Blows Up the World*.
8 Lisa E. Davenport, *Jazz Diplomacy: Promoting America in the Cold War Era* (Jackson: University Press of Mississippi, 2010); Ingrid T. Monson, *Freedom Sounds: Civil Rights Call Out to Jazz and Africa* (Oxford; New York: Oxford University Press, 2007).
9 Clare H. Croft, *Dancers as Diplomats: American Choreography in Cultural Exchange*, Kindle (Oxford; New York: Oxford University Press, 2015); Danielle Fosler-Lussier, *Music in America's Cold War Diplomacy* (Oakland: University of California Press, 2015).
10 The first scholarly interest goes back to the 1990s: Predrag J. Marković, *Beograd između Istoka i Zapada 1948–1965* (Belgrade: Sluzbeni list SRJ, 1996); Aleš Gabrič, *Socialistična kulturna revolucija: Slovenska kulturna politika 1953–1962* (Ljubljana: Cankarjeva založba, 1995); Zoran Janjetović, *Od 'Internacionale' do komercijale: Popularna kultura u Jugoslaviji 1945–1991* (Belgrade: Institut za noviju istoriju Srbije, 2011) framed the political and cultural labels of the Yugoslav musical scene as a hybrid between Western and local identity; Aleksandar Žikić, *Fatalni ringišpil: Hronika beogradskog rokenrola 1959–1979* (Belgrade: Geopoetika, 1999) examined Yugoslav rock music as a cultural, diversionary, and political phenomenon; Reinhard Köchl, Richard Wiedamann, and Peter Tippelt, *Dusko Gojkovic: Jazz ist Freiheit* (Regensburg: ConBrio, 1995) analysed the Yugoslav jazz scene as a medium of personal and artistic liberation in a coercive regime; Aleksandar Raković, *Rokenrol u Jugoslaviji 1956–1968: Izazov socijalističkom društvu* (Belgrade: Arhipelag, 2011) and Siniša Škarica, *Kad je rock bio mlad: Priča sa istočne strane (1956–1970)* (Zagreb: VBZ, 2005)

investigated how Yugoslav rock 'n' roll was transformed from the ideological
enemy to a regime's ally by the Party leaders. More recently, Francesca Rolandi,
Con ventiquattromila baci studied the Italian influences on Yugoslav pop
culture and the transpositions of identities and cross-cultural exchanges in
them.

11 'Shake, Rattle, and Self-Management: Making the Scene in Yugoslavia,' in *Kazaaam!
Splat! Ploof!: The American Impact on European Popular Culture since 1945*, ed.
Sabrina P. Ramet and Gordana Crnković (Lanham, MD; Oxford: Rowman &
Littlefield Publishers, 2003), 181.
12 Kathryn C. Statler, 'The Sound of Musical Diplomacy,' *Diplomatic History* 36, no. 1
(2012): 71, https://doi.org/10.1111/j.1467-7709.2011.01010.x.
13 Croft, *Dancers as Diplomats*, chap. Introduction.
14 Most of the information collected on American performers in Yugoslavia were
confirmed by the 'Jugosvirke Online Collection,' https://jugosvirke.wordpress.
com/, an informal, open access web archive/blog collecting digitized newspaper
excerpts, photographs, concert tickets, and posters of the American artists who
performed in socialist Yugoslavia.
15 Ansari, 'Shaping the Policies of Cold War Musical Diplomacy: An Epistemic
Community of American Composers,' 41–2, 44.
16 Fosler-Lussier, *Music in America's Cold War Diplomacy*, 23.
17 *Ibid.*, 24–5.
18 Country Plan for Yugoslavia 1963, 30 January 1963, Box 45, USIA Subject Files
1953–67, RG 306, NACP, 6–7.
19 'Metropolitan Soprano to Make Four-Month World Trip,' *New York Times*, 9
February 1956.
20 Instruction 161 Dept. of State to Embassy Belgrade, 4 May 1955, 511.683/5–455, Box
2205, CDF 1955–59, RG 59, NACP.
21 'Clothes Makes an Opera as Temperament Shows,' *New York Times*, 4 June 1955;
'The World of Music: Council Seeks Charter,' *New York Times*, 10 July 1955;
Američki ansambli, dirigenti i solisti na Dubrovačkih ljetnim igrama, 1971, File
SAD, KKVI IVS SRH, RG 1410, CSA.
22 Instruction 4063 Dept. of State to Embassy Belgrade, 25 November 1955,
511.683/11–2555, Box 2205, CDF 1955–59, RG 59, NACP.
23 Suradnja Zagrebačke filharmonije sa umjetnicima i ansamblima SAD, 30 September
1971, File SAD; Poznatiji vokalni i instrumentalni solisti koji su do danas učestvovali
na Dubrovačkim ljetnim igrama, n.d., File 1; XX Dubrovačke ljetne igre, 1969, File 1,
KKVI IVS SRH, RG 1410, CSA.
24 Airgram 218 Embassy Belgrade to Dept. of State, 13 September 1963, Box 45, USIA
Subject Files 1953–67, RG 306, NACP, 13.
25 Strani kritičari, publicisti i novinari koji su pratili Dubrovačke ljetne igre, 1966–69,
n.d.; and Ugledne ličnosti i gosti iz inozemstva koji su pratili izvedbe Dubrovačkih
ljetnih igara, 1966–69, n.d., File 1, KKVI IVS SRH, RG 1410, CSA.
26 Bilješka Dubrovačkih ljetnih Igara o posjeti američkog konzula C. Johnsona,
1 June 1968, 02–103/19–68, Box 43, Republički protokol, IVS SRH 1953–90,
RG 280, CSA.
27 Message 74 USIS Belgrade to USIA Washington, 25 March 1963, Box 45, USIA
Subject Files 1953–67, RG 306, NACP.

28 Američki ansambli, dirigenti i solisti na Dubrovačkih ljetnim igrama, 1971, File
    SAD; and Poznatiji vokalni i instrumentalni solisti koji su do danas učestvovali na
    Dubrovačkim ljetnim igrama, n.d., File 1, KKVI IVS SRH, RG 1410, CSA.
29 *Pregled*, February 1959, 30; IES Monthly Progress Report, August 1957, and Status
    of Current Cultural and Sports Projects, IES Report, January 1957, Folder 2, Box 25,
    CU, MC 468, Special Collection, UAL.
30 Airgram 218 Embassy Belgrade to Dept. of State, 13 September 1963, Box 45, USIA
    Subject Files 1953–67, RG 306, NACP, 13; Message 74 USIS Belgrade to USIA
    Washington, 25 March 1963, Box 45, USIA Subject Files 1953–67, RG 306, NACP.
31 Message 44 USIS Belgrade to USIA Washington, 8 January 1965, EDU 14–2 YUGO,
    Box 382, CFPF 1964–66, RG 59, NACP.
32 Frankel to Katzenbach, 24 February 1967, TH29-SA-8, Folder 2, Box 25, CU, MC
    468, Special Collection, UAL.
33 Ansambli na Dubrovačkim ljetnim igrama 1950–69, n.d.
34 XXI Dubrovačke ljetne igre, 1970, File 1, KKVI IVS SRH, RG 1410, CSA.
35 Richardson Jr to Billenbrand, 23 April 1970, Folder 1, Box 26, CU, MC 468, Special
    Collection, UAL.
36 Airgram 218 Embassy Belgrade to Dept. of State, 13 September 1963, 13;
    Memorandum of Conversation Levin, LaSalle Quartet, Jones and Durand Jr, 8 April
    1963, EDX 32, Box 3255, CFPF 1963, RG 59, NACP; Message 74 USIS Belgrade to
    USIA Washington, 25 March 1963; Muzički Biennale Zagreb, 19 April 1965, 967,
    Box 41, RSK SRH 1963–65, RG 1414, CSA.
37 Ansambli na Dubrovačkim ljetnim igrama 1950–69, n.d.; Koncertna direkcija
    Zagreb, 25 October 1966, JS 24, Box 226, RSPKFK 1965–79, RG 1415, CSA; Muzički
    Biennale Zagreb, 1967, File 2, KKVI IVS SRH, RG 1410, CSA.
38 Opera HNK Zagreb, 30 September 1971, 3539/1, File SAD, KKVI IVS SRH, RG
    1410, CSA.
39 'Yugoslavs Sing Praise of "Porgy"'; Joseph N. Acinapura, 'The Cultural Presentations
    Program of the United States,' 29– (MA thesis, Rutgers University, 1970), 29–30.
40 Howard Taubman, 'Cold War on the Cultural Front; At Brussels the US and Russia
    Will Compete or the Minds of Men with Their Arts,' *New York Times*, 21 January
    1958.
41 According to African American writer James Baldwin, 'What has always been
    missing from George Gershwin's opera is what the situation of *Porgy and Bess* says
    about the white world. It is because of this omission that Americans are so proud of
    the opera. It assuages their guilt about Negro and it attacks none of their fantasies'
    (Ellen Noonan, *The Strange Career of Porgy and Bess: Race, Culture, and America's
    Most Famous Opera* [Chapel Hill: University of North Carolina Press, 2012], 1).
42 'Yugoslavs Sing Praise of "Porgy".'
43 American Cultural and Sports Groups Abroad under the President's Fund, January
    1956, Folder 11, Box 24, CU, MC 468, Special Collection, UAL.
44 'Porgy Makes a Hit,' *New York Times*, 23 December 1954.
45 Jack Raymond, 'Porgy Delights Belgrade Crowds,' *New York Times*, 17 December
    1954.
46 Ansambli na Dubrovačkim ljetnim igrama 1950–1969; Muzičko-scenska djela na
    repertoaru Dubrovačkih ljetnih igara 1950–1969, n.d., KKVI IVS SRH, RG 1410,
    CSA.

47 Inspection Report USIS Yugoslavia, 20 November 1959, 16.
48 CP Staff, Activity Report, 13–24 August 1956, Box 25, Folder 1, CU, MC 468, Special Collection, UAL; Opera HNK Zagreb, 30 September 1971; Message 74 USIS Belgrade to USIA Washington, 25 March 1963, Box 45, USIA Subject Files 1953–67, RG 306, NACP.
49 Republičkom sekretarijatu za prosvjetu, kulturu i fizičku kulturu, 14 February 1968, JS-4165, Box 227, RSPKFK 1965–79, RG 1415, CSA.
50 Claudia Gitelman and Martin Randy, eds, *The Returns of Alwin Nikolais: Bodies, Boundaries and the Dance Canon* (Middletown, CT: Wesleyan, 2007).
51 Memorandum Backlund to Re, 19 December 1968, Folder 8, Box 21, CU, MC 468, Special Collection, UAL.
52 Photographs Alwin Nikolais Dance Group in Yugoslavia, Folder 34, Box 346, CU, MC 468, Special Collection, UAL.
53 Allen Robertson, 'Glen Tetley,' in *International Encyclopedia of Dance*, ed. Selma J. Cohen (New York: Oxford University Press, 1998).
54 For a notable debate, see the issue of *Diplomatic History*, 36, no. 1 (2012).
55 Program Plan for Yugoslavia, 27 April 1967, Folder 18, Box 17, CU, MC 468, Special Collection, UAL.
56 Jessica C. E. Gienow-Hecht, 'The World is Ready to Listen: Symphony Orchestras and the Global Performance of America,' *Diplomatic History* 36, no. 1 (2012): 18–19, 22, 24–6.
57 Paul Tingen, 'Miles Davis. The Making of Bitches Brews,' *JazzTimes* 31, no. 4 (2001): 54.
58 Von Eschen, *Satchmo Blows Up the World*, 29–30, 35.
59 The Jazz Ambassadors Program survived in a substantially reduced form after the Cold War within the ECA's American Music Program Abroad (Harm Langenkamp, 'Global Harmony in Silk Road Diplomacy,' in Music and Diplomacy from the Early *Modern Era to the Present*, ed. Rebekah Ahrendt, Mark Ferraguto, and Damien Mahiet [New York: Palgrave Macmillan, 2014], 94).
60 Von Eschen, *Satchmo Blows Up the World*, 31–2.
61 Davenport, *Jazz Diplomacy*, 85.
62 Vučetić, *Koka-kola socijalizam*, 173–4.
63 Ramet, 'Shake, Rattle, and Self-Management,' 135.
64 Vučetić, Koka-kola socijalizam, 173–4, 178–82; Vladimir Dedijer, *Novi prilozi za biografiju Josipa Broza Tita: Sabrana dela Vladimira Dedijera*, vol. 3 (Belgrade: Rad, 1984), 609.
65 Airgram 307 Embassy Belgrade to Dept. of State, 24 July 1970, Box 6, Records Relating to Selected USIA Programs 1953–99, USIA Bureau of Programs, RG 306, NACP.
66 'Yugoslav Concerts,' 18 February 2019, https://jugosvirke.wordpress.com/; Inspection Report USIS Yugoslavia, 20 November 1959, Box 10, Inspection Report and Related Records 1954–62, USIA Inspection Staff, RG 306, NACP, 30; 'Kulturna razmena,' *Pregled*, December 1962, 38.
67 CPP, Area and Country Breakdown, July 1954–September 1966, Folder 11, Box 49, CU, MC 468, Special Collection, UAL; Telegram 694 Dept. of State to Belgrade, 25 February 1957, 511.683/2–1857, Box 2205, CDF 1955–59, RG 59,

NACP; Lewis to Richardson Jr, 17 February 1971, Folder 12, Box 21, CU, MC 468, Special Collection, UAL.

68 Educational and Cultural Profile of Yugoslavia, 27 April 1967, Folder 18, Box 17, CU, MC 468, Special Collection, UAL.

69 Message 86 USIS Belgrade to USIA Washington, 27 June 1966, CUL 16 US, Box 351, CFPF 1964–66, RG 59, NACP.

70 Backlund to Re, 26 September 1968, Folder 8, and Huff to Canter, 27 February 1969, Folder 9, in Box 21, CU, MC 468, Special Collection, UAL.

71 'Blood, Sweat & Tears Wins Ovation in Yugoslav Concert,' *New York Times*, 19 June 1970; Richardson Jr to Billenbrand, 23 April 1970, Folder 1, Box 26, Cu, MC 468, Special Collection, UAL.

72 'Ella Fitzgerald and Peterson Trio Receive Ovation,' *New York Times*, 21 February 1961.

73 A. Tomašek, 'Od baroka do džeza,' *Vjesnik*, 17 July 1970, 6.

74 Joseph N. Acinapura, 'The Cultural Presentations Program of the United States,' 22–3, 24.

75 Despatch 521 Belgrade to Dept. of State, 13 January 1951, 511.68/1–1351, Box 2472, CDF 1950–54, RG 59, NACP.

76 Despatch 936 Belgrade to Dept. of State, 2 April 1952, 511.68/4–252, Box 2472, CDF 1950–54, RG 59, NACP.

77 Razgovor sa predstavnikom Bostonskog simfonija, 9 May 1952, 237, Box 7, Poverljive veze sa SAD i Kanadom, SNK Vlade FNRJ, RG 317, AY.

78 Goranin to Jugokoncert, 24 April 1952, 204, Box 7, Poverljive veze sa SAD i Kanadom, SNK FNRJ, RG 317, AY.

79 Neke primedbe druga Mićunovića o radu KKV, in Zabeleške o razgovoru između Budisavljević Bogdanke i Raymonda Bensona, 19 May 1964, 213/64, Box 237, SAD, Kanada i Latinska Amerika, SSOK, RG 318, AY.

80 Suradnja Zagrebačke filharmonije sa umjetnicima i ansamblima SAD, 30 September 1971.

81 Radina Vučetić,'Trubom kroz Gvozdenu zavesu: prodor đeza u socijalističku Jugoslaviju,' *Muzikologija*, no. 13 (21 January 2012): 53–77, https://doi.org/10.2298/MUZ120229012V.

82 Hixon, *Parting the Curtain*, 29–31 and Rade Ranković, 'Jubilej *Glasa Amerike*,' Glas Amerike, 22 February 2019, www.glasamerike.net/content/voa-serbian-anniversary/1632143.html.

83 McFall to Johnson, 22 August 1950, 511.00/8–950, Box 2238, CDF 1950–54, RG 59, NACP.

84 Washington Report, VOA, 5 May 1972, in Beall to Sites, 24 May 1972, Box 27, USIA Director's Subject Files 1968–72, RG 306, NACP.

85 Voice of America Audience Estimate, December 1966, E-1-66, Box 1, Estimates and Evaluations 1966–78, USIA Office of Research and Evaluation, RG 306, NACP; for scholarly research on VOA broadcasts, see Alan L. Heil Jr, *Voice of America: A History* (New York; West Sussex: Columbia University Press, 2003) and Krugler, *The Voice of America and the Domestic Propaganda Battles, 1945–1953*.

86 A. Ross Johnson, *Radio Free Europe and Radio Liberty: The CIA Years and Beyond* (Washington, DC: Stanford University Press, 2010), 7; see also Richard H. Cummings, *Cold War Radio: The Dangerous History of American Broadcasting*

114 US public diplomacy in socialist Yugoslavia

in Europe, 1950–1989 (Jefferson, NC: McFarland, 2009); Richard H. Cummings, *Radio Free Europe's 'Crusade for Freedom': Rallying Americans Behind Cold War Broadcasting, 1950–1960* (North Carolina: McFarland, 2010).

87 Inspection Report USIS Yugoslavia, 20 November 1959, 19. Only with the eruption of the Balkan Wars did RFE/RL start covering the former Yugoslav territories, and they began broadcasting in Serbian, Croatian, and Bosnian in early 1994, and in Kosovo and Macedonia in 1999 and 2001 ('Then and Now: Free Media in Unfree Societies,' *Radio Free Europe/Radio Liberty*, 22 February 2019, https://pressroom.rferl.org/history).

88 VOA listening in Yugoslavia, October 1952, YO5201, Box 121, Country Projects Files 1951–64, USIA Office of Research and Analysis (hereafter ORA), RG 306, NACP; Worldwide Distribution of Radio Receivers Sets, 31 December 1957, P-105–57, and Radio Listening, 9 November 1960, RN-43–60, Box 4, Research Notes 1958–62, USIA ORA, RG 306, NACP.

89 *Janjetović, Od 'Internacionale' do komercijale*, 74–7; VOA listening in Yugoslavia, October 1952; and The Yugoslav Transistor Contest, 8 March 1962, RN-5–62, Box 4, Research Notes 1958–62, USIA ORA, RG 306, NACP.

90 VOA Listening in Urban Yugoslavia, November 1967, E-7–67, YO6601, Box 41, Africa, Eastern Europe and Multi-Areas, USIA ORA, RG 306, NACP.

91 Radio Listening, 9 November 1960, RN-43–60, Box 4, Research Notes 1958–62, USIA ORA, RG 306, NACP.

92 Report to the President by the President's Committee on International Information Activities, 30 June 1953, FRUS, 1952–54, vol. II, part 2, doc. 368, 1847; Memorandum for the NSC by the Executive Secretary, 1 October 1953, FRUS, 1952–54, vol. II, part 2, doc. 372, 1890.

93 VOA listening in Yugoslavia, October 1952, 70.

94 *Ibid.*, x–xv.

95 *Ibid.*, 59, 69–70.

96 Department of State Publication 3927, August 1950, File 511.00/9–2250, Box 2238, CDF 1950–54, RG 59, NACP.

97 Inspection Report USIS Yugoslavia, 20 November 1959, 19.

98 Zabeleška o emisijama Radio New Yorka, November–December 1950, 5/IX/109/VI-1–82, Box 5, Komisija za međunarodne odnose i veze 1945–90, CK SKJ, RG 507, AY.

99 Mark Taplin, 'Walter Roberts: The Impact of US Cold War Public Diplomacy – "The Most Effective Way of Influencing … Was the Voice of America",' *Global Publicks* website, 22 February 2016, http://globalpublicks.blogspot.hr/2015/02/walter-roberts-impact-of-us-cold-war.html.

100 Yugoslav Reactions to Western Broadcasting, 5 July 1961, RN-15–61, Box 4, Research Notes 1958–62, USIA ORA, RG 306, NACP.

101 Radio Listening: Attitudes of Refugees, July–August 1962, Box 121, Country Projects Files 1951–64, USIA ORA, RG 306, NACP.

102 IRI Intelligence Memorandum, 25 October 1954, IM-1–54, Box 1, Intelligence Bulletins, Memorandums and Summaries 1954–56, USIA ORI, RG 306, NACP.

103 VOA Listening in Urban Yugoslavia, November 1967, 1; Survey of Listening in Yugoslavia, December 1966, YO6601, Box 41, Africa, Eastern Europe and

Multi-Areas, USIA ORA, RG 306, NACP; VOA Listening in Urban Yugoslavia, November 1967.

104 Yugoslav Transistor Contest Draw Large Response, 8 March 1962, RN-5-62, Box 4, Research Notes 1958-62, USIA ORA, RG 306, NACP.

105 Yugoslav Transistor Contest, 30 March 1962, RN-30-62, Box 8, Research Reports 1966-90, USIA Office of Research and Media Reaction, RG 306, NACP.

106 Opštinski komitet SKS Gradskom Komitetu SKS, 26 December 1961, 236, Box 512, Materijali o delovanju inostrane propagande 1958-68, Gradski komitet SKS Beograd, HAB.

107 Informacija o preduzetim merama u vezi neprijateljske propagande na teritoriju opštine Zvezdara, 15 January 1962; Informacija OK Krnjača, June 1961; Informacija o delatnosti strane propagande, 3 May 1962; Opštinski komitet SKS Zemun Gradskom komitetu SKS, 22 January 1962, 01-115/i; and Opštinski komitet SKS Sopot, 12 February 1962, 232, in Box 512, Materijali o delovanju inostrane propagande 1958-68, Gradski komitet SKS Beograd, HAB.

108 Propaganda kapitalističkih zemalja u Jugoslaviji, 1953, 724/1953, Box 44, Materijali komisije za međunarodne veze 1950-59, SSRNJ, RG 142, AY, 24-6.

109 Voice of America Audience Estimate, December 1966, E-1-66, Box 1, Estimates and Evaluations 1966-78, USIA Office of Research and Evaluation, RG 306, NACP; VOA Listening in Urban Yugoslavia, November 1967, i-iii, 4.

110 Reinhold Wagnleitner, *Coca-Colonization and the Cold War: The Cultural Mission of the United States in Austria After the Second World War* (Chapel Hill: University of North Carolina Press, 2000), 211.

111 Airgram 307 Embassy Belgrade to Dept. of State, 24 July 1970, Box 6, Records Relating to Selected USIA Programs 1953-99, USIA Bureau of Programs, RG 306, NACP; Mail Survey of Listeners to MUSIC USA, April 1961, MB-6, Box 1, Country Projects Files 1951-64, USIA ORA, RG 306, NACP.

112 Washington Report VOA, 5 May 1972, in Beall to Sites, 24 May 972, Box 27, USIA Director's Subject Files 1968-72, RG 306, NACP.

113 Orhidea Gaura, 'Vojo Šiljak: Prva zvijezda talk-showa u Hrvatskoj,' *Nacional*, 22 September 2009, http://arhiva.nacional.hr/clanak/print/67442; Vučetić, 'Amerikanizacija u Jugoslovenskoj Popularnoj Kulturi '60-Ih,' 158-60.

5

Yugoslav leaders: (ex)changes and drawbacks

Yugoslavia was among a 'few countries in the world,' explained a 1967 Bureau of Educational and Cultural Affairs report, 'with which the U.S. has such close cultural relations' and where scholars and political and economic leaders have been so exposed to the United States 'through the exchange program.' In its post-Stalinist assessment, Yugoslavia undoubtedly demonstrated 'great courage [...] in meeting its difficulties and applied imagination and adaptability to its problems'; USIA policy generally, and its exchange diplomacy particularly, encouraged the country 'to move ahead toward the creation of a "compromise between Western democratic traditions and proletarian dictatorships".'[1] The long-range exchange program was primarily 'an investment in people': cultural cooperation depended on established ties between American and Yugoslav institutions, and their effectiveness 'in interpreting [...] the needs of their own societies.'[2] Both American and Yugoslav policymakers shared this view. Yugoslav willingness to embark on broad and opulent cultural exchange programs with the United States proved, like in no other bilateral field, to be an irreproachable pragmatic policy on the part of the Yugoslavs that, as this chapter shows, secured a total victory over ideological perplexities.

The Yugoslav Federal Commission for Cultural Relations with Foreign Countries (FCCR)[3] signed, from the mid-1950s on, bilateral exchange programs with several Eastern (the USSR, Poland, Czechoslovakia, Bulgaria, and Rumania) and Western European countries (the United Kingdom, France, Germany, Austria, Belgium, Denmark, and Norway), but also Middle East and African countries such as Syria, Lebanon, and Kenya.[4] This was not the case for the United States. No all-inclusive bilateral agreement was ever signed between the two governments. Moreover, the Yugoslavs adapted to American state–private collaboration in the field of cultural exchanges, and complained about it periodically, but the collaboration proceeded smoothly and efficiently.

Standing between the two governments, USIS provided, together with the Embassy and Consulate, logistical, managerial and, in some cases, financial support. They acted as links between the State Department and Yugoslav leaders coming through the US Foreign Leader Program (FLP), the Foreign Specialist Program (FSP), and the American Specialist Program (ASP). They advised, assisted, and selected grantees for the Experiment in International Living, the Eisenhower Exchange Fellowship, the Salzburg Seminar, the Ford Foundation, and many more, but also invited European Fulbright grantees to lecture in Yugoslavia.[5] The USIS library raised and recruited future grantees, 'favourably influenced by the American books and magazines.'[6] USIS books and pamphlets on American education and universities emphasized 'not only full freedom in our [American] academic life, but also complete liberty in choosing' the courses they liked.[7]

With the 1948 Smith-Mundt Act (PL 402), the US exchange programs became a 'significant aspect of [US] foreign policy'; foreign relations were no longer to be conducted 'between official representatives of foreign governments' exclusively, but rather turned to 'the people's attitudes, their state of progress and education, their level of information, their hopes and expectations.' Cultural exchanges were integrated into 'America's long-range constructive relations with other nations.'[8] Yugoslavia was no exception. The established exchange programs would support Yugoslav independence from Moscow and strengthen its ties with the West. The 1963 USIA Country Plan was unequivocal: the US exchange efforts would balance Soviet exchanges and 'show that the US policies coincided with the best interests of Yugoslavia.' They would 'orient official and public Yugoslav thinking towards Western collective security and economic cooperation,' 'increase Yugoslavia's knowledge of the American democratic institutions,' and 'promote respect for the American cultural traditions and achievements.' Finally, they would 'foster the growth of personal acquaintanceship between political and cultural leaders of both countries.'[9] The focus on Yugoslav leaders proved to be both efficient and effective: the FLP produced immediate results in terms of friendship, human kindness, and eagerness to pursue American interests in Yugoslavia. Going beyond expectations, these programs, while emerging from constructive and affirmative foreign bilateral relations, were unaffected by their occasional deterioration, and even better, proved capable of bringing them back on the right track.

The Foreign Leader Program begins

Talking to Joseph Kendrick from the State Department in May 1958, Josip Defranceski, press counsellor at the Yugoslav Embassy in Washington, expressed the desire of the Yugoslav government 'to expand contacts between the two countries' and asked for more 'scholarships,' 'exchange of scientists,' 'exhibition of paintings,' and other forms of cultural exchange.[10] This unprecedented request surprised the State Department officials. Half a year later, Central Committee member Vlajko Begović approached the American Embassy in Belgrade with an analogous request.[11] The unexpected Yugoslav interests and their agreeable attitude spurred the US Congress to approve the first five FLP grants for 1958.[12] The FLP started in Yugoslavia between June and July 1958, before officially being implemented in the Soviet Union and Poland.[13]

Inspired by Truman's Campaign of Truth to promote a 'full and fair picture' of the United States in the world, Washington inaugurated the FLP in 1949–50. The program began as a series of trips of three months or more around the country, including destinations chosen by the grantee, and ensuring a multivaried experience mixed with professional interests and environmental and social diversity. The itineraries, both flexible and varied, comprised meetings with 'professional counterparts interspersed with tourist visits and small-town hospitality,' and relied on the belief that 'anyone undertaking such a facilitated journey [...], in constant contact with the American people, could only come away favourably influenced.'[14] Renamed in 1965 as the International Visitor Program, and in 2004 as the International Visitor Leadership Program, the leaders' exchange program is, even today, considered the 'Department of State's premier professional exchange program.'[15] As Giles Scott-Smith emphasized, the FLP occupied a 'special place' within the American endeavour of projecting and managing informal power; it revolved around 'personal experience and insight' and created networks among talented, influential political and opinion leaders in Europe and their American counterparts.[16] Between 1950 and 1962, the State Department brought 7,420 leaders from Western Europe to the United States with a global total of 11,475. Of these, 5,122 came from Germany, 420 from France, 324 from Italy, and 279 from the UK, reported Scott-Smith research.[17] Compared to the European average, the Yugoslav numbers are impressive: from 1958 to 1965, at least 184 Yugoslav leaders stayed in the United States, twenty-three per year,[18] compared to thirty-five grants per year in France, twenty-seven in Italy, and twenty-two in the UK.

The FLP, as this chapter reveals, was the most subversive US exchange program in communist Yugoslavia. Remarkably, it was encouraged by the Yugoslav government as it was spurred by American policymakers. Unlike other US exchange programs which, like the Ford or Eisenhower Foundation, submitted to varying degrees of Yugoslav control, the FLP had complete 'freedom in candidate selection.'[19] Travels of top governmental officials, leaders, and specialists were well funded by diem allowances issued as pay cheques in advance by the Embassy. Curiously, the pay cheque granted further baggage allowances giving the grantee the opportunity to bring home books and other material from the United States.[20] In the case of high-level leaders, the Yugoslav government assumed the costs, convinced of the full potential such experience could gain.[21] The 'free selection of itinerary,' and the best treatment given to FLP fellows by the State Department, made this trip enjoyable and desirable. 'We have consciously tried to avoid places,' assured Washington to Embassy Belgrade, 'where [anti-Yugoslav] demonstrations have occurred in the past (Texas, Chicago), or where in our judgement there is a good chance difficulties may arise (Cleveland, Pittsburgh).'[22] To guarantee the best experience, the State Department instructed the local US press to avoid any interviews with Yugoslav leaders, especially with complicated or embarrassing questions.[23] Not surprisingly, in a year or two, the FLP became one of the most wanted and sought-after exchange programs for the Yugoslav ruling elite.

The first years[24]

With bilateral relations running on stable terms, the State Department decided to solve the problematic image Yugoslav journalists were outputting through the press, confident that, even though 'heavily controlled by the Press Law,' Yugoslav journalists would, sooner or later, try a 'break-through.'[25] The 1958 FLP leaders were, almost entirely, 'media and communication leaders.' Ilija Antonijević was the director of Radio Belgrade, Jaša Davico was the editor of *Ekonomska politika*, among the top Yugoslav economic journals, and Tedi Pahor was the editor of *Slovenski Poročevalec*, the predecessor of *Delo*, the major Slovenian newspaper. The feedback collected by the Embassy left US officials enthusiastic: Antonijević became more 'cordial' and 'more knowledgeable – as well as more understanding – about America.' Upon his return, he appeared on radio programmes and was featured in a series of magazine articles lecturing about the United States.[26] 'Broadway didn't disappoint me,' Antonijević reported in a radio interview, 'and I say this as a man who does not easily get enthusiastic about things. [...] The races are mixed. You see the black, the white, the red and the yellow.'[27] And he added in another place, 'The United States and its people taught me how life can be a little more comfortable, but still rewarding in achievements.'[28] The opportunity to explain Yugoslavia to the American people motivated many FLP grantees. The journalist Mirko Ostojić recalled that, while attending a journalism class at Chicago University, 'he was asked by a student whether his government allowed him to leave Yugoslavia and if he would be in trouble [...] for coming to the United States.' Ostojić remained 'more amused than upset by the incident,' but also felt that he had an opportunity to explain his country to the Americans he met.[29]

In 1959, the US government shifted towards a bolder leaders-centred policy. As Chapter 1 explored, the growing coercive legislation that limited free press in Yugoslavia concerned USIS representatives. The Yugoslav Press Law, approved in late 1960, created heated debate on both sides long before it became operational. USIS felt circumstances worsened after 1958. The options on the table were few, so USIS strategy to target Federal Executive Council leaders seemed a worthy one. As the equivalent of the US Cabinet, the Federal Executive Council (FEC) members were the only ones entitled to assure policies in favour of the United States. The FLP invitees reflected such intentions: USIS invited CC member Vlajko Begović, FEC secretaries Leon Geršković, Bogdan Osolnik, and Moma Marković, and first secretary at the FO Anton Kacijan. USIS almost failed to convince Krste Crvenkovski to leave: Kardelj himself, the major Yugoslav ideologist and closest friend of Tito, solicited an uncertain Crvenkovski to accept the FLP invitation.[30] Crvenkovski, FEC Secretary for Education and CC member, was a top cultural leader from Macedonia with great expertise on foreign cultural agreements (he supervised the signing of the Polish–Yugoslav exchange agreement in 1959 in Moscow). He was the perfect leader with whom to start the Fulbright negotiations for Yugoslavia: at his arrival at the State Department in 1960, he was welcomed by Senator William Fulbright and USIA director George Allen.[31] From 29 April to 20 May, Crvenkovski saw the best of the United States: Washington's Smithsonian Institution, the National Gallery of Arts, the Library of Congress. In New York, he visited the Ford and Rockefeller foundations, Columbia University, the Metropolitan Museum of Art, Metropolitan Opera, Museum of Modern Art (MoMA), the United Nations, and obviously, Broadway. He toured Chicago, Los Angeles, the Hollywood MGM, and paid a visit to Disneyland.[32]

USIS was astonished by how profoundly Crvenkovski had changed his 'attitude towards the United States and his working relationship with the Embassy and USIS': he was eager to accept a USIS proposal to prepare English textbooks for Yugoslav schools; he flaunted 'a more thorough knowledge of cultural life in the United States and the purpose of USIA'; and he seemed 'more willing to accept social invitations' from the Embassy and USIS, or to 'instruct his staff' to do so. Above all, he returned optimistically disposed towards the Fulbright negotiations.[33]

The early 1960s

While the Yugoslav government got into a serious diplomatic war with the United States from late 1960 – in a diatribe that persisted up until the Fulbright agreement appeased both sides in November 1964 – Yugoslav interest in the FLP increased spectacularly. Tito's critique of the West for colonial harassment at the 15th UN General Assembly in New York, shifted towards plain anti-Americanism at the First Non-Aligned Conference in Belgrade.[34] Washington fought back, and in June 1962 Congress revoked MFN treatment to Yugoslavia. Bilateral relations were reaching a drowning point, and the FLP in Yugoslavia seemed at risk: the Yugoslav FO prohibited Petar Zdravkovski, a Macedonian government member, from departing under the FLP in 1962, and Yugoslav officials forcefully protested the US individual calls to leaders. Still, for unspoken reasons, the FO let Zdravkovski depart, even though the foreign affairs officers strongly recommended 'that our distinguished political people [...] desist from making the visits in a situation of unresolved issues between the two countries.'[35] Beyond warnings requiring that the FLP calls should obtain a green light on 'the political opportunity and the realization of these exchanges,'[36] nothing really changed. FLP grantees continued to depart in ever increasing numbers, exempted from diplomatic grievances between Washington and Belgrade.

The US–Yugoslav relationship now at risk renewed the Yugoslav–Soviet friendship, which immediately impacted Yugoslav cultural freedoms. Soviet leader Nikita Khrushchev paid the most cordial visit to Tito in October 1962. After Tito returned from Moscow in December 1962, an anti-Western campaign against distortions of socialist reality and 'alien' influence in the arts, press, and literature gained momentum. Speaking at a working factory on 29 December, he warned against foreign infiltration that 'troubled and obscured the purity [...] of socialism.' He went further in his 1962 New Year's Eve message, addressing 'alien and incompatible' Western literary trends.[37]

None of these diplomatic impasses obstructed smooth FLP dynamics. In February and March 1960, the AEC invited the Yugoslav Federal Nuclear Energy Commission to visit the United States through the leader program. Ranković himself allowed the departures; secretary Slobodan Nakićenović and other FNEC members came overseas with the director of the Hot Laboratory at Vinča, Zdenko Dizdar, involved in the negotiations over uranium enrichment and plutonium reprocessing technologies.[38] In a 'welcoming and heartfelt atmosphere,' the FNEC delegation visited the Oak Ridge National Laboratory Tennessee, the Argonne National Laboratory Chicago, the Berkley Radiation Laboratory, the Idaho Reactor Testing Laboratory, and the Dresden

Atomic Power Plant, gave interviews to the press, featured in Voice of America, and appeared on television.[39] The State Department/AEC and the Yugoslav Commission jointly and enthusiastically produced an active cooperation program for the future. The agreement, signed on 19 April 1961, brought $200,000 to the Jožef Stefan Institute in Ljubljana and $150,000 to the Vinča Hot Laboratory in Belgrade.[40] The construction site for the 250 kW TRIGA Mark II light-water research reactor opened at Jožef Stefan in 1961, and started producing radioactive isotopes for use in the medicinal industry and science from 1965 until the present day. US General Atomics provided TRIGA with 20 per cent enriched uranium fuel under the same cooperation agreement.[41] The FNEC–AEC negotiations make a case for how adaptable and functional to bilateral relations the FLP was, conceived as serving as an instrument of soft power rather than having a political goal *per se*. When the FLP exposed 'present and potential leaders' to the 'ideology and techniques of free societies,' as in the case of the FNEC in the United States, it met Yugoslav needs 'for technically and professionally trained personnel' fundamental to developing 'a high level of cultural and scientific achievements.'[42]

Besides surmounting diplomatic complications and exploiting the Yugoslav hunger for technology, the FLP policymakers observed, from the early 1960s, that the Yugoslav regime was in a drift for liberalization. Even before the 1963 constitution was approved, decentralization and federalization entered forcefully into Yugoslav political debate. A 1961 poll suggested that a large percentage of students had serious doubts about the validity of Marxist ideology; one third of the respondents replied that Yugoslavia had no genuine democracy like in Western Europe.[43] Those who left Yugoslavia for the United States pointed to a lack of fundamental personal freedom as one of the regime's most harmful acts, but few were able to name specific losses. They described an atmosphere in which, 'the individual has no freedom,' rather than cataloguing the acts of repression.[44]

American policymakers deemed that much work should be done with leaders 'uncommitted or even anti-American in their present orientation,' not only elected officials but 'party officials, local committee chairmen, and […] potential party leaders' – in other words, 'the sons of local "elite" leaders' who needed to be exposed to 'modern concepts of free society.'[45] This policy direction reflected on the FLP grantees sent abroad between 1961 and 1962. Besides the FEC secretaries involved in the program, such as Herbert Kraus, Secretary for Health, Lidija Šentjurc, Secretary for Social Affairs and Public Utilities, and Pero Djetelić, who later became director of the ideological commission of SAWPY, for the first time republican and local leaders were sent overseas: Djurica Jojkić, president of Vojvodina's Executive Council (EC), Filip Bajković, president of Montenegro's EC, Osman Karabegović, President of Bosnia and Herzegovina People's Assembly, Milutin Baltić and Anka Beruš, members of the Croatian government. Two extremely influential mayors departed on the FLP as well: Većeslav Holjevac from Zagreb (1952–62), and Milijan Neoričić from Belgrade (1961–64). A couple of years later, in 1967, Holjevac signed and supported the Declaration on the Name and Position of the Croatian Language, a request for cultural independency from the Croatian intelligentsia, for which he was expelled from the Party in 1969.

The anti-Western cultural campaign that boomed in 1962 pushed, rather than pulled, more cultural leaders towards the United States. Despite Party criticisms, Yugoslav artists, poets, dramatists, musicians, and actors were less committed to official Party lines.[46] In 1962 and 1963, the American government invited first-class cultural leaders to the United States: Mira Trajlović, dramaturg, theatre director and founder of Belgrade's Atelje 212, renowned for its avant-garde repertoire; Josip Depolo, director of the Dubrovnik Summer Festival, who made great connections with American impresarios and music critics; and Zoran Kržišnik, director of the Modern Art Gallery in Ljubljana.

The State Department recognized that 'editors, and staff of all elements of the press, radio, and television,'[47] were qualified, urbane enough, 'and with ready insight into the work of their Western colleagues,' to be introduced to the 'Western practice of free communication and association without political implications.'[48] USIS in fact struggled with the US treatment in the Yugoslav press from the very beginning. The issue was brought to journalists, editors, government members, the FO, and the Secretariat of Information, quite unsuccessfully. When the Cuban Missile Crisis erupted, Yugoslav press coverage attributed 'wisdom only to Khrushchev,' and accused the United States 'of intransigence,' USIS remarked. Despite the negative bias, USIS remained optimistic: it seemed that, 'both in content and form,' the Yugoslav newspapers were 'coming closer to our [American] norms,' separating news and editorials, and picking from Western press agencies, and even USIS news. Sending influential leaders on the FLP seemed a lucid choice, and intensified between 1962 and 1964. Top leaders were sent abroad, among them Gavro Altman, foreign editor of *Komunist*, the LCY official journal; Alija Nuhbegović, from Sarajevo TV; Miroljub Jevtović, from Radio Belgrade (he later moved to Belgrade TV); Zvonimir Kristl, a foreign reporter from *Vjesnik*; Dragutin Auguštin, deputy chief editor at Zagreb's *Večernji List*; Ivan Šinkovec, from the Slovenian *Delo*; Djordje Radenković, from *NIN*, Belgrade's weekly newspaper; and Bogdan Pešić, from Belgrade's daily *Večernje Novosti*. Upon his return, Pešić became director of the leading Serbian newspaper *Borba*. Such a strategy, PAO Roberts in 1963 was convinced, predisposed 'at least lower echelons' to 'continued close cultural relations with the West.' Roberts was right: the lower-level leaders 'exercised quite some influence on the higher echelons for he [Tito] later disavowed any anti-Western intent.'[49]

The FLP gained momentum by the mid-1960s, specifically after the Party launched a debate about economic reforms. American interests focused on the most vital and energetic Yugoslav leaders. A typical grantee, around 40 years old and with a great career ahead, was considered, within the Yugoslav framework, 'basically a democrat, proud of some [...] achievements of [his] system, but by no means dogmatic or contentious, and essentially pragmatic in outlook.'[50] Revolving around individuals, the FLP caught on immediate investment-return effectiveness. '[P]olite and reserved on their arrival in the United,' the FLP fellows became 'enthusiastic and grateful upon departure,'[51] 'more approachable than heretofore,' with a 'clearer understanding of and more sympathy for the American mentality and U.S. policies.' More friendships allowed the Embassy and USIS 'to expand and develop [...] [the] over-all program more intelligently.' Able to influence the practices of institutions both in the economic and political spheres, these leaders became familiar 'with the U.S. methods and philosophy,' which led to emulation, as Embassy reports underlined.[52] More crucially, the FLP reached Yugoslav representatives beyond the official channels and encouraged them 'to adopt more positive attitudes towards the [exchange] programs in general and the present [Fulbright] negotiations in particular.' As PAO Roberts recalled, Yugoslavia abhorred the possibility of becoming 'an arena for the cold war' which made personal contacts 'at upper and intermediate levels of the hierarchy' quite stressful. The FLP, by enticing an 'understanding attitude,' 'increased confidence,' and by correcting 'misconceptions and superficial judgements' about the United States, served as the launching pad for personal contacts with Yugoslav leaders. Through the FLP, personal contacts became so intense and 'most effective' to the extent that they were the only way to influence 'directly, and often immediately, [...] our foreign policy.'[53]

Yugoslav criticism of too much US autonomy in inviting their leaders did not deflate their enthusiasm for the program. Even concern over presumed Yugoslav embarrassment for those leaders asking to be selected as FLP nominees caused no major disaffection. A case exploded at Central Committee level when Jožef Nadj, Vice President of Vojvodina's Assembly, and Stanka Veselinov, member of the Federal Assembly, first declined, but then pledged for an FLP, before they needed to move to a less important position. 'We should ensure,' stressed the LCY Central Committee, 'that none of our people can offer themselves or accept the invitation of the American officers.'[54] In the Yugoslav government, only the Federal Secretariat for Education and Culture (SEC) remained openly pro-FLP, with words of high praise for the 'direct contacts' and personal initiatives in the US–Yugoslav cultural exchange.[55] Instead, the SEC became critical of the Yugoslav lack of coordination, the obnoxious slowness of the FCCR, and the incapability to attract more American specialists.[56]

From the mid to late 1960s

The 1963 constitution awakened an 'offensive of reform forces' in Yugoslavia.[57] Adopted in April 1963, it renamed the Federation as the Socialist Federal Republic of Yugoslavia and defined the self-management governing structures. The preamble mentioned the sovereign rights of the working people and the nationalities to be exercised through both federal and republican institutions and protected by a newly established constitutional court. This 'complicated formula denied sovereignty to the republics as territorial entities but opened the door to a degree of polycentrism in the governance' by allowing them to manage some social and economic questions 'without federal interference.' Slovenian Edvard Kardelj, as its main author, introduced new rules on the rotation of offices, favoured general decentralization, and pushed for economic reform envisioned to withdraw central planning in favour of more market-driven competition. Kardelj got Vladimir Bakarić, President of Croatia, and the Zagreb 'economic school' to endorse his plan. He also replaced Ranković with Koča Popović as vice president, thus increasing Ranković's isolation among the establishment. Relations between the two had been strained for years.[58] Even if it was a single-party system, US policymakers believed there were symptoms of 'parliamentary democracy' in the rotation system that the new constitution introduced which should be encouraged and stimulated. The State Department trusted that this was a 'transition to a more liberal form of government in Yugoslavia.'[59]

With the USSR sliding towards the neo-Stalinism of the Brezhnev era, Tito remained reluctant about reform, before deciding to take a gamble at the Eighth LCY Congress in December 1964, where he endorsed the principles of market socialism. Nevertheless, he claimed that no one except the Party would control inequalities, and sternly warned against ideological or nationalist deviation. While Tito held talks with the Soviet leadership in Moscow in June 1965, at the very moment 'the Kosygin plans for economic reform in the USSR were in the process of being shelved,' and the Soviet leadership asked Yugoslavia not to stray 'into the capitalist camp,' Belgrade's Federal Assembly brought in a series of economic measures.[60] The 1965 economic reform that Rusinow defined by the oxymoron 'laissez faire socialism,' signed on 24 July 1965, increased the role of the market in the industrial sector, reduced the scope of secondary redistribution by the State, simplified and rationalized foreign trade, and increased its impact on the domestic market. A drastic revision was applied to existing price ratios that were left free to increase in accordance with supply and demand. The tax reform reduced the State's share in the net income of the country's enterprises from 49 to 29 per cent; turnover tax was shrunk to a sales tax on final consumption; taxes on gross personal incomes and social insurance contributions decreased from 17.5 to 10.5 per cent. The government made special efforts to simplify and liberalize foreign trade: the dinar was devalued, and the International Monetary Fund supported the conversions with $80 million in drawing rights, which ultimately brought Yugoslavia, in August 1966, full membership of the General Agreement on Tariffs and Trade (GATT).[61]

Prominent economic leaders who endorsed the 1965 economic reform stayed on an FLP in the early 1960s. Milentije Popović, member of the CC (1948–64) and the FEC, considered by both the State Department and the Embassy as 'one of the most important and influential figures of the Yugoslav government,' and 'Yugoslavia's top economic planner,' went on an FLP in 1961.[62] Nikola Balog was another one: as Undersecretary of State, Secretary for Legislation and Organization, and former Assistant Secretary for General Economic Affairs, Balog was next to the top in the ministry that planned economic legislation, and adviser to the president, with great influence in the field. His contacts with US economic experts and big business representatives, made through a 1963 FLP, strongly influenced his views about a market-driven economy.[63]

It was not the case that many of the mid-level echelons on an FLP in 1964 were involved in economic policy planning. Among them, Rista Aćimović was the general manager at the Yugoslav Bank for Foreign Trade; Krešimir Car was Croatian vice president at the Committee for Tourism; Batric Jovanović was director at the Yugoslav Civil Aeronautics; Milka Kufrin was president of the Federal Committee for Tourism; Ladislav Rupnik was Slovenian director of the Financial and Economic Matters; and Svetozar Pepovski was Assistant Secretary of Labour.

Many old guard pro-centralist communists opposed the 1965 economic reform as they saw decentralization as a path to disintegration. On 1 July 1966, Ranković, chief of the military intelligence services, was dismissed at the Fourth Central Committee Plenum held at Brioni, Tito's summer residence, allegedly for abusing his authority by tapping the President's sleeping quarters. The fall of Ranković hardly hit the proponents of centralized Yugoslavia: the UDBA got reorganized, while more federal power passed to the republics, even intensifying intranational grievances. As Dejan Jović argues, Yugoslavia aimed at a 'radical decentralization of the state,' not only to counter the 'national question,' but because 'an inevitable task of socialism was to succeed in replacing the state with a "self-governing society".' Decentralization and de-etatization was a *'conditio sine qua non'* for a complex system of 'direct, or semi-direct, economic and political democracy via [...] *delegates* and *delegations*.'[64] The replacement of Ranković put more liberties on the political and cultural spot; as Savka Dabčević-Kučar wrote in her memoirs, it seemed as 'if one could breathe more freely.'[65] In the meantime, decentralization took more ground and, in 1966, the federal agencies passed their duties and financial matters to the republics and local government.[66] The interest in local leaders was pushed forward by US policymakers during the mid and late 1960s. The presence of economic leaders such as Dušan Avramov, director at the Federal Food Administration, Nikola Djuverović, Federal Secretary for Foreign Trade, Janez Nedog, president at the District Chamber of Commerce in Ljubljana, Zoran Polić, Federal Secretary at Budget and Administration Organization, and Franc Tretjak, director at the Slovenian Chamber of Commerce Rates, was increasingly high.

In the meantime, USIS shifted its pressure from the Yugoslav press to publishers. In 1963, representatives from McGraw-Hill Book Co., Rand McNally, Princeton University Press, and the American Book Publishers Council, toured Yugoslavia to create new contacts and projects, clear 'misapprehensions,' and promote 'a better selection of American works' for translation in the country. Closer cooperation between the two publishing industries meant 'a greater circulation of American books,' and a chance to reach the entire Yugoslav publishing industry.[67] As a follow-up, USIS invited the top Yugoslav publishers to stay in the United States between 1964 and 1965: Antonije Isaković from *Prosveta*, Ljubica Jurela from *Gradjevinska knjiga*, two publishing houses from Belgrade, Slovenian Zorka Peršić from *Mladinska knjiga*, Croatian Branko Zutić, director at *Školska knjiga*, and also leading journalists from *Komunist*, *Vjesnik*, the LCY journal *Naša Stvarnost*, *Borba*, *Politika*, and *Tanjug*, the Yugoslav News Agency.

The negotiations over the Fulbright Program intensified USIS efforts to bring more academic leaders to the United States as networks became crucial for its implementation. By the mid-1960s, university rectors and faculty deans gained much space on the FLP priority list, with major names such as Kosta Spaić, rector of the Academy of Dramatic Arts in Zagreb, Albert Štruna, rector of Ljubljana University, Slavko Macarol, rector of Zagreb University, Aleksander Trumić, rector of Sarajevo University, and Kiril Miljovski, rector of Skopje University.

In less than ten years, the FLP became one of the most renewed and sought-after US exchange programs; rather than complaining about those involved, the Yugoslavs grumbled about those who were left out. As the influential FO leader Marko Nikezić emphasized, 'Americans need to [ask us] who they should consider as leaders.'[68] The 'stay of our officials,' claimed the Yugoslav cabinet in 1965, served 'the general interests of our country if administered in an organized manner and with the consultation of the interested bodies and organizations.'[69] The Yugoslav government's request for approval of a leader's home institutions (or the FEC and the FO), and a final report upon return, remained more a dream than a reality. Nevertheless, Yugoslavs continued to depart, in ever increasing numbers: thirty leaders in 1965 and forty in 1966.[70] Contacts were appreciated on both sides. When, in late 1966, FEC Secretary for Education and Culture, Janez Vipotnik, returned to Yugoslavia after his stay on the FLP, he wrote to Ambassador Elbrick expressing gratitude for the 'many contacts' and 'frank talks with many great and prominent' Americans.[71] Elbrick was no less enthusiastic: 'visits such the one you have just completed are reflected in the continued good relations between our two countries,' he replied.[72] Senator Fulbright, who Vipotnik met in Washington during his stay, responded in almost same tone to another grateful Vipotnik letter: 'Everyone I know wants good relations with your country. There is much greater interest among my colleagues in your country than you could imagine.' And he concluded: 'your current program is oriented in the right direction,' and 'you will demonstrate with your pragmatic approach [...] that it is possible to develop new and original ways of improving the welfare of the people. I personally am very interested in the success of your country.'[73]

When the State Department started cutting the FLP budget in 1967, its main objective, namely linking the Yugoslav leadership to the United States and providing a network for a positive Fulbright implementation, was already half accomplished. The cuts obviously left the Embassy disappointed, especially at the point when the Yugoslav government became 'less suspicious of and with less desire to control the program.' The US officials protested, emphasizing the value of 'a primary instrument for advancing US policy goals in Yugoslavia [that] [...] could also have an adverse effect in other, more subjective, relationships between the Embassy and the GOY.'[74] A 1967 Embassy memo put it in this way: 'when a rumor reached the Ministry of Foreign Affairs that the IVP [International Visitor Program] was to be sharply cut back,' he prompted the then third-ranking official, Srdjan Prica, 'to personally telephone the Ambassador' and express the strong concern of the Yugoslav government. Without a doubt, argued the Embassy officials, the FLP/IVP was greatly affecting 'the course [of] moderate tendencies in political and economic reforms' in Yugoslavia; the contacts with Yugoslav leaders widened the possibility 'to arrange various cultural programs, often on relatively short notice.' As soon as the number of Yugoslav leaders would become 'large enough to assure mutual support,' the Embassy affirmatively claimed, 'the real effects of that exposure to American life and ideals will be more readily seen.'[75]

The Embassy officers rightly observed that, as historian Scott-Smith argues, the short impact on participants, whether 'positive or negative,' was 'unquestionable.' However, as time passes, and the exchange experience becomes 'one of many variables' that affect political decisions in the long-term, it 'remains difficult to pin down.'[76] Is there, therefore, any way to identify long-lasting influence? I claim that, to find the right answer, we should refocus the question as 'What was the US's main objective in putting these exchanges in place?' USIA Country Plans emphasized the core matter of linking Yugoslavia to the West. In other words, it meant to change the regime by enticing its most progressive and Western-oriented leaders to look for change from within, but through experience gained from the outside. The FLP laid ground for the Fulbright enactment way before other communist countries did. The first enthusiastic impressions from the Embassy ended up being less naive than we might think at an initial glance. Returning from the United States, the Yugoslav leaders encouraged, as in a vicious circle, other contacts and new forms of exchange that, as this chapter demonstrates, were not delayed in coming.

Fulbright comes to Yugoslavia

The Fulbright Program would never have taken hold in Yugoslavia if it was not for the FLP having such a positive and immediate 'favourable effect.'[77] Soon after Congress approved the first five FLP grants to Yugoslavia, in December 1958, the Board of Foreign Scholarships (BFS), a presidentially appointed twelve-member committee to select the Fulbright grantees, 'unanimously concurred in the initiation [of the] Fulbright Agreement with Yugoslavia.'[78] The decision came after almost one year of consultations between the State Department and the Embassy in Belgrade, with the major concern being that the Yugoslavs might intend 'to control the selection of all grantees and [...] attempt across-the board choices of CP members.'[79] At the time the two governments started negotiating over the agreement, the Fulbright Program had already been extended to thirty-eight countries in Western Europe, the Middle East, the Near and Far East, Australia, and Latin America, although without involving any communist country.[80] Since its inception, the program inspired and activated 'the biggest, most significant movement of scholars across the face of the earth since the fall of Constantinople in 1453,' as Ronald McCallum, Senator Fulbright's Oxford tutor, rightly noted.[81] While the FLP/IVP went after short-term influence, the Fulbright Program envisioned 'a long term, slowly maturing effect on potentially influential groups.'[82] Or, as Rade Petrović, former executive secretary at the Yugoslav Binational Commission, claimed, 'the activities of the Fulbright Commission and the Fulbright Program in Yugoslavia were [...] a Western drilling of holes in a socialist "Swiss cheese".'[83]

Senator James William Fulbright gained popularity when, in September 1945, he introduced an amendment to the 1944 Surplus Property Act that envisioned the sales of US surplus property overseas to fund an educational exchange program. Two months later, he replaced his initial proposal with a broader bill, and on 1 August 1946, President Truman signed the Fulbright bill into law. Officially known as the Smith-Mundt Act, the Fulbright scholarship program came into being.[84] Fulbright's concern with mutual scholarly exchanges dated back to his college years. As a student at the University of Arkansas, he applied for a Rhodes Scholarship at the age of twenty. This first international exchange program, founded in 1903 by the British colonial

statesman and businessman Cecil Rhodes, aimed to foster a worldwide commonwealth based on mutual understanding and future leaders' proficiencies, albeit nar-
rowly focused on Anglo-Saxon countries and exclusively white male-oriented. Rhodes
gave students from the British Commonwealth, the United States, and Germany the
opportunity to study at Oxford University. Fulbright's experience at Oxford, from
1925 to 1929, and his ostensible study trips to continental Europe, profoundly influenced his intellectual development and leadership skills. As Fulbright's biographer
Randall Woods pointed out, the spirit of the Rhodes Scholars at Oxford served as an
indelible and long-lasting model in his later quest for internationalism, mutual understanding, and the fostering of strong bonds across cultures and national boundaries.
Fellowships based on international learning became his identity flag in the years to
come.[85] In 1961, the Fulbright-Hays Act (introduced in the House of Representatives
by Wayne Hays from Ohio), officially the Mutual Educational and Cultural Exchange
Act, broadened the categories of foreign leaders and specialists that could participate
in non-profit cultural, artistic, and athletic activities in the United States, supported
the creation of American studies at universities abroad, and simplified the creation of
new agreements. President Kennedy signed it on 25 June 1962 with executive order
11034.[86]

Scholars usually interpreted the Fulbright Program as the corollary of Senator
Fulbright's internationalist Wilsonianism, aimed at fostering the mutual understanding of nations, helping to 'rid the world of the twin evils of parochialism and
nationalism,' combatting 'intolerance and aggression,' and, finally, educating future
leaders in a liberal, internationalist *Weltanschauung*.[87] Besides ideological premises,
the Fulbright Program developed on rationalist foundations, using the surplus wartime economy, particularly the sale of military articles abroad that would otherwise
have been lost. As Sam Lebovic argues, the ideology of liberal universalism resulted
both from US global hegemony and the defeat of fascism; it presumed national asym-
metries and stemmed from an ideology of nationalist globalism. Unquestionably, the
latter was an American cultural practice that subsisted prior to the Cold War, but, with
the Fulbright exchange program, it 'helped lay the groundwork for Cold War cultural
propaganda [and] [...] to making the American Century.'[88]

Tito and Senator Fulbright

In the late 1950s, several favourable conditions propelled the start of the US–Yugoslav
negotiations over the Fulbright Program: the 1958 US–Soviet agreement on cultural
exchanges, the Yugoslav inclination for interstate agreements rather than informal
settlements, and the encouraging reception of the Ford Foundation program after five
years of fruitless negotiations.[89] Congress had originally voted to include Yugoslavia
in the Fulbright Program in 1959, hoping to set a precedent with a communist country.[90] Informal talks commenced when Krste Crvenkovski, Secretary for Education
and Culture, met State Department officials in Washington, DC where he stayed
under the FLP in 1960. Soon after, the two governments exchanged a memorandum
giving formal shape to the talks.[91]

At an early stage, negotiations got stuck over three complications: Yugoslav dinars were not convertible for international travel and staying abroad; the Yugoslavs were reticent about candidate selection; and both parties disagreed over the nationality of the Binational Commission's executive director and secretary. The first impediment was quickly resolved: both sides approved the use of 'excess' currencies owned by the US government in Yugoslavia through PL 480 – the Agreement of the Surplus Agricultural Supplies – to cover travel expenses for Yugoslav grantees (American institutions and the State Department would supply the rest) and full coverage for American grantees in Yugoslavia.[92] The PL 480 Sales Agreements, signed for the first time in 1955, were renewed by amendments every subsequent year, and allowed a favourable currency exchange rate at $1 for 475 Yugoslav dinars, while the official currency exchange rate was around 700 dinars per dollar (at least until 1966 when, due to economic reform, devaluation augmented the exchange rate up to 1,200 per dollar).[93] Candidate selection created apprehension on both sides. The debate over procedures lasted through 1962 and 1963, with the Yugoslavs strongly lobbying and, eventually, winning the right to preselect future Fulbright candidates.[94] The final settlement included a first round of interviews by the Binational Commission and, in a second round, examination of the list by the Ford Commission or Academic Committee, formerly the Yugoslav Commission for Cooperation with the American and Other Foundations, a twenty-two-member group appointed by the Secretary of Education and Culture, gathering distinguished academics and specialists from all republics. Created in 1958 to select candidates for the Ford exchange program, this commission chose Fulbright candidates that best fitted the republican university needs. The final list returned afterwards to the Binational Commission and was forwarded to the BFS in Washington.[95] Regarding the directorship of the Commission, the American side protested to an executive director and secretary of Yugoslav nationality, but ultimately agreed to have in return a Commission's chair of American nationality.[96]

By mid-1964, the major impediments seemed overcome, and the agreement turned into reality on 6 November 1964 in Belgrade, envisioning 'to promote further mutual understanding' between the peoples of both countries 'by a wider exchange of knowledge and professional talents through educational activities.' The Binational Commission set by the agreement consisted of eight equally split members.[97] Yugoslavia was the first socialist country to sign a Fulbright agreement (it started in 1973–74 in the Soviet Union, and 1977 in Hungary), and the only country by 1964 visited by Senator Fulbright, who attended the signing event.

It was a victory moment for bilateral relations and mutual appreciation from both sides. Yugoslav State Secretary Koča Popović proudly emphasized how, as a truly 'progressive personality of the American public and political life' and an early friend of Yugoslavia, Fulbright departed only two days after Johnson was elected President of the United States.[98] Beyond initial intentions, Fulbright's visit to Yugoslavia profoundly shaped his attitude towards communism and what he considered the proper US foreign policy towards regimes in Eastern Europe, Cuba, Vietnam, and the Soviet Union itself. The trip marked a watershed in his thinking about communism and the role the United States should play in the world. As a Cold War case, Yugoslavia helped inform Fulbright about approaches to independent nationalist communism.[99] Fulbright's stay in Yugoslavia was an eminent political event. The senator met chief Party leaders, many of them progressive reformers with pro-Western attitudes – Koča Popović, Marko Nikezić, Edvard Kardelj, and Janez Vipotnik.[100] His meeting with Josip Broz Tito at Brdo Kranj, Slovenia, ended in 'good humour,' and Broz's appreciation for the senator's pro-Yugoslav campaigns at the US Senate Foreign Relations Committee,[101] especially towards his determination to restore the 1963 MFN treaty to Yugoslavia. While the Yugoslav government dissented over US foreign policy in Latin America, the Congo, and Cyprus, Tito admired Senator Fulbright for his flexible position on Cuba, Panama, and China, and his engagement with nuclear disarmament and non-proliferation. Fulbright, in fact, never hid his admiration for Yugoslavia: as he acknowledged to Koča Popović and Vladimir Popović, President of the Committee for Foreign Affairs and International Relations at the FEC, Yugoslavia was a 'pragmatic adjustment,' 'an experiment of worldwide impact,' and a 'bridge between the capitalist and socialist world.'[102] While they disagreed on Berlin, both Tito and Fulbright criticized US foreign policy towards Cuba and pleaded for 'peaceful coexistence' with the Soviet Union.[103] Proud of the first agreement signed with a communist country, Senator Fulbright underscored how the exchanges of intellectuals and leaders would end up being more powerful than diplomatic relations in fostering good relationships. 'Yugoslavia,' he emphasized, could enlighten 'other nations to […] overcome the ideologies that divide them.'[104] Fulbright's 1964 mission to Yugoslavia tackled two issues: as a politician, he corrected misunderstandings that had damaged bilateral relations; as an intellectual, he confirmed his support for a Yugoslavia independent of the Soviet Union, and ultimately left the country even more convinced that the United States should take a different approach to the situation in Vietnam.[105]

The Fulbright Program changed my life (1965–70)

Soon after Senator Fulbright departed, the Binational Commission initiated the first competition in December 1964. The first year of the program (1965–66) provided twelve complete grants for Yugoslav and American postgraduate students, researchers, teaching assistants, lecturers, and professors, twelve additional travel grants for scholarships at US universities, and five grants for American postdoctorate researchers provided by the FCCR.[106] The applicants' interest and number of grants increased rapidly, from eighty-eight applications in 1964 to 215 in 1970. The size of the grants increased as well: in 1967, the Commission provided thirty-eight Yugoslav and sixteen American grants, rising to fifty-five for the Yugoslavs and seventeen for the Americans in 1970. Ultimately, the first five years of the Fulbright Program resulted in 254 grants to Yugoslav and 112 to American professors, scholars, and researchers.[107] As John Lampe pointed out, the Fulbright Program in Yugoslavia was the second largest program in Europe after West Germany.[108]

Numbers show that, between 1965 and 1970, most of the Yugoslav grantees (almost 80 per cent) were picked from the major, and prestigious, Yugoslav universities – Belgrade, Zagreb, and Ljubljana – capitals with a bold presence of

Yugoslav intelligentsia able to make a difference. USIS local effort had a long-lasting presence in these capitals, whether through the libraries (Belgrade and Zagreb), the CPP, or trade fair exhibitions. The Fulbright grantees revealed an unexpected female presence – around 22 per cent – when the Yugoslav academia was male-dominated at around 90 per cent. The data exposed a surprising number of senior scholars, mostly researchers, academics, and lecturers covering more than 50 per cent of total grants,[109] in contradiction to the mission of the Fulbright Program to influence young post-graduate students. It was not the Yugoslav priority though; the Yugoslav Commission members pushed for, and obtained, more grants to senior scholars to meet local university needs.

Nevertheless, the real fight in the Commission was over grants and projects, including Yugoslav studies in the United States, American studies in Yugoslavia, the natural, technical, and technological sciences, the social sciences and education, financial aid to seminars in Yugoslavia, and the arts and human sciences.[110] The Yugoslav authorities, the Academic Commission itself, lobbied and accomplished the prevalence of the natural, technical, and technological science grants that Yugoslav universities needed most, and resisted US pressure for more human and social sciences projects.[111] Numbers were on the Yugoslav side: as deputy director of the Binational Commission, Petar Bošković, stated in 1967, the Ford Foundation was already covering the human and social sciences studies.[112] The Yugoslav scientists who were trained in the United States brought back home not only a stimulating research experience, but remarkable academic contacts. The United States became the Mecca for those ambitious researchers for whom a Fulbright fellowship abroad meant rapid and undisturbed professional advancement.[113] Ranko Bugarski, an English and general linguistics professor at Belgrade University, who retired in 2000, described his Fulbright experience as 'one of the greatest and most cherished experiences of my academic and private life.' Bugarski, who was fellow at University College London in 1962–63, and a Ford Foundation visiting scholar at Columbia University in 1966–67, recalled the Fulbright experience as 'opening up new and lifelong vistas,' and lasting with 'many happy memories.' The 'Fulbright program was,' he evoked, 'a precious endowment to mankind.'[114] Taib Šarić, who retired in 2005 as agronomy professor at the University of Sarajevo, a Fulbright fellow at the Department of Agronomy, Kansas State University, in 1967–68, recalled that, even if he was disappointed that, as he felt, the American people had little interest in other countries and their political systems and way of life, 'I thank the Americans for this kind of intellectual help.'[115]

Gratefulness for the Fulbright experience remained commonplace in many alumni writings and interviews. Petar Grgić, a Fulbright fellow from Zagreb University in 1965–66, once at home, sent a letter to the Binational Commission remembering the experience not only from a professional but also 'from [an] international and human relationship viewpoint.' 'All Americans that I've met,' he underlined, 'were very pleas-ant and fine people,' ready to 'happily help you. They will never let one feel left alone in a foreign country,' he concluded.[116]

As for many others Fulbright alumni worldwide, the Yugoslav Fulbright alumni experienced long and enduring impact. Marijan Bošković, for instance, a 1966–67 fellow from the Zagreb Institute of Food Research and Technologies (Institut za istraživanje i tehnologiju hrane), obtained his MSc in Food Science and Technology at MIT in 1968, thanks to a Fulbright scholarship.[117] The story of Bošković is emblematic: he married an American woman working at the Boston University Medical School, and then returned to Zagreb where he enrolled in a PhD program in biotechnologies. Proficient in English, he translated into Croatian the Apollo 13 space–ground communications during the three live broadcasts by Zagreb RTV in 1970, and interviewed the astronauts when they visited Yugoslavia. Hired by Coca-Cola's European headquarters in Rome in 1972, he stayed in Italy until 1974, then moved to the United States, which turned out to be his last destination. Here, at General Foods (today Kraft Foods), Bošković progressed from research scientist to research principal, and made new discoveries on antioxidants.[118]

As Arndt and Rubin reminded, being a Fulbright alumnus became 'synonymous with self-discovery and, by extension, with self-realization.' The discovery of the self, argued the authors, went hand in hand with the notion of service, 'the commitment to helping humankind' because individual actions could 'make a difference.' This enticed the alumnus to share the experience with others, 'to make it available more widely, and to multiply its potential.'[119]

Yugoslav versus US soft power

In 1969, the Fulbright Program celebrated its fifth anniversary in Yugoslavia. American ambassador, Charles Elbrick, and the President of the Federal Council on Education and Culture, Vukašin Mićunović, exchanged letters and prolonged the program for another four years.[120] In the meantime, John Richardson Jr., Assistant Secretary of State for Educational and Cultural Affairs (and head of the CU), convinced the Yugoslav government to participate in cost-sharing the program. When Richardson visited Belgrade in September, the deal was already done: 20 per cent of Fulbright's annual budget would go on the Yugoslavs. The first arrived in 1970, amounting to 375,000 new dinars; it increased to 525,000 in 1971. 'This decision,' recalled a State Department memo, was 'the first of its kind with a communist country.'[121] Aware of the benefits, the Yugoslavs consented to cost-sharing, when unknown vandals set fire to the Fulbright offices in Belgrade, deteriorating relations inside the Commission. The vandals' acts, committed between 21 and 22 July, caused damage to the facility and a partial loss of files. The Yugoslav government, embarrassed and uncomfortable, moved quickly: Koča Popović and Crvenkovski assured maximum effort in the investigations. The arson, politically motivated, was linked to a group of anti-American, Stalinist hardliners, protesting, according to Embassy sources, the 'sympathy' and 'well-developing ties' between the two countries, and remonstrating the visit to Tito of Vice President Hubert Humphrey.[122] In fact, the Embassy reported a verbal incident the same evening before the attack, when some young people loudly criticized the United States during the television broadcasting of the Apollo 11 moon landing at USIS.[123]

Papers produced by the Yugoslav government unveiled some permanent and obvious tensions within the Commission. Yugoslav members believed the State

Department used the annual appropriations as a 'weapon of political pressure; conscious that the 'Americans have some good reasons' for pursuing it, they deemed that, 'with better organization and coordination,' 'the advantage of the other side [could] be easily minimized.' The main aim, to support and increase the program, was functional to the country's scientific and technological advancement.[124] Such a position seemed anything but conciliatory, with Yugoslav ideological commissions at the CC, the SAWPY, and local city councils, battling what they considered the dangerous cultural penetration of USIS local activities. The hard line towards USIS activities on one hand, and the soft line towards cultural exchanges on the other, was not new on the Yugoslav political front: the divide between Yugoslav centralist and decentralist factions, as between those who believed in centralized political power and economy and those who endorsed more freedom for the republics and economic activities, distinguished the Yugoslav socialist experiment. As Dennison Rusinow argued, the Yugoslav leadership was a 'polycentric polyarchy involving a network of elites,' usually 'open to all except a few minorities excluded by geographical, cultural or self or externally-imposed ethnic or ideological isolation.' Such polyarchy unfolded in an 'impressive number of autonomously organized and institutionally legalized forces, representing divergent interests and values, [...] at all political levels, from commune to Federation.'[125] No surprise then that certain Yugoslav agencies, FO policymakers, and the secretaries of culture and education, subsidized the Fulbright Program as a resource of internationalization, long-term research, technological and industrial advancement, while, concurrently, the ideological commission, more suspicious towards the West, saw the American cultural incursion as public enemy number one.[126] The Yugoslav regime never resolved these tensions.

Unlike in other Western European countries, the Yugoslav Fulbright agreement conceded a great deal of decisional power to select candidates for their own interests. The State Department believed this was worth the gamble as encouraging results attested that, in just a couple of years, Yugoslav Fulbright alumni and US Fulbright specialists spread in every 'Yugoslav republic, in every Yugoslav city, in every Yugoslav university and at most of the university faculties.' Certainly, admitted US policymakers, the Yugoslav leadership participating in the program were 'prepared to gamble that the desired technical advances can be made without a total dislocation of socialist ideology.'[127] As the study grants in the United States became more and more 'avidly sought by Yugoslavs,' Yugoslav leaders became much 'more cooperative [because of] the courtesy and honour extended to them.' The stays in the United States gradually lost 'the stigma of "courting capitalism"' and became a status symbol among the Yugoslav elites.[128]

As the FLP for the Fulbright, the Fulbright Binational Commission in Yugoslavia became a starting point for US public–private cultural exchanges. The boom came immediately after the Commission began its job. The mechanism of exchanges expanded on a new organizational basis that intersected public and cultural diplomacy, but also private foundations, the State Department, and USIA.

State–private networks in the US public diplomacy agenda

The United States has been, since its foundation, the land of private initiative. This became more than evident during the Cold War when 'private allies of the State' worked out a 'system of "grey" propaganda' and engaged in a cultural cold war.[129] Dealing with European nations and societies, these organizations thrived on 'person-to-person familiarization of Americans and Europeans of all strata' and worked to prevent the spread of communism.[130] Private involvement seemed expected in a society with a strong philanthropic and individualistic tradition. As USIA director Streibert wrote to the *New York Times* publisher, Arthur Sulzberger, the victory over hearts and minds demanded 'the cooperation of individual American citizens, business groups, and our many private organizations.'[131]

'The private exchanges,' reminded the State Department in 1967, 'have the added impetus' to 'strengthen ties between institutions' and reach 'key intellectual government officials who play an important role in development and progress in Yugoslavia.'[132] Instead of inhibiting, the lack of one unifying exchange program spurred private initiative: in 1965, more than fifty US exchange programs, of which thirteen were State-based and the rest private and semi-private, were running in Yugoslavia.[133] Yet, other types of US exchanges arrived much earlier: from the early 1950s, the International Technical Cooperation Program, otherwise known as the Technical Cooperation Administration (TCA) or International Cooperation Administration (ICA), trained Yugoslav engineers and experts in the United States, but also sent American and European consultants to Yugoslav production facilities, construction sites, and power plants.[134] From the mid-1950s, USIS became acquainted with, and handed over, several exchange programs bringing American journalists, professors, and specialists to lecture in Yugoslavia. However, it took until the mid-1960s for the Yugoslavs to take these programs seriously: the FCCR got involved, and through the Binational Commission the programs boomed in number. The exchange movement came into being.

The Ford and other 'stories'

Almost concurrently with the start of the FLP negotiations, the Ford Foundation gained momentum; in a couple of years or so, it became the most powerful and attractive US private program in Yugoslavia. Waldemar Nielsen, director of its domestic and overseas programs, visited Belgrade in the winter of 1957, where, approached by FO undersecretary Vladimir Velebit, he initiated dialogue with the Yugoslav government. In mid-October 1958, accompanied by President Robert Goheen from Princeton and Dean Harlan Cleveland from Syracuse University, Nielsen finalized the agreement and interviewed the candidates. To Embassy officers he confided his surprise about the 'overwhelming interest among high-ranking Yugoslavs.'[135] A year later, the first group of twenty-four Yugoslav scholars went on a study tour in the United States. Unlike the Fulbright and the FLP/IVP, Ford grantees developed a specific focus on the humanities and social sciences generally, and education, business and economics, journalism, urbanism, and the arts specifically.[136] From 1959 to 1968, the Foundation granted more than 200 Yugoslavs stays of six to ten months in the United States. Following the 1963 Skopje earthquake, top Yugoslav engineers, architects, and planners, entitled by official Belgrade to rebuild the city, went to American and European universities on a Ford grant.[137]

The Ford experience shaped an entire generation of Yugoslav intellectuals and cultural leaders in a way that is hard to pin down properly. Miladin Životić, Gajo Petrović, Mihailo Marković, and Veljko Korać, philosophers and proponents of an anti-dogmatic Marxism, founders of the heterodox Korčula summer school and the *Praxis* review (1964–74), would become the loudest critics of Titoist Yugoslavia in the aftermath of their Ford experience. Yet the program inspired more than fights for political and intellectual causes: Olja Ivanjicki, Serbian vanguard artist, and Miodrag Protić, founder of the Museum of Contemporary Art in Belgrade, gained in reputation and in fresh, attractive ideas from their US experience. Once back home, Protić wrote to the Ford representatives emphasizing, 'America changed my personality and, in some way, completed it.' Alfred Barr, the founder and first director of the MoMA, became Protić's lifelong friend. Once back in Belgrade, Protić gave birth to a new, fashionable, New-York styled Yugoslav Museum of Contemporary Art; its outdoor cubic architecture, and its indoor thematic and non-chronological artworks sequence, was something never before seen in Yugoslavia. Opened by Ranković on 22 November 1965, Yugoslav National Liberation Day, the museum traced a new concept of outside and inside artistic exhibition.[138]

The case of Savka Dabčević-Kučar makes probably the best point on the long-term influence the exchange program had from within the leadership. Dabčević-Kučar was one of the first women who obtained a PhD in economics in Yugoslavia. Her dissertation, 'J. M. Keynes: The Theorists of State Capitalism,' was certainly an unconventional one. After her 1960–61 Ford experience in the United States and France, she authored and co-authored several books on capitalist economy and Yugoslav integration into the market, such as the 'Decentral and socialist planning: Yugoslavia,' in *Planning Economic Development* (1963) and *The Political Economy of Capitalism* [Politička ekonomija kapitalizma] (1967). As Natasha Deakin wrote to Stanley Gordon after she returned from Yugoslavia in May 1964, Dabčević-Kučar, together with the Slovenian economist Aleksander Bajt, 'opposed increased economic centralization' at the Federal Economic Chamber, and was 'one of the leading spirits' of Croatian CC.[139] In 1967, by taking the presidency of the government of the Socialist Republic of Croatia, she became Europe's first female prime minister. During the 1960s she contributed to the *White Book* [Bijela knjiga], a study in economic reform, with Većeslav Holjevac, Zagreb's mayor and FLP grantee in 1961, yet another leading Croatian pro-market economist. Known for her pro-Western reform stance, in 1971 Dabčević-Kučar imposed herself as one of the leaders of the Croatian Spring, a movement that opposed unitarization and called for economic, cultural, and political rights for Croatia within the Federation. At the Karadjordje residence in Vojvodina, between 30 November and 1 December, Tito condemned the national-democratic movement as 'counterrevolutionary'; its leaders, Miko Tripalo, Dabčević-Kučar, Pero Pirker and many others, were forced to resign. Some 2,000 Party officials were expelled, thousands lost their jobs, around 3,000 students were banished from Zagreb University, its leaders beaten and incarcerated. Dabčević-Kučar was retired in 1975.[140]

Although other US exchange programs focused more on scientific networking and technological advancement turned out to be less politically problematic, they were still pursuing a cultural agenda that benefited US interests in Yugoslavia. Ljubljana University was particularly efficacious in attracting leading and groundbreaking interuniversity projects and courses with American universities. In 1965, Ljubljana's Faculty of Economics established a graduate MBA program, thanks to collaboration with the University of Indiana, with which it also launched a project on agricultural production improvement. The State Department helped financially. The Cornell University Regional Planning Project, backed mainly by the Ford Foundation and developed with the Urban Institute of Slovenia, trained Yugoslav professionals in the United States, and improved projects of urban planning in the Ljubljana metropolitan area.[141] Two other research institutes from Ljubljana, the Institute for Sociology and Philosophy and the Biological Institute, began research projects with the University of Michigan. Zagreb University made great progress in scientific connections overseas: with Western Michigan University, it started educational projects dealing with Yugoslav social, political, and cultural issues; with Portland State College, it launched student exchanges for Serbo-Croatian courses in both countries; while with Pennsylvania University, Zagreb engaged in electrochemical research for engineers.

The research projects involved the most diverse areas of study, from anthropology, linguistics, community development, and industrialization, to American studies, and macroeconomics. The Oak Ridge Institute of Nuclear Studies cooperated with the Yugoslav Federal Council for the Coordination of Scientific Activities on a yearly international conference in Herceg Novi on 'Development of Science and Technology and their Impact on Society'; the Yugoslav Institute for Educational Research conjoined with the University of Pittsburgh in an International Education Project, bringing twelve American professors to Yugoslavia every summer to discuss trends in research. Celebrated American universities were involved in overseas exchange: Harvard University on the Milman Parry Collection Project regarding Yugoslav epic songs, the University of Pennsylvania on social values and local political responsibility, California State College, Louisiana State University, and others.

'Bringing students [...] to the United States,' reminded a State Department memo, 'had an immediate impact 'on the forming of human relations.' But not everything was due to US influence; as the memo underlined, 'certain relaxations have taken place in Yugoslavia to permit their students to come [here] [...] with an open and receptive mind.'[142] The Experiment in International Living, the New York Herald Tribune Youth Forum, the Youth for Understanding Teenage Exchange Program, The Kansas University Theatre Exchange, the Multi-Area Educational Travel Project, and the Interlochen Michigan Music Camp, targeted both university and high school students. Gifted students received support from the Rubin Foundation, and the Hemingway and the Baloković Fund, respectively for talented writers and for those willing to study at Harvard. Meant to introduce 'Yugoslav student leaders to the democratic process,' the student exchanges would convey 'not only a greater appreciation of American education, but also an insight into its broad philosophy and atmosphere.'[143]

Hard science got its piece of cake when, in 1966, the US National Academy of Science signed a memorandum with the Council of Yugoslav Academies to inaugurate mutual research of scholars working in the natural sciences, especially mathematics. The exchanges of communication and mass media leaders, on the other side, were meant to enable 'Yugoslavs to observe the U.S. democratic system of dissemination news and information' and 'bring mutual understanding through free and open communication.'[144] This occurred both through FLP exchanges, as well as through the National Association of Broadcasters and Foreign Radio Television Journalist projects that brought Yugoslav broadcasters for thirty-day stays at American radio and television stations.[145]

With State Department support, these exchange programs gained momentum when the establishment of the Binational Commission provided a legislative, organizational, and logistic setting. While the numbers do not speak to quality impact, their broadness and differentiation leave no doubt about their long-term secondary influence. Yet, to determine such influence requires reaching personal, individual stories, which are rarely 'black and white.' Life is complicated, and so are these stories.

Grey sides of an exchange story

In 1965, the Great Lakes College Association began a close collaboration with Ljubljana University. The project, co-financed by the State Department, organized seminars on political and social issues in both countries, and study trips to the United States. The program was already on the ground in September when five American and ten Yugoslav professors, and more than thirty students of both nationalities, gathered for an eighteen-day seminar in Ljubljana.[146] Three years later, in 1968, Danica Purg, a Slovenian student enrolled at the Political Science College, went to the United States on a GLCA grant, but her stay was all but pleasant. She complained to the Yugoslav vice consul in San Francisco in April that year, and sent several letters to Cvijeto Job, at that time Cultural Affairs Officer at the Yugoslav Embassy. She felt profoundly mistreated during her stay at Kalamazoo College in Michigan. Mike Petrovich, the group escort, behaved like a 'Chetnik,' she wrote.[147] The questions during a VOA radio interview in Washington were 'provocative and unpleasant.' During her visit to State Department headquarters, Purg was upset hearing one US official saying that 'when President Tito dies, national conflicts will explode in Yugoslavia,' and her fellow Yugoslav responded, 'I'm sorry, I won't answer on this because you are being provocative.' During Purg's extensive travels throughout America, in San Francisco, Los Angeles, New Orleans, and New York, she constantly felt surrounded by CIA agents.[148] 'My feelings here are more a protest than a paranoid sickness,' she reported to Job, and continued, 'for the first time in my life I feel what it is like when the "big power" dominates [...]. [At the State Department] our whole discussion was about Yugoslav nationalism. My fellows and I were very angry.' At Hope College, Purg seemed 'disappointed from the very start.' First, because they 'showed two movies about Yugoslavia,' one about the 'natural beauties of our country (made by Pan American),' and the other 'a ten-year-old documentary' full of 'biased statements' over state control of religious practices, over the lack of 'electric kitchen-ranges' and 'fridges' in Yugoslavia. 'The next day,' Purg lamented, 'we had another discussion and were attacked again.'[149] Job brought the issue to Guy Coriden, deputy director at the Soviet and East European Division. As a pro-Western diplomat with much experience in the United States, Job responded with caution. 'Without understating,' he wrote, 'we don't have to exaggerate and create a frightening, unusual [...] hypertrophied show that everyone with whom [the Yugoslavs] gets in contact [...] are CIA and FBI agents and immigrants with hostile intentions.' Certainly, he pointed out, 'it is hard to evaluate the "provocative" questions' because sometimes 'our citizens, coming from another environment, with different habits and traditions, consider as provocative what here is [...] pretty normal.'[150]

Purg returned to the United States many times after that 1968 experience: she completed postgraduate courses at the Harvard Business School, and, as founder and president of the IEDC-Bled School of Management (Slovenia), president of CEEMAN (the Central and East European Management Development Association), and leader of the European Leadership Centre, Purg developed cooperation with the Darden Business School at Virginia University, the Harvard Business School, the MIT Sloan School of Management, Boston University, Babson College, and Claremont University.[151]

In a 2014 email interview, Purg recalled her memories after so many years. From an endpoint perspective she reframed her first experience in the United States: 'I like to remember my stay, [...] the fact that I essentially improved my English, I met some great people there, and I learned a lot.' And resumed, 'it was an unbelievable opportunity I got from the U.S. government.' But then, she remembered the grey side of the story: 'I was shocked by the violence in the United States from the beginning to the end of my stay. When our group arrived [...], we had to stay for four days in a hotel in Washington because of the murder of Martin Luther King. [As] [...] I studied political science, [...] I realized what a loss it was.' She also mentioned 'a young black person threw a bottle at my head, while I was walking in the park.' While on the plane through the United States, Purg spoke with soldiers returning from Vietnam. 'This was another thing that shocked me. Some of them had a nervous breakdown and travelled home to rest, the others spoke to me with great hatred for communism [...] I was offended to hear that.' Finally, at the end of her stay, Robert Kennedy was killed. She recalled, 'I was active in the group of young people – students from Kalamazoo College, preparing his visit to the town for the election campaign, going around the private houses to convince people to vote for him, and finally even giving him a present from Yugoslavia.' In fact, 'these sad events provoked in me some doubts about American democracy, and being an open person, I showed my disappointment and emotions.' Purg remembered the incident at the State Department as 'a long session on Yugoslavia.' The questions 'what will happen after Tito dies,' sounded brutal: 'We lived in a pretty "romantic" environment, we liked President Tito, we didn't feel oppressed by the regime and thought that these were not questions for "guests".' To the question, if she was a Communist Party member, Purg answered:

'Yes, I was a member, but I was accepted in the "party" because I was an exemplary good student, and not out of fanatical, ideological reasons. I believed in justice, in equal opportunities [...]. The fact that I got such a scholarship to the United States was also reflecting that.' Purg concluded: 'My expectations were different visiting the United States the first time, and the disappointment was a consequence of that.' In her later visits, 'I started to see other things, like high-class management education, great professors at Harvard Business School, great artworks, [...] and many universities and management schools.' That time changes the perception of our experience is no surprise: 'Today,' Purg recalls, 'I treasure only good memories of my first trip to the United States. I like to remember nice friends, great professors, the great trips I took throughout the country.' Finally, 'I don't think it was necessary to forward my complaint to the US authorities. I was young, full of ideals about the world and I needed somebody who could understand and comfort me.'[152] Not always do cross-cultural relations broaden mutual understanding. Purg's experience, while being more an exception than a rule, reveals misinterpretations and misapprehensions that come with intercultural communication, the perception of and interaction with the 'other,' and the translation of political identification into ordinary life.

Win-win situation or Cold War necessity?

In late 1966, Charles Frankel, Assistant Secretary of State for Educational and Cultural Affairs, joined an ad hoc Binational Advisory Commission, created in Belgrade by the US and Yugoslav governments, to discuss past cooperation and set new goals.[153] The results were 'encouraging,' and Frankel stated that the Yugoslavs 'well prepared [to] [...] reach ready agreement for major priority fields [...] for the next five to ten years.'[154] Both parties agreed that the exchanges 'had been both successful and useful and had played an important part in the relations of the two nations.' The shared goal was to continue, reinforce, and expand them.[155] Unexpectedly, the Yugoslav government passionately insisted on widening the Ford exchanges, agreed to jointly select Eisenhower Foundation grantees with the American Embassy, and approved seventeen participants to the Salzburg seminar, the only one from a non-Western European country.[156]

At that point, the US government recognized that something new was moving in the Yugoslav political spectrum. The Yugoslav leadership was 'avidly absorbing Western management ideas and technology' in its own socialist self-management system, and increasingly developing it by market principles.[157] Liberal drifts impacted even Yugoslav attitudes towards public opinion surveys. For the first time, in 1966, the Yugoslav Institute for Market Research agreed to get involved in polls commissioned by American agencies.[158]

When the debate over the Vietnam War exploded in Yugoslavia and underpinned severe anti-American denunciations, in political speeches, popular culture, and street demonstrations, the Yugoslav government left intact the affirmative relations with Washington. The Embassy was more than certain this was a positive outcome of the exchange programs.[159] They believed the Yugoslav moderate tendencies, such as the 1965 economic reforms, were reflecting a Western 'influence.' Even though Yugoslav returnees never admitted such American influence during official discussions at the Embassy, they confessed themselves in private talks. While advancing 'in the Party, executive government or academia,' the Yugoslav grantees took along 'the influence of American thought and ideals,' which penetrated and 'moderated traditional communist-socialist values [...] in forms acceptable to that dogma.'[160] But was this enough to create a communist regime with a 'human face'?

The FLP/IVP policymakers were convinced this was a practical solution: Yugoslav government leaders and head academics exposed 'to American life and institutions' would 'increase Yugoslav knowledge and appreciation of U.S. tradition and accomplishments,' and be persuaded 'that the U.S. policies coincide with the best interests of Yugoslavia.'[161] Yet many Party ideologues perceived this agenda as threatening, enticing 'liberalistic pseudo-democracy,' and favouring 'the idea of a multiparty system.' While the FLP involved more and more Yugoslav leaders, vice president Ranković warned, at the Eighth LCY Congress, against 'various demagogues' advocating for 'bourgeois liberal concepts of democracy.' His colleague, Veljko Vlahović, spoke against the 'anti-socialist [...] bacilli of Western political ideas.'[162]

Who were those 'infested' by Western demagogy, applauded and looked for by the US government? What pushed the Yugoslav government to advocate for more potentially threatening exchanges with the United States? USIA estimated the Yugoslav intelligentsia consisted of some 620,000 individuals, with high school or college degrees: doctors, lawyers, engineers, but also teachers, university professors, and students; obviously artists, writers, journalists; then managers, governmental bureaucrats, military and police officers, and leaders of political and social organizations. As Senator Fulbright noted in his 1964 *Report to the Committee on Foreign Relations*, 'the typical Yugoslav leader is an atypical man [...] relatively young, well-educated and multilingual.'[163] With more than two-thirds under the age of forty, the Yugoslav intelligentsia was predominantly urban and middle class (only one-third was of working class or peasant origin).[164] Higher incomes and fringe social benefits made it a privileged group, both economically and socially. As the backbone of the LCY, these future leaders were considered ready to take over the 'Communist Old Guard.' Although most of them were 'hard-boiled,' 'dogmatic and orthodox Marxists,' a sizable number harboured un-Marxist and even anti-Marxist ideas, liberal and national tendencies, and pro-Western attitudes. 'Some of them,' stated the USIA study, were 'increasingly demanding a more liberal handling of domestic problems and an ending of Party control over the country's economic, social and cultural life.' More fundamentally, 'increasing tendencies toward self-identification with Western culture and toward what is called "chauvinistic local nationalism" was gaining major ground. As a fast-growing, aspiring leading force in Yugoslav society, this group could 'prove to be a potent force for the erosion of the Communist status quo in Yugoslavia,' that could eventually be replaced 'by a new orthodoxy' marked with 'pro-Western sentiments and the "bourgeois nationalist deviations".'[165] The USIA prediction was partially correct: as Chapter 6 shows, these leading forces emerged in the 1971 Croatian Spring and 1972 Serbian Liberals movements, but were oppressed just after taking hold.

As Croatian historian Hrvoje Klasić reminded, the 1960s were a missed occasion for the regime to induce a more radical self-reformation. The economic reform turned out less successful than expected: prices increased by 35 per cent, and the managerial establishment remained resistant to guiding principles. Many enterprises did not know how to handle the newly acquired autonomy. Price increases led to a series of strikes all over the country between 1966 and 1968. It was the first time that critics of Party politics, self-management, and bureaucracy came, not only from inside political elites, but from the cultural intelligentsia – the Praxis school – and ordinary citizens.[166] The fact that Yugoslavia had a 'relatively heavy influx of Western tourists and the feedback from the increasing number of Yugoslav workers employed in West European countries,' made many Yugoslavs 'acutely aware of their deprivations,'[167] and exacerbated the possibility of true reform.

Gradual political and economic liberalization, along with decision-making decentralization, periodically swung to criticism of Western influences, imprisonment of political dissenters, and the shutdown of unorthodox journals. In fact, Yugoslav exceptionalism and international prestige grew on a regime that was neither Soviet totalitarianism, nor a Western democracy. Coercion and periodical openness remained at stake until the country's breakdown.[168] This helps us understand why the Yugoslav establishment, from the LCY presidency, the SAWPY, to the FCCR, often expressed contradictory positions on foreign propaganda and cultural exchanges. Research by SAWPY in 1966 estimated that 70 per cent of all foreign propaganda pertained to the United States, while the rest concerned the United Kingdom, the Soviet Union, and France.[169] Praised as necessary, the Yugoslavs staying at American universities could not escape 'the exchange of political opinions.'[170] As the Secretariat of Education reminded in 1968, Yugoslav 'open-policy towards all world countries' was not a 'wise gesture'; it nevertheless 'had long-term results in all areas of economic and social life.'[171] The Party remained critical of foreign propaganda: the LCY condemned 'hostile, illegal propaganda' that attacked 'our country's values and traditions' through 'psychological warfare' run by 'the USIA, the CIA, and NATO's Atlantic Institute,' together with emigrant organizations of '*ustasha,*' '*chetniks,*' and '*volksdeutchers.*'[172] The fifth Plenary session of the Presidency in 1969 agreed to move for 'a sort of self-protection of our self-management socialist society,'[173] yet contradicted the 1969 LCY Congress which stated: 'the openness of our community [...] and our willingness to enter into free trade with all countries and, above all, the free circulation of people, ideas and experience – is an expression of the strength of our free self-governing society.' Even, the LCY continued, if risking 'various non-socialist and ideologically reactionary attitudes, and covert or openly hostile activities.'[174] The inner contradiction seemed insolvable: when the dictatorship opened towards the world, it became instantly vulnerable to anything that could eventually question or shake its legitimacy, ultimately leading its leaders to neither isolation, nor a complete system of political freedoms; the core issue was the strength of a self-governing society, not a self-governing free individual.

The US–Yugoslav cultural exchanges expose Yugoslav contradictions between pragmatic policies and ideological perplexities; as this chapter proves, the first overwhelmed the latter. If, at first glance, both sides appeared authentically satisfied, negotiations over the Fulbright Program revealed power-dependent interactions. The Yugoslavs struggled and prevailed in the Binational Commission, maximizing access to American expertise. The Embassy and USIS proved excellent intermediaries between American private actors and their Yugoslav counterparts, particularly through personal contact. Personal contacts made friendships, and 'the intellectual curiosity and disarming friendliness of the American students,' were 'positive factors in building better relationships among Americans and Yugoslavs.'[175] The exchange programs were based on the premise that only soft power could win over hearts and minds. Not surprisingly, the US grantees were 'expected to maintain a high image of technical and scientific superiority, but at the same time raise the image of personal, moral, humanistic values in the United States, which years of propaganda in this part of the world have helped distort.'[176] Even the benefits that Yugoslav scientists gained in the United States, considerably advancing Yugoslav technological development, was a soft-power revenue; as the Embassy underlined in 1969, 'a concrete indication of the [Yugoslav] government's attitude is the fact that, at considerable cost and with little internal struggle, it is contributing eight scholarships for Americans to study in Yugoslavia.'[177]

Yugoslav policies were mainly driven by pragmatic considerations. In 1969, the Federal SEC explained:

> We give special attention to these relations because of: a) the obvious necessity of using the results of American science and technology for our development, especially in the context of reforms; b) the stability of these relations that are not directly subject to political oscillations [...]; c) the maintenance and exchange of scientific, educational and cultural relations with the American intellectual and influential elites (especially at the American universities), which is mostly liberal and has a positive attitude towards us and our relations with the United States, strengthens and safeguards our valuable political position in the public and political life of the United States.[178]

The numbers at stake remained high: in 1967, the United States accommodated the major number of Yugoslav students – 194 to 222 – after East Germany.[179] In 1970, more than fifty Yugoslavs stayed abroad on Fulbright, Rubin, and Eisenhower grants, and more than 400 Yugoslavs flew overseas under some US exchange program. The fact that the 'Americans acted co-ordinately to include their political and ideological goals [...] to influence [...] our future leaders,' did not bother the FCCR at all.[180] As the Yugoslav ambassador, Veljko Mićunović, emphasized, 'the development of our country' required 'the use of the highly developed science, technology and culture of the United States.' And pragmatically, he concluded: 'the improvement of our political relations, which conditions and allows the liberalization of contacts and travels, gives it a real foundation.'[181]

Notes

1 CU program planning and budgeting system – FY69 Program Recommendations for Yugoslavia and Turkey, 27 April 1967, Folder 18, Box 17, Bureau of Educational and Cultural Affairs (hereafter CU), Manuscript Collection 468 (hereafter MC), Special Collection, University of Arkansas Library (hereafter UAL).
2 Report of the Binational Advisory Commission, 2 December 1966, Folder 17, Box 17, CU, MC 468, Special Collection, UAL, 10.
3 Originally 'Savezna komisija za kulturne veze s inozemstvom.'
4 Box 64, Razmjena naučnih radnika, Savjet za kulturu i nauku NRH 1956–1961, RG 1599, CSA.
5 Despatch 212 Embassy Belgrade to Dept. of State, 17 October 1960, 511.683/10–1760, Box 1074, CDF 1960–63, RG 59, NACP, 10.
6 Despatch 53 Consulate Zagreb to Dept. of State, 26 November 1957, 511.683/11–2657, Box 2205, CDF 1955–59, RG 59, NACP.
7 *Pregled*, June 1961, 38; List of Reference Materials, in Airgram 81 Dept. of State to All Diplomatic and Consular Posts, 13 July 1962, 511.00/7–1362, Box 1046, CDF 1960–63, RG 59, NACP; Airgram 682 Dept. of State to Certain Diplomatic and Consular Officers, 7 October 1950, 511.00/10–750, Box 2238, CDF 1950–1954, RG 59, NACP.
8 Memorandum Battle to Averell, 9 April 1963, EDX 2, Box 3254, Central Foreign Policy Files (hereafter CFPF) 1963, RG 59, NACP, 3–4.
9 Despatch 48 Embassy Belgrade to Dept. of State, 30 July 1957, 511.683/7/3057, Box 2205, CDF 1955–59, RG 59, NACP.
10 Memorandum of conversation Defranceski and Kendrick, 26 May 1958, 511.68/5–2658, Box 2204, CDF 1955–59, RG 59, NACP.
11 Despatch 235 Embassy Belgrade to the Dept. of State, 20 November 1958, 511.683/11–2057, Box 2205, CDF 1955–59, RG 59, NACP.
12 Murphy to Secretary of State, 25 October 1957, 511.683/10–2557, Box 2205, CDF 1955–59, RG 59, NACP.
13 Study Annual Programs Division, 1 July–30 June 1958, Folder 14, Box 26, CU, MC 468, Special Collection, UAL.
14 Giles Scott-Smith, *Networks of Empire: The US State Department's Foreign Leader Program in the Netherlands, France and Britain 1950–1970* (Brussels: P.I.E. Peter Lang, 2008), 21, 78.
15 'About IVLP,' Bureau of Educational and Cultural Affairs, Department of State, 26 January 2019, http://eca.state.gov/ivlp.
16 Scott-Smith, *Networks of Empire*, 21, 26.
17 Giles Scott-Smith, 'The US State Department's Foreign Leader Program in France during the Early Cold War,' in *Les Relations Culturelles Internationales Au XXe Siècle: De La Diplomatie Culturelle à l'acculturation*, ed. A. Dulphy et al. (Brussels: P.I.E. Peter Lang, 2010), 72.
18 This data was collected by intersecting diverse archival material, mainly Box 1074 and Box 2205, CDF 1955–59, RG 59, NACP; Box 610 and 640, SIV 1953–90, RG 130, AY; Box 142 and Box 320, CU, MC 468, Special Collection, UAL; Box 45, USIA Subject Files 1953–67, RG 306, NACP; and the periodical *Pregled*, 1959–1969.

19 Despatch 212 Embassy Belgrade to the Dept. of State, 17 October 1960, 511.683/
    10–1760, Box 1074, CDF 1960–63, RG 59, NACP, 2.
20 Mr Crvenkovski visit to the United States, SAD f/1960, Box 237, SAD, Kanada i
    Latinska Amerika, SSOK, RG 318, AY.
21 Popović to FEC, 18 January 1960, 9327, and Rešenje o putovanju Krste
    Crvenkovskog u SAD, 26 March 1960, Box 640, SIV 1953–90, RG 130, AY.
22 Telegram 08175 Dept. of State to Embassy Belgrade, 15 September 1961, 511.683/
    9–1561, Box 1074, CDF 1960–63, RG 59, NACP; Despatch 212 Embassy Belgrade to
    Dept. of State, 17 October 1960, 511.683/10–1760, Box 1074, CDF 1960–63, RG 59,
    NACP, 14.
23 Airgram G-94 Dept. of State to Embassy Belgrade, 25 November 1958, 511.683/
    11–458, Box 2205, CDF 1955–59, RG 59, NACP.
24 The list and descriptions of the FLP grantees result from criss-crossing the US and
    Yugoslav archival sources, as information was randomly scattered in the documents.
    From the Archives of Yugoslavia, these were: boxes 2, 124, 145, RG 472; boxes 237
    and 240, RG 318; box 61, RG 319; and boxes 610 and 640, RG 130. From the US
    National Archives, these were: boxes 1074, 2204, and 2205, CDF 1955–59, RG 59;
    from the UAL, the boxes 142 and 320, CU, MC 468; and the periodical *Pregled* from
    1959–1969.
25 The Key Elements of Population, 27 April 1967, Folder 18, Box 17, CU, MC 468,
    Special Collection, UAL.
26 Despatch 224 Embassy Belgrade to Dept. of State, 12 November 1958, 511.683/
    11–1258, Box 2205, CDF 1955–59, RG 59, NACP.
27 'Broadway,' in Despatch 380 Embassy Belgrade to Dept. of State, 19 February 1959,
    511.683/2–1959, Box 2205, CDF 1955–59, RG 59, NACP.
28 Despatch 380 Embassy Belgrade to Dept. of State, 19 February 1959, 511.683/2–
    1959, Box 2205, CDF 1955–59, RG 59, NACP.
29 Dept. of State Memorandum of conversation Hughes and Ostojić, 9 December 1958,
    511.683/12–958, Box 2205, CDF 1955–59, RG 59, NACP.
30 Odlazak u SAD, 22 February 1960, SAD g/1960, Box 237, SAD, Kanada i Latinska
    Amerika, SSOK, RG 318, AY.
31 SAD i/1960, Box 237, SAD, Kanada i Latinska Amerika, SSOK, RG 318, AY.
32 Mr Crvenkovski visit to the United States, SAD f/1960, Box 237, SAD, Kanada i
    Latinska Amerika, SSOK, RG 318, AY.
33 Despatch 212 Embassy Belgrade to Dept. of State, 17 October 1960, 511.683/
    10–1760, Box 1074, CDF 1960–63, RG 59, NACP, 6.
34 *Vjesnik*, 23 September 1960, 3–4; 'Dobrodoslica, ali … – svjetka javnost o
    Beogradskoj konferenciji,' *Vjesnik*, 7 September 1961, 4.
35 Nikezić to Zeković, 26 October 1962, 435748, Box 640, SIV 1953–90, RG 130, AY.
36 Secretary of FEC to Kardelj, Todorović, and Istok, 22 November 1962, 337, Box 640,
    SIV 1953–90, RG 130, AY.
37 *Vjesnik*, 1 January 1963; The Yugoslav Intelligentsia: An Appraisal, June 1965, Box
    25, Research Reports 1966–90, USIA OR and Media Reaction, RG 306, NACP,
    16; 'Tito: Moramo ukloniti sve što smeta našem pravilnom razvoju,' *Vjesnik*, 30
    December 1962, 1–2; Chronology of Cultural Policy in Yugoslavia, in Park to Cody,
    27 March 1963, M-32–63, Box 1, Research Memoranda 1963–99, USIA OR and
    Media Reaction, RG 306, NACP.

38 FO to FEC, 16 February 1960, 9698, file 1062, Box 640, Međunarodni odnosi 1953–70, SIV 1953–90, RG 130, AY; Andrew Koch, 'Yugoslavia's Nuclear Legacy: Should We Worry?,' *The Nonproliferation Review* 4, no. 3 (1997): 124, https://doi.org/10.1080/10736709708436687.
39 Stručni izvještaj sa puta po SAD, March 1960, SAD 1960, SAD 1957, Files 1565, and A. Moljk, Kratki izvještaj o putu delegacije SKNE po Americi, 22 April 1960, SAD 1960, SAD 1957, Files 1565, 2–3, in Box 438, Međunarodna saradnja, SAD 1955–64, SKNE, RG 177, AY.
40 Farley to Nakićenović, 31 March 1960, 00277/60, SAD 1960, SAD 1957, Files 1565, Box 438, Međunarodna saradnja, SAD 1955–64, SKNE, RG 177, AY; Zabeleška za sekretara druga Veljka Zekovića o pozivima višim državnim rukovodiocima, 9 August 1961, 424501, and FCNE to the AEC, 17 June 1960, 03–969/1 in Box 640, Međunarodni odnosi 1953–70, SIV 1953–90, RG 130, AY.
41 Izvještaj SKNE SIV-u o radu 1964. godine, file 995, Box 601, Međunarodni odnosi, SIV 1953–90, RG 130, AY, 1–4.
42 Summary of Principal Action Recommendations, 13 July 1961, Folder 2, Box 46, CU, MC 468, Special Collection, UAL.
43 Review of USIA Research, April 1963, R-34–63 (P), Box 13, Research Reports 1966–90, USIA OR and Media Reaction, RG 306, NACP, 7–8.
44 Refugee Views on Life in Yugoslavia, 30 April 1963, R-27–63, Box 13, Research Reports 1966–90, USIA OR and Media Reaction, RG 306, NACP, 13.
45 *Ibid.*
46 Key Elements of Population, 27 April 1967.
47 Summary of Principal Action Recommendations, 13 July 1961.
48 Key Elements of Population, 27 April 1967.
49 Message 74 USIS Belgrade to USIA Washington, 25 March 1963, IAE Yugoslavia Belgrade, Box 45, USIA Subject Files 1953–67, RG 306, NACP.
50 Dept. of State Instruction 142 to Embassy Belgrade, 2 December 1958, 511.683/12–258, Box 2205, CDF 1955–59, RG 59, NACP.
51 Dept. of State Memorandum of conversation Frol, Grabcanovic, Petrovic and Jorgensen, 12 June 1961, 511.683/6–1261, Box 1074, CDF 1960–63, RG 59, NACP.
52 Despatch 73 Embassy Belgrade to Dept. of State, 6 August 1959, Box 2, Eastern Europe, CU, Microfilm Collection (hereafter MC), Roosevelt Institute for American Studies, Middelburg, The Netherlands (hereafter RIAS).
53 Despatch 212 Embassy Belgrade to Dept. of State, 17 October 1960, 511.683/10–1760, Box 1074, CDF 1960–63, RG 59, NACP.
54 Primedba druga Marka na informaciju 222, 21 November 1962, IX, 109/VI-100, Box 6, KMOV, CK SKJ, RG 507, AY.
55 Pro Memoria, SAD 2/1960, Box 237, SAD, Kanada i Latinska Amerika, SSOK, RG 318, AY.
56 Exchange program, 19 June 1964 and Saradnja sa komisijom za kulturne veze, 19 June 1964, Box 237, SAD, Kanada i Latinska Amerika, SSOK, RG 318, AY.
57 Bilandžić, *Hrvatska moderna povijest*, 451; for more insights, see John R. Lampe, *Yugoslavia as History: Twice There Was a Country*, 2nd ed. (Cambridge: Cambridge University Press, 2000), 276–98.
58 Leslie Benson, *Yugoslavia: A Concise History* (Basingstoke; New York: Palgrave Macmillan, 2001), 108; Bilandžić, *Hrvatska moderna povijest*, 452–3.

59 Key Elements of Population, 27 April 1967.
60 Benson, Yugoslavia, 108–10; Bilandžić, Hrvatska moderna povijest, 451–2.
61 Rusinow, The Yugoslav Experiment 1948-1974, 176–9; Lampe, Prickett, and Adamović, Yugoslav–American Economic Relations Since World War II, 72–103. The GATT acts, from 1995, under the World Trade Organization (WTO).
62 Ante Batović, 'Od Ekonomske Reforme Do Brijunskog Plenuma – Američki i Britanski Izvještaji o Hrvatskoj (1964–1966),' Historijski Zbornik 63, no. 2 (2010): 539–60.
63 Airgram 218 Embassy Belgrade to Dept. of State, 13 September 1963, IAE-Yugoslavia, Box 45, USIA Subject Files 1953–67, RG 306, NACP.
64 Jović, 'Communist Yugoslavia and its "Others",' 19.
65 Savka Dabčević-Kučar, '71. – hrvatski snovi i stvarnost, vols 1 and 2 (Zagreb: Interpublic, 1997), 84; Hrvoje Klasić, Jugoslavija i svijet 1968 (Zagreb: Ljevak, 2012), 23–7.
66 Komisija za kulturne veze sa inostranstvom, 27 July 1966, 06–23; O likovnoj saradnji sa inostranstvom, 19 July 1966, 652–6; and Sredstva za strane nastavnike i lektore, 12 December 1966, 01–638-1/1966, in Box 226, RSPKFK, RG 1415, CSA.
67 Message 38 USIS Belgrade to USIA Washington, 3 December 1963, IAE-Yugoslavia, Box 45, USIA Subject Files 1953–67, RG 306, NACP.
68 Nikezić to FEC, 6 October 1964, 434554, Box 640, SIV 1953–90, RG 130, AY.
69 Predlog zaključaka o postupku za ostvarivanje programa vlade SAD 'Leaders' Exchange,' 15 February 1965, 01–271, Box 640, SIV 1953–90, RG 130, AY.
70 Latinovic to SSOK, 22 June 1966, Box 237, SAD, Kanada i Latinska Amerika, SSOK, RG 318, AY.
71 Vipotnik to Elbrick, 10 November 1966, Box 237, SAD, Kanada i Latinska Amerika, SSOK, RG 318, AY.
72 Elbrick to Vipotnik, 3 December 1966, Box 237, SAD, Kanada i Latinska Amerika, SSOK, RG 318, AY.
73 Fulbright to Vipotnik, 4 November 1966, Box 237, SAD, Kanada i Latinska Amerika, SSOK, RG 318, AY.
74 Airgram 252 Embassy Belgrade to Dept. of State, 28 September 1965, Box 2, Eastern Europe, CU, MIC, RIAS.
75 Airgram 359 Embassy Belgrade to Dept. of State, 24 November 1967, Box 2, Eastern Europe, CU, MIC, RIAS.
76 Scott-Smith, Networks of Empire, 26.
77 Wyman to Lyon, 6 September 1957, 511.683/9–657, Box 2205, CDF 1955–59, RG 59, NACP.
78 Telegram 2647 Dept. of State to Embassy Belgrade, 5 December 1958, 511.683/11–2058, Box 2205, CDF 1955–59, RG 59, NACP. Today known as the Fulbright Foreign Scholarship Board, it gathers US specialists, mostly academic scholars, writers, lawyers, and communication specialists, who administer the program, in cooperation with the State Department's ECA, the bi-national Fulbright Commissions and Foundations, and the Public Affairs Sections of the US embassies abroad.
79 Despatch 415 Embassy Belgrade to Dept. of State, Feb. 24, 1958, 511.683/2–2458, Box 2205, CDF 1955–59, RG 59, NACP.

80 Fact Sheet on the IEEP, April 1966, Folder 11, Box 103, CU, MC 468, Special Collection, UAL.
81 Eric Sevareid, CBS commentary, 18 May 1976, in Haynes B. Johnson and Bernard M. Gwertzman, *Fulbright: The Dissenter* (Garden City, NY: Doubleday, 1968), 108.
82 Wyman to Lyon, 6 September 1957, 511.683/9-657, Box 2205, CDF 1955-59, RG 59, NACP.
83 Rade Petrović. Interview by Author. Telephone interview. 28 August 2014.
84 Randall B. Woods, 'Fulbright Internationalism,' *Annals of the American Academy of Political and Social Science* 491, The Fulbright Experience and Academic Exchanges (1987): 25-6.
85 Randall B. Woods, *Fulbright: A Biography* (Cambridge: Cambridge University Press, 1995), 9, 35-6.
86 The New Authority provided by the Fulbright-Hays Act in Instruction 4352 Dept. of State to All American Diplomatic Posts, 21 November 1961, 511.003/11-2161, and Airgram 2792 Dept. of State to All American Diplomatic Posts, 13 September 1962, 511.003/9-1362, Box 1050, CDF 1960-63, RG 59, NACP.
87 Woods, 'Fulbright Internationalism,' 23.
88 Sam Lebovic, 'From War Junk to Educational Exchange: The World War II Origins of the Fulbright Program and the Foundations of American Cultural Globalism, 1945-1950,' *Diplomatic History* 37, no. 2 (2013): 280-312, https://doi.org/10.1093/dh/dht002.
89 Telegram 532 Belgrade to Secretary of State, 6 November 1958, 511.683/11-2058, Box 2205, CDF 1955-59, RG 59, NACP. The US-Soviet agreement, signed on 17 January 1958, included exchanges in science and technology, agriculture, medicine and public health, radio and television, motion pictures, exhibitions, publications, government, youth, athletics, scholarly research, culture, and tourism. As an executive agreement, not a treaty, it did not require US Senate ratification and so avoided a prolonged debate in a forum that had witnessed the challenges of McCarthyism only a couple of years before (Yale Richmond, *US-Soviet Cultural Exchanges, 1958-1986: Who Wins?* [Boulder, CO: Westview Press, 1987], 133-7.)
90 FO to FEC, 11 June 1959, 91842, Box 640, Međunarodni odnosi 1953-1970, SIV 1953-90, RG 130, AY.
91 Pro Memoria from US Government to the Government of Yugoslavia, 7 July 1960, 511.683/6-2660, and Telegram 038335 Dept. of State to Embassy Belgrade, 7 June 1960, 511.68/6-760, Box 1074, CDF 1960-63, RG 59, NACP; FO to FEC, 19 December 1963, 91430/3, Box 640, Međunarodni odnosi 1953-1970, SIV 1953-90, RG 130, AY.
92 The Need for a Policy Decision re the Conversion of 'Excess' Currencies, 27 February 1961, and Agreements Signed from Beginning of Program, 31 March 1961, Folder 3, Box 46, CU, MC 468, Special Collection, UAL; Zabeleška o Fulbrajtovom programu, Aug. 21, 1967, Box 61, Kulturno-prosvetne veze sa inostranstvom 1967-1971 (hereafter KPVI), SSOK 1960-1971, RG 319, AY.
93 Savezni sekretarijat za finansije, 27 September 1963, 08-2830/1, Box 240, SAD, Kanada i Latinska Amerika 1953-67, SSOK, RG 318, AY; Godišnji izvještaj jugoslovensko-američke komisije za Fulbrajtov program (1.1965-10.1966), 12 May 1967, Box 61, Kulturno-prosvetne veze sa inostranstvom 1967-1971, SSOK 1960-1971, RG 319, AY.

 94 Look specifically to 511.003/7–1662, Box 1050, CDF 1960–63, RG 59, NACP,
     and EDX 4/48–4460, Box 3254, CFPF 1963, RG 59, NACP; and, on the Yugoslav
     side, Godišnji izvještaj Jugoslovensko-americke komisije za Fulbrajtov program,
     12 May 1967, Box 61, and KPVI 1967–71, SSOK, RG 319, AY, 8 and Elaborati o
     međunarodnim vezama, May 1968, Box 34, Sednice Saveznog saveta 1968, SSOK
     1960–1971, RG 319, AY, 72.
 95 Zabeleška o sprovodjenju i produženju ugovora o Fulbrajtovom programu, 1968,
     Box 61, KPVI 1967–71, SSOK 1960–1971, RG 319, AY; Saradnja SFRJ-SAD u oblasti
     obrazovanja (Fulbrajtov program), November 1970, 021/1, Box 61, KPVI 1967–71,
     SSOK 1960–1971, RG 319, AY, 20–1.
 96 Grbić to Wheeler, 1963, Box 240, SAD, Kanada i Latinska Amerika 1953–67,
     SSOK, RG 318, AY and Vipotnik to Elbrick, 9 November 1964, Box 1, Komisija za
     prosvetnu razmenu između SFRJ i SAD, RG 472, AY.
 97 Agreement between the Government of the USA and the Government of the FSRY,
     9 November 1964, Box 1, Komisija za prosvetnu razmenu između SFRJ i SAD, RG
     472, AY.
 98 Popović to General Secretary of the President, 22 October 1964, 441257, Box I-3-
     a/107–132, Prijemi stranih ličnosti i delegacija, KPR, RG 837, AYBT.
 99 Carla Konta, 'Nice to Meet You, President Tito … Senator Fulbright and the
     Yugoslav Lesson for Vietnam,' in The Legacy of J. William Fulbright: Policy,
     Power, and Ideology, ed. David J. Snyder, Alessandro Brogi, and Giles Scott-Smith
     (Lexington: University Press of Kentucky, 2019).
100 See reports to Josip Broz Tito from 24 October to 3 November 1964, Box I-3-
     a/107–132, Prijemi stranih ličnosti i delegacija, KPR, RG 837, AYBT.
101 Zabeleška o razgovoru Predsednika SFRJ Josipa Broza Tita sa predsednikom SPKS
     SAD, James William Fulbrightom, 14 November 1964, Box I-3-a/107–132, Prijemi
     stranih ličnosti i delegacija, KPR, RG 837, AYBT.
102 Informacija povodom prijema senatora Fulbrighta, 14 November 1964, 611/8, Box
     I-3-a/107–132, Prijemi stranih ličnosti i delegacija, KPR, RG 837, AYBT; Bogetić,
     Jugoslavensko-američki odnosi 1961–1971, 174–7.
103 Zabeleška o izlaganju Predsednika SFRJ Josipa Broza Tita u razgovoru sa
     predsednikom SPKS SAD, James William Fulbrightom, and Zabeleška o razgovoru
     Predsednika SFRJ Josipa Broza Tita sa predsednikom SPKS SAD, 14 November
     1964, Box I-3-a/107–132, Prijemi stranih ličnosti i delegacija, KPR, RG 837, AYBT.
104 Izjava senator J. W. Fulbrighta povodom potpisivanja sporazuma, 9 November 1964,
     Box 1, Komisija za prosvetnu razmenu između SFRJ i SAD, RG 472, AY.
105 Konta, 'Nice to Meet You, President Tito.'
106 Informacija o Fulbrightovom programu, 16 June 1965, 1203, Box 640, SIV 1953–90,
     RG 130, AY.
107 Yugoslav–American Commission Meeting, 21 January 1965, and 42nd Meeting, 11
     June 1970, Box 2, Komisija za prosvetnu razmenu između SFRJ i SAD, RG 472, AY;
     Godišnji izvještaj Jugoslovensko-američke komisije za Fulbrajtov program, 12 May
     1967, AY, 8; Izvještaj o realizaciji programa razmene u oblasti prosvete između SFRJ
     i SAD, 1970, Box 61, KPVI 1967–71, SSOK 1960–1971, RG 319, AY.
108 Lampe, Yugoslavia as History, 292–3.
109 These data were obtained by intersecting archival sources from Box 2, 124, 145, RG
     472, AY; Box 240, RG 318, AY and Box 61, RG 319, AY.

110 Saradnja SFRJ-SAD u oblasti obrazovanje, November 1970, 15.

111 Informacija o sprovođenju zadataka iz programa razmene u oblasti prosvete između SFRJ i SAD, 2 June 1969, in Predlog za učešće u finansiranju programa razmene, 11 June 1969, 01.1092, Box 640, SIV 1953–90, RG 130, AY.

112 Izvještaj o boravku u SAD druga Petra Boškovića, in Rukavina to Mićunović, 10 January 1968, Box 61, KPVI 1967–71, SSOK 1960–1971, RG 319, AY.

113 Airgram 413 Embassy Belgrade to Dept. of State, 16 August 1969, Box 2, Eastern Europe, CU, MIC, RIAS, 1–4. This was particularly remarked to me by Rade Petrović, former member of the Binational Commission, in his telephone interview on 25 August 2015.

114 Ranko Bugarski. Interview by author. Email interview, 27 August 2015.

115 Taib Šarić. Interview by author. Email interview, 25 August 2015.

116 Airgram 359 Embassy Belgrade to Dept. of State, 24 November 1967, Box 2, Eastern Europe, CU, MIC, RIAS. For more on Fulbright alumni gratitude see, for instance, Arthur P. Dudden and Russell R. Dynes, eds, *The Fulbright Experience 1946–1986: Encounters and Transformations* (New Brunswick, NJ: Transaction Publishers, 1987); Richard T. Arndt and David Lee Rubin, *The Fulbright Difference: 1948–1992* (New Brunswick, NJ; London: Transaction Publishers, 1993).

117 Twenty Years of the Commission for Educational Exchange between the USA and Yugoslavia, Belgrade 1984, Box 10, Series III, J. William Fulbright FSB Records, MC 1279, UAL, 58.

118 Paula Gordon, 'Dr. Marijan Ante Bošković – In Memoriam,' *Translation Journal* 12, no. 4 (October 2008), http://translationjournal.net/journal/46boskovic.htm.

119 Arndt and Rubin, *The Fulbright Difference*, 6.

120 Elbrick to Mićunović, 19 December 1968, and Mićunović to Elbrick, 19 December 1968, Box 1, Komisija za prosvetnu razmenu između SFRJ i SAD, RG 472, AY.

121 Richardson Jr to Dept. of State, 3 October 1969, Folder 5, Box 21, CU, MC 468, Special Collection, UAL; Fulbright Commission to Federal Council on Education and Culture, 11 January 1971, 4/021–2, Box 61, KPVI 1967–71, SSOK 1960–1971, RG 319, AY. It was common in Yugoslav financial history that the Yugoslav national bank substituted the old devalued currency by a new one called simply the 'new dinar.'

122 Airgram 413 Embassy Belgrade to Dept. of State, 16 August 1969, 1–4; Federal Council on Education and Culture to Gagović, 22 July 1969, 34/69, Box 640, SIV 1953–90, RG 130, AY.

123 Razgovor načelnika III Uprave DSIPa R. Radovića sa g. I. Tobinom, July 22, 1969, Box 61, KPVI 1967–71, SSOK 1960–1971, RG 319, AY.

124 Produženje sporazuma o Fulbrajtovom programu, 21 November 1967, Box 1, Komisija za prosvetnu razmenu između SFRJ i SAD, RG 472, AY; Zabeleška o sprovodjenju i produženju ugovora o Fulbrajtovom programu, 1968, Box 61, KPVI 1967–71, SSOK 1960–71, RG 319, AY.

125 Rusinow, *The Yugoslav Experiment 1948–1974*, 346.

126 Saradnja SFRJ-SAD u oblasti obrazovanja, November 1970, 20–1, 23.

127 Airgram 366 Embassy Belgrade to Dept. of State, 8 October 1970, Box 2, Eastern Europe, CU, MIC, RIAS.

128 Airgram 969 Embassy Belgrade to Dept. of State, 15 August 1968, Box 2, Eastern Europe, CU, MIC, RIAS.

129 Scott W. Lucas, 'Beyond Freedom, beyond Control, beyond the Cold War: Approaches to American Culture and the State–Private Network,' *Intelligence and National Security* 18, no. 2 (2003): 66, https://doi.org/10.1080/02684520412 331306740. See also Helen Laville and Hugh Wilford, eds, *The US Government, Citizen Groups and the Cold War: The State–Private Network* (London; New York: Routledge, 2006).
130 Report on the Program Planning Conference, 4 February 1954, Box 3, USIA Subject Files 1953–67, RG 306, NACP.
131 Streibert to Sulzberger, 4 January 1956, Box 13, USIA Subject Files 1953–67, RG 306, NACP. Many bright historiographical accounts have framed the role of the private players and the intelligentsia as autonomous subjects, as well as their interference with the state power network like the European Congress for Cultural Freedom. For this, see Giles Scott-Smith and Hans Krabbendam, eds, *The Cultural Cold War in Western Europe, 1945–1960* (London; Portland, OR: Frank Cass Publishers, 2003); and Luc van Dongen, Stephanie Roulin, and Giles Scott-Smith, eds, Transnational Anti-Communism and the Cold War: Agents, Activities, and Networks (Basingstoke; New York: Palgrave Macmillan, 2014).
132 Report on Relations of Private Exchange to CU Objectives, 27 April 1967, Folder 18, Box 17, CU, MC 468, Special Collection, UAL.
133 Summary of Educational Exchange between Yugoslavia and the United States, 2 December 1966, Folder 17, Box 17, CU, MC 468, Special Collection, UAL.
134 Summary of Educational Exchange, 2 December 1966; 'Jugoslavija – SAD,' *Pregled*, November 1962, 63; boxes 2705 and 2706, CDF 1960–63, RG 59, NACP; and boxes 238 and 240, SAD, Kanada i Latinska Amerika, SSOK, RG 318, AY. This is a completely neglected area of study, partially addressed in Lampe, Prickett, and Adamović, *Yugoslav–American Economic Relations Since World War II.*
135 Despatch 415 Embassy Belgrade to Dept. of State, 24 February 1958, 511.683/2–2458, and despatch 569 from Embassy Belgrade to Dept. of State, 16 May 1958, 511.683/5–1658, Box 2205, CDF 1955–59, RG 59, NACP.
136 Yugoslav exchange program of the Ford Foundation, April 1960, Report 010916, Box 18976, Unit 85, Rockfeller Archive Center, New York (hereafter RAC); Suggestions for the Yugoslav exchange program, 24 January 1961, Grants 00001.
137 Private Sector Forum, 27 April 1967, Folder 18, Box 17, CU, MC 468, Special Collection, UAL.
138 Vučetić, 'Amerikanizacija u Jugoslovenskoj Popularnoj Kulturi '60-Ih,' 167. Vučetić, *Koka-kola socijalizam*, 234–7.
139 Memorandum Deakin to Gordon, 29 October 1964, Grants 0004, RAC, 8.
140 Yugoslav scholarship development program, 31 October 1961, Grants 0001, RAC; 'Savka Dabčević-Kučar,' *Hrvatski biografski leksikon* (Leksikografski zavod Miroslav Krleža, 1993), 9 February 2019, http://hbl.lzmk.hr/clanak.aspx?id=4288; Dabčević-Kučar, *'71. – hrvatski snovi i stvarnost*, vol. 1, 254–83.
141 M. Stierli, V. Deskov, and V. Kulić, *Toward a Concrete Utopia: Architecture in Yugoslavia, 1948–1980* (New York: MoMA, 2018).
142 Key Elements of Population, 27 April 1967.
143 Program Plan for Yugoslavia, 27 April 1967, Folder 18, Box 17, CU, MC 468, Special Collection, UAL.

144 *Ibid.*
145 This list has been created by criss-crossing several archival resources: Izvještaj Dvonacionalne savetodavne komisije za dugoročno planiranje obrazovne, naučno-tehničke i kulturne saradnje između SFRJ i SAD, 2 December 1966, Box 237, SAD, Kanada i Latinska Amerika 1953–67, SSOK, RG 318, AY; Summary of Educational Exchange, 2 December 1966; and Private Sector Forum, 27 April 1967.
146 Coriden to Richardson Jr, 27 January 1970, Folder 12, Box 21, CU, MC 468, Special Collection, UAL.
147 As a Serbian paramilitary group that engaged in guerilla warfare during both world wars, in post-war Yugoslavia Chetnik was commonly used to indicate a political enemy of the regime.
148 Zabeleška o razgovoru Bogomira Liovića sa Danicom Purg, 5 July 1968, 26/68, Box 43, Republički protokol, IVS SRH 1953–90, RG 280, CSA.
149 Purg to Job, 25 May 1968, Box 43, Republički protokol, IVS SRH 1953–90, RG 280, CSA. The documentary Purg quotes was *Wings to Yugoslavia (Pan Am Airways)*, 16 mm (US: Kodachrome, 1964), www.youtube.com/watch?v=o7vHzk_hbuM, 9 February 2019.
150 Povodom zabeleške Generalnog konzulata SFRJ u San Franciscu od 28. maja 1968, Aug. 5, 1968, 09/592, Box 43, Republički protokol, Izvršno Vijeće Sabora SRH 1953–1990, RG 280, CSA.
151 'About IEDC,' www.iedc.si/about-iedc, 10 February 2019.
152 Danica Purg. Interview by author. Email interview, 6 June 2014.
153 Airgram 374 Embassy Belgrade to Dept. of State, 13 December 1966, Box 17, Folder 17, CU, MC 468, Special Collection, UAL.
154 Frankel to Katzenbach, 23 Dec 1966, Folder 5, Box 21, CU, MC 468, Special Collection, UAL.
155 Report of the Bi-national Advisory Commission, 2 December 1966, Folder 17, Box 17, CU, MC 468, Special Collection, UAL.
156 Kulturno-prosvetna saradnja SFRJ i SAD 1950–65, in Poseta Charlesa Franklina – Materijali, 11 May 1966, 416844, Box 237, SAD, Kanada i Latinska Amerika 1953–67, SSOK, RG 318, AY.
157 Airgram 366 Embassy Belgrade to Dept. of State, 8 October 1970.
158 Memorandum of conversation, 67049, 13 January 1967, YO6601, Box 41, Africa, Eastern Europe and Multi-Areas, USIA ORA, RG 306, NACP.
159 Airgram 969 Embassy Belgrade to Dept. of State, 15 August 1968; Airgram 366 Embassy Belgrade to Dept. of State, 8 October 1970; for Yugoslav anti-American demonstrations against the Vietnam conflict, see James Mark et al., '"We Are with You, Vietnam": Transnational Solidarities in Socialist Hungary, Poland and Yugoslavia,' *Journal of Contemporary History* 50, no. 3 (2015): 439–64, https://doi.org/10.1177/0022009414558728.
160 Airgram 359 Embassy Belgrade to Dept. of State, 24 November 1967, Box 2, Eastern Europe, CU, MIC, RIAS.
161 Program Plan for Yugoslavia, 27 April 1967.
162 'Vodeću ulogu SK ostvariti svakodnevnom aktivnošću,' Vjesnik, 14 October 1964, 1, 3; 'Referat Sekretara CK SKJ druga Aleksandra Rankovića,' and 'Referat člana Izvršnog komiteta CK SKJ druga Veljka Vlahovića,' *Vjesnik*, 14 December 1964.

163 James W. Fulbright, *Yugoslavia 1964: Report to the Committee on Foreign Relations, United States Senate* (Washington, DC: US Government Printing Office, 1965), 7–9.
164 The Yugoslav Intelligentsia: An Appraisal, June 1965, 7.
165 *Ibid.*, 15, 18.
166 Klasić, *Jugoslavija i svijet 1968*, 28–9.
167 Refugee Views on Life in Yugoslavia, April 30, 1963, 13–14. 'Contact between the Yugoslav people and the much more prosperous countries of Western Europe is so frequent that it would be difficult for them not to be aware of the contrast. Inferences can be drawn with more confidence about the relative importance of different sources of discontent,' emphasized the report (20–1).
168 On the limits of Yugoslav exceptionalism, see Armina Galijaš, Rory Archer, and Florian Bieber, *Debating the End of Yugoslavia* (London; New York: Routledge, 2016); and the excellent Vesna Drapac, *Constructing Yugoslavia: A Transnational History* (London; New York: Palgrave Macmillan, 2010).
169 Informacija o problemima vezanim za inostranu propagandnu u našoj zemlji, 15 April 1966, 16/2–1966, Box 256, Komisija za politički i idejno-vaspitni rad 1966, SSRNJ, RG 142, AY.
170 Informacija o naučnoj i kulturno-prosvetnoj saradnje Jugoslavija-SAD, 14 December 1967, 5, Box 61, SSOK 1960–71, RG 319, AY.
171 Elaborat o međunarodnim vezama nekih kulturnih i prosvetnih organizacija i institucija, May 1968, US 4 BJ, Box 34, SSOK 1960–71, RG 319, AY, 6.
172 Oreč and Mićović, *Inostrana propaganda u Jugoslaviji* in Materijal za razmatranje na petoj sjednici Komisije, September 1968, 15–143/10–69, Box 2, XXVI-K.2/1–5, Komisija PSKJ za političku propagandu i informativnu delatnost 1965–78, CK SKJ, RG 507, AY, 31–2.
173 Inostrana propaganda prema Jugoslaviji, December 1969, Box 2, XXVI-K.2/1–57, Komisija PSKJ za političku propagandu i informativnu delatnost 1965–78, CK SKJ, RG 507, AY, 3.
174 Mate Oreč and Vojislav Mićović, Inostrana propaganda u Jugoslaviji, Sept. 1968, 2–3.
175 Airgram 119 Embassy Belgrade to Dept. of State, 16 August 1966, Box 2, Eastern Europe, CU, MIC, RIAS.
176 Airgram 969 Embassy Belgrade to Dept. of State, 15 August 1968.
177 Airgram 413 Embassy Belgrade to Dept. of State, 16 August 1969.
178 Program posjete ambasadora SAD Williama Leonharta i supruge, 26 November 1969, Box 43, Republički protokol, IVS SRH 1953–90, RG 280, CSA.
179 The Educational and Cultural Profile of Yugoslavia, 27 April 1967, Folder 18, Box 17, CU, MC 468, Special Collection, UAL.
180 Pripremanje razgovora o kulturnoj suradnji sa SAD, 1970, file SAD (unregulated files), Komisija za kulturne veze s inozemstvom IVS-a SRH, RG 1410, CSA.
181 Materijal i neke sugestije u vezi programiranja saradnje sa SAD u prosvetno-naučnoj i kulturnoj oblasti, Nov. 15, 1966, Box 237, SAD, Kanada i Latinska Amerika 1953–67, SSOK, RG 318, AY.

6

Beyond the 1960s

Take two or three dry wafers of the five-year plan and be sure that all agriculture has been completely squeezed out of them; smear them with the stuffing of industry [...]: pass through a masher the unlimited number of cheap workers and at least the same number of slightly more expensive administrators; add one gram of expensive leadership to this; dilute to fifty percent liquid using economic criminality. Afterwards mix this with a reliable foreign currency expert of no morals; then roll it flat with the dependable director with no school education. Take care that the mass remains flexible and manageable, adding fresh slogans all the time. Shape the cake as self-management and put it into the oven. In order to prevent over-cooking – dampen it with the juice of American aid. Since the baked cake does not have a special appearance, you will have to glaze it with the economic reform. The icing is prepared from a crushed standard of living, chopped culture and peeled education. If the icing cracks, touch it up with new measures [...]. Decorate the cake with flowers of economic experts and models of cars, villas and cabins. [...] If you want it to taste better, drink the juice of the glorious past [...] and in case of bad digestion take some pills of Marxism [...]. Vomiting is forbidden.

'Economic Cake à la Yugoslavia,' *Paradoks*, satirical monthly youth
magazine, banned in summer 1966, Zagreb[1]

In 1966, during a comfortable and friendly meeting at the US Embassy in Belgrade, a group of Yugoslav journalists explained to American officials how the Yugoslav press was not free in the Western sense. As they convincingly argued, they were 'all young and communists,' but their generation remained critical of the 'current conditions [...] and impatient for change.'[2] Yet reform was reluctant to arrive. While embarking on a set of internal transformations from the mid-1960s on, Yugoslavia failed 'to implement substantial and comprehensive changes,' Hrvoje Klasić claims. Without 'respecting and encouraging pluralism, with a growing gap between theory and practice, the reform[s], of which much was expected, only intensified the already present antagonisms.'[3]

In fact, the Party leadership remained divided over three critical issues: decentralization and further federalization, along with the splitting of political power; economic reform towards a market-led socialism; and the degree of democratic expression permitted to heterodox Marxist political and cultural elites. The dissident and critical voices of Yugoslav socialism, diverse in origin and often clashing with one another, accelerated from the mid-1960s. One faction emphasized liberalization and market reform; others strove for the republics' rights to greater autonomy. These differences weakened the reform movement, preventing the parties involved from providing mutual support and joint action. Both State Department and USIA officials remained mere observers; the US priority was to 'keep Tito afloat,' and, only in the second instance, to nudge its institutions towards Western liberal-democratic traditions. Nevertheless, this two-fold strategy prioritized Yugoslav independence towards the Soviet Union, especially when, from the late 1960s, the Brezhnev Doctrine turned its attention towards Yugoslavia.

The anti-LCY movements obviously gained huge press attention in the United States and became an opportunity for political pressure from Washington to criticize the lack of individual freedom in Yugoslavia. Yet the dissident movements, as we shall see, never openly called US and Western liberal democracies their inspiration. Certainly, many of the proposed, then rejected and suppressed, reforms implied more pluralism in the Yugoslav political and cultural arena. The US policymakers and field officers considered these requests to be directly inspired by US public diplomatic policies, striving to influence the regime from outside to entice change from within. Many dissidents, such as Savka Dabčević-Kučar and the Praxis protagonists, were once US grantees. Others, such as Mihajlo Mihajlov, but the Praxis philosophers as well, enjoyed good relations, even friendships with the US representatives in Yugoslavia. As for the Praxis school, their public polemic, based on Marxist assumptions, stood in contradiction to Western philosophical and ideological values. Certainly, as Scott-Smith pointed out, the exchange programs were not a 'decisive factor in terms of political effect,' given 'too many other variables'. Nevertheless, 'the political effect of exchanges' continued Scott-Smith, 'fell into a gap between quantitative analysis (statistical assessments and hard data) and qualitative analysis (personal judgment).'[4] The exchange programs were just an aspect of US public diplomacy in Yugoslavia, and as a soft-power medium they attached to many other forms of cultural persuasion: the USIS libraries, personal contacts policies, cultural events, exhibitions, and information dissemination, all indirectly putting more irons in the fire.

The late 1960s: dissidents on fire

As Croatian historians Tihomir Cipek and Katarina Spehnjak note, dissent in Yugoslavia profoundly differed from that of other Eastern European countries. After the Soviet Union lost its dominant influence here in 1948, the reasons for motivated dissent and opposition suddenly imploded. Due to Yugoslavia's special position between the two superpowers, the Yugoslav opposition movements received less support from the West compared to, for instance, the Polish resistance. The fact that political opportunities in Yugoslavia were less restrictive than in other countries of state socialism – more freedom to import literature, more available entertainment and everyday consumer goods, and the ability to travel overseas – they nonetheless inhibited the creation of a coherent opposition movement.[5]

After Djilas in 1954, the Mihajlov case was the second, a deliberately planned anti-LCY dissidence case that gained immediate international press coverage when it exploded in early 1965. Mihajlo Mihajlov (1934–2010), born into a family of Russian emigrants, was a professor of Russian literature at the coastal University of Zadar. His 1964 cultural exchange trip to the Soviet Union radically impacted his world view and intents: thanks to the 'thaw that accompanied Khrushchev's destalinization campaigns, he collected an astonishing volume of literature, novels, stories, memoirs, and songs, about the camps by survivors and others.' Belgrade's literary magazine *Delo* published two Mihajlov articles in its first two issues of 1965; entitled *The Moscow Summer 1964* (Leto moskovsko 1964), the articles described his Soviet journey and argued that the first concentration camps were those of the Soviets, and not the Nazis, constructed in 1921.[6] Soviet diplomats were outraged, and the two issues immediately withdrawn. Accused by Tito of 'Djilasism' and 'reactionary thought,' Mihajlov was expelled from the university soon after.[7] On 26 March, the Zadar public prosecutor brought him to court for 'damaging the reputation of a foreign country,' and, under article 125 of the Press Law, for disseminating 'written material in contravention of an already-announced ban' (he sent copies of his writings to Italian right-wing editor Giovanni Volpe).[8] *Delo* soon dissociated itself from the 'politically untrue and ill-intentioned interpretations with which Mihajlov's travelogue was partly burdened,' and apologized.[9] Once free, after being imprisoned for a year, Mihajlov gathered a group of heterodox intellectuals such as Danijel Ivin, Francis Zenko, Marijan Batinić, Leonid Sheikh, Mary Čudina, Davor Aras, Jovan Barović, and Predrag Ristić to start the first legal opposition journal in Yugoslavia, in summer 1966. *Nova misao* [The New Thought], intended to critically re-examine the lawful conduct of the ruling elites. He failed, some participants were arrested, but only Mihajlov was brought to trial, and then imprisoned from 1967 to 1970, then again for shorter periods in 1970, 1972 to 1973, and from 1975 to 1978. Finally, in 1978, he left Yugoslavia for the United States, and was awarded by the International League for Human Rights for his democratic activism.[10]

As an Embassy report emphasized in August 1965, Mihajlov was Western-oriented, well connected to Western media (the *New York Times* often published his anti-LCY remarks) and invited to speak at Columbia University and the University of California at Berkeley. He was passionately opposed to the LCY and its elites.[11] In the United States he taught Russian literature and philosophy at Yale, Ohio State University, and the University of Virginia, as well as in Western Europe until 1985. Before returning to Serbia in 2001, after the removal of President Slobodan Milošević, he served as a Radio Free Europe analyst.[12]

While the Mihajlov case mostly revolved around individual dissidence, the cases of *Perspektive* and *Praxis* exposed an intellectual network, the first Slovenian, the second

Croatian, which unmasked philosophical weaknesses and contradictions within Yugoslav communism. *Perspektive*, a cultural review from Ljubljana, was founded in 1960 by Taras Kermauner, a Slovenian literary historian and philosopher. In 1964, the magazine shifted towards harsh criticism of Party deviations, asking for more open discussions. Vida Tomšič, President of the Slovenian LC, called it 'a return to a multi-party system' and an attack on 'the principle of democratic centralism in the League of Communists.'[13] The editorial board was dismissed, but the newly appointed one was unwilling to end the rebellion. Soon, *Perspektive* became a cause célèbre by publishing a satirical poem which defined Yugoslav Communism as 'socialism à la Louis XIV,' and its Party as 'proprietors of soul torments.'[14] Three weeks later, on 22 May 1964, *Perspektive* was suppressed, and the new editor-in-chief Tomaž Salamun and regular contributor Jože Pučnik arrested for 'fomenting hostile propaganda.' Pučnik, one of the most outspoken Slovenian critics of Tito's dictatorship and the lack of civil liberties in Yugoslavia, was imprisoned for seven years, and later forced into exile.[15] On 9 June, ten former editors and contributors signed a declaration requesting less coercion and bureaucratic monopoly over culture, and more democratization in the field. Another eighty-seven Slovenian poets, writers, essayists, critics, and scientists joined the list. However, the action passed 'in silence and contempt,' and the ban was not lifted.[16]

Praxis: 'network is power'[17] or the power of networks

Among Yugoslav dissident journals, *Praxis* holds a special place, for its transnational character, international prestige, and long-term impact. Founded by a group of Zagreb philosophers, and subsequently extended to Belgrade in 1964, its main protagonists included Gajo Petrović and Rudi Supek, and editorial board members such as Branko Bošnjak, Danko Grlić, Milan Kangrga, Ivan Kuvačić, Danilo Pejović, and Predrag Vranicki.[18] *Praxis* was published in two editions: a Yugoslav one (1964–74), and a foreign one (*Praxis International*, 1965–73). Both were suppressed following the Croatian Spring (1971) and the Downfall (purge) of Serbian Liberals (1972).

By breaking with Stalinist tradition at the philosophical Bled Conference in 1960, *Praxis* advocated an 'authentic' Marxist theory and praxis, and its humanistic and dialectical elements resolved to fight Stalinism and bureaucracy.[19] Initially, the emphasis was on general philosophical matters; however, from the mid-1960s on, social and political questions arose, together with ontological and anthropological inquiries. As Petrović wrote in 1967, 'philosophy is still necessary as a living thought that penetrates the fundamental issues of the contemporary world; [that] becomes a human revolutionary work.'[20] The *Praxis* philosophers remained opened-minded, tackling other philosophical debates like their Western counterparts. As Mihailo Marković asserted, *Praxis* was a 'remarkable, courageous, creative magazine' that contributed to debates on 'political philosophy, the theory of revolution, democracy, nation and ethnic relations.'[21]

US policymakers were quite involved in the Praxis movement and their Korčula Summer School. Miladin Životić, Petrović, Marković, and Veljko Korać were all

Ford Foundation grantees in the 1960s. The philosophical and political experience among American, mainly leftist, university professors and students, left a compelling impact on these Marxist philosophers. The Korčula Summer School, which prepared the launch of the journal, was first organized in 1963 (though not on the island of Korčula, but in Dubrovnik). In a couple of years, it emerged as a modern agora among philosophers and intellectuals from both East and West.[22] Marxist philosophers from the United States, such as Herbert Marcuse and Howard Parsons, participated at the second Summer School of July 1964, on a State Department grant. After his Korčula experience, Parsons published *Humanistic Philosophy in Contemporary Poland and Yugoslavia* in the 1966 issue of the American Institute for Marxist Studies.[23] The Korčula School crafted an extensive network-building community.

Financed by the Croatian Republic, the school was held in a quite rudimentary environment: in 1965, participants lamented the lack of water and electricity for a few days, the schedule was messy, there was no newspaper coverage, and no Soviet and Czechoslovak presence. However, 'the primary interest [for the] non-Marxists present at the Korčula Summer School,' emphasized the American Consulate Zagreb, 'was the desirability of such contacts between Marxist and non-Marxist [Western] philosophers,' like father Giuseppe Wetter, a Vatican Jesuit, or Allan Gouldner, a Ford fellow from Washington University, St Louis, who came to Korčula to explore the possibility of obtaining financial support from the Ford Foundation for the summer school, which were eventually denied.[24]

Accused by Croatian Party leaders of establishing 'a philosophical elite and to set themselves up as the arbiters of Yugoslav destiny,'[25] criticism of Praxis members exceeded, argued the American Consulate, 'the customary bounds of self-criticism in communist countries.' As for the Praxists themselves, they deemed theirs a 'loyal opposition [...] within the Marxist-Leninist framework.'[26] And even within this framework, Praxis entered the debate, with Western and US values and ideologies, as no other intellectual group had done before in Yugoslavia: the authors believed in the 'necessity of scrupulous criticism of everything existing.'[27] Their major denunciation of Yugoslav socialism was the poor attention to civil rights, and the lack of democracy and freedom attained by more liberal bourgeois states. For the Praxists, the right to strike was a symbol of strength, rather than of weakness; however, the future of socialist societies lay in the withering away of the Party, not the establishment of a multiparty system. Praxis philosophers remained critical towards the evils of capitalism, as well as consumer and mass culture materialism. Nevertheless, the multiparty system was a worthy discussion issue, especially the free choice between parties in elections. More importantly, as the 1964 second issue of *Praxis* underlined, the democratic institutions in Yugoslavia could not ensure real democracy without the people's participation and their exercise of dissent.[28]

Besides transatlantic connections with US philosophers such as Marcuse and Parsons, the Praxists entertained personal, affable relationships with the US representatives in Zagreb. In a May 1966 meeting at the Zagreb Consulate, Petrović and Pejović openly reported to US officials about their plan to spend some weeks in Moscow with 'more liberal Soviet philosophers who are not given as free a reign as their counterparts in Yugoslavia,' whereas, earlier that month, Petrović met some American philosophers at Notre Dame University.[29] Danilo Marković and other Praxists occasionally dined with Embassy officers, intimately, as the Embassy reported, discussing the future of *Praxis*. Networking and open discussion inspired those meeting in the most positive way, recalled the Consulate and Embassy officials.[30]

The Praxis group represented the most avant-garde and radical Marxist criticism against the LCY during its existence. Yet, despite its radicalness, argues Rei Shigeno, the group never became a political opposition to the Party, partially because their political strategy was largely a consequence of their interpretation of Marx's philosophy, but mostly because they hesitated to move their criticism onto political grounds. While claiming that it was necessary to abolish the Party as it monopolized decision-making power and alienated the universal human being, they never incorporated these standpoints into some particular political body.[31] Or, as Renata Salecl put it, they 'called for a programme to abolish the gulf between the ideal and the real,' but opposed and 'criticized the establishment in the name of a purified version of the establishment's own ideology.'[32]

The Nixon era

In the name of a country's right to pursue its own path to socialism, Tito harshly condemned the Soviet's invasion of Czechoslovakia of August 1968. As twenty years before, the Yugoslav 'No' to the Soviets and the threat of the Brezhnev Doctrine of restricted sovereignty, forced the Yugoslav Foreign Office to discuss once more a possible Soviet military invasion of Yugoslavia. Ambassador Elbrick in Belgrade assured US backing in such a case.[33] Yugoslav advocacy of the Prague Spring helped to bring 'back on track' Yugoslav–US bilateral relations, which had been on a downward spiral after the Six-Day War of June 1967, when Israel was attacked by its neighbouring states, Egypt (UAR), Jordan, and Syria.[34] The US 1968 endorsement of Tito's regime threw open 'all doors for those American enterprises' willing to establish their affiliates in Yugoslavia.[35] In the spirit of this cooperation, in May 1969, the Yugoslav Secretariat for Foreign Trade sent its first economic delegation to the United States to meet with Federal Reserve and EXIM bank representatives,[36] while a US economic delegation visited Yugoslavia in November of that year.[37] President Nixon's visit to the Far East, India, and Romania in 1969, and US space successes of Apollo 11, galvanized pro-American sentiments and helped foster a climate for increased cooperation.[38]

After taking office in January 1969, President Richard Nixon made foreign policy his primary, priority agenda. Like his former rival President Kennedy, Nixon became far more interested in foreign policy than domestic affairs. His efforts towards normalization of relations with the Soviet Union and the People's Republic of China culminated in 1972. Nixon's Shanghai Communiqué, issued during his visit to Beijing in February, announced a desire for open, normalized relations. His visit to China was widely televised and viewed. The announcement of the Beijing summit immediately improved relations with the Soviet Union. Not long after, Soviet premier Leonid

Brezhnev invited Nixon to Moscow. Nixon's 'triangulation,' his 'low-profile' policy based on a 'community of balance,' was finally producing results: the Soviet fear of improved relations between China and the United States led the Russians to improve their own relations with Washington. The President and First Lady arrived in Moscow on 22 May for an historic first-ever meeting. The Strategic Arms Limitation Talks I and Anti-Ballistic Missile Treaty, which resulted from the summit, culminated in the first comprehensive limitation pact signed by the two superpowers, and in banning the development of systems designed to intercept incoming missiles. The two leaders proclaimed a new era of 'peaceful coexistence'; Nixon truly believed that only diplomatic détente could temper the Cold War. Such a policy, put in place by his Secretary of State and National Security Adviser, Henry Kissinger, eased Cold War tensions. These developments were in line with many Americans favouring a lower profile in world affairs after the Vietnam War, which drew to an end between 1973 and 1975, with the last withdrawal of US military personnel.[39]

Nixon's détente policy reflected on relations between Washington and Belgrade. On 27 October 1971, Tito was cordially welcomed at Maryland's Andrews Air Force Base, before proceeding to Camp David for the rest of the day. Kissinger himself arranged the meeting to avoid protests of Yugoslav émigrés to which the Marshal was particularly sensitive.[40] World news headlines highlighted the 'spirit of Camp David.' The next day, Tito 'was received with a very elaborate military reception that included a marching band in colonial red coats.'[41] But the crucial talks occurred during the evening reception in Tito's honour when Yugoslav Foreign Minister Mirko Tepavac pulled aside Secretary of State William Rogers to speak with him in private. Via Rogers, Tito and Tepavac succeeded in informing Nixon about the fear of the Soviets at the highest level in Yugoslavia, despite the positive words exchanged at official meetings in Belgrade. Tepavac referred to Brezhnev's visit to Belgrade between 22 and 25 September 1971, when 'he criticised the liberal attitudes of the Yugoslav press and softness on "imperialism" as the key disadvantages of Yugoslav internal and foreign policy.'[42] In the final joint statement, Yugoslavia avoided 'any appearance of moving closer to the Eastern bloc.' Yugoslav leaders declined any Soviet suggestion of a 'friendship agreement,' but insisted on clarifying that 'this was a negotiation between two sovereign states.' When Brezhnev 'inquired about the possibility of a new Balkan pact between Yugoslavia, Albania, Romania and Greece,' Tito dismissed the proposal straightaway, surprised 'that the Soviets even considered it to be realistic, especially the inclusion of Greece.' Mijalko Todorović, President of the Federal Assembly, expressed great concern and criticism of Soviet attitudes, arguing that 'the Soviets had not changed their strategy towards Yugoslavia,' and that Brezhnev had more interest in strengthening their position than furthering bilateral negotiations. As Ante Batović reminded, 'there was no real dialogue between the two delegations.' Yet, as the FEC concluded, the meeting successfully resisted 'Soviet efforts to interfere in Yugoslavia while affirming Yugoslav positions and long-term policy towards the Soviet Union.'[43]

Tepavac's intervention at the White House dinner confirmed Nixon's impression of 'how scared' the Yugoslavs were of possible Soviet intervention in response to domestic unrest or Tito's death. 'So scared, in fact, that they could never speak of it in public.'⁴⁴ The fear of Russia was real, but these coordinated messages were put in place to increase US and Western support for Yugoslavia ('Yugoslav military officials would later use similar tactics in their dealings with NATO,' Batović argues).⁴⁵ On 30 October, Nixon and Tito released a joint communiqué confirming US interest in an 'independent and non-aligned position and policy of Yugoslavia,' and emphasized Yugoslavia's non-alignment as 'a significant factor in international relations.' The statement set out the principles for bilateral relations: 'respect for national independ-ence and state sovereignty,' 'indivisibility of peace and mutuality,' 'negotiation in respect to the interests of all countries,' and 'full equality regardless of differences [...] of a state's socio-political system.'⁴⁶

To circumvent the steady ups and downs in Yugoslav–American relations and establish them on a more stable basis, Tito and Nixon agreed to engage in 'continuous consultations,' 'intensive exchange visits of state leaders,' and 'permanent contacts between the two presidents.' Free from ideological burdens, and led by mutually pragmatic interests and goals, they approved the efforts to enlarge and advance bilateral economic and industrial cooperation, trade, joint ventures, and joint third markets exchanges. The development of long-term scientific, educational, and cultural cooperation was no doubt of importance. The joint communiqué, later referred to as the Washington Declaration (recalling Belgrade's 1955 Yugo–Soviet Declaration), had great political weight, and was released by the White House only on a special occasion. The document laid ground for long-term, advantageous, and stable bilateral relations during the Nixon administration and afterwards.⁴⁷

The end of the US propaganda issue

The renewed Tito–Nixon partnership ameliorated Yugoslav concern about 'dangerous' American propaganda. Excellent economic relations returned, with cooperation between the two countries covering issues from traffic, urban planning, environmental protection, and oceanography, to science teaching, computer application, industry, petrochemistry, and electronics.⁴⁸ Appointed by President Nixon, the new USIA director visited Yugoslavia in September 1969 to reassure the Federal Assembly that the new administration would fight in Congress for continuing cultural programs.⁴⁹ Thanks to his charming personality and soft skills, Shakespeare convinced the Yugoslav government to open, in addition to Belgrade, Zagreb, and Novi Sad, American Libraries in Ljubljana, Skopje, and Sarajevo.⁵⁰ Only seven years before, Secretary of Information Bogdan Osolnik dismissed such a request as 'out of the question.'⁵¹ John Richardson Jr., the newly appointed Assistant Secretary of State for Cultural and Educational Affairs, together with Guy Coriden, Director of the Office of European Exchange Programs at the State Department, visited Belgrade just after Shakespeare departed. The talks at the Yugoslav FO reinforced mutual understanding.⁵²

Frank Shakespeare took over the USIA after a long career in broadcasting. He put 'new emphasis on television to help sell the American way of life,' using commercials, and was mainly concerned with endorsing the American cause in Vietnam. He trans-ferred more decision-making power to the local PAO because 'our man on location should know better than the supporting forces in Washington.'[53] Re-evaluation of the book program became one of his priorities. Assigned to James Burnham, editor of the conservative *National Review*, the program, attracting harsh left-liberal criticism, introduced, for the first time, top conservative intellectuals on the USIS agenda. Burnham warned that the 'absence of conservative writers and books means that an entire dimension of contemporary American life [...] is virtually left out,' especially since 'most of the conservative writers tend to support basic U.S. international policies.' Works by Russell Davenport, John Adams, Alexander Hamilton, Thomas Carlyle, Winston Churchill, Russell Kirk, Edmund Burke, Frank Meyer, Friedrich Hayek, Ludwig Von Mises, and many others, appeared for the first time on Yugoslav bookshelves. Shakespeare launched theoretical classic liberalism, libertarianism, limited government, and anti-Keynesianism, in the USIS battle for hearts and minds abroad.[54] Under his directorship, the two governments engaged in a mutual project on implementing educational TV in Yugoslavia under the auspices of US private broadcasters and universities; the culmination was the 1971 Zagreb Fair, with an exhibition on 'technology in the schools.'[55]

The Brezhnev Doctrine brought Yugoslavia and the United States closer to one another than ever. A profound turnaround occurred in cultural and cooperation endeavours. For the first time, the LCY ideological commission stopped focusing on US propaganda: the debate turned towards putting self-management into practice at the transversal level of administration.[56] The FCCR was abolished in 1971, and cultural relations with the foreign countries passed to republic and local government. As the Brezhnev Doctrine surfaced, debate over foreign influence became much less important. The USIS gained momentum, and on 5 June 1970 the two governments signed an agreement establishing a USIS post in Ljubljana. Two years later it was the turn of USIS Skopje, opened in May 1972, while, on 18 July 1973, Sarajevo got its own USIS library.[57] The ninety-page long *Report of the Yugoslav Delegation for the Talks on Cultural Cooperation with the United States*, that the Yugoslavs released in November 1973, envisioned and described such a vast cooperation program with the United States as had never been done before.[58]

The Croatian Spring and the Downfall of Serbian Liberals

Following the 1965 economic reform, Ranković's fall, and the contraction of the centralistic faction, the Yugoslav economy accepted some market mechanisms, a little private entrepreneurship was allowed, and political life got somewhat liberalized. These policies relaxed the barriers of international travel and permitted a relatively tolerant cultural policy. The effects were twofold: on the one hand, groups of activists in civil society strengthened their political engagement, and significant student protests occurred in 1968; on the other, the reforms enticed the Party leadership of the constituent republics to intensify their demands for national autonomy. Both tendencies proliferated in the early 1970s.

The movement known as the Croatian Spring was an old dispute over Yugoslav unity and Croatian national autonomy. Only nine months after the removal of

Ranković, a group of 130 influential Croatian poets and linguists, eighty of whom were communists, published a *Declaration on the Status and Name of the Croatian Standard Language* (March 1967), both as a quest for national autonomy and the independent status of the Croatian language.[59] In mid-1971, the reformist wing of the League of Communists of Croatia (LCC) sought the application of further market reform measures, concurrently advancing the idea of transitioning the highly central-ized Yugoslav federation in the confederation. The reformists soon attracted broad political support – from the Society of Writers, to the intellectual elite, and students – thereby becoming the most massive dissident movement ever. Its leaders emerged among the Party intelligentsia, led by Savka Dabčević-Kučar, Miko Tripalo, and Pero Pirker, among intellectuals such as Vlado Gotovac and Marko Veselica, and student organizations like Dražen Budiša and Ivan Zvonimir Čičak. When the Croatian Spring enticed other national movements in Vojvodina and Bosnia and Herzegovina, Tito took action: the 'Karadjordje cut' (Sječa u Karadjordjevu), in December 1971, led to massive incarceration, thousands losing their jobs, and some 25,000 Party expulsions. Matica Hrvatska literary and cultural review and student organizations were shut down, while editorial boards were replaced by new ones. Harassment continued in the late 1970s and early 1980s, resulting in the 'Croatian silence.' While cut into pieces, the reform movements ultimately led to constitutional reforms that gave the republics a stronger position against central government than they had before. In 1974, the Yugoslav Assembly adopted a new constitution containing a high degree of confederal elements.[60]

The US Consulate stayed clear of any attempts by Spring leaders to involve them in their agenda. As Ante Batović reported, in September 1971, Ivan Zvonimir Čičak and his brother Neno visited the Consulate to ask for exchanges with American universi-ties. 'Čičak suggested that a delegation of American students could attend a student gathering in Dubrovnik in October.' The lack of time and information, 'and political sensitivities,' led the Consulate to politely decline the invitation. The Dubrovnik gath-ering, Batović acknowledged, was the forum that shaped the ideas of the 1971 student movement.[61]

After the Croatian Spring – or MASPOK (mass movement) – was repressed, Tito turned towards those political leaders in Serbia who were suspected of criticising fed-eral centralism and demanding reduced Party monopoly. Considered as not willing to condemn the Spring, on 18 October 1972, the newspapers published a letter penned by Tito calling for 'democratic centralism' and greater LCY control over society. On 26 October, Marko Nikezić, president of the CC of Serbia, his Secretary Latinka Perović, and secretary of the LC City Committee of Belgrade Bora Pavlović, resigned.[62] New withdrawals of Party leaders considered to be liberals followed: younger politicians such as Mirko Čanadanović and Orhan Nevzati, but also, older, experienced com-munists like Koča Popović, Milentije Popović, Mijalko Todorović, Mirko Tepavac, and many more. Soon, Nikezić and Tepavac went on pre-retirement leave, while Perović dedicated herself to writing her doctoral dissertation. Isolated and accused of anti-Titoism, the group continued to convene at Koča Popović's apartment. He later described the purge as the shutdown of 'legitimate representatives of the democratic orientation' in the LC in Serbia and Yugoslavia. Centred around *Ekonomska politika* (*Economic Policy*), a weekly magazine founded in 1952, the group was considered a forum for more capitalist economic solutions. Critics suggested they were covertly peddling political liberalism.[63] The repression went transnational, and an entire generation of Yugoslav pro-Western politicians were replaced – Slovenian Stane Kavčić, Croatians Dabčević-Kučar and Tripalo, and Macedonian Krste Crvenkovski. Many editors-in-chief were dismissed: Aleksandar Nenadović from *Politika*, Frane Barbieri from *NIN*, Mirko Stamenković from *Novosti*, Ljubomir Veljković from *Ekonomska politika*, Draljub Era Ilić from RTV Belgrade, and Slobodan Glumac from *Borba*.[64]

Unsurprisingly, many members of that group had been somehow involved in the US public diplomacy network. Koča Popović, long-serving Secretary of State (1953–65), helped to restore and stabilize the Yugoslav–US partnership in the Eisenhower era; Marko Nikezić, who substituted for Popović in 1965 (leaving office in 1968), served as Yugoslav ambassador to Washington between 1958 and 1962, playing a crucial role during the Fulbright negotiations; and Krste Crvenkovski, an FLP grantee in 1960, began formal Fulbright negotiations with the US government.[65]

According to Perović, the Downfall epitomized a long-term struggle among the Serbian LC between the dominant centralist fraction, represented by Dobrica Ćosić, and Ranković before him, and a liberal fraction, corresponding to leaders such as Nikezić, Koča Popović, and Milovan Djilas, which endorsed a vision of an autonomously led market economy, political federalism, and liberalization. The latter – 'unwanted elites,' Perović argued – ultimately failed in making their case, though their legacy provided a foundation for the tradition of Serbian liberal democracy.[66]

With the Brezhnev Doctrine in the air, and US international endorsement, Tito's leadership turned to solving internal assessments that menaced his political authority and relied on Kardelj's new constitutional project to solve tense relations between the Federation and the republics, as well as those between the Party and the State. Kardelj's 1974 constitution, argues Dejan Jović, implemented the Yugoslav commitment to the Marxist ideology of dissolving the State. The trend of decentralization, he claims, followed Marxist beliefs 'that the state should be decentralized and weakened until it was finally replaced by a self-managing society.'[67] While abandoning the anti-American rhetoric over propaganda, the LCY turned against the Soviet Union as its major menace, while serving the US foreign policy strategy as a non-orthodox communist state.

As Rinna Kullaa explains, Washington remained a mere observer of the Croatian Spring and Downfall movement;[68] however, it seems undeniable that the USIA policy agenda in Yugoslavia left a mark on these leaders, compromised, in one way or another, by their experience with or in the United States. Any US support for Yugoslav disaggregating forces exacerbated the problem of what would happen if Tito died or resigned. Even though diverse in content and strategy, Eisenhower's New Look, Kennedy's 'flexible response,' and Nixon's détente, contemplated Yugoslav independence from Moscow, and, therefore, its national sovereignty under Tito, as an anti-Soviet Cold War feature. The impact of USIA and USIS worked in long-term ways. Indeed, both the Serbian 'liberals' and the Croatian 'springers,' as well as Slovenian dissidents revolving around *Perspektive*, remained attached to their views of democratic pluralism and a market economy. In the late 1980s and early 1990s, they emerged as protagonists of the new wave of liberal democratic parties in Serbia, Croatia, and Slovenia. *Perspektive* journalist Jože Pučnik returned to Slovenia in the late 1980s, where he became leader of the Democratic Opposition of Slovenia, a platform of parties that defeated the communists in the first free elections in 1990. Franjo Tudjman, imprisoned after Karadjordje, became Croatia's first president; Čičak affirmed himself as leader of the Croatian Helsinki Committee for Human Rights; Budiša founded the Croatian Social-Liberal Party; while Dabčević-Kučar, Tripalo, and Dragutin Haramija became founders of the new Croatian People's Party. With the collapse of the Soviet Union and the Cold War in demise, these leaders faced the transition towards democracy, sometimes by embracing, other times by rejecting, Western liberal standards, in a nation-building process full of tensions that we have still not fully understood.

Notes

1 Reported in Airgram 13 Consulate Zagreb to Dept. of State, 19 July 1966, PPB 10–2 YUGO, Box 433, CFPF 1964–66, RG 59, NACP.
2 Airgram 935 Embassy Belgrade to Dept. of State, 31 May 1966, PPB 9 YUGO, Box 433, CFPF 1964–66, RG 59, NACP.
3 Klasić, *Jugoslavija i svijet 1968*, 450.
4 Giles Scott-Smith, 'Mapping the Undefinable: Some Thoughts on the Relevance of Exchange Programs within International Relations Theory,' *The Annals of the American Academy of Political and Social Science* 616, no. 1 (2008): 191, https://doi.org/10.1177/0002716207311953.
5 Katarina Spehnjak and Tihomir Cipek, 'Disidenti, opozicija i otpor – Hrvatska i Jugoslavija,' *Časopis za suvremenu povijest* 39, no. 2 (2007): 262–3.
6 Mihajlo Mihajlov, 'Now it Can Be Told – By the Russians,' *New York Times*, 14 March 1965.
7 Telegram 1593 Embassy Belgrade to Secretary of State, 8 March 1965, PPV 12, Box 434, CFPF 1964–66, RG 59, NACP.
8 Telegram 1608 Embassy Belgrade to Secretary of State, 29 March 1965, PPV 12 – PPV 1–2, Box 434, CFPF 1964–66, RG 59, NACP.
9 Telegram 1593 Embassy Belgrade to Secretary of State, 8 March 1965; for more details, see Srđan Cvetković, *Portreti disidenata* (Belgrade: Institut za noviju istoriju Srbije, 2007), 239–312.
10 Richard Eder, 'Mihajlov is Given New 4-Year Term by Belgrade Court,' *New York Times*, 20 April 1967; Mihajlo Mihajlov, 'Punished for Publishing Abroad,' *New York Times*, 12 February 1971; 'Yugoslav Writer Given Jail Term,' *New York Times*, 10 February 1972; Mihajlo Mihajlov, 'Rights Come First,' *New York Times*, 8 April 1978.
11 Airgram 177 Embassy Belgrade to Dept. of State, 24 August 1965, POL 29 YUGO – EDU 9–3 YUGO, Box 382, CFPF 1964–66, RG 59, NACP.
12 'Mihajlo Mihajlov, 76; Writer and Dissident in Yugoslavia,' *New York Times*, 8 March 2010.

13 Airgram 139 Consulate Zagreb to Dept. of State, 7 April 1964, INFO 12 YUGO, Box 417, CFPF 1964–66, RG 59, NACP.

14 Airgram 166 Consulate Zagreb to Dept. of State, 20 May 1964, PPV 12 YUGO–PPV 1–2 YUGO, Box 444, CFPF 1964–66, RG 59, NACP.

15 *Ljubljanski Dnevnik*, 2 June 1964.

16 Airgram 177 Consulate Zagreb to Dept. of State, June 23, 1964, PPV 12 YUGO – PPV 1–2 YUGO, Box 444, CFPF 1964–66, RG 59, NACP; *Delo*, 18 May 1964, 3; *Delo*, 20 May 1964, 6.

17 Marcel Castells, *The Rise of the Network Society* (West Sussex: Wiley-Blackwell, 2011).

18 The editorial advisory board consisted of, among others, the French philosopher of Greek origin Kostas Axelos, the German Marxist philosopher Ernst Bloch, the German-born American humanistic philosopher Erich Fromm, the Marxist French intellectuals Lucien Goldman and Henri Lefebvre, the world leading pragmatic thinker Jürgen Habermas, the Budapest school philosopher Agnes Heller, the Polish anti-Marxist philosopher and inspiration of the Solidarity movement Leszek Kolakowski, and the German-American philosopher, sociologist, and political theorist, member of the Frankfurt School of Critical Theory, Herbert Marcuse. For a broader debate on the Praxis legacy, I recommend Corinna Gerbaz Giuliano, 'Philosophy and Politics – the Experience of the Publication Review «Praxis» (1964–1974),' *Eidos* 2, no. 2 (2018): 159–70.

19 Mihailo Marković, 'Neobjavljenji intervju: Praxis – Kritičko mišljenje i delanje,' *Filozofija i društvo* 14, no. 1 (2010): 3; Predrag Vranicki, *Historija Marksizma*, vol. 2 (Zagreb: Cekade, 1987), 368–410.

20 Gajo Petrović, 'Na početku novog godišta,' *Praxis*, no. 1–2 (April 1967), 5; for major insights, see Gajo Petrović, 'Čemu Praxis,' *Praxis*, no. 10–11 (1971); and Luka Bogdani et al., *Aspekti Praxisa: Refleksije Uz 50. Obljetnicu* (Zagreb: Filozofski fakultet Sveučilišta u Zagrebu, 2015).

21 Marković, 'Neobjavljenji intervju,' 4; Bogdani et al., *Aspekti Praxisa*, 32, 39.

22 Milan Kangrga, *Šverceri vlastitog života: Refleksije o hrvatskoj političkoj kulturi i duhovnosti* (Belgrade: Res publica, 2001), 215–34.

23 Airgram 144 Consulate Zagreb to Dept. of State, 4 March 1965, PPV 12 YUGO-POL 12 YUGO, Box 444, CFPF 1964–66, RG 59, NACP.

24 Airgram 43 Consulate Zagreb to Dept. of State, 31 August 1965, PPB 7 YUGO, Box 433, CFPF 1964–66, RG 59, NACP, 1–7.

25 Airgram 262 Consulate Zagreb to Dept. of State, 7 June 1966, PPB 7 YUGO-PPB 9 YUGO, Box 433, CFPF 1964–66, RG 59, NACP.

26 Airgram 43 Consulate Zagreb to Dept. of State, 25 July 1965, PPB 9 YUGO-POL 15 YUGO, Box 433, CFPF 1964–66, RG 59, NACP, 4.

27 Milan Kangrga, 'O metodi i domašaju jedne kritike,' *Praxis*, no. 2 (1964), 239–306.

28 Miladin Životić, 'Socijalizam i masovna kultura,' *Praxis* no. 2 (1964), 258–68; Howard Parsons, 'Sloboda i demokracija' (189–202), Slobodan Stojanović, 'Sloboda i demokracija u socijalizmu' (203–13), and Danilo Pejović, 'Socijalizam i inteligencija' (214–27), in *Praxis*, no. 2 (1964).

29 Airgram 241 Consulate Zagreb to Dept. of State, 17 May 1966, PPB 7 YUGO-USSR-PPB 9 YUGO, and Airgram 880 Embassy Belgrade to Dept. of State, 2 May 1966, PPB 9 YUG, in Box 433, CFPF 1964–66, RG 59, NACP.

30 Airgram 64 Embassy Belgrade to Dept. of State, 19 July 1966, PPB 9 YUGO, Box 433, CFPF 1964–66, RG 59, NACP.
31 Rei Shigeno, 'On the Conception of Politics of the Praxis Group – Exposing the Limits of its Universalism,' *European Studies* 1 (2001): 81–98.
32 Renata Salecl, *The Spoils of Freedom: Psychoanalysis and Feminism After the Fall of Socialism* (London; New York: Routledge, 1994), 60.
33 Bogetić, *Jugoslavensko-američki odnosi 1961–1971*, 258–67.
34 Bogetić and Životić, *Jugoslavija i Arapsko-Izraelski Rat 1967*.
35 Bilješka o razgovoru Milan Kovačevića sa Steven E. Steinerom, 12 June 1969, 04–332/1–1969, Box 43, Republički protokol, IVS SRH 1953–90, RG 280, CSA.
36 Izvještaj o poseti privredne delegacije SFRJ Kanadi i SAD-u, May 1969, 1964, Box 43, Republički protokol, IVS SRH 1953–90, RG 280, CSA.
37 Delegacija privrednika iz Sjedinjenih Američkih Država, 27 October 1969, XXV-10/773–1969, Box 43, Sjeverna i Južna Amerika 1967–69, Savjet IVS-a za odnose s inozemstvom, RG 1409, CSA.
38 Airgram 413 Embassy Belgrade to Dept. of State, 16 August 1969, Box 2, Eastern Europe, CU, MIC, RIAS.
39 Robert D. Schulzinger, 'Détente in the Nixon-Ford Years, 1969–1976,' in *The Cambridge History of the Cold War 2*, ed. Melvyn P. Leffler and Odd Arne Westad (New York: Cambridge University Press, 2010), 373–94; for a deeper analysis, see Raymond L. Garthoff, *Détente and Confrontation: American–Soviet Relations from Nixon to Reagan* (Washington, DC: Brookings Institution, 1994); and Jeremi Suri, *Power and Protest: Global Revolution and the Rise of Detente* (Cambridge, MA; London: Harvard University Press, 2009).
40 Memorandum for the Record, 13 September 1971, FRUS, 1969–76, Vol. XXIX, doc. 231.
41 Ante Batović, *The Croatian Spring: Nationalism, Repression and Foreign Policy Under Tito* (London; New York: I. B. Tauris, 2017), 199.
42 *Ibid.*, 197.
43 *Ibid.*, 198.
44 Editorial note, 29 October 1971, FRUS, 1969–76, Vol. XXIX, doc. 233.
45 Batović, *The Croatian Spring*, 201.
46 Memorandum for the President's Files, 30 October 1971, FRUS, 1969–76, Vol. XXIX, doc. 234; Dragan Bogetić, 'Razgovori Tito-Nikson Oktobra 1971. Političke Implikacije Vašingtonske Deklaracije,' *Istorija 20. Veka*, issue 2 (2011): 169–70.
47 Bogetić, 'Razgovori Tito-Nikson Oktobra 1971,' 169–71.
48 Informacija o naučno-tehničkoj saradnji između SFRJ i SAD, 21 October 1971, str.pov. 107/14, Box 45, Savjet IVS za odnose s inozemstvom 1967–73, RG 1409, CSA.
49 Zabeleška o prijemu g. Frenka Šekspira kod druga Marka Bulca, 10 September 1969, 432742, Box 61, SSOK 1960–71, RG 319, AY.
50 Shakespeare to Derwinski, 9 January 1970, Box 13, USIA Director's Subject Files 1968–72, RG 306, NACP.
51 Neka pitanja informativne-propagandne delatnosti SAD u FNRJ, 24 October 1962, Box 240, SAD, Kanada i Latinska Amerika 1953–1967, SSOK, RG 318, AY, 36–37.
52 Informacije i predlozi za posetu J. Richardsona, 17 September 1969, 432890, Box 61, SSOK 1960–71, RG 319, AY.

53 Loomis to Hayes, 6 January 1970, Box 13, USIA Director's Subject Files 1968–72, RG 306, NACP; for further analysis, see also Cull, *The Cold War and the United States Information Agency*, 293–309.

54 Leonard Sloane, 'USIA Sends Commercials Abroad with TV Shows,' *New York Times*, 16 August 1970; Specer Rich, 'USIA Orders Overseas Libraries to Balance Collection,' *Washington Post*, 25 April 1970; Frank Shakespeare, 'Television and the New Diplomacy,' 1970, Box 14, USIA Director's Subject Files 1968–72, RG 306, NACP; and Shakespeare to Henry Loomis, 24 June 1970, James Burnham, Analysis of USIA Program Books for Overseas Use, 1969, Some Conservative Books, April 1970, in Box 13, USIA Director's Subject Files 1968–72, RG 306, NACP. For an overall debate on US public diplomacy in the 1970s, see Hallvard Notaker, Giles Scott-Smith, and David J. Snyder, eds, *Reasserting America in the 1970s: US Public Diplomacy and the Rebuilding of America's Image Abroad* (Manchester: Manchester University Press, 2016).

55 Izvještaj Saveznog saveta za obrazovanje i kulturu, 4 May 1971, 2549, Box 228, RSPKFK, RG 1415, CSA.

56 K-40/41/43/44/45/46/49, Materijali ideološke komisije, Ideološka komisija VIII, CK SKJ, RG 832, AY.

57 Sporazum između vlade SFRJ i vlade SAD o osnivanju američkog informativnog centra u Ljubljani, 6 June 1970, 133/2–01, Box 44; Sporazum između Vlade SFRJ i Vlade SAD o osnivanju informativnog centra SAD u Skopju, 11 May 1972, 09–424/1–1972, Box 45; Sporazum između Vlade SFRJ i SAD o osnivanju Informativnog centra SAD u Sarajevu, 13 September 1973, 226/2–01, Box 46, in Savjet IVS za odnose s inozemstvom 1967–73, RG 1409, CSA.

58 Izvještaj jugoslavenske delegacije za vođenje razgovora o kulturnoj saradnji između SFR Jugoslavije i SAD, November 1973, SAD (unordered series), KKVI IVS-a SRH, RG 1410, CSA; Osnovna pitanja i koncept razgovora o kulturnoj saradnji SRFJ i SAD, 1972, 9.624/72, Box 45, Savjet IVS za odnose s inozemstvom 1967–73, RG 1409, CSA.

59 Dragutin Lalović, ed., *Hrvatsko i Jugoslavensko 'Proljeće' 1962–1972* (Zagreb: Društvo 'Povijest izvan mitova,' 2014), 54–9.

60 Tihomir Ponoš, *Na Rubu Revolucije: Studenti '71* (Zagreb: Profil, 2007); Drapac, *Constructing Yugoslavia*, 230–3; Batović, *The Croatian Spring*. For testimonies from its leaders, see Miko Tripalo, *Hrvatsko Proljeće*, 2nd ed. (Zagreb: Globus, 1990); and Dabčević-Kučar, *'71. – hrvatski snovi i stvarnost*. On the US press reporting, see James Feron, 'Purges go deep into Croatian life,' *New York Times*, 7 February 1972.

61 Batović, *The Croatian Spring*, 209.

62 'Moramo ukloniti sve što smeta jedinstvu SKJ,' *Borba*, 17 October 1972, 1, 5; 'Usvojene ostavke Marka Nikezića i Latinke Perović,' *Borba*, 26 October 1972, 1.

63 Aleksandar Nenadović and Koča Popović, *Razgovori s Kočom* (Zagreb: Globus, 1989), 151–58; Igor Lasić, 'Mirko Tepavac: I ovoj kontrarevoluciji štošta će se osvetiti,' *Novosti*, 3 June 2013, 702, http://arhiva.portalnovosti.com/2013/06/mirko-tepavac-i-ovoj-kontrarevoluciji-stosta-ce-se-osvetiti/, 6 June 2019.

64 Mijat Lakićević, *Ispred vremena* (Belgrade: Fond za otvoreno društvo, Srbija, 2011).

65 Jakovina, *Socijalizam na američkoj pšenici*, 59–60.

66 Latinka Perović, *Dominantna i neželjena elita: Beleške o intelektualnoj i političkoj eliti u Srbiji (XX–XXI)* (Belgrade: Dan Graf, 2015). Perović wrote about her personal memories of the 1972 events in her memoirs, including Latinka Perović, *Zatvaranje*

kruga: ishod političkog rascepa u SKJ 1971/1972 (Sarajevo: Svjetlost, 1991); but see also interviews such as Latinka Perović, *Snaga Lične Odgovornosti* (Belgrade: Helsinški odbor, 2008); and Olivera Milosavljević, *Činjenice i tumačenja: Dva razgovora sa Latinkom Perović, Svedočanstva* (Belgrade: Helsinški odbor za ljudska prava u Srbiji, 2010).

67 Dejan Jović, 'The Disintegration of Yugoslavia. A Critical Review of Explanatory Approaches,' *European Journal of Social Theory* 4, no. 1 (2001): 101–20, https://doi.org/10.1177/13684310122225037; Dejan Jović, *Yugoslavia: A State That Withered Away* (West Lafayette, IN: Purdue University Press, 2008).

68 Rinna Kullaa, 'US Intelligence Estimates of "The Crises in Croatia" and its Relationship to Détente in East–West Relations Across Europe 1971–1972,' in *Hrvatsko Proljeće 40 Godina Poslije*, ed. Tvrtko Jakovina (Zagreb: CZD Miko Tripalo, FFZG, FPZSZ, PFSZ, 2012).

Conclusion

Political power may change hands overnight, and economic and social life may soon follow, but people's personalities, shaped by the communist regime they lived under, are slower to change. Their characters have so deeply incorporated a particular set of values, a way of thinking and of perceiving the world that exorcising this way of being takes an unforeseeable length of time. [...] Democracy is not like an unexpected gift that comes without effort. It must be fought for. And that is what makes it so difficult.

Slavenka Drakulić, Croatian feminist activist and writer[1]

I never quite understood why the Yugoslavs allowed us to do that.

USIS PAO Walter Roberts[2]

We live in an era of soft skills. Soft skills – namely the personal attributes that enable someone to interact effectively and harmoniously with other people – are cooperative features of soft power. There is no soft power without personal ascendance, the attraction of who you are, and who you speak for.

As this book shows, US public diplomacy in Yugoslavia was a story of soft skills rendered as soft-power endeavours. The USIA mission flourished in the climate of reduced Yugoslav resistance to US influence, but only after accepting the American partnership that helped to pull back Soviet interference in the post-1948 assessment. As David Engerman argues, the Cold War 'was fought on neutral ground or, more precisely, to make neutral ground less so.' In fact, with 'no hopes of transforming the antagonists themselves, the American–Soviet conflict became a bipolar one in which the poles themselves were off limits.' After establishing their outer borders, the superpowers started competing for those outside any camp.[3]

In Franco's Spain, for instance, USIA put in place a strategy that counteracted the anti-American tendencies of Franco's opposition, while maintaining relations with groups and individuals 'who wielded influence – either present or potential – over the government's decisions, international matters, or over public opinion.' The strategy, which emerged in the Yugoslav case as well, 'held a number of glaring contradictions'[4] – namely, how could USIA remain a credible proponent of democracy and not clash with the dictatorship?

The soft power of a country, argues Joseph Nye, hinges on three major resources: its culture, when it becomes attractive to others; its political values, when they move hearts and minds at home or abroad; and its foreign policies, but only 'when others see them as legitimate and having moral authority.'[5] This makes soft power dependent on 'willing interpreters and receivers' that, usually, are prone to engage in exchanges that are perceived, at least by the majority, as being non-political. Yet, how can we evaluate if the attraction by soft power produced the 'desired policy outcomes'? There is no other way than to judge on a case-by-case basis, argues Nye, but with a conscience about the persistent gap 'between power measured as resources and power judged as the outcome of behavior.' In fact, soft-power attraction often relies on 'a diffuse effect, creating a general influence rather than producing an easily observable specific action.'[6] Sometimes its diffusion is spread and involves way too many actors; other times we cannot measure attractiveness that may be both the cause and consequence of certain behavioural outcomes; or, simply because, while culture could be 'a tool of diplomacy' possibly 'instrumentalized to achieve a state's goals in foreign policy,'[7] the reverse could happen – namely, culture to exploit diplomacy networks for its own affirmation.

USIS in Yugoslavia was far more interested in creating networks over the long-term, rather than undermining the Yugoslav dictatorship in the first place. Working in socialist Yugoslavia was quite a gamble, USIS field officers reported:

> Perhaps [the] best [way to] describe the situation in Yugoslavia is by a story that I told a USIA director when he asked me: 'How is it to work in Belgrade?' And my answer was, at the time, if you travel from Sofia to Rome, Belgrade looks like Rome. But if you travel from Rome to Sofia, Belgrade looks like Sofia. [...] At the time I came [in 1960], I had the distinct feeling that while of course, I worked in a Communist country, in many respects our USIS program in Yugoslavia was more like a USIS program in Austria than in Budapest.[8]

Such a perception arose from the difficulty, for both foreign observers and domestic ideologues, of framing the Yugoslav experiment between permanent, consensual criteria. Titoist Yugoslavia constructed its identity on three basic pillars: self-management, non-alignment, and 'confederalized federalism.' All three of them were inspired by the desire to be different from interwar Yugoslavia and the Soviet Union, as Dejan Jović recognized.[9] However, the Yugoslav inclination towards 'bold and imaginative' experimentation created a series of dilemmas on how economic modernization could coexist without the institutional or social breakdown of the regime, and how, consequently, individual and national freedom would relate to these modernization processes.[10] American endorsement of Tito's regime involved a calculated risk in both political and economic terms, and was repeatedly subject to attacks from both Congressional and public critics, such as the Yugoslav émigré community, particularly at times when Tito endorsed vital international issues that appeared identical with, or very close, to those of the Soviet Union.

The establishment of Washington's public diplomacy in Yugoslavia coincided with, and stemmed from, a profound transformation of US strategy towards anti-Stalinist Yugoslavia. Early USIS projections strived for the 'real emergence of that country as a democratic, independent member of the world community, cooperating with and adhering to the United Nations, and willing to contribute fully to the establishment of international peace and wellbeing.'[11] This mindset was held by all US administrations during the Cold War – both Republican and Democrat. The objective was threefold: to assist Yugoslav national independence; to 'exert an influence' over its 'present and future leadership' by pushing its institutions 'along more democratically representative and humanistic lines,' with increasing ties to the West; and to extract 'maximum benefit' from its significant role as 'a disturbing influence upon the political and ideological unity of the Soviet-dominated international Communist movement.'[12] Indeed, Yugoslavia remained a model for the 1956 Budapest uprising and the 1968 Prague Spring.

Speaking in Geir Lundestad's terms, Yugoslavia entered neither the 'empire by invitation' nor the 'empire by imposition.'[13] However, the great pull towards the United States, and the cultural networking put in place by the USIA/USIS agenda, enticed a bold development of Yugoslav social science that, consequently, impacted critical thought and opposition. As Cipek and Spehnjak recounted, the political opposition spurred, from the 1960s on, at the major universities, when political science, and then sociology, acknowledged the importance of psychology and the conduct of public opinion polls at republic institutes. Many socio-humanist scientists, coming back from their stays at American and West European universities, imported the critical scientific apparatus of the social sciences. The latter proliferated, especially in Ljubljana, Zagreb, and Belgrade.[14]

Transnational connections with fellows and critical thinkers in the United States became crucial to the Yugoslav dissident movement – for Mihajlo Mihajlov, the Praxists, the Croatian Springers, and the Serbian Liberals, as well as for the leadership involved in the FLP and other US exchange programs.[15] These movements never took a radical position against the government, but they requested challenging reforms. Yet liberalization had a different meaning in Yugoslavia, since the 1965 economic reform and the political federalization following the 1963 and 1974 constitutions did not intend to shift the country towards a liberal, constitutional democracy, or a multiparty system.

In such circumstances, US public diplomacy, acting as an external attraction and delivering values, messages, ideas, and lessons, aimed to transform the Yugoslav regime from within. It was conceived as a long-term policy. As the exchange programs became a pragmatic and desired endeavour of Yugoslav struggle for the country's development, the Yugoslav government almost totally abandoned negative anti-American rhetoric.[16] The USIA Country Plan suggested an ambitious project aimed at changing the mindset of Yugoslav leaders. By the late 1960s, more than fifty US cultural exchange programs had been enacted. Capable of balancing bilateral relations, the exchange programs became first-hand tools of soft power for both sides, involving, as for the FLP, more than 200 Yugoslav leaders by 1966. USIS, the Embassy, and the Fulbright Commission, as this study shows, worked in symbiosis over logistics, management, and support. If the FLP was unilateral, relying on the Embassy and State Department, the Fulbright Program emerged as 'a more truly binational project,' focused on long-term influence, and involving a great network of US private institutions, foremost the universities.[17] The 1964 Fulbright agreement, negotiated by top Yugoslav FO officials, was the first ever signed with a communist country, the first ever in the presence of Senator Fulbright, the first ever co-financed by a communist country (from 1970 on), and the only one with a Yugoslav national chairing the Binational Commission. Study and research in the United States advanced many Yugoslav careers, while concurrently channelling Western cultural and political ideas. Moreover, since other Eastern European countries looked to Yugoslavia as a mirage of freedom and welfare, Washington judged they could gain leverage for these ideas beyond the Iron Curtain.[18]

Attractive to so many eager audiences, the USIS libraries and its field activities presented the American way of life at multiple at multiple levels of society: through the Zagreb and Belgrade trade fairs, through American performers on Yugoslav stages, through Voice of America broadcasts, and through the personal contact policies that co-opted Yugoslav leaders for the exchange programs. Created by USIA policymakers as public libraries with circulating books, as research centres with arranged amusement and educational programs, USIS posts offered a full cultural experience, spanning music, film-lending, lectures, and exhibitions. As places of alternative culture, the libraries combined silent reading with research and discussion; the field officials operated at the crossroads of local, regional, and federal government, managing daily successes and failures with soft skills and grace, as personal interviews have revealed. The Yugoslav Party ideologists and executive leaders, who considered the American centres as threatening national security, were prevented from shutting them in the name of the Yugoslav non-aligned vocation. Western cultural contamination was, therefore, regarded as a by-product of such a policy.

Outside the libraries, USIS invested in a cultural agenda that looked all but political. Financed by a specifically crafted President's Fund, the CPP aimed to dismantle racial and cultural prejudices about the United States and projected American artistic unconventionality as world-leading. American classical performers, actors, and dancers defended US prestige abroad, while advancing private motives. These artists affirmed themselves at major Yugoslav festivals and cultural events, while, on the other hand, Yugoslav impresarios made the American appearances a matter of their own prestige. Interpersonal and intercultural relations produced extraordinary results. This turned out true, especially for the jazz concerts which, mostly arranged by private impresarios, counted on the State Department/USIS's occasional support; the latter turned them into a Cold War statement over domestic African American civil rights advancement.

If the classical and jazz concerts, ballet, and theatre groups coming to Yugoslavia through the CPP were not regarded as a potential political risk by Yugoslav cultural leaders, likewise interested in reciprocal cooperation, the same could not be said for Yugoslav VOA broadcasts, which raised political anxieties and caused uproar. Voice of America, as with other USIS field-centred activities, remained in limbo between approbation and restriction, in a political space where the boundaries of freedom and margins of coercion fluctuated. No firmly established criteria defined what was totally forbidden, tolerated, or implicitly not recommended. Such grey areas were discussed among Party factions, in the political arena where decisions were made, but apparently never solved.

Such inner contradictions are best described by Yugoslav attitudes towards different features of US public diplomacy in the 1960s: as the 1960 Yugoslav Press Law was reducing USIS margins of liberty, and the ideological commissions harshly criticised American propaganda, the Yugoslav government pushed to intensify the US–Yugoslav exchange programs, and sent hundreds of Yugoslavs to the United States.

Yugoslav experimentation with liberalization ended up being a contradiction. In fact, as Valerie Bunce argues, Yugoslavia was, by regional socialist standards, 'unusually decentralized, unusually liberalized, and unusually situated with respect to East–West economic and political-military rivalries.'[19] The apparent contradictory position on US propaganda was only a collateral effect of such policies. In search of a new identity, Yugoslavia rebranded its national self-management and non-aligned socialism.[20] Such rebranding consisted, as Vesna Drapac emphasizes, of a delicate balancing act in which Titoism was less a philosophy of politics than a response to changing circumstances and pressures. Titoism, she claims, ended up being a 'synthesis of communism and Yugoslav nationalism,' a calculation between ideology, expediency, self-interest, and maintaining peaceful relations within centralistic and federalization forces, and externally with the United States and the Soviet Union.[21] The US cultural penetration contributed to shaping that experiment. The mutual (dis)trust between the two partners over the decades covered in this study emerged from them belonging to opposing ideological factions. Ultimately, this was overcome by pragmatism, realpolitik, and, to some extent, shared appreciation. For the founders of its way to socialism, Yugoslavia was a product of Marxist exceptionalism; for US policymakers, it was an experiment worth gambling with.

While, domestically, the USIA struggled in making its policy prerogatives a matter of executive strategy, in Yugoslavia its efforts became a key feature for the attainment of Washington's short, middle, and long-term policy goals. Senator Fulbright's advocacy in Congress for Yugoslav interests, for instance, and Yugoslav lobbying in the Fulbright Commission for their university needs, attest to how both the Americans and Yugoslavs were ready to gamble their own ideological stances for issues of realpolitik shrouded in 'mutual understanding' and 'active peaceful coexistence.'

The imposed, often arbitrary, limits to the American cultural agenda display both the regime's invisible boundaries of coercion and American keenness to overcome them. The discrepancy between the perception and reality of Tito's dictatorship remains, until this day, largely contested in the debates over Yugoslav memory, Tito, and Yugoslav nostalgia.[22] 'Nothing in the Balkans,' reminded PAO Roberts, 'is ever black or white – there are only shades of grey.'[23] Investigating these shades, which evolved from the binaries of the Cold War, helps us understand the distinctiveness that shaped Yugoslav bilateral relations with the United States and the Soviet Union.

As this study proves, these relationships became viable through cultural interactions and interchanges, especially when traditional diplomacy applied soft skills and soft-power diplomacy as its fundamental and irreplaceable feature.

Notes

1 Drakulić, *How We Survived Communism and Even Laughed*, xvii.
2 Taplin, 'Walter Roberts: US Public Diplomacy in Yugoslavia.'
3 David C. Engerman, 'Ideology and the Origins of the Cold War, 1917–1962,' in *The Cambridge History of the Cold War*, ed. Melvyn P. Leffler and Odd Arne Westad, Reprint, vol. 1 (Cambridge: Cambridge University Press, 2012), 33.
4 Lorenzo Delgado Gomez-Escalonilla, 'Modernizing a Friendly Tyrant: US Public Diplomacy and Sociopolitical Change in Francoist Spain,' in *US Public Diplomacy and Democratization in Spain: Selling Democracy?*, ed. Francisco Javier Rodriguez Jimenez, Lorenzo Delgado Gomez-Escalonilla, and Nicholas J. Cull (New York: Palgrave Macmillan, 2015), 81–3.
5 Nye, *The Future of Power*, 123.
6 Nye, *Soft Power*, 27, 34. This means, suggests Nye, that 'public polls can measure the existence and trends in potential […] resources, but they are only a first approximation for behavioral change in terms of outcomes. Where opinion is strong and consistent over time, it can have an effect, but its impact in comparison to other variables can only be determined by careful process tracing of the sort that historians do' (Joseph S. Nye, 'Responding to My Critics and Concluding Thoughts,' in *Soft Power and US Foreign Policy: Theoretical, Historical and Contemporary Perspectives*, ed. Inderjeet Parmar and Michael Cox [London; New York: Routledge, 2010], 218).
7 Depkat, 'Cultural Approaches to International Relations: A Challenge?,' 177.
8 Taplin, 'Walter Roberts: US Public Diplomacy in Yugoslavia.'
9 Jović, 'Communist Yugoslavia and its "Others".' While the disintegration and political legitimacy of Yugoslavia was not this book's concern, some excellent studies have been done in the field, namely Sabrina P. Ramet and Ljubiša S. Adamović, *Beyond Yugoslavia: Politics, Economics, and Culture in a Shattered Community* (Boulder, CO: Westview Press, 1995); Sabrina P. Ramet, *Balkan Babel: The Disintegration of Yugoslavia from the Death of Tito to the Fall of Milosevic*, 4th ed. (Boulder, CO: Westview Press, 2002); Sabrina P. Ramet, *The Three Yugoslavias: State-Building and Legitimation, 1918–2005* (Washington, DC; Bloomington: Indiana University Press, 2006); Dejan Djokić, *Yugoslavism: Histories of a Failed Idea, 1918–1992* (London: Hurst&Co. Publishers, 2003); Lenard J. Cohen and Jasna Dragović-Soso, *State Collapse in South-Eastern Europe: New Perspectives on Yugoslavia's Disintegration* (West Lafayette, IN: Purdue University Press, 2007).
10 Rusinow, *The Yugoslav Experiment 1948–1974*, vii.
11 USIE Country Paper, 3 July 1950, 511.68/7–350, Box 2472, CDF 1950–54, RG 59, NACP.
12 Kohler to Kennan, 12 October 1961, FRUS 1961–1963, Vol. XVI, Eastern Europe; Cyprus; Greece; Turkey, doc. 102, 213.
13 Geir Lundestad, *The Rise and Decline of the American 'Empire': Power and its Limits in Comparative Perspective* (Oxford; New York: Oxford University Press, 2012); and

Geir Lundestad, *The United States and Western Europe Since 1945: From Empire by Invitation to Transatlantic Drift* (Oxford: Oxford University Press, 2003).

14 Spehnjak and Cipek, 'Disidenti, opozicija i otpor – Hrvatska i Jugoslavija,' 260–1.

15 For this, see the conclusions in Yugoslav Opinion Leader Study, 1968–69, YO6801, Box 41, Africa, Eastern Europe and Multi-Areas, USIA ORA, RG 306, NACP.

16 Informacija o poseti dr. Charlesa Franklina, 18 May 1966, in Poseta Charlesa Franklina – Materijali, 11 May 1966, 416844, Box 237, SAD, Kanada i Latinska Amerika 1953–1967, SSOK, RG 318, AY.

17 Instruction A-110 Dept. of State to Embassy Belgrade, 3 February 1958, 511.683/2–358, Box 2205, CDF 1955–59, RG 59, NACP.

18 Airgram 969 Embassy Belgrade to Dept. of State, 15 August 1968, and Box 2, Eastern Europe, CU, MIC, RIAS, 14; Airgram 413 Embassy Belgrade to Dept. of State, 16 August 1969, Box 2, Eastern Europe, CU, MIC, RIAS, 1–4.

19 Valerie Bunce, *Subversive Institutions: The Design and the Destruction of Socialism and the State* (Cambridge: Cambridge University Press, 1999), 53. Bunce further explains that the destruction of socialism following the collapse of the Soviet Union derived from two basic factors: institutional design of socialism as a regime, a state, and a bloc, and the rapid expansion during the 1980s of opportunities for domestic and international change.

20 Melissa Aronczyk, *Branding the Nation: The Global Business of National Identity* (Oxford; New York: Oxford University Press, 2013).

21 Drapac, *Constructing Yugoslavia: A Transnational History*, 227.

22 On these issues, see Stefan Troebst, Augusta Dimou, and Maria Todorova, eds, *Remembering Communism: Private and Public Recollections of Lived Experiences in Southeast Europe* (Budapest: CEU Press, 2014); Maria Todorova and Zsuzsa Gille, *Post-Communist Nostalgia* (New York: Berghahn Books, 2012); and Luthar and Pusnik, *Remembering Utopia*.

23 Roberts, *Tito, Mihailovic, and the Allies*. On this perspective, see also John B. Allcock, *Explaining Yugoslavia* (New York: Columbia University Press, 2000).

Select bibliography

Archival collections

National Archives, College Park, MD, United States

Department of State Records: Central Decimal Files 1950–54; Central Decimal Files 1955–59; Central Decimal Files 1960–63; Central Foreign Policy File 1963; Central Foreign Policy Files 1964–66; Central Foreign Policy Files 1967–69

United States Information Agency Records: Office of Research and Analysis; Voice of America; Office of Administration; Office of the Assistant Director for Radio and Soviet Orbit; Information Center Service/English Teaching Division; Office of Research and Media Reaction/Research Memoranda 1963–99; Country and Subject Files; Book Translation Program; Office of Research and Media Reaction/Briefing Papers; Information Center Service/Exhibits Division; Information Center Service (Administrative Files 1949–67); Information Programs/Publications 1950–2000; Library Program Division/Records relating to Exhibits 1955–99; Library Program Division/Records Relating to Culture Centers 1946–88; Office of Research/Special Reports 1953–97; Office of Research and Media Reaction; Office of Policy and Plans/Program Coordination Staff; Office of Administration/Interagency/Congressional Reports; Inspection Staff; Library Program Division; Office of Research and Analysis/Research Notes 1958–62; Office of Research and Evaluation; Office of Research/Country Project Correspondence 1952–63; Office of Research and Intelligence

University of Arkansas Library, Special Collection, Fayetteville, AR, United States

J. William Fulbright Foreign Scholarship Board Records

Bureau of Educational and Cultural Affairs: CU Organization and Administration; Cultural Presentations Program; Fulbright Program; Special Programs; Post Reports; Reports, Surveys, and Correspondence: State Department Programs

Arhiv Jugoslavije/Archives of Yugoslavia, Belgrade, Serbia

CK SKJ Ideološka komisija

CK SKJ Komisija PSKJ za političku propagandu i informativnu delatnost 1965–78

CK SKJ Komisija za međunarodne odnose i veze CK SKJ 1945–90

SSRNJ: Materijali komisije za međunarodne veze 1950–59; Komisija za politički i idejno-vaspitni rad 1966

Savezno izvršno veće / vijeće 1953–90

Komisija za prosvetnu razmenu između SFRJ i SAD (Fulbrajtova komisija)

Savet akademija nauka i umetnosti SFRJ

Savet za nauku i kulturu Vlade FNRJ

Savezni savet za obrazovanje i kulturu (1960–71)
Savezni sekretarijat za obrazovanje i kulturu

Arhiv Josipa Broza Tita/Josip Broz Tito Archives, Belgrade, Serbia

Kabinet Predsednika Republike

Istorijski Arhiv Beograda/Historical Archives of Belgrade, Belgrade, Serbia

Skupština Grada Beograda Sekretarijat za kulturu
Gradski komitet SKS Beograd

Hrvatski Državni Arhiv/Croatian State Archives, Zagreb, Croatia

CK SKH: Komisija za agitaciju i propagandu; Idejno-politička pitanja i ideološki rad; Međunarodni odnosi i spoljna politika
Sabor SRH – Republičko vijeće
Izvršno Vijeće Sabora NRH/SRH
Izvršno Vijeće Sabora SRH
SSRNH: Izvršni odbor Narodne fronte Hrvatske; Komisija za idejno-političi odgoj; Komisija za međunarodnu suradnji; Komisija za štampu i izdavačku djelatnost
Komisija za kulturne veze s inozemstvom Izvršnog Vijeća Sabora SRH
Ministarstvo za nauku i kulturu
Predsjedništvo Vlade NRH
Republički sekretarijat za prosvjetu, kulturu i fizičku kulturu

Roosevelt Institute for American Studies, Microfilm Collection, Middelburg, The Netherlands

Bureau of Educational and Cultural Affairs
USIA (Cold War Era Special Reports)
OSS/State Department Intelligence and Research Reports

Nacionalna i Sveučilišna Knjižnica/National and University Library, Zagreb, Croatia

Periodical collection

Sveučilišna Knjižnica Rijeka/University of Rijeka Library, Rijeka, Croatia

Periodical collection

Nada Apsen-Pintarić Private Collection, Zagreb, Croatia

Online archival collections

Memory of the World, Praxis Library (https://praxis.memoryoftheworld.org)
Jugosvirke web archive/blog (https://jugosvirke.wordpress.com/)

Governmental documents

Chatten, R., L. Herrmann, T. Markiw, F. Sullinger, and United States Information Agency. *The United States Information Agency: A Commemoration: Public Diplomacy, Looking Back, Looking Forward.* Washington, DC: United States Information Agency, 1999.

Departments of State, Justice, and Commerce, the Judiciary, and Related Agencies Appropriations for Fiscal Year 1978: Hearings before a Subcommittee of the Committee on Appropriations, United States Senate, 95th Congress, First Session. Washington, DC: US Government Printing Office, 1977.

'Inaugural Address of John F. Kennedy,' *The Avalon Project at Yale Law School*, 26 February 2018. https://web.archive.org/web/20070514235348/http://www.yale.edu/lawweb/aval on/presiden/inaug/kennedy.htm, accessed 10 October 2019.

Public Papers of the Presidents of the United States: Harry S. Truman, 1950. Washington, DC: Government Printing Office, 1965.

United States Department of State. *Foreign Relations of the United States, 1917–1972. Public Diplomacy, World War I.* Washington, DC: United States Government Printing Office, 2014. http://history.state.gov/historicaldocuments/frus1917-72PubDip, accessed 10 October 2019.

———. *Foreign Relations of the United States, 1946. Eastern Europe, the Soviet Union.* Vol. VI. Washington, DC: United States Government Printing Office, 1969. http://digital.library.wisc.edu/1711.dl/FRUS.FRUS1946v06, accessed 10 October 2019.

———. *Foreign Relations of the United States, 1948. Eastern Europe; The Soviet Union.* Vol. IV. Washington, DC: United States Government Printing Office, 1974. http://digital.library.wisc.edu/1711.dl/FRUS.FRUS1948v04, accessed 10 October 2019.

———. *Foreign Relations of the United States, 1949. Eastern Europe; the Soviet Union.* Vol. V. Washington, DC: United States Government Printing Office, 1976. http://digital.library.wisc.edu/1711.dl/FRUS.FRUS1949v05, accessed 10 October 2019.

———. *Foreign Relations of the United States, 1950. Central and Eastern Europe; The Soviet Union.* Vol. IV. United States Government Printing Office, 1980. http://digital.library.wisc.edu/1711.dl/FRUS.FRUS1950v04, accessed 10 October 2019.

———. *Foreign Relations of the United States, 1951. Europe: Political and Economic Developments.* Vol. IV. Part 2. Washington, DC: United States Government Printing Office, 1985. http://digital.library.wisc.edu/1711.dl/FRUS.FRUS1951v04p2, accessed 10 October 2019.

———. *Foreign Relations of the United States, 1952–1954. Eastern Europe; Soviet Union; Eastern Mediterranean.* Vol. VIII. Washington, DC: United States Government Printing Office, 1988. http://history.state.gov/historicaldocuments/frus1952-54v08, accessed 10 October 2019.

———. *Foreign Relations of the United States 1952–1954. National Security Affairs.* Vol. II. Part 2. Washington, DC: United States Government Printing Office, 1984. https://history.state.gov/historicaldocuments/frus1952-54v02p2, accessed 10 October 2019.

———. *Foreign Relations of the United States, 1955–1957. Central and Southeastern Europe.* Vol. XXVI. Washington, DC: United States Government Printing Office, 1992. http://history.state.gov/historicaldocuments/frus1955-57v26, accessed 10 October 2019.

———. *Foreign Relations of the United States, 1955–1957. Foreign Economic Policy; Foreign Information Program.* Vol. IX. Washington, DC: United States Government Printing

Office, 1989. http://history.state.gov/historicaldocuments/frus1955-57v09, accessed 10 October 2019.

——. *Foreign Relations of the United States, 1958–1960. Eastern Europe; Finland; Greece; Turkey.* Vol. X. Part 2. Washington, DC: United States Government Printing Office, 1993. http://history.state.gov/historicaldocuments/frus1958-60v10p2, accessed 10 October 2019.

——. *Foreign Relations of the United States, 1961–1963. Eastern Europe; Cyprus; Greece; Turkey.* Vol. XVI. Washington, DC: United States Government Printing Office, 1994. http://history.state.gov/historicaldocuments/frus1961-63v16, accessed 10 October 2019.

——. *Foreign Relations of the United States, 1961–1963. Organization of Foreign Policy; Information Policy; United Nations; Scientific Matters.* Vol. XXV. Washington, DC: United States Government Printing Office, 2001. http://history.state.gov/historicaldocuments/frus1961-63v25, accessed 10 October 2019.

——. *Foreign Relations of the United States, 1964–1968. Eastern Europe.* Vol. XVII. Washington, DC: United States Government Printing Office, 1996. http://history.state.gov/historicaldocuments/frus1964-68v17, accessed 10 October 2019.

——. *Foreign Relations of the United States, 1969–1976, Volume XXIX, Eastern Europe; Eastern Mediterranean, 1969–1972.* Washington, DC: United States Government Printing Office, 2007. https://history.state.gov/historicaldocuments/frus1969-76v29, accessed 10 October 2019.

——. *Foreign Relations of the United States: Diplomatic Papers, 1945. Europe.* Vol. V. Washington, DC: United States Government Printing Office, 1967. http://digital.library.wisc.edu/1711.dl/FRUS.FRUS1945v05, accessed 10 October 2019.

——. *Dictionary of International Relations Terms.* 3rd ed. [Washington, DC]: Department of State Library, 1987.

VIII Kongres Saveza komunista Jugoslavije. Stenografske beleške. Beograd: Kultura, 1965.

Oral sources

Apsen, Nada. Interview by author. Oral interview. Zagreb, Croatia, 31 May 2014.
Bašić, Sonja. Interview by author. Telephone and email interview. Zagreb, Croatia, 26 November 2013.
Bugarski, Ranko. Interview by author. Email interview. 27 August 2015.
Nikolić, Petar. Interview by author. Oral interview. Belgrade, Serbia, 5 July 2014.
Nikolić, Zdenka. Interview by author. Email interview. Zagreb, Croatia, 3–27 June 2014.
Petrović, Rade. Interview by Author. Telephone interview. 28 August 2014.
Purg, Danica. Interview by author. Email interview. 6 June 2014.
Šarić, Taib. Interview by author. Email interview. 25 August 2015.

Newspapers and periodicals

Borba
Corriere della Sera
Delo
Ekonomska politika

Select bibliography

Glas Amerike
Glas Istre
Komunist
Life
Ljubljanski dnevnik
New York Times
Novosti
Oko
Politika
Praxis
Pregled
Telegram
Vjesnik
Washington Post

Video material

Wings to Yugoslavia (Pan Am Airways), 16 mm (US: Kodachrome, 1964), www.youtube.com/watch?v=o7vHzk_hbuM, accessed 9 February 2019.

Books and articles

Acinapura, Joseph N. 'The Cultural Presentations Program of the United States,' 29–. MA thesis. Rutgers University, 1970.

Alexander, Jeffrey C. *The Civil Sphere*. New York: Oxford University Press, 2006.

Allcock, John B. *Explaining Yugoslavia*. New York: Columbia University Press, 2000.

Ansari, Emily Abrams. 'Shaping the Policies of Cold War Musical Diplomacy: An Epistemic Community of American Composers.' *Diplomatic History* 36, no. 1 (2012): 41–52. https://doi.org/10.1111/j.1467-7709.2011.01007.x, accessed 10 October 2019.

Appy, Christian G. *Cold War Constructions: The Political Culture of United States Imperialism, 1945–1966*. Amherst: University of Massachusetts Press, 2000.

Arndt, Richard. *The First Resort of Kings: American Cultural Diplomacy in the Twentieth Century*. Washington, DC: Potomac Books, 2007.

Arndt, Richard T., and David Lee Rubin, eds. *The Fulbright Difference: 1948–1992*. New Brunswick, NJ; London: Transaction Publishers, 1993.

Aronczyk, Melissa. *Branding the Nation: The Global Business of National Identity*. Oxford; New York: Oxford University Press, 2013.

Auerbach, Jonathan, and Castronovo Russ, eds. *The Oxford Handbook of Propaganda Studies*. New York: Oxford University Press, 2013.

Barnhisel, Greg. *Cold War Modernists: Art, Literature, and American Cultural Diplomacy*. New York: Columbia University Press, 2015.

Barnhisel, Greg, and Catherine Turner, eds. *Pressing the Fight: Print, Propaganda, and the Cold War*. Amherst and Boston, MA: University of Massachusetts Press, 2012.

Batančev, Dragan. 'A Cinematic Battle: Three Yugoslav War Films from the 1960s.' MA thesis. Central European University, Budapest, 2012.

Batović, Ante. 'Od Ekonomske Reforme Do Brijunskog Plenuma – Američki i Britanski Izvještaji o Hrvatskoj (1964 – 1966).' *Historijski Zbornik* 63, no. 2 (2010): 539–60.

———. *The Croatian Spring: Nationalism, Repression and Foreign Policy Under Tito.* London; New York: I.B. Tauris, 2017.

Bekić, Darko. *Jugoslavija u Hladnom ratu: Odnosi s velikim silama 1949–1955.* Zagreb: Globus, 1988.

Belmonte, Laura A. 'Exporting America: The US Propaganda Offensive, 1945–1959.' In *The Arts of Democracy: Art, Public Culture, and the State,* edited by Casey N. Blake, 123–49. Washington, DC; Philadelphia: Woodrow Wilson Center Press; University of Pennsylvania Press, 2007.

———. 'Selling Capitalism: Modernization and US Overseas Propaganda, 1945–1959.' In *Staging Growth: Modernization, Development, and the Global Cold War,* edited by D. C. Engerman, N. Gilman, M. E. Latham, and M. H. Haefele, 107–28. Amherst; Boston: University of Massachusetts Press, 2003.

———. *Selling the American Way: US Propaganda and the Cold War.* Philadelphia: University of Pennsylvania Press, 2010.

Benson, Leslie. *Yugoslavia: A Concise History.* Basingstoke; New York: Palgrave Macmillan, 2001.

Berghahn, Volker. 'The Debate on "Americanization" among Economic and Cultural Historians.' *Cold War History* 10, no. 1 (2010): 107–30. https://doi.org/10.1080/14682740903388566, accessed 10 October 2019.

Bilandžić, Dušan. *Hrvatska moderna povijest.* Zagreb: Golden Marketing, 1999.

Bogdani, Luka, Lino Veljak, Karlo Jurak, Borislav Mikuli, Nikola Cerovac, and Raul Rauni. *Aspekti Praxisa: Refleksije Uz 50. Obljetnicu.* Zagreb: Filozofski fakultet Sveučilišta u Zagrebu, 2015.

Bogetić, Dragan. *Jugoslavensko-američki odnosi 1961–1971.* Belgrade: Institut za savremenu istoriju, 2012.

———. *Jugoslavija i Zapad 1952–1955: Jugoslovensko približavanje NATO-u.* Belgrade: Institut za savremenu istoriju, 2005.

———. *Jugoslovensko-američki odnosi u vreme bipolarnog detanta 1972–1975.* Belgrade: Institut za savremenu istoriju, 2015.

———. *Nova strategija spoljne politike Jugoslavije 1956–1961.* Belgrade: Institut za savremenu istoriju, 2006.

———. 'Razgovori Tito-Nikson Oktobra 1971. Političke Implikacije Vašingtonske Deklaracije.' *Istorija 20. Veka,* issue 2 (2011): 159–72.

Bogetić, Dragan, and Aleksandar Životić. *Jugoslavija i Arapsko-Izraelski Rat 1967.* Belgrade: Institut za savremenu istoriju, 2010.

Bogle, Lori Lyn. *The Pentagon's Battle for the American Mind: The Early Cold War.* College Station: Texas A&M University Press, 2004.

Brogi, Alessandro. *Confronting America: The Cold War Between the United States and the Communists in France and Italy.* Chapel Hill: University of North Carolina Press, 2011.

Bunce, Valerie. *Subversive Institutions: The Design and the Destruction of Socialism and the State.* Cambridge: Cambridge University Press, 1999.

Campbell, John C. *Successful Negotiation, Trieste 1954: An Appraisal by the Five Participants.* Reprint. Princeton: Princeton University Press, 2016.

Castells, Marcel. *The Rise of the Network Society.* West Sussex: Wiley-Blackwell, 2011.

Castillo, Greg. *Cold War on the Home Front: The Soft Power of Midcentury Design.* Minneapolis: University of Minnesota Press, 2010.

Ceh, Nick. *US Diplomatic Records on Relations with Yugoslavia during the Early Cold War.* New York: Columbia University Press, 2001.

Changhe, Su. 'Soft Power.' In *The Oxford Handbook of Modern Diplomacy*, edited by Andrew F. Cooper, Jorge Heine, and Ramesh Thakur, 544–58. Oxford: Oxford University Press, 2013.

Cialdini, Robert B. *Influence: The Psychology of Persuasion.* New York: HarperCollins, 2009.

Cohen, Lenard J., and Jasna Dragović-Soso. *State Collapse in South-Eastern Europe: New Perspectives on Yugoslavia's Disintegration.* West Lafayette, IN: Purdue University Press, 2007.

Cohen, Lizabeth. *A Consumers' Republic: The Politics of Mass Consumption in Postwar America.* New York: Vintage Books, 2003.

Colomina, Beatriz, Ann Marie Brennan, and Jeannie Kim, eds. *Cold War Hothouses: Inventing Postwar Culture, from Cockpit to Playboy.* New York: Princeton Architectural Press, 2004.

Corke, Sarah-Jane. *US Covert Operations and Cold War Strategy: Truman, Secret Warfare and the CIA, 1945–53.* New York: Routledge, 2007.

Corkin, Stanley. *Cowboys as Cold Warriors: The Western And US History.* Philadelphia: Temple University Press, 2004.

Costigliola, Frank. 'US Foreign Policy from Kennedy to Johnson.' In *The Cambridge History of the Cold War*, edited by Melvyn P. Leffler and Odd Arne Westad, 2:111–33. Cambridge: Cambridge University Press, 2012.

Croft, Clare H. *Dancers as Diplomats: American Choreography in Cultural Exchange.* Kindle. Oxford; New York: Oxford University Press, 2015.

Cull, Nicholas J. 'Public Diplomacy before Gullion. The Evolution of a Phrase.' In *Routledge Handbook of Public Diplomacy*, edited by Nancy Snow and Philip M. Taylor, 19–23. New York; London: Routledge Taylor & Francis, 2009.

———. *The Cold War and the United States Information Agency: American Propaganda and Public Diplomacy, 1945–1989.* Cambridge; New York: Cambridge University Press, 2009.

Cummings, Richard H. *Cold War Radio: The Dangerous History of American Broadcasting in Europe, 1950–1989.* Jefferson, NC: McFarland, 2009.

———. *Radio Free Europe's 'Crusade for Freedom': Rallying Americans Behind Cold War Broadcasting, 1950–1960.* North Carolina: McFarland, 2010.

Cvetković, Srđan. *Portreti disidenata.* Belgrade: Institut za noviju istoriju Srbije, 2007.

Dabčević-Kučar, Savka. *'71. – hrvatski snovi i stvarnost.* Vols 1 and 2. Zagreb: Interpublic, 1997.

Davenport, Lisa E. *Jazz Diplomacy: Promoting America in the Cold War Era.* Jackson: University Press of Mississippi, 2010.

Dedijer, Vladimir. *Novi prilozi za biografiju Josipa Broza Tita: Sabrana dela Vladimira Dedijera.* Vol. 3. Belgrade: Rad, 1984.

Depkat, Volker. 'Cultural Approaches to International Relations: A Challenge?' In *Culture and International History*, edited by Jessica C. E. Gienow-Hecht and Frank Schumacher, 175–97. New York; Oxford: Berghahn Books, 2004.

Dimić, Ljubodrag. *Jugoslavija i Hladni rat.* Belgrade: Arhipelag, 2014.

Dimitrijević, Bojan. 'Jugoslavija i NATO 1951–1958. Skica intenzivnih vojnih odnosa.' In *Spoljna politika Jugoslavije: 1950.-1961.*, edited by Slobodan Selinić, 255–74. Belgrade: Institut za noviju istoriju Srbije, 2008.

Dizard, Wilson P. Jr. *Inventing Public Diplomacy: The Story of the US Information Agency.* Boulder, CO: Lynne Rienner Publishers, 2004.

Djokić, Dejan. *Yugoslavism: Histories of a Failed Idea, 1918–1992.* London: Hurst&Co. Publishers, 2003.

Doherty, Thomas. *Cold War, Cool Medium: Television, McCarthyism, and American Culture.* New York: Columbia University Press, 2005.

Dongen, Luc van, Stephanie Roulin, and Giles Scott-Smith, eds. *Transnational Anti-Communism and the Cold War: Agents, Activities, and Networks.* Basingstoke; New York: Palgrave Macmillan, 2014.

Drakulić, Slavenka. *How We Survived Communism and Even Laughed.* New York; London: W. W. Norton & Company, 1991.

Drapac, Vesna. *Constructing Yugoslavia: A Transnational History.* London; New York: Palgrave Macmillan, 2010.

Duda, Igor. 'Konzumerizmom do konzumizma? Potrošačka kultura u Hrvatskoj od 1950-tih do 1980-tih.' In *Potrošačka kultura i konzumerizam*, edited by Snježana Čolić, 83–105. Zagreb: Institut društvenih znanosti Ivo Pilar, 2013.

———. *Pronađeno blagostanje: svakodnevni život i potrošačka kultura u Hrvatskoj 1970–ih i 1980–ih.* 2nd ed. Zagreb: Srednja Europa, 2014.

———. *U potrazi za blagostanjem: o povijesti dokolice i potrošačkog društva u Hrvatskoj 1950 – ih i 1960 – ih.* 2nd ed. Zagreb: Srednja Europa, 2014.

Dudden, Arthur P., and Russell R. Dynes, eds. *The Fulbright Experience 1946–1986: Encounters and Transformations.* New Brunswick, NJ: Transaction Publishers, 1987.

Elder, Robert E. R. *The Information Machine: The United States Information Agency and American Foreign Policy.* New York: Syracuse University Press, 1968.

Ellwood, David W., and Rob Kroes. *Hollywood in Europe: Experiences of a Cultural Hegemony.* Amsterdam: Vu University Press, 1994.

Elteren, Mel van. 'Rethinking Americanization Abroad: Toward a Critical Alternative to Prevailing Paradigms.' *The Journal of American Culture* 29, no. 3 (2006): 345–67.

Engerman, David C. 'Ideology and the Origins of the Cold War, 1917–1962.' In *The Cambridge History of the Cold War*, edited by Melvyn P. Leffler and Odd Arne Westad, 1:20–43. Reprint. Cambridge: Cambridge University Press, 2012.

Eschen, Penny Von. *Satchmo Blows Up the World: Jazz Ambassadors Play the Cold War.* Cambridge, MA; London: Harvard University Press, 2004.

Farlow, Jonathan M. *I've Seen it All at the Library: The View from Behind the Desk.* Jefferson, NC: McFarland & Company, Inc., 2015.

Ferguson, Niall. 'Think Again Power.' *Foreign Policy*, February 2003.

Fosler-Lussier, Danielle. *Music in America's Cold War Diplomacy.* Oakland: University of California Press, 2015.

Fousek, John. *To Lead the Free World: American Nationalism and the Cultural Roots of the Cold War.* Chapel Hill: University of North Carolina Press, 2000.

Fulbright, James W. *Yugoslavia 1964: Report to the Committee on Foreign Relations, United States Senate.* Washington, DC: US Government Printing Office, 1965.

Gabrič, Aleš. *Socialistična kulturna revolucija: Slovenska kulturna politika 1953–1962.* Ljubljana: Cankarjeva založba, 1995.

Gaddis, John L. *Strategies of Containment: A Critical Appraisal of American National Security Policy During the Cold War*. Kindle. New York: Oxford University Press, 2005.

Galijaš, Armina, Rory Archer, and Florian Bieber. *Debating the End of Yugoslavia*. London; New York: Routledge, 2016.

Garthoff, Raymond L. *Détente and Confrontation: American–Soviet Relations from Nixon to Reagan*. Washington, DC: Brookings Institution, 1994.

Gienow-Hecht, Jessica C. E. 'Shame on US? Academics, Cultural Transfer, and the Cold War: A Critical Review.' *Diplomatic History* 24, no. 3 (2000): 465–94. https://doi.org/10.1111/0145-2096.00227, accessed 10 October 2019.

———. 'The World is Ready to Listen: Symphony Orchestras and the Global Performance of America.' *Diplomatic History* 36, no. 1 (2012): 17–28.

Gitelman, Claudia, and Martin Randy, eds. *The Returns of Alwin Nikolais: Bodies, Boundaries and the Dance Canon*. Middletown, CT: Wesleyan, 2007.

Giuliano, Corinna Gerbaz. 'Philosophy and Politics – the Experience of the Publication Review «Praxis» (1964–1974).' *Eidos* 2, no. 2 (2018): 159–70.

Glancy, Mark. *Hollywood and the Americanization of Britain: From the 1920s to the Present*. London; New York: I. B. Tauris, 2015.

Gomez-Escalonilla, Lorenzo Delgado. 'Modernizing a Friendly Tyrant: US Public Diplomacy and Sociopolitical Change in Francoist Spain.' In *US Public Diplomacy and Democratization in Spain: Selling Democracy?*, edited by Francisco Javier Rodriguez Jimenez, Lorenzo Delgado Gomez-Escalonilla, and Nicholas J. Cull, 63–92. New York: Palgrave Macmillan, 2015.

Graham, Sarah E. *Culture and Propaganda: The Progressive Origins of American Public Diplomacy, 1936–1953*. London; New York: Routledge, 2016.

Grandits, Hannes, and Karin Taylor, eds. *Yugoslavia's Sunny Side: A History of Tourism in Socialism (1950s–1980s)*. Budapest; New York: Central European University Press, 2010.

Haddow, Robert H. *Pavilions of Plenty: Exhibiting American Culture Abroad in the 1950s*. Washington, DC: Smithsonian, 1997.

Hamilton, Shane. 'Supermarket USA Confronts State Socialism: Airlifting the Technopolitics of Industrial Food Distribution into Cold War Yugoslavia.' In *Cold War Kitchen: Americanization, Technology, and European Users*, edited by Ruth Oldenziel and Karin Zachmann, 137–59. Cambridge, MA: MIT Press, 2011.

Hart, Justin. *Empire of Ideas: The Origins of Public Diplomacy and the Transformation of US Foreign Policy*. Oxford; New York: Oxford University Press, 2013.

Hayden, Craig. *The Rhetoric of Soft Power: Public Diplomacy in Global Contexts*. Lanham, MD: Lexington Books, 2011.

Heil, Alan L. Jr. *Voice of America: A History*. New York; West Sussex: Columbia University Press, 2003.

Hildenbrand, Suzanne. *Reclaiming the American Library Past: Writing the Women In*. Norwood, NJ: Ablex Publications, 1996.

Hixon, Walter L. *Parting the Curtain: Propaganda, Culture, and the Cold War, 1945–1961*. New York: Palgrave Macmillan, 1997.

Huijgh, Ellen. *Public Diplomacy at Home: Domestic Dimensions*. Leiden; Boston, MA: Brill, 2019.

Huntington, Samuel P. *The Clash of Civilizations and the Remaking of World Order*. 3rd ed. New York: Simon & Schuster, 2011.

Iriye, Akira. 'Culture.' *Journal of American History* 77, no. 1 (1990): 99–107.

———. 'Culture and International History.' In *Explaining the History of American Foreign Relations*, edited by Frank Costigliola and Michael Hogan, 214–25. Cambridge: Cambridge University Press, 1991.

Jakovina, Tvrtko. *Američki komunistički saveznik: Hrvati, Titova Jugoslavija i Sjedinjene Američke Države 1945–1955*. Zagreb: Profil, 2003.

———. 'Narodni kapitalizam protiv narodnih demokracija. Američki super-market na Zagrebačkom velesajmu 1957. godine.' In *Zbornik Mire Kolar Dimitrijević*, edited by Damir Agičić, 469–79. Zagreb: FF Press, 2003.

———. 'Razgovor s Cvijetom Jobom, dugogodišnjim diplomatom i veleposlanikom FNRJ/ SFRJ.' *Časopis za suvremenu povijest* 35, no. 3 (2003): 1031–48.

———. *Socijalizam na američkoj pšenici*. Zagreb: Matica Hrvatska, 2002.

———. *Treća Strana Hladnog Rata*. Zagreb: Fraktura, 2011.

Janjetović, Zoran. *Od 'Internacionale' do komercijale: Popularna kultura u Jugoslaviji 1945–1991*. Belgrade: Institut za noviju istoriju Srbije, 2011.

Jimenez, Francisco J. R., Lorenzo D. Gomez-Escalonilla, and Nicholas J. Cull. *US Public Diplomacy and Democratization in Spain: Selling Democracy?* New York: Palgrave Macmillan, 2015.

Johnson, Haynes B., and Bernard M. Gwertzman. *Fulbright: The Dissenter*. Garden City, NY: Doubleday, 1968.

Jović, Dejan. 'Communist Yugoslavia and its "Others".' In *Ideologies and National Identities: The Case of Twentieth-Century Southeastern Europe*, edited by John Lampe and Mark Mazower, 277–302. Budapest: Central European University Press, 2013. http://books.openedition.org/ceup/2438, accessed 10 October 2019.

———. 'The Disintegration of Yugoslavia. A Critical Review of Explanatory Approaches.' *European Journal of Social Theory* 4, no. 1 (2001): 101–20. https://doi. org/10.1177/13684310122225037, accessed 10 October 2019.

———. *Yugoslavia: A State That Withered Away*. West Lafayette, IN: Purdue University Press, 2008.

Kangrga, Milan. *Šverceri vlastitog života: Refleksije o hrvatskoj političkoj kulturi i duhovnosti*. Belgrade: Res publica, 2001.

Klasić, Hrvoje. *Jugoslavija i svijet 1968*. Zagreb: Ljevak, 2012.

Koch, Andrew. 'Yugoslavia's Nuclear Legacy: Should We Worry?' *The Nonproliferation Review* 4, no. 3 (1997): 123–8. https://doi.org/10.1080/10736709708436687, accessed 10 October 2019.

Köchl, Reinhard, Richard Wiedamann, and Peter Tippelt. *Dusko Gojkovic: Jazz ist Freiheit*. Regensburg: ConBrio, 1995.

Kolešnik, Ljiljana, ed. *Socijalizam i modernost: umjetnost, kultura, politika 1950.-1974*. Zagreb: Institut za povijest umjetnosti, 2012.

Konta, Carla. 'Nice to Meet You, President Tito … Senator Fulbright and the Yugoslav Lesson for Vietnam.' In *The Legacy of J. William Fulbright: Policy, Power, and Ideology*, edited by David J. Snyder, Alessandro Brogi, and Giles Scott-Smith. Lexington: University Press of Kentucky, 2019.

———. 'Yugoslav Nuclear Diplomacy Between the Soviet Union and the United States, 1950–1965.' *Cahier Du Monde Russe* 60, no. 3–4 (2020): forthcoming.

Krige, John. 'Atoms for Peace, Scientific Internationalism, and Scientific Intelligence.' *Osiris* 21, no. 1 Global Power Knowledge. Science and Technology in International Affairs (2006): 161–81.

Kroes, Rob. *If You've Seen One, You've Seen the Mall: Europeans and American Mass Culture*. Urbana; Chicago: University of Illinois Press, 1996.

———. 'Imaginary Americas in Europe's Public Place.' In *The Americanization of Europe: Culture, Diplomacy, and Anti-Americanism After 1945*, edited by A. Stephan, 337–59. New York; Oxford: Berghahn Books, 2007.

Krugler, David F. *The Voice of America and the Domestic Propaganda Battles, 1945–1953*. Columbia: University of Missouri Press, 2000.

Kullaa, Rinna. *Non-Alignment and its Origins in Cold War Europe: Yugoslavia, Finland and the Soviet Challenge*. London; New York: I. B. Tauris, 2012.

———. 'US Intelligence Estimates of "The Crises in Croatia" and its Relationship to Détente in East–West Relations Across Europe 1971–1972.' In *Hrvatsko Proljeće 40 Godina Poslije*, edited by Tvrtko Jakovina. Zagreb: CZD Miko Tripalo, FFZG, FPZSZ, PFSZ, 2012.

Lacy, Dan. 'The Role of American Books Abroad.' *Foreign Affairs* 34, no. 3 (1956). www.foreignaffairs.com/articles/united-states/1956-04-01/r-le-american-books-abroad, accessed 10 October 2019.

Lakićević, Mijat. *Ispred vremena*. Belgrade: Fond za otvoreno društvo, Srbija, 2011.

Lalović, Dragutin, ed. *Hrvatsko i Jugoslavensko 'Proljeće' 1962–1972*. Zagreb: Društvo 'Povijest izvan mitova,' 2014.

Lampe, John R. *Yugoslavia as History: Twice There Was a Country*. 2nd ed. Cambridge: Cambridge University Press, 2000.

Lampe, John R., Russell O. Prickett, and Ljubiša S. Adamović. *Yugoslav–American Economic Relations Since World War II*. Durham, NC: Duke University Press, 1990.

Langenkamp, Harm. 'Global Harmony in Silk Road Diplomacy.' In *Music and Diplomacy from the Early Modern Era to the Present*, edited by Rebekah Ahrendt, Mark Ferraguto, and Damien Mahiet. New York: Palgrave Macmillan, 2014.

Larson, David L. *United States Foreign Policy Toward Yugoslavia: 1943–1963*. Lanham, MD: University Press of America, 1979.

Laville, Helen, and Hugh Wilford, eds. *The US Government, Citizen Groups and the Cold War: The State-Private Network*. London; New York: Routledge, 2006.

Lebovic, Sam. 'From War Junk to Educational Exchange: The World War II Origins of the Fulbright Program and the Foundations of American Cultural Globalism, 1945–1950.' *Diplomatic History* 37, no. 2 (2013): 280–312. https://doi.org/10.1093/dh/dht002, accessed 10 October 2019.

Lees, Lorraine M. *Keeping Tito Afloat: The United States, Yugoslavia, and the Cold War*. University Park, PA: Pennsylvania State University Press, 2005.

Leffler, Melvyn P. *A Preponderance of Power: National Security, the Truman Administration, and the Cold War*. Stanford, CA: Stanford University Press, 1993.

———. 'The Emergence of an American Grand Strategy, 1945–1952.' In *The Cambridge History of the Cold War*, edited by Melvyn P. Leffler and Odd Arne Westad, Reprint ed., 1:67–89. Cambridge: Cambridge University Press, 2012.

Lucas, Scott W. 'Beyond Freedom, beyond Control, beyond the Cold War: Approaches to American Culture and the State-Private Network.' *Intelligence and National Security* 18, no. 2 (2003): 53–73. https://doi.org/10.1080/02684520412331306740, accessed 10 October 2019.

Lundestad, Geir. *The Rise and Decline of the American 'Empire': Power and its Limits in Comparative Perspective*. Oxford; New York: Oxford University Press, 2012.

——. *The United States and Western Europe Since 1945: From Empire by Invitation to Transatlantic Drift.* Oxford: Oxford University Press, 2003.

Luthar, Breda. 'Shame, Desire and Longing for the West. A Case Study of Consumption.' In *Remembering Utopia: The Culture of Everyday Life in Socialist Yugoslavia*, edited by Breda Luthar and Maruša Pušnik, 341–77. Washington, DC: New Academia Publishing, 2010.

Luthar, Breda, and Marusa Pusnik, eds. *Remembering Utopia: The Culture of Everyday Life in Socialist Yugoslavia.* Washington, DC: New Academia Publishing, 2010.

Mark, James, Péter Apor, Radina Vučetić, and Piotr Osęka. '"We Are with You, Vietnam": Transnational Solidarities in Socialist Hungary, Poland and Yugoslavia.' *Journal of Contemporary History* 50, no. 3 (2015): 439–64. https://doi.org/10.1177/ 0022009414558728, accessed 10 October 2019.

Marković, Mihailo. 'Neobjavljeni intervju: Praxis – Kritičko mišljenje i delanje.' *Filozofija i društvo* 14, no. 1 (2010): 3–16.

Marković, Predrag. 'Najava bure: studentski nemiri u svetu i Jugoslaviji od Drugog svetskog rata do početka šezdesetih godina.' *Tokovi Istorije*, issue 3–4 (2000): 51–62.

Marković, Predrag J. *Beograd između Istoka i Zapada 1948–1965.* Beograd: Sluzbeni list SRJ, 1996.

Masey, Jack, and Conway L. Morgan. *Cold War Confrontations: US Exhibitions and Their Role in the Cultural Cold War.* Baden, Switzerland: Lars Müller Publishers, 2008.

Mates, Leo. *Međunarodni odnosi socijalističke Jugoslavije.* Belgrade: Nolit, 1976.

Mattern, Janice Bially. 'Why "Soft Power" Isn't So Soft: Representational Force and the Sociolinguistic Construction of Attraction in World Politics.' *Millennium: Journal of International Studies* 33, no. 3 (2005): 583–612. https://doi.org/10.1177/030582980503 30031601, accessed 10 October 2019.

May, Elaine T. *Homeward Bound: American Families in the Cold War Era*, revised ed. New York: Basic Books, 2008.

Melissen, Jan. *The New Public Diplomacy: Soft Power in International Relations.* London: Palgrave Macmillan, 2005.

Melissen, Jan, and Jian Wang. *Debating Public Diplomacy: Now and Next.* Leiden; Boston, MA: Brill, 2019.

Milosavljević, Olivera. *Činjenice i tumačenja: Dva razgovora sa Latinkom Perović: Svedočanstva.* Belgrade: Helsinški odbor za ljudska prava u Srbiji, 2010.

Monson, Ingrid T. *Freedom Sounds: Civil Rights Call Out to Jazz and Africa.* Oxford; New York: Oxford University Press, 2007.

Needell, Allan A. '"Truth is Our Weapon": Project TROY, Political Warfare, and Government–Academic Relations in the National Security State.' *Diplomatic History* 17, no. 3 (1993): 399–420. http://dx.doi.org/10.1111/j.1467-7709.1993.tb00588.x, accessed 10 October 2019.

Nelson, Richard, and Foad Izadi. 'Ethics and Social Issues in Public Diplomacy.' In *Routledge Handbook of Public Diplomacy*, edited by Nancy Snow and Philip M. Taylor, 334–51. New York; London: Routledge, 2008.

Nenadović, Aleksandar, and Koča Popović. *Razgovori s Kočom.* Zagreb: Globus, 1989.

Nilsson, Mikael. *The Battle for Hearts and Minds in the High North: The USIA and American Cold War Propaganda in Sweden, 1952–1969.* Leiden: Brill, 2016.

Ninkovich, Frank A. *The Diplomacy of Ideas: US Foreign Policy and Cultural Relations, 1938–1950.* Cambridge; New York: Cambridge University Press, 1981.

Njegić, Radmila. 'Razvoj Stanovništva Beograda u Posleratnom Periodu.' *Godišnjak Grada Beograda*, issue 11–12 (1964): 219–44.

Noonan, Ellen. *The Strange Career of Porgy and Bess: Race, Culture, and America's Most Famous Opera*. Chapel Hill: University of North Carolina Press, 2012.

Notaker, Hallvard, Giles Scott-Smith, and David J. Snyder, eds. *Reasserting America in the 1970s: US Public Diplomacy and the Rebuilding of America's Image Abroad*. Manchester: Manchester University Press, 2016.

Novak, Bogdan C. *Trieste 1941–1954: La lotta politica, etnica e ideologica*. Milano: Mursia, 2013.

Nye, Joseph S. Jr. 'Responding to My Critics and Concluding Thoughts.' In *Soft Power and US Foreign Policy: Theoretical, Historical and Contemporary Perspectives*, edited by Inderjeet Parmar and Michael Cox, 215–27. London; New York: Routledge, 2010.

———. *Soft Power: The Means to Success in World Politics*. 2nd ed. New York: Public Affairs, 2009.

———. *The Future of Power*. Reprint. New York: PublicAffairs, 2011.

Oldenziel, Ruth, and Karin Zachmann. *Cold War Kitchen: Americanization, Technology, and European Users*. Cambridge, MA: MIT Press, 2009. https://books.google.hr/books?id=9dDgAAAAMAAJ, accessed 10 October 2019.

Osgood, Kenneth. *Total Cold War: Eisenhower's Secret Propaganda Battle at Home and Abroad*. Lawrence: University Press of Kansas, 2006.

Parry-Giles, Shawn J. *The Rhetorical Presidency, Propaganda, and the Cold War, 1945–1955*. Westport, CT; London: Praeger, 2001.

Patterson, Patrick H. *Bought and Sold: Living and Losing the Good Life in Socialist Yugoslavia*. Ithaca, NY: Cornell University Press, 2011.

———. 'Making Markets Marxist? The East European Grocery Store from Rationing to Rationality to Rationalizations.' In *Food Chains: From Farmyard to Shopping Cart*, edited by Warren Belasco and Roger Horowitz, 196–216. Philadelphia: University of Pennsylvania Press, 2010.

Perišić, Miroslav. *Diplomatija i kultura: Jugoslavija: prelomna 1950*. Belgrade: Institut za noviju istoriju Srbije, 2013.

Perović, Jeronim. 'The Tito–Stalin Split: A Reassessment in Light of New Evidence.' *Journal of Cold War Studies* 9, no. 2 (2007): 32–63. https://doi.org/10.1162/jcws.2007.9.2.32, accessed 10 October 2019.

Perović, Latinka. *Dominantna i neželjena elita: Beleške o intelektualnoj i političkoj eliti u Srbiji (XX–XXI)*. Belgrade: Dan Graf, 2015.

———. *Snaga Lične Odgovornosti*. Belgrade: Helsinški odbor, 2008.

———. *Zatvaranje kruga: ishod političkog rascepa u SKJ 1971./1972*. Sarajevo: Svjetlost, 1991.

Petrović, Vladimir. '"Pošteni posrednik". Jugoslavija između starih i novih spoljnopolitičkih partnerstava sredinom pedesetih godina.' In *Spoljna politika Jugoslavije: 1950–1961.*, edited by Slobodan Selinić, 462–71. Belgrade: Institut za noviju istoriju Srbije, 2008.

Ponoš, Tihomir. *Na Rubu Revolucije: Studenti '71*. Zagreb: Profil, 2007.

Prime, Rebecca. *Hollywood Exiles in Europe: The Blacklist and Cold War Film Culture*. New Brunswick, NJ: Rutgers University Press, 2014.

Svetozar Rajak. 'From Regional Role to Global Undertakings: Yugoslavia in the Early Cold War.' In *The Balkans in the Cold War*, edited by Svetozar Rajak et al., 65–86. London: Palgrave Macmillan, 2017.

———. 'No Bargaining Chips, No Spheres of Interest: The Yugoslav Origins of Cold War Non-Alignment.' *Journal of Cold War Studies* 16, no. 1 (2014): 146–79. https://doi. org/10.1162/JCWS_a_00434.

———. *Yugoslavia and the Soviet Union in the Early Cold War: Reconciliation, Comradeship, Confrontation, 1953–1957.* London; New York: Routledge, 2011. https://doi.org/10.10 80/14682745.2011.569155.

Raković, Aleksandar. *Rokenrol u Jugoslaviji 1956–1968: Izazov socijalističkom društvu.* Belgrade: Arhipelag, 2011.

Ramet, Sabrina P. *Balkan Babel: The Disintegration of Yugoslavia from the Death of Tito to the Fall of Milosevic.* 4th ed. Boulder, CO: Westview Press, 2002.

———. 'Shake, Rattle, and Self-Management: Making the Scene in Yugoslavia.' In *Kazaaam! Splat! Ploof!: The American Impact on European Popular Culture since 1945*, edited by Sabrina P. Ramet and Gordana Crnković, 173–97. Lanham, MD; Oxford: Rowman & Littlefield Publishers, 2003.

———. *The Three Yugoslavias: State-Building and Legitimation, 1918–2005.* Washington, DC: Bloomington: Indiana University Press, 2006.

Ramet, Sabrina P., and Ljubiša S. Adamović. *Beyond Yugoslavia: Politics, Economics, and Culture in a Shattered Community.* Boulder, CO: Westview Press, 1995.

Richmond, Yale. *US–Soviet Cultural Exchanges, 1958–1986: Who Wins?* Boulder, CO: Westview Press, 1987.

Robbins, Louise S. 'The Overseas Libraries Controversy and the Freedom to Read: US Librarians and Publishers Confront Joseph McCarthy.' *Libraries & Culture* 36, no. 1 (2001): 27–39. https://doi.org/10.1353/lac.2001.0021, accessed 10 October 2019.

Roberts, Walter. *Tito, Mihailovic, and the Allies.* Kindle. Durham, NC: Duke University Press, 1987.

Robertson, Allen. 'Glen Tetley.' In *International Encyclopedia of Dance*, edited by Selma J Cohen. New York: Oxford University Press, 1998.

Rolandi, Francesca. *Con ventiquattromila baci: L'influenza della cultura di massa italiana in Jugoslavia (1955–1965).* Bologna: Bononia University Press, 2015.

Ross Johnson, A. *Radio Free Europe and Radio Liberty: The CIA Years and Beyond.* Washington, DC: Stanford University Press, 2010.

Rosteck, Thomas. *See It Now Confronts McCarthyism: Television Documentary and the Politics of Representation.* 2nd ed. Tuscaloosa; London: University of Alabama Press, 1994.

Rusinow, Dennison I. *The Yugoslav Experiment 1948–1974.* Berkeley: University of California Press, 1978.

———. *Yugoslavia: Oblique Insights and Observations.* Pittsburgh: University of Pittsburgh Press, 2008.

Salecl, Renata. *The Spoils of Freedom: Psychoanalysis and Feminism After the Fall of Socialism.* London; New York: Routledge, 1994.

Schulzinger, Robert D. 'Détente in the Nixon-Ford Years, 1969–1976.' In *The Cambridge History of the Cold War 2*, edited by Melvyn P. Leffler and Odd Arne Westad, 373–94. New York: Cambridge University Press, 2010.

Scott-Smith, Giles. 'Mapping the Undefinable: Some Thoughts on the Relevance of Exchange Programs within International Relations Theory.' *The Annals of the American Academy of Political and Social Science* 616, no. 1 (2008): 173–95. https://doi. org/10.1177/0002716207311953, accessed 10 October 2019.

———. *Networks of Empire: The US State Department's Foreign Leader Program in the Netherlands, France and Britain 1950–1970*. Brussels: P.I.E. Peter Lang, 2008.

———. 'The US State Department's Foreign Leader Program in France during the Early Cold War.' In *Les Relations Culturelles Internationales Au XXe Siècle: De La Diplomatie Culturelle à l'acculturation*, edited by A. Dulphy, R. Frank, M. A. Matard-Bonucci, and P. Ory, 71–8. Brussels: P.I.E. Peter Lang, 2010.

Scott-Smith, Giles, and Hans Krabbendam, eds. *The Cultural Cold War in Western Europe, 1945–1960*. London; Portland, OR: Frank Cass Publishers, 2003.

Seib, Philip. *Toward a New Public Diplomacy: Redirecting US Foreign Policy*. New York: Palgrave Macmillan, 2009.

Shaw, Tony. *Hollywood's Cold War*. Amherst: University of Massachusetts Press, 2007.

Shaw, Tony, and Denise J. Youngblood. *Cinematic Cold War: The American and Soviet Struggle for Hearts and Minds*. Lawrence: University Press of Kansas, 2014.

Shigeno, Rei. 'On the Conception of Politics of the Praxis Group – Exposing the Limits of its Universalism.' *European Studies* 1 (2001): 81–98.

Sluga, Glenda. *The Problem of Trieste and the Italo-Yugoslav Border: Difference, Identity, and Sovereignty in Twentieth-Century Europe*. New York: SUNY Press, 2001.

Smith, Tony. *America's Mission: The United States and the Worldwide Struggle for Democracy*. Expanded ed. Princeton: Princeton University Press, 2012.

Snow, Nancy, and Philip M. Taylor, eds. *Routledge Handbook on Public Diplomacy*. New York; London: Routledge Taylor & Francis, 2009.

Spehnjak, Katarina. 'Posjeta Josipa Broza Tita Velikoj Britaniji 1953. godine.' *Časopis za suvremenu povijest* 33, no. 3 (2001): 597–631.

Spehnjak, Katarina, and Tihomir Cipek. 'Disidenti, opozicija i otpor – Hrvatska i Jugoslavija.' *Časopis za suvremenu povijest* 39, no. 2 (2007): 255–97.

Spring, Dawn. *Advertising in the Age of Persuasion: Building Brand America, 1941–1961*. New York: Palgrave Macmillan, 2011.

Statler, Kathryn C. 'The Sound of Musical Diplomacy.' *Diplomatic History* 36, no. 1 (2012): 71–5. https://doi.org/10.1111/j.1467-7709.2011.01010.x, accessed 10 October 2019.

Stierli, M., V. Deskov, and V. Kulić. *Toward a Concrete Utopia: Architecture in Yugoslavia, 1948–1980*. New York: Moma, 2018.

Stone, David R. 'The Balkan Pact and American Policy.' *East European Quarterly* 28, no. 3 (1994): 393–405.

Suri, Jeremi. *Power and Protest: Global Revolution and the Rise of Detente*. Cambridge, MA; London: Harvard University Press, 2009.

Škarica, Siniša. *Kad je rock bio mlad: Priča sa istočne strane (1956–1970)*. Zagreb: VBZ, 2005.

Taplin, Mark. 'Walter Roberts: George Kennan and Public Diplomacy – "Basically, George Kennan was an Old-Line Diplomat",' *Global Publicks* website, 22 February 2016. http://globalpublicks.blogspot.hr/2015/02/walter-roberts-george-kennan-and-public.html, accessed 10 October 2019.

———. 'Walter Roberts: The Impact of US Cold War Public Diplomacy – "The Most Effective Way of Influencing … Was the Voice of America",' *Global Publicks* website, 22 February 2016. http://globalpublicks.blogspot.hr/2015/02/walter-roberts-impact-of-us-cold-war.html, accessed 10 October 2019.

———. 'Walter Roberts: US Public Diplomacy in Yugoslavia – "We Had Quite a Program There",' *Global Publicks* website, 22 February 2016. http://globalpublicks.blogspot.hr/2015/02/walter-roberts-us-public-diplomacy-in.html, accessed 10 October 2019.

——. 'Walter Roberts: USIS Magazines and Exhibits in Yugoslavia – "I'm Red-Faced. I Apologize.",' *Global Publicks* website, 22 February 2016. http://globalpublicks.blogspot. hr/2015/02/walter-roberts-usis-magazines-and.html, accessed 10 October 2019.

Taubman, Howard. 'Cold War on the Cultural Front; At Brussels the US and Russia Will Compete or the Minds of Men with Their Arts.' *New York Times*, 21 January 1958.

Tiemeyer, Phil. 'Launching a Nonaligned Airline: JAT Yugoslav Airways between East, West, and South, 1947–1962.' *Diplomatic History* 41, no. 1 (2017): 78–103. https://doi. org/10.1093/dh/dhv061, accessed 10 October 2019.

Tingen, Paul. 'Miles Davis. The Making of Bitches Brews.' *JazzTimes* 31, no. 4 (2001): 46–57.

Tobia, Simona. *Advertising America: The United States Information Service in Italy (1945–1956)*. Milan: LED Edizioni Universitarie, 2009.

Todorova, Maria, and Zsuzsa Gille. *Post-Communist Nostalgia*. New York: Berghahn Books, 2012.

Tomlin, Gregory M. *Murrow's Cold War: Public Diplomacy for the Kennedy Administration*. Kindle. Lincoln: University of Nebraska Press, 2016.

Tomlinson, John. *Cultural Imperialism: A Critical Introduction*. London: A&C Black, 2001.

Tripalo, Miko. *Hrvatsko Proljeće*. 2nd ed. Zagreb: Globus, 1990.

Troebst, Stefan, Augusta Dimou, and Maria Todorova, eds. *Remembering Communism: Private and Public Recollections of Lived Experiences in Southeast Europe*. Budapest: CEU Press, 2014.

'UN Conference on Atomic Energy, Geneva August 8–20, 1955.' *Bulletin of the Atomic Scientists* 11, no. 8 (1955): 274–313.

Vranicki, Predrag. *Historija Marksizma*. Vol. 2. Zagreb: Cekade, 1987.

Vučetić, Radina. 'Amerikanizacija u Jugoslovenskoj Popularnoj Kulturi '60-Ih.' Belgrade, 2011.

——. *Coca-Cola Socialism: Americanization of Yugoslav Culture in the Sixties*. Budapest; New York: Central European University Press, 2017.

——. 'Kauboji u partizanskoj uniformi: američki vesterni i partizanski vesterni u Jugoslaviji šezdesetih godina 20. veka.' *Tokovi Istorije*, issue 2 (2010): 130–51.

——. *Koka-kola socijalizam: Amerikanizacija jugoslavenske popularne kulture šezdesetih godina XX veka*. Belgrade: Službeni glasnik, 2012.

——. 'Trubom kroz Gvozdenu zavesu: prodor džeza u socijalističku Jugoslaviju.' *Muzikologija*, no. 13 (21 January 2012): 53–77. https://doi.org/10.2298/MUZ1202 29012V, accessed 10 October 2019.

Wagnleitner, Reinhold. *Coca-Colonization and the Cold War: The Cultural Mission of the United States in Austria After the Second World War*. Chapel Hill: University of North Carolina Press, 2000.

Wall, Wendy L. *Inventing the 'American Way': The Politics of Consensus from the New Deal to the Civil Rights Movement*. Oxford: Oxford University Press, 2008.

Winkler, Allan M. *The Politics of Propaganda: The Office of War Information, 1942–1945*. New Haven, CT: Yale University Press, 1978.

Woods, Randall B. *Fulbright: A Biography*. Cambridge: Cambridge University Press, 1995.

——. 'Fulbright Internationalism.' *Annals of the American Academy of Political and Social Science* 491, The Fulbright Experience and Academic Exchanges (1987): 22–35.

Wulf, Andrew J. *US International Exhibitions during the Cold War: Winning Hearts and Minds through Cultural Diplomacy*. Lanham, MD: Rowman & Littlefield Publishers, 2015.

Zimmerman, William. *Open Borders, Nonalignment, and the Political Evolution of Yugoslavia*. Princeton Legacy Library. 2nd ed. Princeton: Princeton University Press, 2015.

Žikić, Aleksandar. *Fatalni ringišpil: Hronika beogradskog rokenrola 1959–1979*. Belgrade: Geopoetika, 1999.

Index

Note: literary works can be found under authors' names

Index

EU authorised representative for GPSR:
Easy Access System Europe, Mustamäe tee 50,
10621 Tallinn, Estonia
gpsr.requests@easproject.com

www.ingramcontent.com/pod-product-compliance
Lightning Source LLC
Chambersburg PA
CBHW070844300326
41935CB00039B/1436